Market Microstructure in Practice

Market Microstructure in Practice

Editors

Charles-Albert Lehalle
Capital Fund Management, France

Sophie Laruelle
Université Paris-Est Créteil, France

NEW JERSEY • LONDON • SINGAPORE • BEIJING • SHANGHAI • HONG KONG • TAIPEI • CHENNAI

Published by

World Scientific Publishing Co. Pte. Ltd.

5 Toh Tuck Link, Singapore 596224

USA office: 27 Warren Street, Suite 401-402, Hackensack, NJ 07601

UK office: 57 Shelton Street, Covent Garden, London WC2H 9HE

Library of Congress Cataloging-in-Publication Data

Lehalle, Charles-Albert.

Market microstructure in practice / Charles-Albert Lehalle (Capital Fund Management, France) & Sophie Laruelle (Universite Paris-Est Creteil, France).

pages cm

Includes bibliographical references and index.

ISBN 978-9814566162 (hardcover : alk. paper)

1. Capital market. 2. Finance. 3. Stock exchanges. I. Laruelle, Sophie. II. Title.

HG4523.L44 2013

332'.0415--dc23

2013031361

British Library Cataloguing-in-Publication Data

A catalogue record for this book is available from the British Library.

In-house Editor: Chye Shu Wen

Typeset by Stallion Press

Email: enquiries@stallionpress.com

Printed in Singapore

About the Editors

Currently Senior Research Manager at Capital Fund Management (CFM), **Charles-Albert Lehalle** is an international expert in market microstructure and optimal trading. Formerly Global Head of Quantitative Research at Crédit Agricole Cheuvreux, and Head of Quantitative Research on Market Microstructure in the Equity Brokerage and Derivative Department of Crédit Agricole Corporate Investment Bank, he has been studying the market microstructure since regulatory changes in Europe and in the US took place. He provided research and expertise on this topic to investors and intermediaries, and is often heard by regulators and policy-makers like the European Commission, the French Senate, the UK Foresight Committee, etc.

Currently Assistant Professor at Université Paris-Est Créteil (UPEC), **Sophie Laruelle** defended her PhD in december 2011 under the supervision of Gilles Pagès on analysis of stochastic algorithms applied to Finance. During her PhD, she made two contributions on market microstructure in collaboration with Charles-Albert Lehalle: The first one on the optimal allocation among dark pools and the second on optimal posting price in the limit order book. Then she worked at Ecole Centrale Paris with Frédéric Abergel on agent-based models and now she continues to work on applications of stochastic approximation theory, notably in market microstructure for building trading algorithms.

About the Contributors

Romain Burgot graduated from ENSAE in 2006, and he started to get curious about market microstructure during his time at ENSAE. He worked directly in this field as a quant analyst and consequently observed the establishment of whole equity trading fragmentation in Europe. He took part in the first stages of building a team of efficient researchers in the domain. He helped in market data processing, visualization, modeling and robust statistical estimations for benchmarked agency brokerage execution algorithms. His main interests lie in volume volatility spread joint dynamics, the influence of tick size on trading and helping regulators get understanding in equity trading evolutions.

Stéphanie Pelin works as a Quant Analyst in the Quantitative Research team of Kepler Cheuvreux. For the past four years, she has conducted quantitative analysis on Corporate Brokerage strategies, focusing on stocks' liquidity characterization or price guaranteed interventions. She regularly published documents where pertinent issues in financial markets' microstructure were investigated, in particular with regards to fragmentation and European equity markets regulation, e.g. MiFID. Stéphanie graduated with a B.Sc. from Paris Dauphine University; majoring in Applied Mathematics and Financial Markets. She started her professional experience by studying energy products in an Asset Management firm.

Matthieu Lasnier was admitted at the Ecole Normale Superieure in Lyon and he graduated as an engineer from ENSAE. He holds the Master of Science in Financial Mathematics at the University Denis Diderot-Paris 7. Currently a quantitative analyst at Kepler-Cheuvreux, Matthieu Lasnier's fields of expertise include the study of the price formation process with a focus on market impact questions. He has been working with the quantitative research team of CA Cheuvreux in New York and in Paris since 2009. His core field is financial mathematics, in particular statistical analysis of high-frequency financial data. The questions he faces overlap with the design of statistical arbitrage strategies, the optimization of execution trading algorithm, as well as the study of the market impact. In the context of raising fragmentation of the European equity markets, he is a contributor to *Navigating Liquidity*.

Contents

Foreword

Robert Almgren, President and Cofounder of Quantitative Brokers

Fragmentation, the search for liquidity, and high-frequency traders: These are the realities of modern markets. Traditional models of market microstructure have studied the highly simplified interaction between an idealized market maker or specialist, and a stream of external orders that may come from noise traders or informed traders. In the modern marketplace, the market itself is replaced by a loosely coupled network of visible and hidden venues, linked together by high frequency traders and by algorithmic strategies. The distinction between market makers who post liquidity and directional traders who take liquidity no longer exists. All traders are searching for liquidity, which may be flickering across many different locations with varying latencies, fill probabilities, and costs. That is the world which this book addresses, treating these issues as central and fundamental rather than unwelcome complexities on top of a simple framework.

This market evolution is furthest along in equity markets, thanks in large part to their size, social prominence as indicators of corporate value, and large variety of active traders from retail investors to sophisticated proprietary operations and large fundamental asset managers. Regulation has also been most active in equity markets, most importantly Reg NMS in the US and MiFiD in Europe. Other asset markets, such as foreign exchange, futures, and fixed income, are further back along this pathway, but it is clear that the direction of evolution is toward the landscape treated in this book, rather than back to simpler times. Regulation will continue to shape the further development of all these markets, and all market participants have an interest in increasing the broad understanding of the underlying issues by regulators as well as each other.

The central focus of the book is liquidity: Loosely speaking, the ease and efficiency with which large transactions can be performed. For any real user of the market this is the primary concern, although academic researchers may focus on other aspects. Thus fragmentation and high frequency trading are addressed from this point of view. Throughout the book, the emphasis is on features of the marketplace that are of tangible and pressing concern to traders, investors, and regulators.

The authors have extensive personal experience of the development of the European equity markets, as traders and as participants in conversations with regulators and other interested parties. They bring this experience to bear on every aspect of the discussion, as well as deep quantitative understanding. The resulting book is a unique mixture of real market knowledge and theoretical explanation. There is nothing else out there like it, and this book will be a central resource for many different market participants.

Bertrand Patillet, Deputy Chief Executive Officer of CA Cheuvreux until April 2013

MiFID I removed the freedom of national regulators to maintain the secular obligation to concentrate orders on historical markets. In this way, the regulation, without a doubt, lifted the last regulatory obstacle preventing Europe from experiencing — for better or for worse perhaps — the macro- and micro-structural changes already at work on North American markets. This complete shift in paradigm was to render obsolete our savoir-faire and knowledge of how equity markets work.

We needed to observe, analyse, understand, and, to a certain extent, anticipate and foresee the consequences of the transformations underway that would drastically change the structure of inter and intra-market liquidity and thus the nature of the information conveyed by order books, the right reading of which is vital to obtaining the best price for our clients. Only then, could we redefine our approach to best execution, and adapt our behaviour and our tools.

We could not have achieved this task without resources hitherto the monopoly of certain hedge funds or derivatives desks, but unknown to agency brokers, namely profiles capable of extracting useful information from market data in order to better model new behaviours, validate or invalidate intuitions and ultimately provide our traders with buy or sell decision-making tools in these exceedingly complex markets. This is why, as early as 2006, we decided to form a team of quantitative analysts with strong links to the academic world, and headed by Charles-Albert, newly hired at Crédit Agricole Cheuvreux. This move was to transform our execution practices beyond our expectations and place us among the leaders.

Before MiFID II imposes new rules for structuring financial markets, this book provides a point of view, far from the preconceived ideas and pro domo pleas of such and such a lobby, on market microstructure issues — the subject of impassioned, fascinating, and as yet unclosed debate — which will interest all those, who, in one respect or another, are concerned with improving how equity markets work.

Philippe Guillot, Executive Director, Markets Directorate, Autorité des marchés financiers (AMF)

When Charles-Albert asked me to write a foreword for his book on markets microstructure, in which many of the topics are reminiscent of the uncounted hours spent discussing them while we were at Cheuvreux, he specifically asked for one (alas, only one) of the many analogies I use to help people getting a grasp on microstructure. A good proportion comes from comparing the electronics markets to aviation, with a big difference worth noting: At the beginning of aviation, as Igor Sikorsky said, the chief engineer was almost always the chief test pilot, which had the fortunate result to eliminate poor engineering at an early stage in aviation (could we do something similar for algos?). When comparing the two today, what is probably missed the most in the markets microstructure is common sense.

How can this be illustrated through MiFID? At first glance, one clear beneficiary of MiFID is Mr Smith. When he bravely buys 500 shares of Crédit Agricole, the reduction in tick sizes that occurred in the previous years means that rather than having to pay 6.95€ per share when he crosses the spread, he now buys them at 6.949€ (he still crosses the spread but, because his dealing size remained smaller than the Average Trade Size, he still buys from the best offer) and saves a whopping 0.5€ every times he deals. Unfortunately, whenever he does so, he is never sure that the price he has dealt at is the one he has seen on his screen nor that the marketplace where he has dealt is the one on which he was looking at the price. Add to that some literature on HFT, predatory strategies and flash crashes: No wonder the markets have lost Mr Smith's confidence. Where is the analogy with aviation?

When today's engineers build an Airbus A380, they could really simplify the problems by building it without windows when only one out of six passengers sits next to one of them. The body of the plane would not have to be reinforced around the panels and a lot of weight would be saved. Add to that the reduction of drag when flying and you could expect that some of these savings would be passed to the passengers, maybe 0.5€ every time he buys a plane ticket.

Sadly, Mr Smith and many of his fellow travellers are not yet ready to fly in a windowless plane for a 0.5€ saving (you may have also noticed that on automatic tube lines there is always a huge windowpane at the front of the train in the unlikely event that there is a risk of a head on crash with another train). Even if it is technically possible today to fly a plane without a pilot, even if every serious accident that occurred in this century has a human error to its origin, the plane industry has realised how important it is to keep the trust of customers.

Today, the markets have lost the trust of their most precious customer, the most humble link in the markets ecosystem: The uninformed trader. The ecosystem is damaged and repairing it will be our biggest challenge of the coming years. Although politicians may decide to make big bold changes, technicians and regulators have to carefully use their considerable weight on the delicate levers of markets microstructure.

Charles' and Sophie's book on markets microstructure will improve our knowledge and consequently help us to tweak these potentiometers. In promoting better education, this book is at the roots of restoring trust in the markets.

Albert J. Menkveld, Professor of Finance at VU University Amsterdam and Research Fellow at TI-Duisenberg School of Finance

We go to markets to buy and sell. Perhaps the oldest market still around is the farmer's market. Even New York City has them with farmers driving their vans out to Manhattan to sell their wares at the local square amid high-rises. It is a pleasant experience to go out on a sunny day and buy your veggies fresh from the farmer.

That seems a far way off from modern securities markets. Exchanges have moved from floor trading to servers that match incoming buy and sell orders. These orders, in turn, were submitted through electronic channels after traders typed them into their terminals. Better yet, it seems that even the 'typing' is increasingly left to robots to gain speed. So, in today's markets, decisions are taken and trades go off at sub-millisecond speed. The clock speed of a human brain is about 100 milliseconds.

The market place itself changes at a speed that is hard to keep up with. Practitioners, academics, and regulators all wonder whether these new electronic markets are better. But what is the appropriate measure? To an economist, securities markets should get the assets in the hands of those who have highest value for them (given budget constraints). The assets should be allocated optimally. Furthermore, an important by-product of trading is 'price discovery'. Prices reveal information about the fundamental value of a security. They help shareholders discover poor management and take appropriate action.

This book provides a perspective on today's markets. It reviews institutional changes, discusses them, and provides color through real-world examples. It focuses mostly on European securities markets. This does not make it less relevant in a global context as the issues are very similar outside of Europe.

This perspective is an important contribution to the public debate on modern markets. In the end, we might have gained from automated markets as costly human intermediaries are replaced by computers. And when a robot monitors the market for us, we will have more time to go out and enjoy the farmer's market.

Preface

Charles-Albert Lehalle, Senior Research Manager at Capital Fund Management and former Global Head of Quantitative Research at Crédit Agricole Cheuvreux

This book results from the conjunction of recent academic research and day to day monitoring of the equity market microstructure evolutions. Academic research targeted simultaneously the emergence of a scientific framework to study the impact of market design and agent behaviours on the price formation process (see [Lehalle *et al.*, 2010b] [Lehalle, 2012]), and to model and control the execution costs and risks in such an ecosystem (see [Lehalle, 2008] [Lehalle, 2009] [Guéant *et al.*, 2012b] [Guéant *et al.*, 2012a] [Bouchard *et al.*, 2011]). This book aims to keep its content not too technical. Readers interested in a deeper quantitative approach will find more details and pointers in the Appendix.

Market microstructure monitoring has been motivated by brokerage-oriented business needs. One of the roles of an intermediary is to provide unbiased advices on available investment instruments; an execution broker should provide independent analyses on the price formation process. It sheds light on the market valuation of financial instruments. This is one of the reasons why this books owes a lot to Crédit Agricole Cheuvreux' Navigating Liquidity series ([Lehalle and Burgot, 2008] [Lehalle and Burgot, 2009b] [Lehalle and Burgot, 2009a] [Lehalle and Burgot, 2010] [Lehalle *et al.*, 2010a] [Lehalle *et al.*, 2012]). Moreover, internal discussions at CA Cheuvreux (mainly with Bertrand Patillet and Philippe Guillot) as well as intense debates with regulators and policy makers (like Laurent Grillet-Aubert and Kay Swinburne) on the consequences of recent evolutions of the microstructure, required us to mix these academic and practical viewpoints to find at least partial answers.

Academics usually do not answer questions that broad. They choose one specific case or one market context and try to model and explain it as much as they can. It does not mean that they have no intuition. But they cannot afford to claim anything without strong evidence, and the never-ending fluctuations of regulations and market conditions do not help. Interactions with academics are nevertheless of paramount importance in making progresses to answer regulators and policy makers' questions.

Public lectures are no less crucial to mature the outcome of the dialog with academics — especially when attendees are smart, talented students. It was my luck that Nicole El Karoui and Gilles Pagès gave me the opportunity to teach market microstructure and quantitative trading in their famous Master of Arts Programme in Mathematical Finance since 2006, and a few years later that Bruno Bouchard suggested I address the same topics in front of students of University Paris Dauphine. My understanding of market microstructure, adverse selection, and optimal trading progressed a lot thanks to passionate discussions with experts like Robert Almgren, Thierry Foucault, Albert Menkveld, and Ivar Ekeland. The latter invited me to give a one-week lecture at a summer school at the MITAC-PIMS (University of British Columbia), giving birth to challenging exchanges about statistics of high frequency processes and stochastic control with Bruno Bouchard, Mathieu Rosenbaum, and Jérôme Lebuchoux.

Conferences play an important role in the maturation of ideas. The 2010 Kolkata Econophysic Conference on Order-driven Markets enriched my viewpoints on the study of market structure thanks to Frederic Abergel, Fabrizio Lillo, Jim Gatheral, and Bernd Rosenow. The CA Cheuvreux TaMS (Trading and MicroStructure) workshop at the Collège de France and the FieSta (Finance et Statistiques) seminar at Ecole Polytechnique, driven by Mathieu Rosenbaum, Marc Hoffman, and Emmanuel Bacry, contributed to create a small group of researchers in Paris focussed on the topics of this book. It has been strengthened by the organization of the 2010 and 2012 "Market Microstructure: Confronting Many Viewpoints" Paris Conferences, under the auspices of the Louis Bachelier Institute.

The collaborative process giving birth to academic papers demands to confront one's viewpoints with co-authors. It is a strong source of new ideas and breakthroughs. This book hence owns a lot to Ngoc Minh Dang, Olivier Guéant, Julien Razafinimanana, Mauricio Labadie, Joaquin Fernandes-Tapia, Weibing Huang, Jean-Michel Lasry, Pierre-Louis Lions, Aimé Lachapelle, Gilles Pagès, and Sophie Laruelle. The day-to-day work in an algo trading quant team is made of debates to sharpen a common understanding of the price formation process. Not only the co-authors of this book, but Edouard d'Archembaud, Dana Croize, Nicolas Joseph, Matthew Rowley, and Yike Lu took part of this wonderful adventure. Yike had enough energy and a wide enough knowledge to read the last version of this book, giving us last minute comments, correcting our English and helping us to clarify some points.

Last but not least, the tone of this book owns a lot to my previous life in automotive and aerospace industry, during which Robert Azencott taught me how to use applied mathematics to discover relationships on the fly inside high dimensional datasets. It is worth to mention the similarity between the realtime control of the combustion of an automotive engine (with the need to inject enough fuel to produce the desired energy, taking care to not inject too much fuel to avoid pollution and degradation of the combustion process) and the optimal trading of a large order (buying or selling fast enough to extract the expected alpha of the market, but not too fast to avoid market impact, disturbing the price formation process at its own disadvantage). These proximity may be why eight years ago, when I considered to switch to the financial industry, Jean-Philippe Bouchaud told me I would find interesting to study market microstructure and optimal execution; I thank him a lot for that.

Sophie Laruelle, Assistant Professor at Paris-Est Créteil University (UPEC) in the Laboratory of Analysis and Applied Mathematics (LAMA)

How did I come to be concerned about market microstructure? The answer to this question begins with the answer to how I come to be concerned about financial mathematics.

I began a course at Rouen University in 2002 in mathematics and in 2004, with the enforcement of the reform about university autonomy in France, I started a bachelor's degree in applied mathematics with economics and finance. As I liked these new fields, I decided to continue my course in this way with a master's degree in actuaries and mathematical engineering in insurance and finance still at Rouen university, then in Paris at UPMC (Paris VI university) with the so-called Master "Probabilities and Finance" in 2007 and finally with a PhD in 2008 under the supervision of Gilles Pagès on numerical probabilities applied to finance because I wanted to extend my knowledges in this field.

I began to work on stochastic approximation theory and I met Charles-Albert Lehalle in 2009 owing to Gilles Pagès; we started to work together on our first paper on optimal split of volume among Dark Pools. I discovered in this way market microstructure, starting with the different types of trading destination and their associated characteristics. Then I collaborated with Charles to do the practical work associated to his course on quantitative trading in the Masters course "Probabilities and Finance" in 2010: We used a market simulator to teach to students the implemetation of trading strategies, in front of real market data. Then we worked on optimal posting price of limit order with Gilles and Charles (our second paper), still using stochastic approximation algorithm to solve this execution problem.

In parallel, I attended to several conferences on market microstructure and I talked at some of them. I found the community interested in this subject is diversified: Economists, mathematicians, physicists... Confronting these different viewpoints is very enriching and compatible.

The market microstructure gives to academics and professionals new problematics to deal with in modeling, mathematical and computational viewpoints: Which price model to use (the dynamics in high frequency data is not the same as on a daily basis), how to take into account the price discretization (tick size), which statistics to use (problems like signature plot and Epps effect), which model to take into account the market impact, how to take into account the market fragmentation (Lit Pools, Dark Pools), how to model the limit order book, how to model the interactions between the different market participants, how to build optimal trading strategies (optimal control or forward optimization) and how to implement them, how to understand the impact of trading strategies on the market (like the flash crash in May, 6 2010), etc. This list is not exhaustive and there are lots of other questions that the study of market microstructure produces. There is still work to be done to better understand and model all its characteristics with both empirical studies and academic contributions while discussing too with regulators. The mixing of different kinds of studies and people make market microstructure a rich and active environment. We tried in this book to deliver keys to understanding the basis of all these questions in a quantitative yet accessible way.

Introduction

Liquidity in Question

Liquidity is a word often used in the context of financial markets. Nevertheless, it is not that simple to define with accuracy. Some simple qualitative definitions exist, like this one: An asset is *liquid* if it is easy to buy and sell it. We immediately see the importance of liquidity: If an investor valued an asset at one price, and wants to buy and hold it for a few months before selling it, he needs to quantify its associated *liquidity risk*. How much will he really have to pay to buy it once he makes the investment decision? It may take days to finds the needed liquidity in the market, and during this period the price can change in an adverse way. Moreover potential sellers may have the same information as the investor (or deduce that the price should go up, by observing the dynamics of the orderbooks) and consequently if the buyer is not stealthy enough, they can offer to sell at worse prices for the buyer. This last effect is known as *Market Impact*. Finally, when he wants to sell the asset, will the market remember that he bought so many shares and offer only unfavorable prices?

Seen from a very short term view, we can consider the *Bid-Ask spread* (i.e., the distance between the best bid and the best ask price) as a proxy of liquidity, however it does not put enough emphasis on the quantities available to buy or sell at these levels of prices. A *round trip cost* (net loss on an immediate buy then sell, see Figure 1) of a given quantity is for sure a better proxy of liquidity. But it is not just a number: If we compute this over several quantities, we get a curve associating a price to each possible demanded quantity.

When seeking liquidity and the desired quantity is not instantaneously available in the public quotes or electronic orderbooks, the investor will have to split his large order in *slices*, through time and

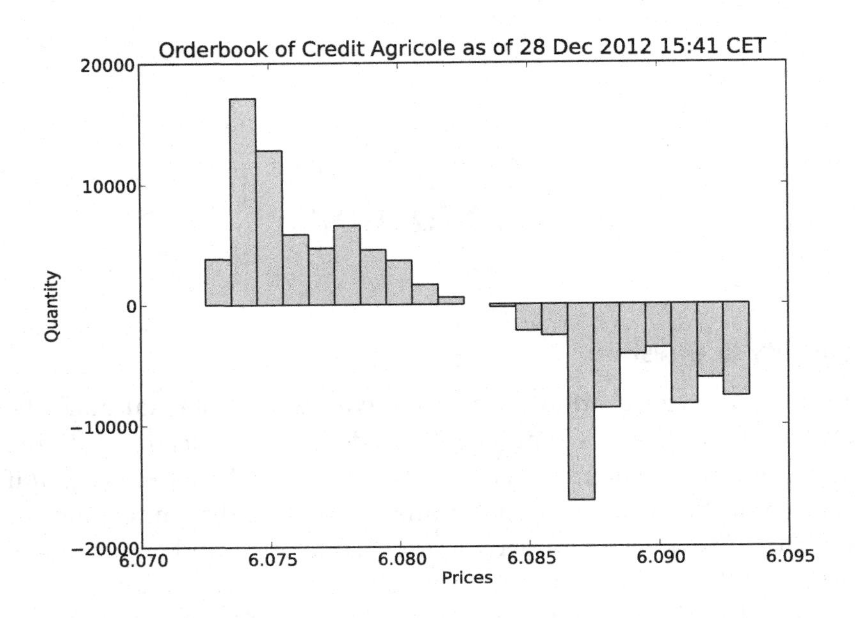

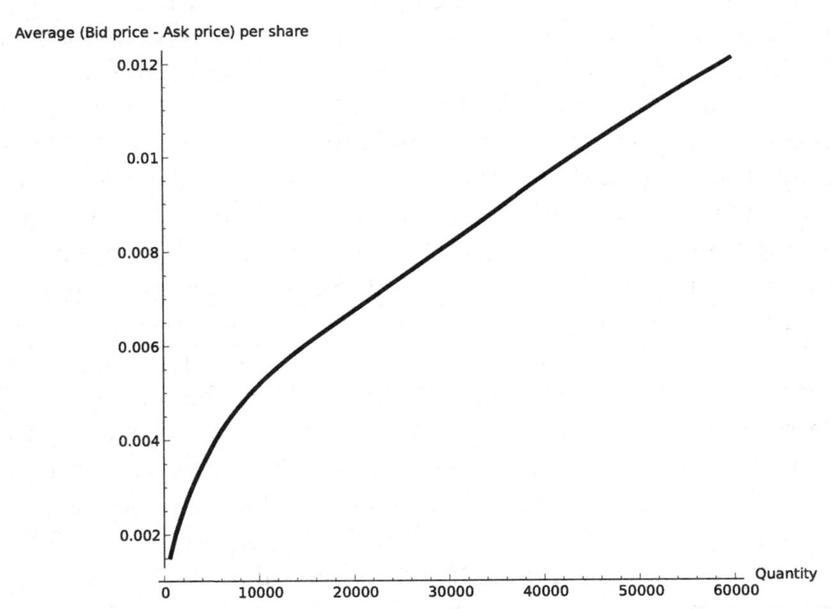

Figure 1. A typical roundtrip curve (bottom), for Crédit Agricole as of 28 December 2012 15:41 CET. The corresponding orderbook is at the top.

through trading venues or counterparts. Anticipating the optimal slicing taking into account market risk and market liquidity is addressed by *optimal trading theory* (see Chapter 3, Section 3.3). Such a mathematical optimization can embed Market Impact models, but does not say which one to use. A very key characteristic of the market impact is how resilient the liquidity is: If I consume liquidity on an asset within half an hour, moving the price because of my impact, how much time will we need to wait for the price to come back?

Qualitatively it is clear that the *decay* of the market impact coming from a large buy order is not the same in an increasing market than in a decreasing one. From a microscopic viewpoint, it can be explained by the level of *synchronization* of the buy order with other orders. If the large buy order in question faces a market context during which many other market participants also send buy orders, the impact will be permanent. If during the same period of time most market participants are sending sell orders, the impact of the large buy order can be almost invisible. The only way to notice the *market impact* of a large order is to average it over enough market configurations such that the specific contexts will balance each other, revealing the intrinsic value and amplitude of this impact (Section 3.2 of Chapter 3 covers synchronization effects and market impact measurements). The market impact is a major factor of the *Price Formation Process*: A buying or selling pressure that is not consistent with market participants' current consensus will only generate temporary impact. When the same pressure is coherent with participants' viewpoints, nobody will push back the price: The impact will be permanent. Such an exploratory process provides information to all the observers of not only the transaction prices, but of the whole offer and demand dynamics.

Oscillating prices observed in the markets thus come from temporary imbalances between buyers and sellers, that could (in theory) be suppressed if these investors would have been more synchronized. Such market impact can be profited from *market makers*, buying to the early sellers, and selling a short while later to buyers. Such an action reduces meaningless oscillations of the price arising from temporary market impact. Such market makers are nevertheless exposed to risk as they cannot anticipate the price move due to an unexpected news event between the arrival of sellers and buyers. Microstructure theory [O'Hara, 1998] explains the consequences of this relationship between market risk and market makers' bid-ask spread.

The loop is now almost closed: If we accept market makers, most of the temporary oscillations of the price will be reduced to a bid-ask spread related to the intrinsic risk of the traded asset. Liquidity is now consistent with the fundamental value of this asset, and no more an endogenous quantity. Unfortunately this is not as good as it seems. First, this means that the liquidity of some assets cannot exceed some threshold related to their market risk. Hence a market in which all assets would be very liquid is a chimera, close to the chimeric efficient markets described by Grossman and Stiglitz in [Grossman and Stiglitz, 1980] (at the lowest time scale, market dynamics have to contain enough inefficiency to reward participants improving the informational contents of the price formation proces). Second it is well known that some arbitrage are never implemented because of frictions: What if such frictions can prevent market makers from scalping price oscillations efficiently enough?

This pending question came to the attention of regulators a few years after 2000. Some friction costs had been identified: The monopoly of the exchanges resulted in high fees and low quality of service. Reg NMS in the US and MiFID in Europe emerged around 2005: Implementing competition among trading venues would be the way to lower explicit and implicit friction costs so that market makers could improve their efficiency, and consequently increase globally the liquidity of all equity markets.

The outcome of this new microstructure surprised most of the market participants. The nature of liquidity itself changed into a highly fragmented system that called the efficiency of market makers into question. This book covers important aspects of these changes, with a focus on European markets, with three major questions:

1. How do we describe quantitatively a fragmented market? (Chapter 1)
2. How do we understand relationships between characteristics of such a market? (Chapter 2)
3. How do we optimize trading in such an environment? (Chapter 3)

We answer these questions using data monitoring the fragmentation of European markets, and by covering important events on other markets, like the *Flash Crash* in the US (see Chapter 2, Section 2.4.3). We emphasize the methodology, so the reader can study the continuing evolution of markets (which is beyond the scope of this book). A detailed scientific Appendix exposes important concepts and tools, providing to the reader some basis in applied mathematics and quantitative analysis to understand the roots and mechanisms of the important tools used in the book. The bibliography of the Appendix allows a passionate reader to explore the topic in much greater depth.

Microstructure from a Regulatory Standpoint

Without a doubt, substantial changes in the market microstructure have occurred since 2005 in the US and in Europe. The symptoms are not the same, but there are some shared roots: The price formation process has been affected by fragmentation following regulatory changes, and the market liquidity itself suffered from the financial crisis. A new type of agent, namely "high-frequency traders" (HFT), acting as market makers but in most cases without obligations, has blurred the usual roles of each layer of the market structure (see Figure 2).

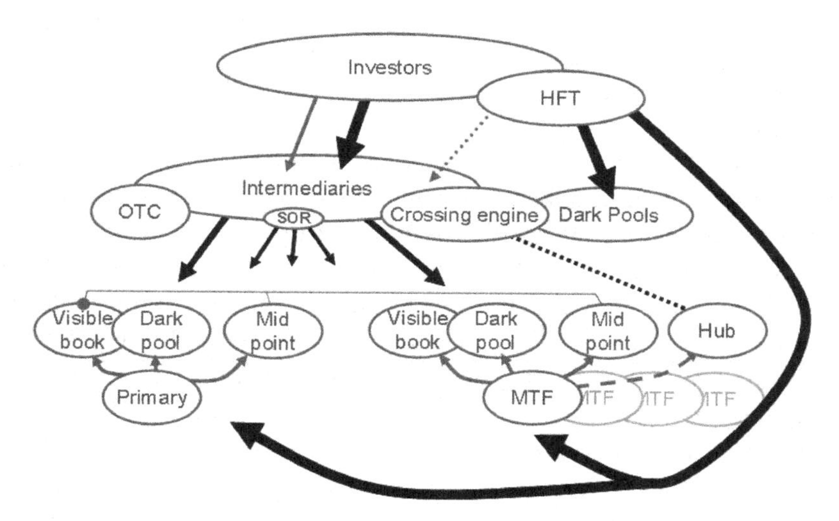

Figure 2. Diagram of a fragmented market microstructure.

The consequences of the changes in the microstructure are different in the US and Europe, mainly because of local regulations.

In the US, the Flash Crash on 6 May 2010 showed that a market organized around a pre-trade consolidated tape can also have its weak points (see Chapter 2, Section 2.4.3). In Europe, outages have shown that without shared information among agents, it is very difficult to obtain a robust price formation process. Some facts seem to be undeniable:

- HFT (High Frequency Trading) is the price to pay for fragmentation; it is not possible to put trading venues in competition without agents building high-frequency liquidity bridges across them. The potential negative externalities of their activity have to be questionned, this book takes time to review them.
- The main question is: How much should market participants and the overall market structure agree to pay to support these kinds of high frequency liquidity bridges?
- Once this threshold is fixed, plenty of ways can be used to adjust the level of HFT activity, one of these being the tick size; this book also explores this essential component of the market design (see Chapter 1, Section 1.3).
- The impact of market design is not limited to intraday trading. Undoubtedly, the price formation process, and the availability of liquidity plays a large role in the price moves. The link between systemic risk and intraday activity is explored in Section 2.4 of Chapter 2.
- The PFP (Price Formation Process) is mainly driven by information. From the viewpoint of one investor: On the one hand, sharing information is better for his own market impact and the likelihood to be adversely selected. On the other hand using information from other market participants to launch a buy when they sell (or the reverse), the better it is for his trading process. The crucial role of timing and the optimal way to schedule trading and liquidity seeking are covered Sections 3.2 and 3.3 of Chapter 3. In the US, the existence of the consolidated tape organizes how information is shared among agents; it allows them to make synchronous decisions and strengthens the price formation process. Europe

needs a way to share information without relying on primary markets alone. A consolidated post-trade tape is a good option that could leverage on fragmentation to improve the robustness of the price formation process.

A Recent Appetite of Regulators and Policy-Makers for Electronic Markets

Regulators and policymakers are comfortable demanding the recording and storage of information on the behavior of market participants; this mood favors a market design organized around competing electronic markets. On paper this type of market design provides traceability of the transactions everaging the usual benefits of competition (price pressure and run for quality). Again on paper, the two other archetypal models — a highly concentrated model (typically the French one from five years ago) or an intricate and high latency network of bilateral counterparts (think about the UK markets a few years ago) — would probably be expensive or too "dark", respectively. In reality, transparent information on the price formation process (not only reporting transactions as soon as they occur, but also disseminating the full depth of the order-books at pre-trade) and the appetite of competing trading venues for liquidity providers opened the door to liquidity arbitrageurs, mainly known as "High Frequency Traders" (HFT).

Because "liquidity bridges" have to be established between available trading venues to ensure that a bid price somewhere is not greater than an ask one elsewhere (or an available ask being lower than an available bid), the arbitrageur will take half of the differences between the two prices and "improve" the level of information of other participants having access to fewer venues. The less such cross-trading venue arbitrages exist, the more blindly a market participant can send an order to any venue: He effectively delegates the information search to arbitrageurs (HFTs), and agrees to pay for this "service". Since HFTs mechanically increase fragmentation, their activity can be monitored by the effective fragmentation of markets. A "Fragmentation Efficiency Index" (FEI) is presented in Chapter 1, Section 1.1.3; inspired by the concept of entropy used in physics

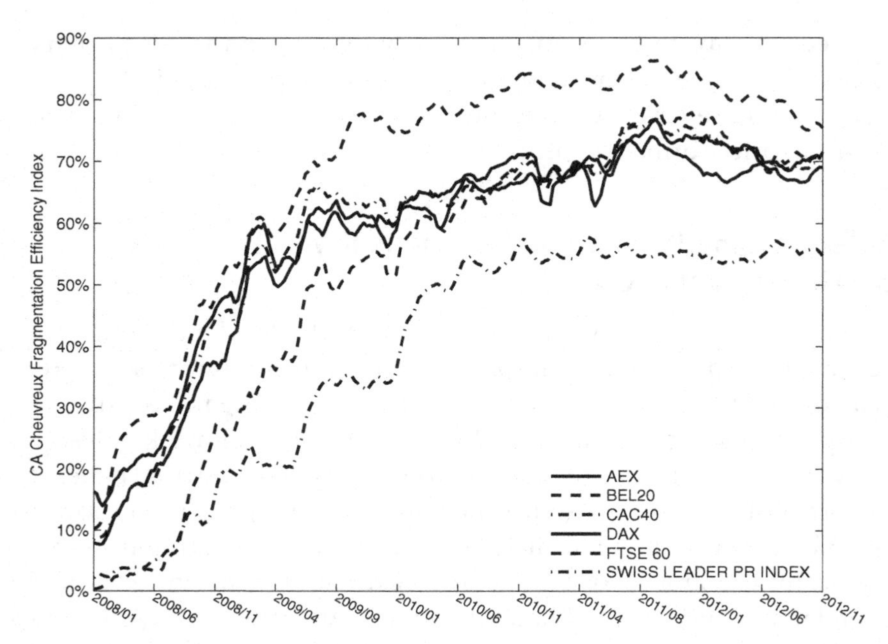

Figure 3. History of the Fragmentation Efficiency Index on main European markets.

to measure the level of heterogeneity of an environment it can be efficiently used that for. In short: The higher the index (maximum is 100%), the more blindly an order can be sent to a venue, while the lower its value (minimum is 0%), the more carefully an order has to be split. Figure 3 shows the recent trend in the FEI in Europe.

It can be seen that the liquidity offered on the components of the three main European indexes shows a two-slope trend: The first one (fast) during 2008, the other one (slower) from the beginning of 2009.

The sequencing of different auction mechanisms (fixing, continuous, trading at last, etc.) is also an important component of the market design, influencing the way market participants provide and consume liquidity. While the third part of this section is dedicated to an in-depth study of fixing auction mechanisms, one has to remark here that Asian markets are gradually converging to common trading hours when possible (for instance, Tokyo and Singapore in 2011). Competition to capture flows of investors wishing to invest on Asian-driven market factors can be enough to drive convergence in terms of auction types and sequencing.

Worldwide Consolidation: An Electronic Trading Global Timeline

Markets have faced significant changes in the last forty years, both in terms of regulation and technology. Key steps of these evolutions are indicated in the timeline in Table 1. Different typefaces are used to mention the type of change:

- `this style for technological changes;`
- **this style for newcomers** (increasing fragmentation);
- *this style for merger* (somehow decreasing fragmentation).

The first column indicates the corresponding speed of processors over the years, and their computational throughput (MIPS: million of instructions per second) which increases according to Moore's law.

Note that more events and more mergers occur in recent years.

Table 1. Chronology.

2 MHz 0.64 MIPS	**1970s:**	US/`Introduction of the NYSE's "designated order turnaround" system (DOT)` that routed orders electronically to the floor.
16–40 MHz 5 MIPS	**1980s:**	Automation of index arbitrage and development of program trading.
	1986:	France/`Introduction of the CAC trading system` (fully-computerised matching engine).
233 MHz 100 MIPS	**1990s:**	US/Introduction of the Electronic Communication Networks.
	1992:	`Initiation of the FIX protocol`: International real-time exchange of information.
1.3–3.8 GHz 1700 MIPS	**2000s:**	US/Decimalisation of prices.
	June 2001:	Creation of the Committee of European Securities Regulators (CESR), which will be replaced by ESMA under MiFID II.
2.6-3.6 GHz 9000 MIPS	**April 2004:**	Adoption of the MiFID directive at the EU level.
	2005:	US/Rules promoting national market system are consolidated into RegNMS.
	June 2005:	US/**BATS Trading** is formed.

(*Continued*)

Table 1. (*Continued*)

2.4 GHz 22 000 MIPS	**February 2006**:	*Archipelago becomes NYSE Arca* after the NYSE's buyout.
	June 2006:	*NYSE (New York Stock Exchange) and Euronext merge to become NYSE Euronext.*
	July 2006:	Publication of implementing measures for MiFID.
3 GHz 2*22 000 MIPS	**July 2007**:	Launch of **Chi-X Amsterdam** and **Chi-X London**.
	August 2007:	**One participant makes 80% of Chi-X Amsterdam's trades.**[1]
	September 2007:	The same participant reaches 15% of all Dutch trades and drives Chi-X's increase in market share in Amsterdam.
	November 2007:	Deadline for the industry to apply the directive. Launch of **Chi-X Paris**.
3.2 GHz 2*24 000 MIPS	**August 2008**:	Launch of **Turquoise** in Europe.
	October 2008:	US/**Knight Link** is the No. 1 Dark Pool in share volume.
	November 2008:	Launch of **BATS** Trading Europe and **Xetra Mid-Point**.
2.93 GHz 76 383 MIPS	**March 2009**:	Market-making agreements on Turquoise expire. Its market share drops.
	May 2009:	Launch of **Nasdaq OMX** Europe.
	June 2009:	Tick war: BATS and Turquoise activate a gradual reduction in tick sizes, leading to a tacit agreement between exchanges under the FESE.
	July 2009:	A former Goldman Sachs programmer is arrested by the FBI with a USB key containing algorithmic trading codes.
	August 2009:	US/Flash orders appear on the Nasdaq Stock Exchange.
	October 2009:	Launch of **NYSE ARCA** Europe.
	November 2009:	Launch of **Knight Link**, first Systematic Internaliser in Europe.

(*Continued*)

Table 1. (*Continued*)

3.33 GHz 147 600 MIPS	**January 2010:**	Turquoise offers futures and options on Norwegian stocks and an index on Turquoise derivatives. US/The SEC sends a request for comments on market microstructure.
	April 2010:	The CESR also sends questions to participants on market microstructure.
	May 2010:	May 6th: Flash Crash.
	July 2010:	*Closure of Nasdaq OMX Europe.*
	September 2010:	Findings on the May 6th events are reported by the CFTC and the SEC.
	December 2010:	The European Commission launches a public consultation for the revision of MiFID (MiFID II). *BATS Global and Chi-X Europe enter exclusive merger talks.*
3.33 GHz 147 600 MIPS	**February 2011:**	End of the EC consultation. Regulatory change in Spain for Chi-X to get clearing and settlement.
		Feb. 18th: London Stock Exchange and Turquoise merge. Deutsche Boerse and NYSE Euronext confirm advanced merger discussions.
		Feb. 22nd: Outage on the Italian Stock Exchange.
		Feb. 25th: Outage on the London Stock Exchange.
	May 2011:	Markus Ferber appointed as rapporteur for MiFID II.
		His conclusions are to be presented to the ECON (European Parliament's Economic and Monetary Affairs Committee).
	June 2011:	**June 13th and 15th: Outages on Chi-X.**
		June 20th, 21st and 27th: Outages on NYSE Euronext.
	August 2011:	India/first regulatory approval for Smart Order Routing.
	September 2011:	Turquoise offers futures and options on the FTSE 100 index.
	October 2011:	Proposal for MiFID II is unveiled by the European Commission. It contains one directive, and one regulation.

(*Continued*)

Table 1. (*Continued*)

November 2011:	*Final decision on the BATS-Chi-X merger from the UK Competition Commission. BATS Global and Chi-X Europe successfully closed their deal.*
April 2012:	ESMA guidelines issued for MiFID II. Both BATS and Chi-X Europe to launch fully interoperable clearing.
May 2012:	Amendment deadline for MiFID II.
July 2012:	ECON committee vote on MiFID II.
End of 2012:	Trialogue process to reach agreement on MiFID II.
January 2013:	Inter Continental Exchange (ICE) offer to buy Nyse-Euronext.
January 2014:	Earliest indicated implementation of MiFID II.

Source: *High-Frequency Trading and The New Market Makers*, A. Menkveld, 2011.

Changes in the Microstructure

The microstructure of a market is defined as the way the different traders share their responsibilities and their roles. The rules are defined by the regulators and under these rules (mainly respecting regulatory-defined constraints), each trader works to maximize his utility (i.e., a risk vs. reward balance).

In the field of equity markets (European and US markets), the traders are usually divided into two main categories (see [Harris, 2002]):

- The agents (brokers and buy-side traders);
- The principals (utilitarian traders, speculators, dealers and "noise" traders).

The characteristics of liquidity available on a given stock are a mix of the trading rules, the type of traders trading it, and the properties of the underlying asset (i.e., the listed firm: Its sector, its level of risk, etc). Hence changes in regulation, corporate governance decisions (modifying the capital structure of the firm), or more technical decisions (split or reverse split of shares) can modify the liquidity of a stock.

Defining Best Execution

MiFID, which came into effect on 1 November 2007, changed most of the rules for the equity market through the introduction of two main guidelines:

- The liberalization of trading venues: By abolishing the concentration rules in place in some European countries, MiFID enabled the creation of "alternative" trading venues.
- The concept of "best execution", which is not clearly defined in the regulatory framework, as each broker is allowed to draw up its own definition, thus providing access to the market through a clearly defined "best execution policy".

The various outcomes of these changes were unexpected. The liberalization of the trading venues did not lead to the creation of numerous alternative venues (the financial crisis clearly did not encourage investors to finance the creation of alternative venues), but a small number of such venues (Chi-X, Turquoise, BATS Europe, NASDAQ-OMX), each of which offers more than one "liquidity pool" (visible pools, anonymous ones, etc). Most primary markets also offer alternate liquidity pools.

In short: Rather than giving rise to a high level of competition, the liberalization of trading venues spread the liquidity among a few venues, which rapidly split "their" markets into niches.

As most final investors'[1] needs consist of a mix of different liquidity pools, the agents (i.e., brokers and buy-side traders) inherited the crucial role of consolidating the liquidity. It is worth noting that the fragmentation followed a very similar path in the US, even if the "equivalent" regulation (Reg NMS) came into effect two years earlier.

---

[1] Final investors are investors who will keep their position for long, they are more interested on dividends rather than on buying low and selling high; their decisions are triggerred at a largest time scale than the one of orderbook dynamics.

The role of the financial crisis, even if it is difficult to isolate, may be a very important common factor to explain the almost simultaneous emergence of such a microstructure in both regions.

In addition, the concept of best execution focused on "immediate price improvement", which is dedicated to aggressive orders and based on snapshots of visible orderbooks. This was clearly a rational way to define best execution before the fragmentation of the market. However, after a few years, we think that the definition of best execution has to change, given, on the one hand, the importance of capturing liquidity passively, and, on the other, the lack of information recorded in snapshots (hidden orders have increased by 30%, from 2007 to 2011 according to NYSE Euronext, since some market participants, especially high frequency traders use mirrored orders and hidden ones).

At present, best execution is first and foremost a matter of offering consolidated access to liquidity for both passive and aggressive orders. Large brokers offer access to an internal crossing engine, in order to value the "natural liquidity" provided by their clients. The "value" of flows originated by final investors comes from the fact that they do not look at the state of the orderbook to take decisions. Since their investment process takes place at a larger scale than the trading process, such large buyers and sellers have a much higher probability of crossing their orders with little market impact. On the other hand, if a large buyer exposes its flow in a pool filled with more "opportunistic" players (i.e., investors with a very short investment horizon), the opportunistic players can make a profit by using the information that a big order has just entered the market (buying "in front" of the large investor and selling back to him few hours latter at an higher price). Consequently, there is an apparent disincentive for large investors to be exposed to flows originated by faster players, explaining the success of large broker BCNs (Broker Crossing Networks) as far as such pools are "HFT-free guaranteed". They also give access to a maximum number of pools (including dark ones) via trading algorithms and Smart Order Routers (SOR).

With the increasing complexity of the microstructure, it is difficult to define exactly the right benchmark to use to compare an average price to. Besides, it seems that best execution can no longer be limited to the split of an aggressive order according to an instantaneous snapshot of several orderbooks. Adverse selection, passive split, reversal are measurements that should be used to rank the performance of a trading process. The concept of "efficient execution" can only be defined on a long time scale (and not instantaneously) and has to be related to the investment style of the originator of the order.

In the realm of market microstructure, the clearing and settlement channels play a major role, as it is meaningless to compare millisecond-time stamped orderbooks of two venues that do not share the same clearing and settlement costs and risks. Most of the market participants stressed that MiFID did not provide a clear way to rank the efficiency of a trading process as a whole.

The importance of the market microstructure stems from the fact that we all entrust this market of markets with the price formation process. This process is one of the mechanisms at the heart of capitalism: It should, by balancing supply and demand via the occurrence of deals between traders, form prices that constitute a fair view of the value of the exchanged assets. To guide traders to

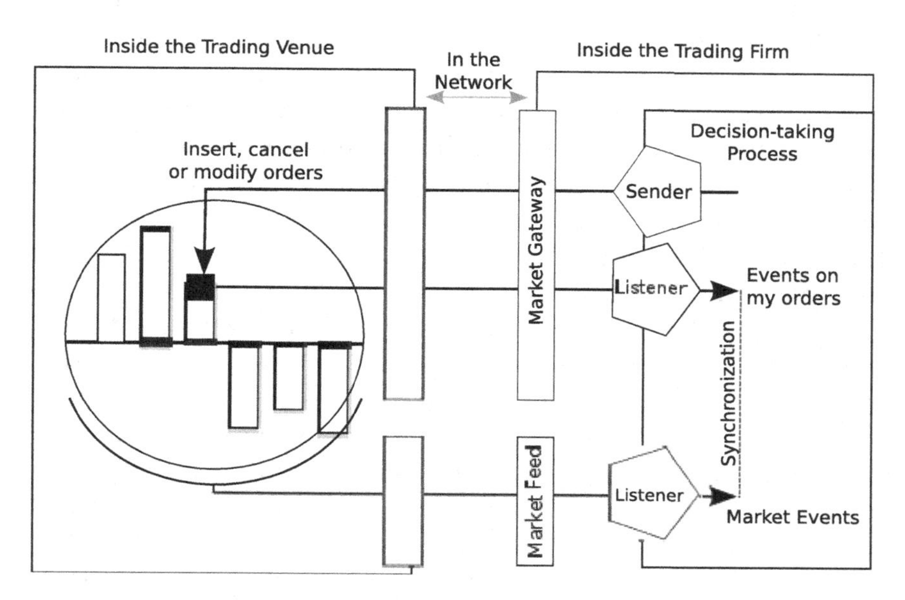

Figure 4. Diagram of the decision-making framework for automated trading.

decide at which prices and for which quantities they have to place orders, the market has to provide them with information prior to the trades and then make public the information that a given trade took place.

The paradox is that, on the one hand, the more information that is available to the traders, the better the price formation process (PFP) will theoretically be, but, on the other hand, each trader fears "information leakage" and the threat of being front run or having excessive price impact. Market design is clearly at the heart of this contradiction: The microstructure should allow enough information to be shared by all investors to ensure a fair PFP, but the interest of each investor has to be protected from information leakage. Reorganizing the market microstructure is thus a difficult and subtle task, involving changes in the way information goes from one trader to all other market participants and vice versa.

It is clear that any investor will primarily be concerned with protecting his own interest, participating with stealth in the PFP, but some investors are less capable of protecting themselves, especially if this protection involves heavy technological investments. The issue of protection of all investors can only be resolved through regulation, and MiFID aimed at this protection with the concept of pre-trade and post-trade transparency. Demanding all participants (the investors themselves, intermediaries, and trading venues) to publish enough ex ante and ex post information has been a good move towards guaranteeing a fair price formation process. While the constraints on pre-trade transparency are clear, there is a consensus about the difficulty of obtaining efficient post-trade transparency. Another principle underlined by MiFID was to use the size of an order as a proxy for the level of maturity of a trader: The larger an order, the more autonomous the investor is; the smaller the order, the more the originator of the order has to be protected.

Two elements recently shook up these principles (the sharing of information and the relationship between the size of an order and the maturity of its originator): "Dark Pools" (whose activity is detailed in Chapter 1, Section 1.4) and high frequency traders (studied in Chapter 2, Section 2.3). The former do not publish the same level of information as the other liquidity pools, and the latter are highly

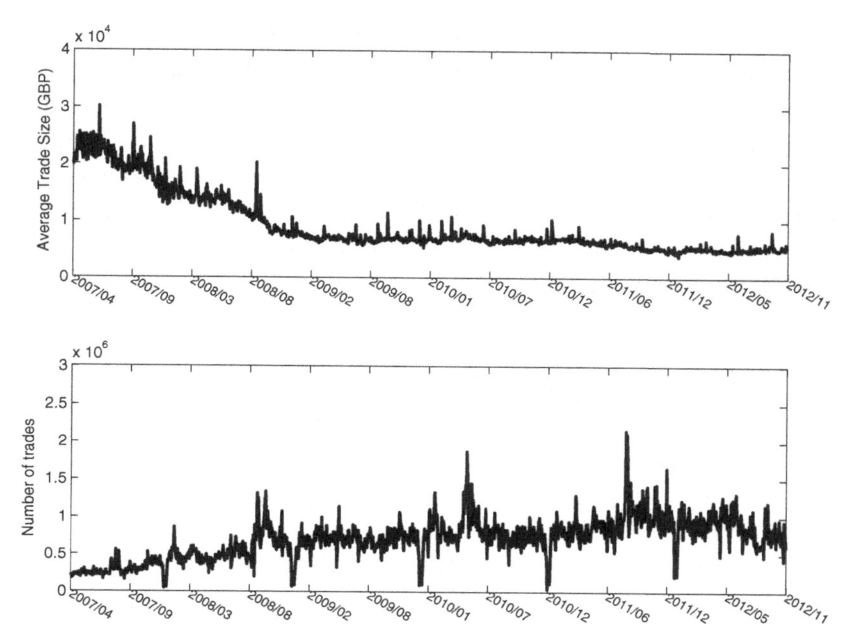

Figure 5. Indicators of Average Trade Size (ATS) and daily number of trades for the components of the FTSE 100.

informed investors using only very small orders (the increase in the number of trades independently of the decreasing average trade size is often considered as evidence of the increasing activity of HFT, see Figure 5).

Redefining the Roles: An Agent is Now Both Liquidity Taker and Liquidity Provider Simultaneously

Dark Pools are a new component of the market microstructure. Since there is no official definition of Dark trading, the term can be used to cover all OTC trade or just trades occurring in a multilateral trading facilities (MTF) governed by a waiver allowing it to match orders without pre-trade transparency (when the size of the order is small enough) as long as the price of the deals is imported from a visible reference market. The rationale of such a rule is that from a theoretical point of view, deals at imported prices do not participate in the price formation process.

Dark Pools and high frequency traders share a common point: They blur the quality of the liquidity available in orderbooks; they thus modify the usual definitions of liquidity providers and liquidity consumers. The trading activity of HFT updates limit orderbooks at a higher rate than the round trip for any non co-located observer. The snapshot of the limit orderbooks you take into account to make decisions does not, in most cases, reflect the state of the book when your order actually reaches it. Figure 1.17 (on p. 63) shows the typical routing logic followed by an order:

1. Snapshot the state of the orderbooks; say that time τ is needed for this information to reach the decision taker,
2. Make a decision; say that time ϵ is needed,
3. The order is sent, but takes time τ to reach the orderbook.

Summing all these durations the order will reach the matching engines of the trading venues with a delay of $2\tau + \epsilon$. The decision taking process can be accelerated using more powerful computers (or dedicated hardwares like FPGAs), but the time taken to carry information from one point to an other is constrained by the laws of physics. Thus when the orderbook update frequency f is larger than two times the traveling time the information (i.e., $f > 1/(2\tau)$) the decision making process does not use the proper information to decide where and how to route an order. Hence the "picture" of the orderbook taken in step (1) has to be replaced by real-time estimates of the quantity that is really available in the books at each price (see [Lehalle, 2012] for a review of literature proposing such models). That being said there is not that much difference between a Lit Pool (giving access to the state of its orderbook, blurred by hidden orders and mirrored quantities) and a Dark Pool publishing its hosted trades immediately. This is a shift in the paradigm: Before fragmentation, one could send an order to a market knowing that it would be a liquidity provider or a liquidity consumer. Now, when an order is sent to the market, the present information only gives an estimate of its probability of capturing aggressive or passive flows.

As it has been explained: Such a situation has to occur once the trading frequency crosses a given threshold. This is a well-known result of information theory known as the "Nyquist-Shannon sampling theorem". Restated in trading terms, it says that:

Proposition 1 (Nyquist-Shannon sampling theorem). *As soon as the frequency of the changes in the orderbook of a trading venue is greater than half of the inverse of the latency between an observer of the venue, the observer loses information.*

Our Nyquist-Shannon trading threshold formula is consequently:

$$\textit{Orderbook update frequency threshold} = \frac{1}{2}\frac{1}{\textit{latency to the exchanges}}.$$

This implies that if a trader is at a "distance" (i.e., latency) of 2 ms from a trading venue, he has complete information as soon as the orderbook update frequency is lower than 250 Hz. If not, the time for him to receive the information and to send back an order is higher than the time to the next update.

Definition 1 (Nyquist-Shannon latency bound). *We will call the Nyquist-Shannon latency bound of an orderbook the latency needed to fulfill the eponymous threshold:*

$$\textit{Nyquist-Shannon latency bound} = \frac{1}{2}\frac{1}{\textit{Orderbook update frequency}}.$$

Figure 6 shows the variations of the number of updates of the orderbook (top five levels on each side) per second (i.e., frequency in Hertz) for two liquid stocks (one listed in the UK, and the other in Paris) during the day. It is greater than 250 Hz during most of the day, which implies a *Nyquist-Shannon latency bound* of 2 ms.

Given that the roundtrip (time go go from one place to another and to travel back to the initial point; see Figure 1) from Paris to London, is around 8 ms (in 2012), the orderbook update frequency threshold is 125 Hz. It means that any matching engine updated more than 125 times per second in London will not be seen from Paris with enough accuracy to take deterministic decisions. It partially explains why NYSE-Euronext moved its data center from Paris to the suburbs

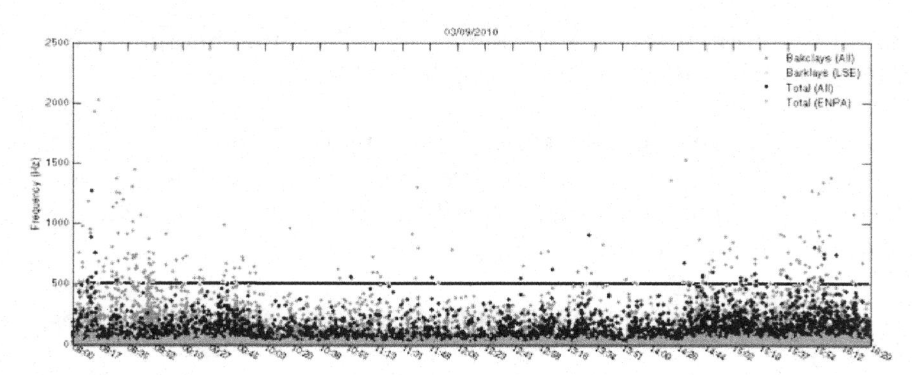

Figure 6. Intra-day frequency of update of the top five levels for two large caps in Europe (on their primary market and on a consolidated tape): 500 Hz (horizontal line) is a common value, its associated latency bound is 1 ms.

of London: it eases the smart order routing process between Chi-X, BATS Europe and Euronext-Paris orderbooks.

Dark Pools also contribute to this blurring of definitions: On sending an order to such a liquidity pool, the only information you have is the probability of being a liquidity provider or liquidity consumer. This uncertainty about the nature of the contribution of an order to the price formation process is now so high that a new type of order is available (for instance on Xetra and NYSE Arca Europe): "Book or cancel". Such an order is canceled if it happens to consume liquidity. The necessity of such a type of order can be read as acceptance by most of the market participants that they cannot know in advance if a limit order will be marketable or not.

These two points emphasize the importance of post-trade transparency: The fact that a trade occurred at a given price for a given size gives clear deterministic information on the price formation process. The weight of such an information in a decision-making process is far greater than that of a snapshot of an orderbook: At present, pre-trade transparency carries less importance than post-trade transparency. Unfortunately, the quality of post-trade transparency in Europe is lower than for its pre-trade counterpart.

Dark Pools do not provide pre-trade transparency (they import the price from an external venue because the pre-trade transparency of such a venue is theoretically considered to be a good proxy for the nature of the liquidity they are able to provide), but do provide post-trade transparency, and are thus more compatible with the new trading landscape than it is widely believed. Dark Pools are liquidity pools for which the price formation process takes place anonymously, and their outcomes (deals) are publicly reported, as for "Lit" Pools. Some investors may feel more comfortable dealing under the cloak of anonymity, in order to minimize the amount of information they give to HFT.

Towards a Paradigm Shift: A Blurring of Roles

Not only has the frontier between liquidity providers and liquidity consumers become less clear-cut with the change of microstructure, but the separation of roles between the different operators and intermediaries of the market has become blurred.

The previous situation was simple enough (Figure 7). There were:

- Primary markets with listing and surveillance capabilities;
- Intermediaries in charge of pairing interests between investors in-house (via OTC trades for instance) or on visible markets.

In this simple pre-MiFID model, the market share of OTC trades was not clearly known and often underestimated by observers

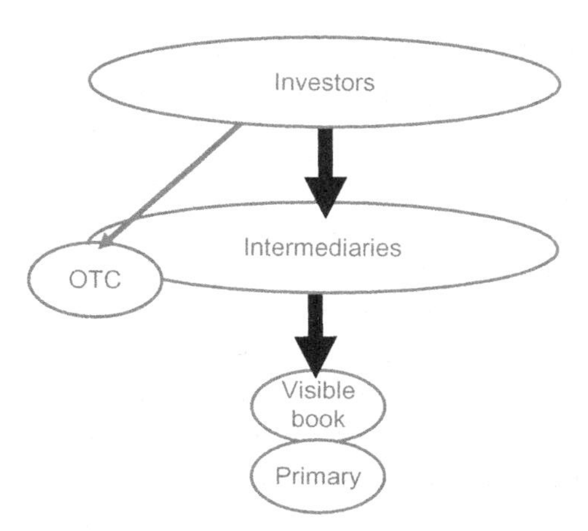

Figure 7. Idealized view of a non-fragmented microstructure.

(investors and corporates alike). Now the roles are less clear-cut (Figure 2):

- MTFs have been created by investment banks (e.g., Turquoise), brokers, overseas exchanges (e.g., BATS Europe and NASDAQ-OMX), or independent shareholders;
- European primary markets also govern or own MTFs with visible (NYSE-Arca) or anonymous books (e.g., SmartPool or Xetra midpoint);
- A proportion of previously OTC trades now takes place in the "crossing engines" of brokers, some of which are regulated as MTFs;
- Brokers are struggling to give their clients a consolidated view of the pools, given that each client needs a specific mix of liquidity pools;
- MTFs offer more than one trading pool (mid-points and Dark Pools) and also give access to the crossing engines of some brokers (such as TQ Lens);
- The HF traders, part of investment firms or funds (thus being formally considered as investors), are now closer to being part of the price formation process (i.e., their role is closer to that of intermediaries).

The fact that a system has become more complex is not a bad thing in itself. On the contrary, it is often an opportunity to achieve progress. For instance, if you are able to use a plane instead of a car, you will be able to reach more destinations and to follow new trajectories, although flying a plane is more difficult than driving a car.

In the field of market design, one must bear in mind that each participant will try to optimize his own utility. This is the root of liberalism, popularized by the welfare theorem: In a well-organized market, the fact that each player aims to maximize his own utility will lead to an efficient state for all concerned, without there being a need for dialogue. When the complexity of the market microstructure increases, one must ensure that the relationship between the utility of each player and the efficiency of the whole system is preserved. The change in positioning of some players, such as the high frequency traders (HFT) which simultaneously drift from being investors to market operators and to the leading clients of trading venues, can be considered a danger from this point of view. As was the case in the US in August 2008, exchanges can maximize their utility (i.e., increasing the satisfaction of their clients) by offering "flash orders" to HFT as if they were market operators. Since the latter retain the utility function of a regular investor, their use of such information leakage to their own interest will not benefit the efficiency of the market. When the positioning and the role of a player in the market changes, the regulator should ensure that this will not cause efficiency leakage in the system.

In addition, competent entities have to be clearly designated to carry out market surveillance. Primary markets claim that they support most of the costs of surveillance. Those costs are clearly shared by brokers, which also have regulatory constraints of this nature. Moreover, the primary market receive revenues generated by market data. The diversity of incentives and interests makes it difficult for the regulators and policy-makers to anticipate the impact of a change of rule.

Impact on Liquidity

The price formation process (PFP) has long been studied by academics and practitioners. A consensus seems to exist around the idea that the PFP consists of the impact of each trade occurring in the market, combined with the variation of the "fair price" of the listed asset [Bouchaud *et al.*, 2002]. This "fair price" is very difficult to estimate and the role of a large broker as an intermediary is to provide information about the fair price via financial analysis (i.e., "research") on the one hand and to concentrate a large part of the liquidity (i.e., execution) on the other. It positions such brokers at the crossroads of the two main forces driving the PFP. In order to give a simple view of the PFP, we split it into two phases (see Figure 8):

- The deals impact the price (through the balance between buyers and sellers, and liquidity-providing orders and liquidity-consuming ones) in conjunction with moves of the bid ask spread.

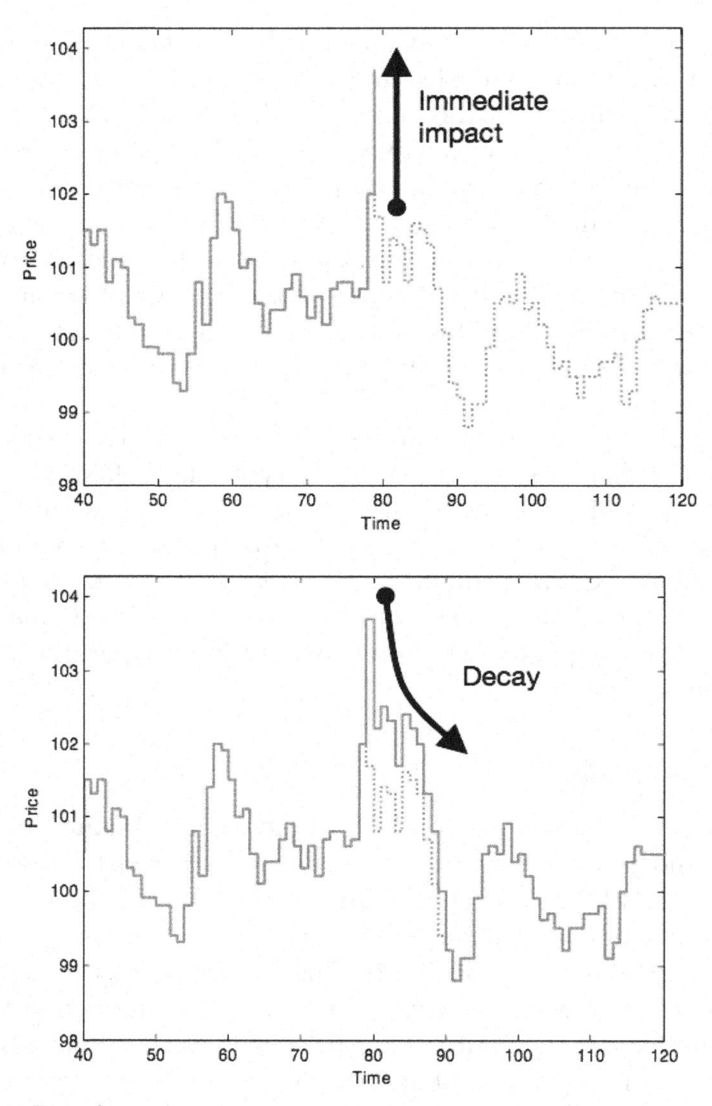

Figure 8. Price formation process in two steps: Immediate impact (top) and then decay (bottom).

This is often named the "immediate price impact" (as presented in [Smith *et al.*, 2003]).

- Liquidity returns (or not, as the case may be) according to the distance between the best bid and ask prices and investors' view of the "fair price". This leads to a "decay" of the impact, also termed the "resilience" of the limit orderbook.

As illustrated in Figure 8, the price impact of a deal can be absorbed rapidly if the impacted price is far from investors' views of the fair price, generating a temporary market impact, or can move the price permanently if their views of the fair price move in accordance with the new quoted prices.

The role of post-trade transparency is underlined here: Potential traders have to be warned that the latest price is not in line with their view, so that they can send limit orders to the market (i.e., provide liquidity to it) and bring the price back to a more efficient level.

The faster the information is propagated, the sooner the impact will decay thanks to investors having a view of the fair price, or which utility function is consistent with this liquidity providing role. For instance, market markers with inventory-keeping constraints can contribute to the decay of the price impact without having any view of the fair price.

As a result, the more investors with views of the fair price are part of the PFP, the more likely the decay after a deal will reduce the price impact rapidly. If the horizon of an investor is longer than a jump in the price, he will probably contribute to the subsequent decay. Conversely, the inventory of a market maker has to be larger than the turnover of a jump in price to allow it to contribute to the decay.

The growing contribution of HFT to the price formation process can be seen as a threat to the stability resulting from the decay in price impacts. HFT do not necessarily have a view on the fair price of the stock they deal, and high-frequency market makers have small inventory limits. It does not mean that it is never the case (see [Brogaard *et al.*, 2012][Menkveld, 2010] for more details): Seen from a market microstructure perspective an high frequency arbitrage technique could be to detect the isolated market impact of one trade on the price of one isolated stock, thus the HFT is able to provide liquidity on this stock since he can hedge his position in other stocks (or sectors) that have not been impacted by the trade. Intra-day arbitrage can be read as a way to propagate market

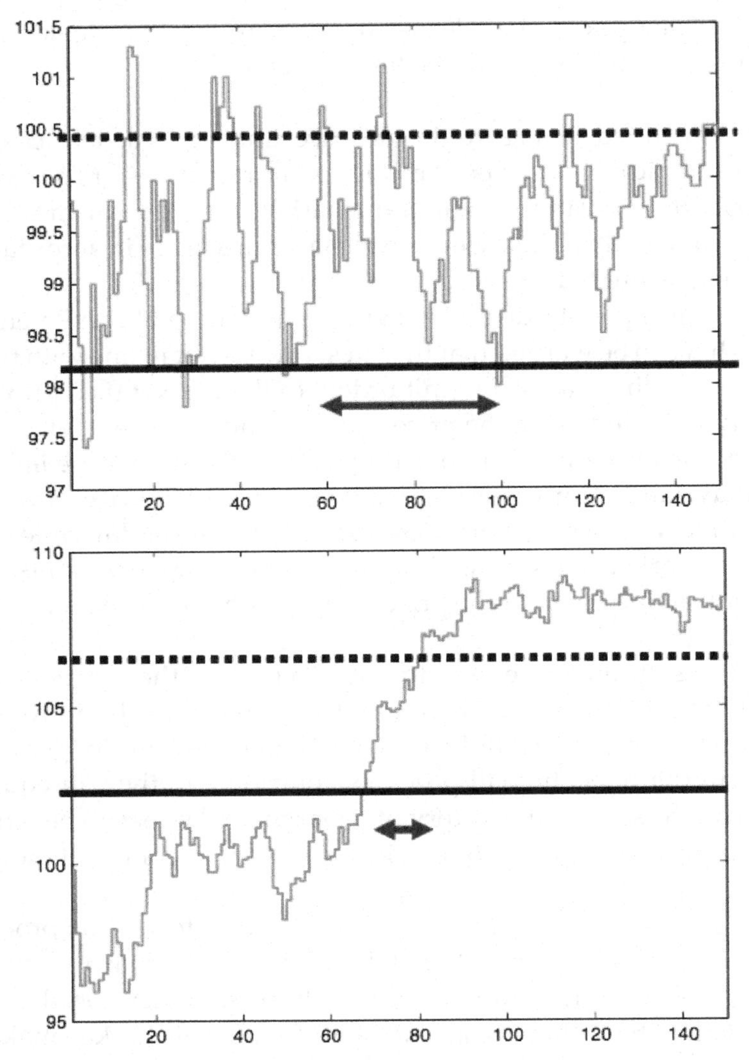

Figure 9. The horizon of trend following strategies is lower than the one of trend reverting ones.

impact from one stock to the others, hence being a proper way to convey information market-wide. Nevertheless the shorter their horizon is, the less they will be able to provide liquidity to decay the impact of the trades. They will act as "market impact followers" rather than "market impact reverters". Instead of *making the market* (i.e., providing liquidity ex-ante), HFT is more likely propagating meaningful market impact (i.e., removing liquidity ex-post). This observation questions the possible contribution of the HFT to the stability of markets.

Chapter 1

Monitoring the Fragmentation at Any Scale

1.1. Fluctuations of Market Shares: A First Graph on Liquidity

1.1.1. *The market share: A not so obvious liquidity metric*

The fragmentation of a market usually occurs at different scales.

- At the scale of the market operators: New operators appear in the early phases (like Archipelago, Direct Edge, BATS in the US and Turquoise and Chi-X in Europe), then some of them merge to try to handle the fixed costs linked to operating market places.
- At the scale of trading venues: The same market operator (like Nyse-Euronext in Europe) can operate different trading venues (like the Nyse-Euronext Lit orderbook, plus Smartpool, plus Nyse-Arca). Typical BCN (Broker Crossing Network) are trading venues appearing because of fragmentation.
- At the scale of the orderbooks: The same trading venue can offer more than one orderbook. This is the case for most European RM (Regulated Markets) and MTF (Multilateral Trading Facilities). Chi-X offers Chi-X Lit and Chi-Delta (a Dark Pool) in Europe.
- At the scale of orders themselves, since when fragmentation increases, it is more and more necessary to split an order not just through time (to minimize its market impact, see Chapter 3, Section 3.3); but also through *space*, to spread the order among all the available orderbooks compatible with an execution policy, chasing liquidity.

Measuring fragmentation is thus not straightforward, since there is one adequate metric for each scale. Market share is nevertheless the most used metric. Monitoring the market share of each venue is a convenient way to understand the way the transactions migrate from one destination to another; it is an important component of the dynamic of the fragmentation of a market.

The market share is even not easy to define on one stock.

Definition 1 (Market Share). *If N trading venues $\mathcal{T}(1), \ldots, \mathcal{T}(N)$ offer trading on the same stock k, we can compute the Market Share $\mathfrak{M}^k(n;d)$ of the trading venue n on this stock during day d using the value of the transactions on the stock during this same day. Noting $(S^k_\ell, V^k_\ell, \tau^k_\ell, \delta^k_\ell)_{1\leq \ell \leq L(d)}$ the $L(d)$ trades of the day, where S is the price, V the quantity, τ the time and δ the index of the trading venue on which the trade occurred (i.e., $\delta^k_\ell = n$ if the ℓth transaction on security k during day d occurred on trading venue $\mathcal{T}(n)$), we can write the market share of the nth trading venue on the stock k between time t_1 and t_2:*

$$\mathfrak{M}^k(n;[t_1,t_2]) = \frac{\sum_{t_1 \leq \tau^k_\ell \leq t_2} S^k_\ell V^k_\ell \cdot \mathbf{1}_n(\delta^k_\ell)}{\sum_{t_1 \leq \tau^k_\ell \leq t_2} S^k_\ell V^k_\ell} \tag{1.1}$$

where $\mathbf{1}_a(b)$ is the indicator function: $\mathbf{1}_a(b) = 1$ when $a = b$, zero elsewhere. Formally, the market share for a day d is just $\mathfrak{M}^k(n;[t_1,t_2])$ with t_1 the first time of the day and t_2 the last one.

We can first notice that the market share in value (i.e., $\mathfrak{M}^k(n;[t_1,t_2])$) is not far from the market share in number of shares *over a period during which the price does not change a lot.*

$$\mathfrak{M}^k(n;[t_1,t_2]) \simeq \frac{\sum_{t_1 \leq \tau^k_\ell \leq t_2} V^k_\ell \cdot \mathbf{1}_n(\delta^k_\ell)}{\sum_{t_1 \leq \tau^k_\ell \leq t_2} V^k_\ell}, \quad \text{when } \forall \ell : S^k_\ell \simeq S.$$

Another simple way to compute a market share is to do it *per trade*:

$$\mathfrak{M}^k_t(n) = \frac{\sum_{1 \leq \ell \leq T} \mathbf{1}_n(\delta^k_\ell)}{T}. \tag{1.2}$$

It is of importance to recognize that the market share relies on the interval of time considered too: The market share during the first hour of trading is usually not the same than the one on the last hour of trading (Section 2.1.2 in Chapter 2, shows how the market is subject to an intraday rhythm).

Moreover, taking into account the fixing auctions changes the computation of the market share, mostly because one venue usually has a monopoly in the fixing auctions.[1] If a trading venue $\mathcal{T}(n)$ has an average market share of $m(n)$ during the fixing auctions, and if the fixing auctions weight for q in the overall exchange of the day (chart (a) of Figure 1.1 given some numerical values for this in Europe),

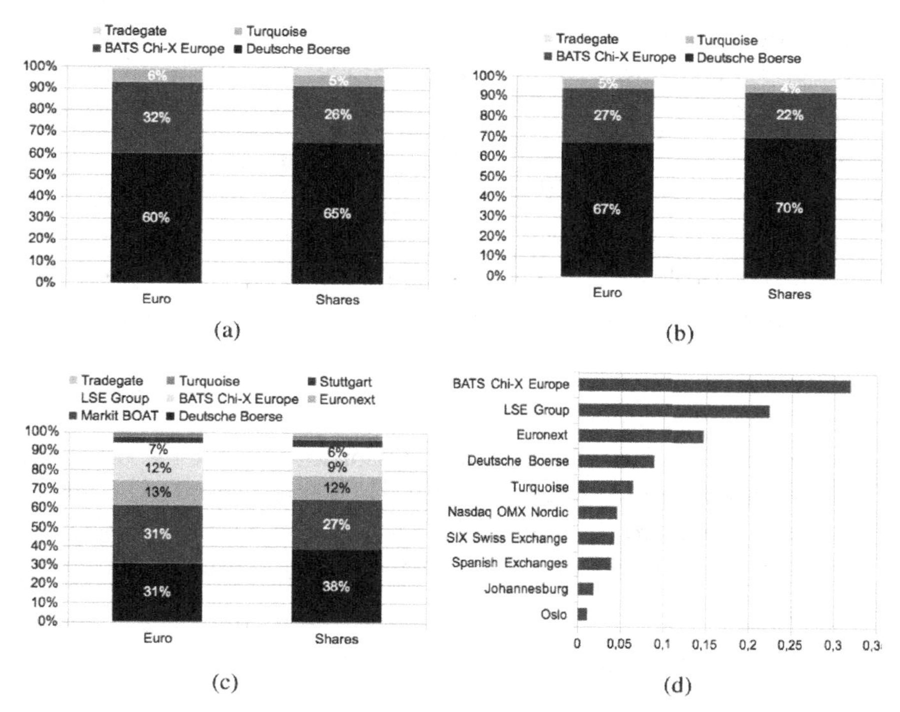

Figure 1.1. (a) Market shares of main venues on the DAX components (visible venues, continuous auctions only), (b) Market shares of main venues on the DAX components (visible venues, continuous and fixing auctions), (c) Market shares of main venues on the DAX components (all traded volumes), (d) Market shares in Euros of European venues (EuroStoxx600 + FTSE100 components).

Source: Reuters monthly liquidity report, June 2012.

[1]The historical markets: Nyse-Euronext on French stocks, the London Stock Exchange on UK-listed stocks, the Deutsche Boerse on German stocks, etc.

then on average ($\mathbf{T} = \sum_{1\le\ell\le T} S_\ell^k V_\ell^k$ is the average daily turnover for the stock on the whole market):

$$\begin{aligned}\mathfrak{M}(n;\text{ex-fixing}) &\simeq \frac{(1-m(n)p)\mathfrak{M}(n)\mathbf{T}}{(1-p)\mathbf{T}} \\ &\simeq \frac{1-m(n)\,p}{1-p}\cdot\mathfrak{M}(n;\text{all included}).\end{aligned}$$

Another important decision in computing a market share on more than one stock is to choose a weighting scheme for the stocks:

- The most natural weighting with respect to the upper definition is to weight according to the daily turnover of considered stocks $1 \le k \le K$:

$$\mathfrak{M}^{1,\dots,K}(n) = \frac{\sum_{1\le k\le K} \mathbf{T}^k\, \mathfrak{M}^k(n)}{\sum_{1\le k\le K} \mathbf{T}^k},$$

- It is also possible to weight the market share of a stock k according to a weight w_k in a given index $\mathfrak{I}$:

$$\mathfrak{M}^{\mathfrak{I}}(n) = \sum_{k\in\mathfrak{I}} w_k \cdot \mathfrak{M}^k(n),$$

  the weight in an index being often proportional to the free-float or to the market capitalization of the stock, it is not equal to its daily turnover (see chart (b) of Figure 1.1).
- Another way of weighting is to give the same weight to each stock considered:

$$\mathfrak{M}_u^{1,\dots,K}(n) = \frac{1}{K}\sum_{1\le k\le K} \mathfrak{M}^k(n).$$

Figure 1.2 shows four different ways to measure the market share on the same basis for UK listed stocks. First the considered universe of stock is of importance: charts (a) and (d) use the same metric (the traded value), but on two different universes (the FSTE 100 — i.e. the Local Main Index — and the whole universe of stocks listed on the London Stock Exchange). It is obvious that the result is not similar, showing that the fragmentation is not the same for all stocks.

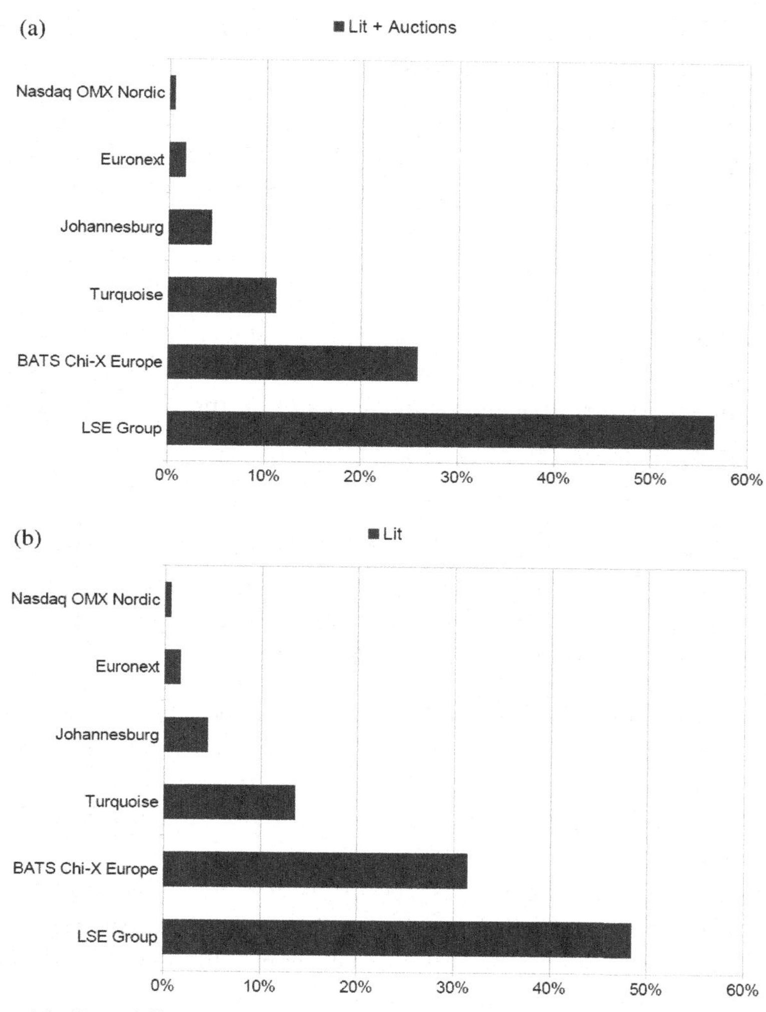

Figure 1.2. Two different market shares measurements for the UK-listed stocks in March 2013: (a) Including all visible trades (continuous and fixing auctions), and (b) including continuous auctions only. If a trader wants to know a proxy for the probability to have an order send during continuous actions executed, he needs to use figures of Figure (b), not (a).

Typically fragmentation increases with liquidity: the more liquid, the more fragmented. Section 2.3 in Chapter 2 provides a metric dedicated to study the homogeneity of the fragmentation across an index, the coverage.

To assess whether a metric is adequate, it is important to go back to the question the metric is supposed to answer:

- If we want to analyze the positioning and revenue of each trading venue, the market share all included can be of importance, even if in terms of revenue, the trading fees are usually not the same during the fixing auctions as during the continuous ones.
- If we want to estimate *the probability that, when a trade occurs on security k, it is on trading venue* $\mathcal{T}(n)$, then it can be better to not sum the fixing auctions with the continuous ones, and to follow two indicators: the market share during the fixing auctions and the one ex-fixing. Just note that in this case, the natural measure of market share is $\mathfrak{M}_t^k(n)$ of formula (1.2).
- If we want to estimate that *the probability that, when a unit of currency (Euro, dollar) is traded on security k, it is on trading venue* $\mathcal{T}(n)$, then the classical market share in value (i.e. $\mathfrak{M}^k(n)$) is the proper one, even if it can be better to make one measurement during the fixing auction (especially if there is 100% chance to be traded on a specific venue during the fixing) and another for the intraday.

This list shows that the market share measurement is clearly linked to trading optimization: It is a rough estimate of *where the market participants are trading, on average*. Section 3.3.2 in Chapter 3 shows how to be more subtle in using analytics to optimize smart order routing.

Besides, two of the listed meanings of the market shares are about *"estimating the probability that...."* To use them properly, we should take profit of the knowledge of probability estimations that is available in the literature.

Theoretical development: Estimation of a proportion and its confidence intervals. See Appendix A.7 for more details.

1.1.2. *Phase 1: First attempts of fragmentation*

Once MiFID allowed the creation of new market operators in the equity markets, Europe has seen many new trading venues. To understand how it impacted the microstructure, it is enough to focus on Chi-X, Turquoise, BATS Europe, and NASDAQ-OMX Europe.

Table 1.1. Main MTF launch dates.

Primary market	Chi-X	Turquoise	BATS
France	28 Sept. 2007	29 August 2008	14 Nov. 2008
UK	29 June 2007	29 August 2008	7 Nov. 2008
Germany	30 March 2007	29 August 2008	19 Nov. 2008
Netherlands	30 March 2007	29 August 2008	14 Nov. 2008
Belgium	4 July 2008	29 August 2008	14 Nov. 2008
Finland	4 April 2008	29 August 2008	5 Dec. 2008
Sweden	14 March 2008	29 August 2008	5 Dec. 2008
Switzerland	23 Nov. 2007	29 August 2008	28 Nov. 2008
Denmark	20 June 2008	29 August 2008	5 Dec. 2008
Norway	20 June 2008	29 August 2008	5 Dec. 2008

This is not to downplay the existence of other trading platforms, but to shed light on main mechanisms that took place during the fragmentation of European equity markets and influenced market participant behaviors.

Not all European stocks have been open to trading simultaneously, Table 1.1 gives open dates for three venues. It means that members of the historical exchanges had to follow a progressive calendar to open access to such venues. This asynchronous fragmentation allows us to do some comparative studies, like the one conducted on UK and Spanish markets in, Chapter 2, Section 2.4.1. That is also why it is interesting to study the fragmentation following a country-driven breakdown, since most often trading venues opened trading country by country.

One simple statistic to follow the fragmentation of European markets is thus the market share of the historical markets on each main index of each country (Figure 1.3).

It is obvious that the market share of historical markets decreased continuously since the beginning of competition. To go beyond this simple observation, we need to try to understand the goals and the stakes of fragmentation. If MiFID did not have a singular simple goal, it can nevertheless be said ex post that it targeted:

- The implementation of competition to halt the monopolistic position of historical exchanges.
- The promotion of a pan-European microstructure.

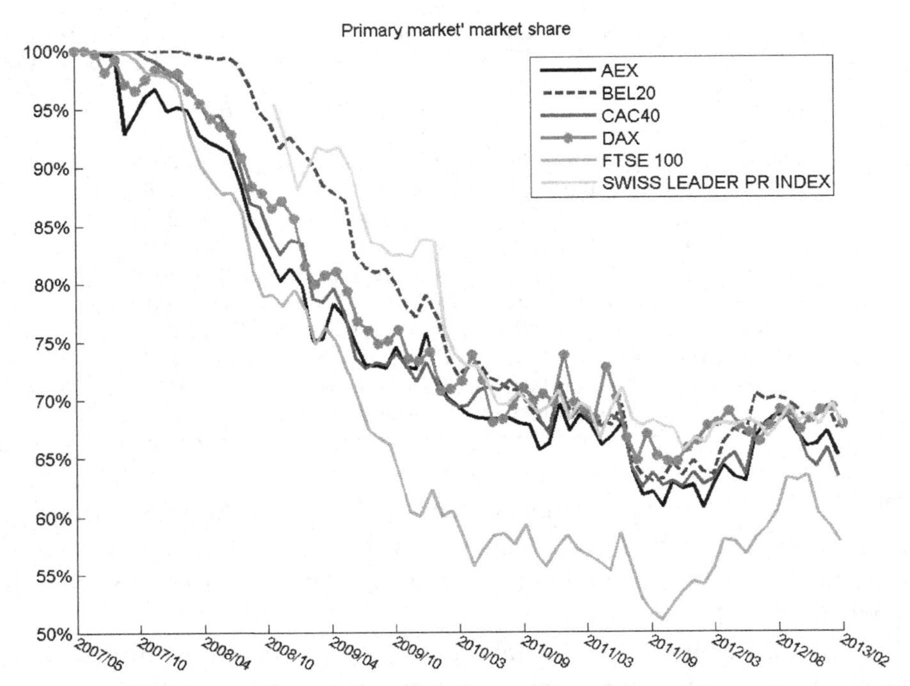

Figure 1.3. Market shares of the historical European exchanges on the usual regional indices.

Four years later, these two goals had been more or less been fulfilled:

- The Chi-X and BATS Europe merger created a large European platform in 2012 (this platform did not existed before MiFID, and continuously challenges its competitors);
- The LSE Group new includes the London Stock Exchange, the Borsa Italia and Turquoise, offering trading on all European stocks.

With Nyse-Euronext (despite the failure of its merger with Deutsche Boerse in 2012[2]), these three firms dominate European equity markets.

This does not mean that the complexity of trading decreased with the emergence of three concentrated actors: they managed to offer

[2]The probable merger with ICE in 2013 will change Euronext Equity market positioning in Europe.

a large diversity of trading pools, segmenting the liquidity to create niche markets. Each of these niche market offers a specific mix of liquidity between two kinds:

- The "natural liquidity", coming directly from investors buying and selling for medium to long term held positions (weeks to months);
- The "opportunistic liquidity", offered by the new high frequency traders and market makers (see [Menkveld, 2010]).

Since there is a debate around the significance and definition of these two kinds of liquidity, market operators identified quite early that their clients would be receptive to siloed offers: one market for the *"lemon liquidity"* and another for the *"cheery liquidity"* (in [Akerlof, 1970]'s words). It is for instance why the LSE Group maintains trading on Turquoise on stocks already listed on the LSE; it implicitly told investors that the LSE orderbooks will contain more cherries and Turquoise more lemons. Thanks to this split, each market participant should be able to create his own mix of liquidity, depending on its needs. This segmentation supported the creation of mid-point Dark Pools, Buy-side only pools, size-priority books, and random-auctions.

Usually, increasing the number of degrees of freedom of a problem allows one to find a better resource allocation. Consequently increasing the number of pools, each of them offering a different "nature" of liquidity can be seen as a positive evolution of the microstructure. Nevertheless the complexity of the allocation decision increases with the degrees of freedom of the problem. The cost to provide an aggregated view and access to liquidity in European equity markets increased with this kind of fragmentation. Smart order routing, best execution proof, understanding the significance of the trading flows on a listed firm are all more complex in 2012 than they were in 2006.

An outstanding property of the fragmentation is that MiFID opened the door to this complexity with very few and simple mechanisms: Best execution, three statuses for trading venues, and pre-trade transparency rules.

Best execution

Unlike in the US, the European Commission did not provide a "consolidated tape[3]" to the market participants. Neither did it demand the trading venues to systematically route orders that could be (according to this consolidated tape) obtain a better price elsewhere. One good reason for this is that the diversity of clearing and settlement channels in Europe (with a diversity of complex tariffs) implied potential inversion of "best prices" once all the costs have been taken into account (i.e., a good price cleared and settled via an expensive channel can be worse than expected).

The concept of Best Execution thus replaced the US trade-through rule: In Europe the intermediaries disclose their "Best Execution Policy" (i.e., the way they will route and split orders across trading venues). Hence a "meta competition" among best execution policies take place on top of the competition between trading venues. This two-layered competition is designed to put pressure on intermediaries and trading venues to offer the best mix of liquidity to the final investor, thus improving the PFP (Price Formation Process).

If such a competition can, on paper, drive the microstructure to a more efficient state, the convergence to such a state is slower than on a one-layered competition. Hence the "Best Execution" driven organization of European market participants relies on so many parameters that it is complex to understand how efficiently it is in place.

Types of trading venues

MiFID also constrained a transaction to occur:

- On a RM (Regulated Market), that hosts a matching engine that executes orders on a public orderbook; RM are responsible for the integrity of the PFP (they are in charge of circuit breakers, for instance);

---

[3]The "consolidated tape" contains a consolidation of all the most competitively priced limit orders available at exchanges. It forms the NBBO (National Best Bid and Offer), so that any market participant knows where to find the best price for a given quantity.

- On an MTF (Multilateral Trading Facility), in a matching engine executing orders on a public orderbook, most often (implicitly or explicitly) pegged to the state of the orderbooks in RMs;
- By SIs (Systematic Internalizers) in accordance with bilateral agreements between counterparts, one of them being a market maker;
- Or Over The Counter (OTC).[4]

Regardless of the type of agents and the place on which the transaction occurred, it has to be reported and disseminated in an effort to increase the rationality of the PFP.

The logic of this split put the emphasis on the deals generated on regulated markets. On the one hand, it probably made it more difficult for MTFs to attract market participants; on the other hand, it eased their operations since they had less obligations and regulatory constraints.

Two main facts disturbed the planned organization of markets:

- The size of the OTC market surprised most observers, even after some double counting had been taken into account. The bad organization of post-trade transparency pushed most of actors to try to reduce OTC deals one way or the other.[5]
- Very few participants applied for the status of Systematic Internalizers, because of the pre- and post-trade transparency constraints attached to it. Market makers involved in bilateral trading do not like to disseminate information about their inventory, especially in the post-crisis world.

Put side to side, these two facts reshaped post-MiFID fragmentation in a binary configuration of RMs and MTFs.

---

[4]In MiFID 2, another status is planned to host transactions: The OTF (Organized Trading Favility) one. The OTF would be inbetween MTF and OTC.

[5]Note that in Italy, the Financial Transaction Tax put in place in mid-2013 for OTC deals was twice of the one for other transactions. It thus decreased dramatically the number of OTC trades.

Pre-trade transparency

The last important concept supported by MiFID is a high demand of pre-trade transparency, i.e., the disclosure of the state of the orderbook to traders. In short, the principle underlying this demand is that the more information is disclosed to decision makers (i.e., traders), the more rational their actions will be, and thus the more "efficient" the price formation process (in the sense that the emerging price will be closer to the "fair" price).

In the spirit of MiFID, a price can be formed by executing a liquidity demanding order against a resting order in an orderbook if and only if the state of the orderbook is disclosed to all market participants. Some exemptions exist:

- The 'large in scale waiver', stating that large orders can rest in orderbooks without transparency. It is thus possible to have fully hidden orders, provided that they are large enough.
- The 'order management facility waiver', to protect facilitating trades[6] from information leakage.
- The 'negotiated trade waiver', that have to be priced within the volume weighted spread of a reference market.
- The 'reference price waiver', allowing hidden orders of any size in an orderbook, provided that they do not *form a price* via the confrontation of offer and demand. Note that they can be traded at a fixed external price, the transparency is thus *delegated* to the reference trading venue. Dark Pools operate under this waiver.

Post-trade transparency

Another obligation of paramount importance for the price formation process is the post-trade publication of any transaction *as soon as possible* in a public way to disseminate the information across market participants. Regulators and policy makers see this post-trade dissemination as a way to ensure that investors and traders make rational choices since they will have the proper level of

[6]Facilitation is a temporary and not systematic market making-like activity, generally conducted by brokers.

information on the last price at which participant just agreed to trade (and for which size).

Unfortunately, the way investors think about post-trade dissemination is not straightforward:

- On one hand they would like to have as much information as possible to make rational decisions;
- On the other hand they would like to keep the information related to *their trades* private, since they fear that participants with shorter investment horizons can profit from this information.

Idealized market impact seen as in [Gabaix *et al.*, 2006] cannot harm the large asset manager selling a huge quantity of shares to a market maker since the market maker will sell back to other investors during the next day, impacting the price to hedge its market risk. In practice, things are more complicated: A large asset manager splits any large orders in temporal slices (with duration usually less than one day of trading) and in lists of names. Say it is a buy order; observing the first half day of trading could allow other participants to anticipate the pressure to come that will move the price up. They may thus begin to buy earlier than they originally planned in order to avoid exposure to this price move thus impacting the price, impacting themselves the price in a negative way for the original asset manager.

Moreover, a market maker accepting large orders will be reluctant to let other market participants know that he just bought a large number of shares: Everyone will know that he now has to hedge it.

One possibility is to have a single post-trade tape with little information on the venue that hosted each transaction. For instance have one unique post-trade tape with few information on the trading venue who hosted to transaction could be a good proposal. Unfortunately this is not the case: The trading venue in which the trade occurred is always available. Hence the more fragmented the market, the more visible the counterparties in a pool. For instance, a niche trading pool dedicated to market makers (or another to large buy-sides) would imply that most trades in it are hedging (or the start of a large portfolio transition).

For sure this effect played a role in the low number of firms that have applied for Systematic Internalizer in Europe, and the small increase in the number of alternative trading venues. It has been more comfortable for market participants to have one venue like Chi-X simultaneously hosting visible orderbooks (i.e., *Lit Pools*), a Dark Pool and totally hidden orders. The trades occurring in these three pools will be mixed into the same post-trade channel, delivering less specific information.

Two failures in the MiFID early years

1) Turquoise Trading: From Investment banks to the London Stock Exchange

The first months of MiFID saw the creation of two MTFs: Turquoise and NASDAQ-OMX Europe. Turquoise was founded by large investment banks (BNP Paribas, Citi, Credit Suisse, Deutsche Bank, Goldman Sachs, Merrill Lynch, Morgan Stanley, Société Générale, and UBS); its founders initially had an agreement to perform the market making on Turquoise themselves. Not being intra-day trading professionals, they did not offer the expected liquidity on day one, and the intraday pattern on Turquoise was very different from the one on other trading platforms at the beginning (see Figure 1.4).

Turquoise intraday volume curve was more related to intraday volatility than the volume curves of other trading venues, showing that the market makers operating on this pool were more risk averse than others.

After one year of operation (in March 2009), these dedicated market makers stopped their operations, Figure 1.5 shows the immediate impact on the market share of this MTF. See Figure 1.6 (with Chi-X and NASDAQ OMX market shares) as an element of comparison. The Turquoise story stopped after it was bought by the London Stock Exchange Group in December 2009.

Turquoise is now an important component of the LSE Group offer. Offering trading on stocks already listed on the LSE, this group has been the first one to offer double listing after Euronext merged all its orderbooks[7] in January 2009.

[7] Before January 2009, some European stocks like Alcatel TODO:check were double listed by Euronext on its Paris and Amsterdam books.

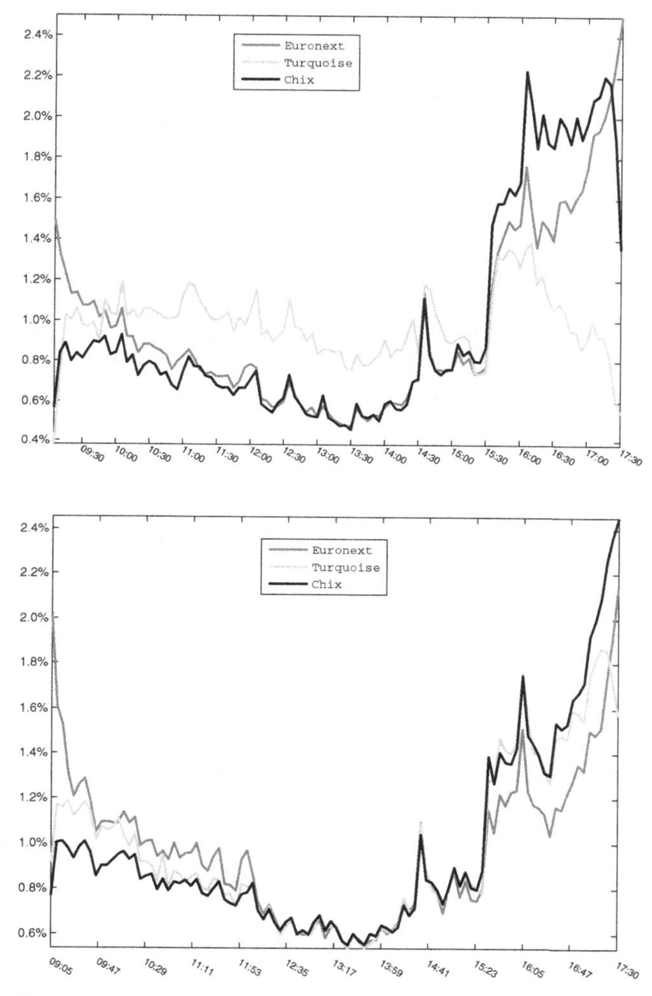

Figure 1.4. Turquoise intraday volume curve compared to other European trading venues (top: in early 2009; bottom: in 2012).

2) NASDAQ-OMX Europe: When technology is not enough

NASDAQ-OMX took part of the post-MiFID fragmentation from September 2008 to May 2010, operating the "Nasdaq-OMX MTF Europe" trading venue. Like BATS Europe trying to make the most of its overseas experience, NASDAQ wanted to provide an MTF recycling some US-based concepts.

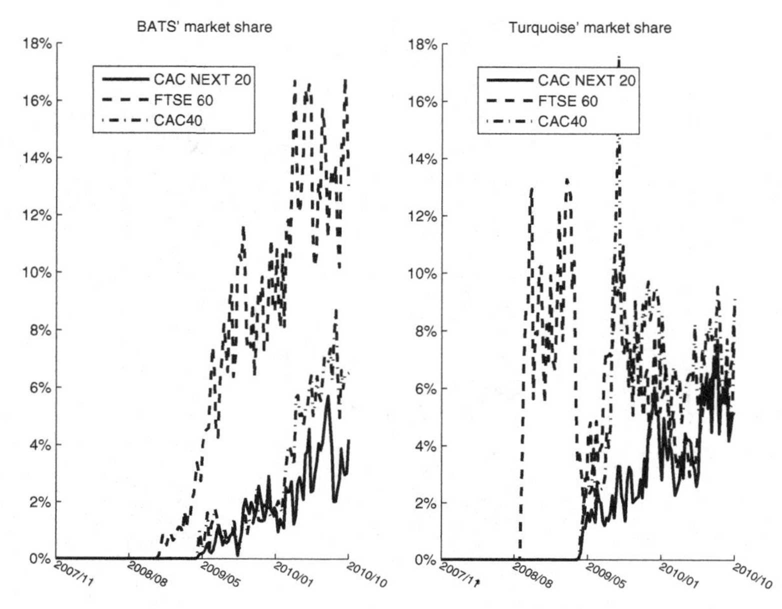

Figure 1.5. Market share of BATS Europe (left) and Turquoise (right) on different segment of liquidity for the first years of fragmentation in Europe.

The first interesting NASDAQ-OMX offer was a SOR (Smart Order Router) on the MTF side, very close to a "trade-through rule view" of MiFID. This initiative was not very popular since the routing principles in Europe are defined more by the "Best execution policies" than by blink routing (see Section 1.1.2 for more details). Despite innovative initiatives, this MTF has not been profitable fast enough; it almost never crossed 1% of market share on its whole perimeter.

At the end of 2010, we could see the roles of the major players for 2012: The LSE Group, Euronext and Deutsche Boerse as large historical exchanges, BATS Europe and Chi-X as challengers.

1.1.3. *Phase 2: Convergence towards a European offer*

Entropy of the market microstructure

It is obvious that if five trading venues are available for a given stock, the maximum level of fragmentation is attained when one-fifth of trades occur on each venue, and the lowest level of fragmentation when all deals are carried out on one venue only. As often in quantitative finance, it is worth looking at statistical thermodynamics (the

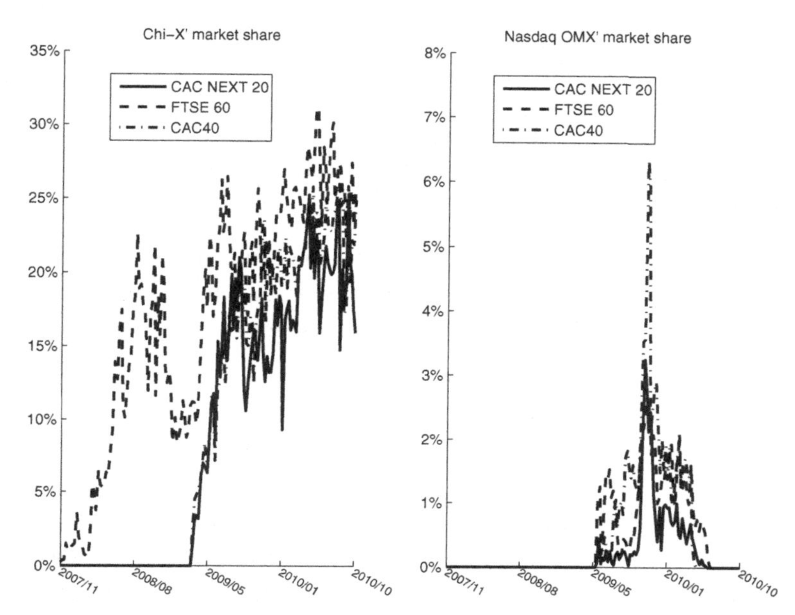

Figure 1.6. Market share of Chi-X trading (left) and NASDAQ-OMX MTF (right) on different segment of liquidity for the first years of fragmentation in Europe.

source of the Brownian Motion and Black-Scholes formulae) to see if measurements are available to answer our needs.

It is worth noting that mathematicians and physicists have a common methodology for measuring the dispersion of matter or the level of randomness of a phenomenon. This is called "entropy". Entropy measures the level of "disorder" (i.e., fragmentation) in a system. If the consolidated market is considered a "system", it is perfectly ordered should all transactions take place on a single venue and its "disorder" increases with its fragmentation. For a given stock, when 70% of trades take place on one venue, 20% on a second and 10% on a third, its entropy will be 0.34, according to the following formula defined by Kolmogorov and Shannon, the entropy is:

$$\text{Entropy} = -\sum_{n=1}^{N} \mathfrak{M}_n \log \mathfrak{M}_n$$

where $\mathfrak{M}_n$ is the market share of the nth venue.

Theoretical development: Entropy. See Appendix A.1 for more details.

The Fragmentation Efficiency Index: A metric summarizing fragmentation

Entropy is often renormalized by a constant; we therefore propose the constant be the maximum entropy possible for a market with N different venues, i.e. $\log(N)$. This gives us the following formula for normalized entropy:

$$H = -\frac{1}{\log N}\sum_{n=1}^{N} \mathfrak{M}_n \log \mathfrak{M}_n.$$

Thus, for our example of a stock with a breakdown across three venues of 70/20/10, the renormalized entropy is 72%. More than a formula, this normalized entropy — which we will refer to as the FEI (Fragmentation Efficiency Index) — can be used to produce

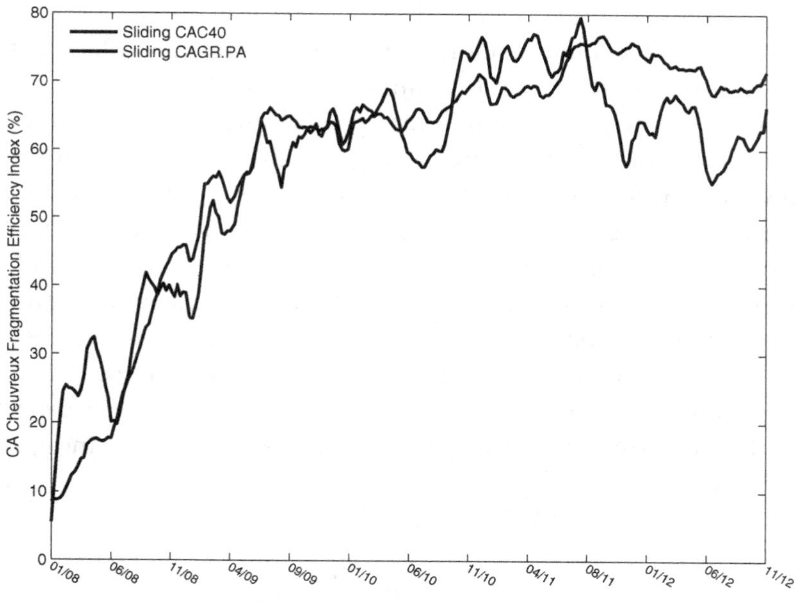

Figure 1.7. Comparison of the variations of the renormalized entropy of the CAC 40 and of the Crédit Agricole S.A. share.

Table 1.2. Values of the Fragmentation Efficiency Index (FEI) for typical distributions of market shares.

Breakdown by venue (%)	FEI value	Breakdown by venue (%)	FEI value
25/25/25/25	100%	70/20/5/5	63%
50/50	100%	64/24/5/5/1	60%
25/25/25/25/0	86%	70/20/10/0	58%
70/20/10	73%	80/10/5/5	51%

meaningful analysis of the history of a stock's fragmentation, for instance compared to the one of an index (see Figure 1.1c on p. 31).

Examples: Table 1.2 gives some typical values for the Fragmentation Efficiency Index (FEI). It is worth noting that the FEI scores the fragmentation state of a liquidity pool relative to what it could be given the number of available venues. For instance, the FEI for a breakdown of 70/20/10 across three venues is 73%, while the same breakdown with four available venues (i.e., 70/20/10/0) yields 58%. The threshold to include a new MTF in the FEI has been set at 1% market share.

Figure 1.8 below shows the past values of the FEI for the six main European indexes. The pan-European Euro STOXX 50 is, due to its composition, more fragmented than any country-related index: Its FEI is over 65% split across 12 venues. We can also see the impact the end of Turquoise's liquidity agreement (March 2008) had on the other indices.

Using such a metric is a good way to quantify the fragmentation on a segment in a single figure. Insofar as it reproduces the essence of fragmentation in terms of its physical source of inspiration (entropy), the main fragmentation events will leave their mark on the FEI.

Fragmentation of what?

Naturally analysts refer to fragmentation as how an order has to be split to find enough liquidity to be fulfilled as soon as possible. Section 1.1.1 in this Chapter, giving several possible definitions of *market shares*, shows that one of them is close to the average fraction of one Euro, traded on European markets, that is traded on one specific venue. In this sense trading is fragmented.

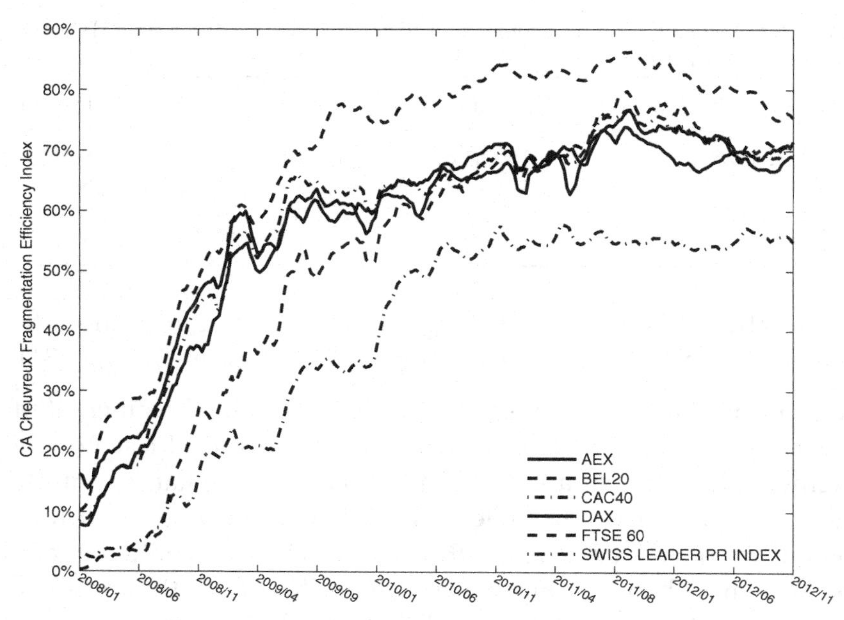

Figure 1.8. Comparison of the variations of the FEI for the main local European indices.

The upper Fragmentation Efficiency Index measures how traded euros are split between different venues. Another important aspect of fragmentation has to be underlined: The dispersion of means to access liquidity. For a market participant, establishing a connection with each trading platform has a cost. Hence the convergence of communication protocols is of paramount importance. From this viewpoint, Europe was highly fragmented during the first years of MiFID and slowly began to offer a smaller number of protocols to connection to its markets. Nevertheless the technology needed to trade in Europe is *fragmented* in different directions:

- Application protocols: XDP, ITCH, EBS, Pitch, EMDI, RWF;
- Network protocols: Multicast UDP vs. TCP. Furthermore, the venues that do use multicast UDP, have different initialization steps and implementations to handle lost (and unordered) messages;
- Compression protocols: FAST vs. ZLIB vs. none (other compression protocols are rarely used in the industry).

In a 2012 white paper [Cohen and Wolcough, 2012], eTrading Software underlines that *"with all these differences, it is understandably difficult to implement a common feed handler that will serve most of the existing venues (sic) API protocols for market data"*.

1.1.4. *Phase 3: Apparition of broker crossing networks and Dark Pools*

Fragmentation in Europe appeared to evolve similarly to a network of mobile phone operators: A few firms owning the "hardware" (i.e., technology) and a wide range of offerings (including niche products) operating on this network. The London Stock Exchange group is archetypal in this; one technology (Millenium IT) supports a lot of orderbooks: The usual LSE one, the Turquoise Lit and Dark ones covering all UK listed stocks, including the one of the Milan Stock Exchange one. Similarly, BATS Europe and Chi-X Europe share the same technology between four orderbooks (the Lit and Dark of each venue), and Nyse-Euronext uses the same technology for the Nyse and Euronext Paris, Lisbon, Brussels and Amsterdam books, plus Nyse-Arca.

The rise of high frequency traders, being partly prop trading teams and partly high-tech market makers (see Chapter 2, Section 2.3), in conjunction with a global decrease of liquidity in Europe for economic reasons dulled the trust traditional investors had in the integrity of the price formation process. The Flash Crash (see Chapter 2, Section 2.4.3) sharpened the vague idea that some specific investors (the "HFTs"), earning part of the bid-ask spread (see [Menkveld, 2010]), necessarily took this profit from other market participants.

The financial crisis endangered the profitability of traditional brokers, who have seen their technological costs increasing because of the investments demanded to be able to offer trading to all the new orderbooks, to efficiently route client orders to an adequate mix of them, and to be able to prove it.

How HFT activity promoted trading outside of visible pools

Phase 2 of fragmentation created different pools of liquidity, each of them hosting orders issued by a specific mix of investors. Like

Akerlof's "market for lemons" [Akerlof, 1970], MTFs offered "second hand liquidity" where historical pools hosted more cherries, "first hand liquidity". Executing brokers, suffering from an increase in their fixed costs (due to the fragmentation) and from a decrease in global asset under Management (because of the crisis), have been tempted to open pools marketed as "100% first hand liquidity". Only some of them could meet the associated expenses: The technology, the staff demanded by the regulation, and the marketing. They created the first BCNs (Broker Crossing Networks).

BCNs host not only "natural liquidity", but sometimes prop trading flows originating from the Investment Banks owning the operating broker of each pool. Afraid of the prospect of losing market share, MTFs (and some historical exchanges, like Euronext) launched Dark Pools. Some brokers then converted their BCNs into MTF Dark Pools, to assure their clients that no prop trading desk had a too clear view on the incoming flows.

The last phase of MiFID one has thus been:

- The stabilization of the technological means in few hands,
- the rise of powerful BCNs,
- and the conversion of some of them into regulated (MTF) Dark Pools.

This restructuring of the European landscape was not fully in original plans of the European Commission. The MiFID Review, already planned to expand fragmentation to other asset classes, came in time to adjust the rulebook on Equity markets. HFT, tick sizes, maker/taker fees, Dark Pools, and other unexpected aspects of European fragmentation has to be scrutinized.

Small and mid-caps: Catching up main indexes

Figures 1.9 and 1.10 shows the evolution of the market share of historical markets on the components of a market-capitalization driven split of the 600 most liquid European stocks (according to the composition of the DJ EuroStoxx in February 2013). It is clear that fragmentation followed the same path for all capitalization segments, in three steps:

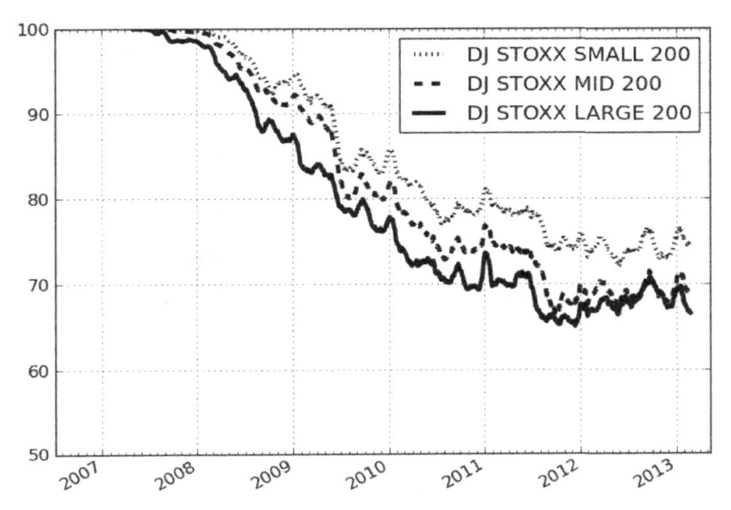

Figure 1.9. Market share of the primary market on the three capitalization segments of the EuroStoxx 600.

- Until mid-2009, large caps were significantly more fragmented than small and mid caps;
- After mid-2009, the erosion of primary markets for small caps slowed down;
- In mid-2012, the difference between mid and large caps became very low.

Theoretical development: Measuring Liquidity Discrepancies. See Appendix A.8 for more details.

Appendix A.8 gives more details about a means to measure liquidity discrepancies amongst the components of an index and Section 2.3.1 (in Chapter 2) conducts such an analysis. Section 2.3.1 comments on the way HFTs expand their activity from highly liquid to less liquid instruments.

At this stage of the analysis, two main reasons explaining the difference between these three segments of stocks need to be underlined:

1. To be able to provide liquidity on the ask side (i.e., using sell orders) without being officially a market maker, often necessary

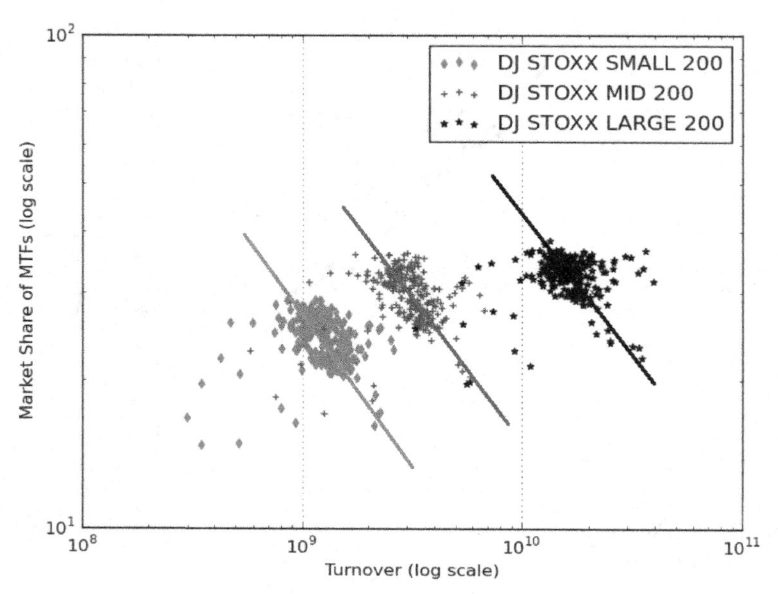

Figure 1.10. Market share on MTFs with respect to turnover for three EuroStoxx indices; one point is one day of 2011. The scale is log-log, disclosing multiplicative relationships.

to borrow shares. It is thus easier to do it when the borrowing cost is cheap rather than when it is expensive, but the borrowing cost decreases with the number of shares available on the market (i.e., with the *free float* of the stock). It implies an asymmetry in the provision of liquidity for a stock; providing it at the bid is "free" but at the ask you potentially have to borrow shares, which is not in line with the utility function of a high frequency market maker (see [Guéant *et al.*, 2012a]). During short selling bans in Europe (mid August 2011) some HFT firms applied for a status close to the one of market maker provided by MTFs to allow HFTs to provide "naked" liquidity on the ask side. The lack of a European market making status opens such regulatory holes.

2. To compensate for unbalanced inventories, HFTs and market makers have the capability to buy or sell correlated financial instruments. A typical case is to hedge a positive inventory on the cash components of an index by selling future contracts on the same index. The bid-ask spread being commonly smaller on

the future market than on the cash market, it is a convenient way to be able to offer more liquidity on stocks. It is thus easier to sustain unbalanced inventories on stocks that are part of indices or with a market capitalization large enough so that they are the underlying of future contracts.

These two reasons make it easier for liquidity arbitrageurs like HFTs to accept an inventory risk on large market caps than on small ones. They explain the different fragmentation levels for different capitalization levels.

Theoretical development: Log-Linear Regression. See Appendix A.9 for more details.

To investigate the relationship between liquidity and fragmentation further, one can take each day of 2011 forming pairs with (1) the market share of the MTFs on one of the three given capitalization-driven indices and (2) the traded amount the same day. Figure 1.10 is the result of such a scatter plot with the daily traded amount on the x-axis and the market share of the MTFs on the y-axis. A log-log scale has been used to discover multiplicative relationship between these two variables.

A first observation is that each of the three capitalization-driven index is clearly separate from the others: *The larger the capitalization, the larger the market share of the MTFs*, on average. A second order relation is made concrete by lines: inside each index, the *larger the daily traded amount, the smaller the market share of MTFs*. In fact the relationship between the two variables inside each index is of this kind:

$$\text{Market Share of MTFs} = \frac{b_i}{\text{Turnover}^{\gamma}} + \epsilon,$$

where b_i is an "intercept" specific to each index (would be to each stock if one would zoom inside the components of the indices), γ is a *universal* slope (i.e. independent from the index or the stock), and ϵ a "noise" term capturing exogenous effects (i.e. any good reason for a stock to not follow this power law).

This means that during high volume days, historical markets capture more trades than alternative venues. This comes from (1) a race to liquidity (investors coming back to historical markets during liquidity stresses, to be sure to find liquidity), (2) investors more present during high volume days having less mature trading processes.

It is remarkable that the way fragmentation evolves with respect to liquidity is two fold:

- Comparing two different stocks: The fragmentation increases with the capitalization of a stock,
- for one given stock, comparing one trading day to another, the fragmentation decreases during high volume days.

From division to union

We have seen that MiFID enabled the creation and development of multiple new trading platforms, bringing competition to markets. After this huge and rapid evolution, things appear to have stabilized, and a new trend towards venue consolidation emerged. The merged entities seek to survive the fierce competition and make gains in technology, and the future of markets seems to lie in fewer but bigger competitors.

Europe already saw the London Stock Exchange buying Turquoise in February 2011. The same month, the London Stock Exchange migrated to the Millennium IT Technology platform for the main UK orderbook. Turquoise had migrated to this system five months before. This new technology brought a positive combination of a reduction in latency to 126 microseconds for order acknowledgment and a potential threefold increase in capacity of volume handled. However, the move came at a cost with Turquoise suffering an outage on Monday 4 October 2010.

With their merger, LSE and Turquoise were only the first movers in a wave of potential consolidation. Two other major mergers in European markets are currently in the spotlight. The first would link up BATS and Chi-X Europe. Negotiations went exclusive in December 2010, and the UK's Office of Fair Trading referred BATS and Chi-X Europe's proposed merger to the Competition Commission in June

2011. The Commission gave its approval and BATS acquired Chi-X in November 2011. Note that they had to face the same problems as the LSE and Turquoise in terms of technology migration; shortly after the two venues declared that BATS technology would be chosen for both platforms, Chi-X suffered a wave of outages following more than four years without any major technical glitches. Both exchanges have experienced technical issues in December 2011 and January 2012.

The second merger concerned Deutsche Boerse and NYSE Euronext. Advanced talks were confirmed in February 2011. NASDAQ-OMX Group and Intercontinental Exchange (ICE) made an alternative offer to NYSE Euronext in April 2011, which was rejected. Deutsche Boerse shareholders approved the proposed combination in mid-July 2011. However, the European Commission rejected the offer because of the potential monopoly in the derivatives business that this merger could create.

In January 2013, ICE launched an offer to buy Nyse-Euronext, mainly focused on its derivative business. After this merger, the market equity business of Euronext should become independent, leading to another consolidation phase in Europe.

In addition to the aforementioned two European examples, the merger wave has also affected exchanges around the world. The LSE and Canada's TMX were to merge at the end of June 2011. However this plan fell through when the required two-thirds majority of shareholders was not reached. A second offer for TMX from Maple Group, a consortium of domestic banks, was refuled twice, but finally received the backing of the TMX board at the end of October. Mergers giving birth to international groups show how important size is in today's worldwide fragmentation landscape. In an attempt to compete with the more developed Brazilian Stock Exchange, South American markets (Chile, Colombia, and Peru) launched a single access point for investors on 30 May 2011. This represents the first example of cooperation for these markets. In response to the increasing presence of alternative venues in the Japanese market (Chi-X increased its market share from 0.8% in January 2011 to 1.7% in June 2011), the Tokyo Stock Exchange (91.2% in June) and the Osaka Securities Exchange (5.3% in June) reached agreement on a merger in November 2011. An offer from the Singapore Exchange to buy the

Australian Stock Exchange was aborted after it was rejected by the Australian Treasurer in April 2011. Some interpreted this refusal as a risk and damaging for the country's appeal to foreign investors.

Exchanges are not the only ones to dream of becoming bigger, investment firms and clearing houses are also part of trend. Two US proprietary trading firms merged in 2011, namely Madison Tyler and Virtu Financial, confirming the increasing challenge of technological investment in order to make profits and stay in competition. In addition, US group Getco acquired the British proprietary firm Automat in July 2011. After several months of rumors, in early September 2011 the London Stock Exchange confirmed preliminary talks with LCH.Clearnet; the LSE Group finally acquired LCH.Clearnet in late 2012.

The trend towards getting bigger to become stronger thus extends to primary markets, alternative venues, investment firms and clearing houses, underscoring the mainly technological challenges that markets participants face. It is a sign that operating fixed costs are difficult to bear, especially in the post-financial-crisis context.

1.2. Smart Order Routing (SOR), A Structural Component of European Price Formation Process

1.2.1. *How to route orders in a fragmented market?*

Focus on atomic orders

Most large orders are now temporally split by traders using decision support tools and trading algorithms. It is well known that this split has to follow a few rules:

- On one hand, the market impact of orders has to be estimated (no temporal split leading to a large order that would impact the market and depreciate the price obtained);
- On the other hand, the market risk has to be considered: Waiting too long can expose the order to adverse moves in the price.

A subtle balance must be found between these two effects. Practitioners and academics have proposed to use a parameter called

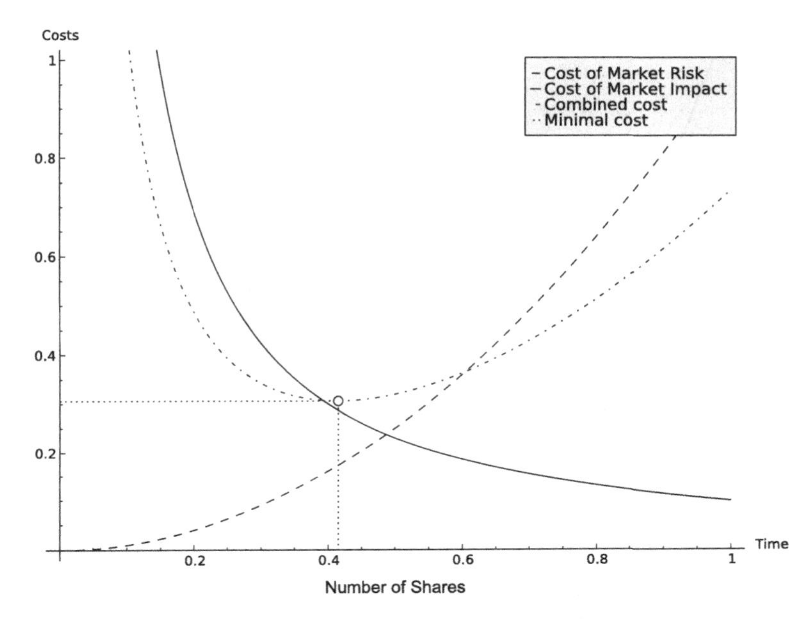

Figure 1.11. Market impact vs. market risk.

"risk aversion", whose meaning is similar to that used in portfolio allocation: If you fear risk (high risk aversion), you will accept paying a high market impact to reduce your exposure to future risk. If you are ready to accept risk (low risk aversion), you will accept being exposed to market risk and try to use time to reduce your market impact. Figure 1.11 shows how the market impact and the market risk vary with the time you take to trade a given number of shares (horizontal axis) as a fraction of one day. The mix dotted line is the combined cost: For this arbitrary risk aversion parameter, we see the line decreasing first (it is worth waiting) before increasing (the market risk after 42% of the day does not balance the expected gain in market impact). Because the market risk and the market impact are not linear functions of the time and the quantity to be traded, and because volume and volatility experience the usual intra-day variation, solving this optimisation leads to optimal trading curves that are not straight lines. Figure 1.12 shows two trading curves corresponding to two different values for the risk aversion parameter (see [Lehalle, 2009]). Before market fragmentation, large orders were

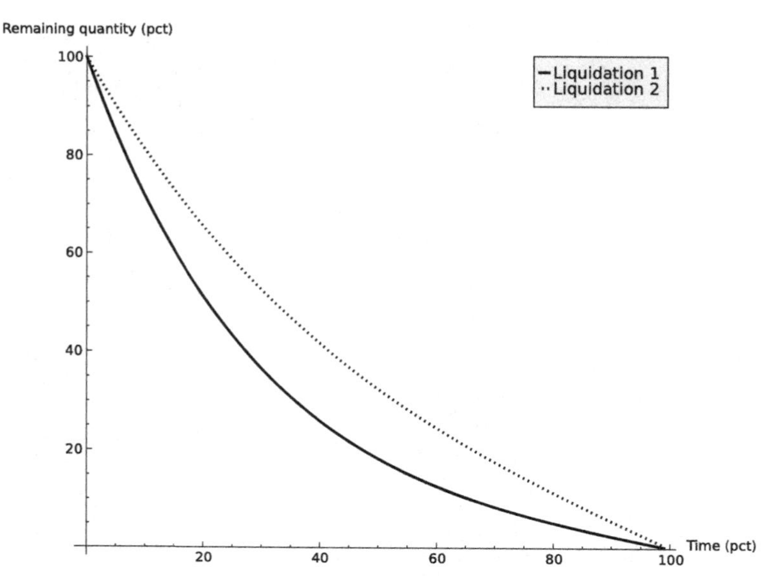

Figure 1.12. Some optimal trading schedules associated with different risk aversion parameters.

only temporally split according to such optimisation schemes, but now each temporal slice itself (each "atomic order", also called "child order", "slice" or "occurrence") has to be split and sent to different trading destinations according to the liquidity they offer. The next section is dedicated to an explanation of the mechanisms that take place during this spatial split.

Using a Smart Order Router (SOR)

Assuming that each "slice" is sent at the best instant given the information available to the trader and his decision support systems, assuming also that this slice has a well-defined "limit price" and exact quantity, it is possible to focus on the best way to split the quantity among available trading venues. It is obvious that such a split will be optimal if:

- It obtains a price better than or equal to the asked price;
- it finishes the order as soon as possible (because the temporal aspect has been solved at a higher level).

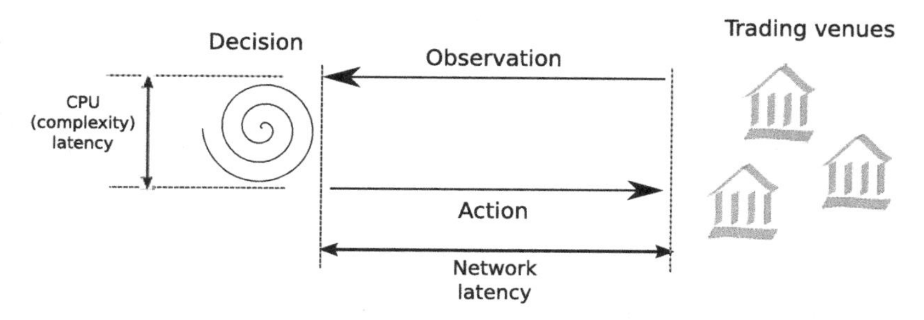

Figure 1.13. Functional diagram of a smart order router.

The best way to use the liquidity available in alternate venues is to avoid to consume a whole limit of price on the main trading destination if volume is available at the same price on another venue: It will accelerate the execution, improve the price and minimize the footprint of the overall execution in the market. The standard device to achieve such an optimization is named Smart Order Router (SOR). See Figure 1.13 for a stylized diagram of how a typical SOR works. Other tactics such as multi-destination icebergs, liquidity seekers, etc., can also be used to fragment a parent order. Such tactics can be seen as restrictions (for icebergs) or extensions (for liquidity seekers or SOR). The specific feature of an SOR is that it is an agnostic device: It takes a limit or market order and splits it with advanced knowledge of the state of the liquidity on the trading destinations that are ready to trade. An SOR order is like a new type of order giving access to an aggregated view of a large set of trading venues. An SOR can be customized for different uses, mainly via a selection of trading destinations and some split options. The better understood the capabilities of each trading destination are, the better an SOR will be able to comply with users' needs. An SOR is not only a "fire and forget" device: It also needs to be able to prove that every decision made is in accordance with the agreed-upon "execution policy". To comply with MiFID, the choices made by the SOR and the relevance of the execution policies must also be reviewed. Such a trading tool thus needs to be properly connected to large data warehouse recording policies, snapshots of the state of the market, decisions made and executions obtained. Figure 1.14 is a simplified view of the components of an SOR: The decision-making part has to

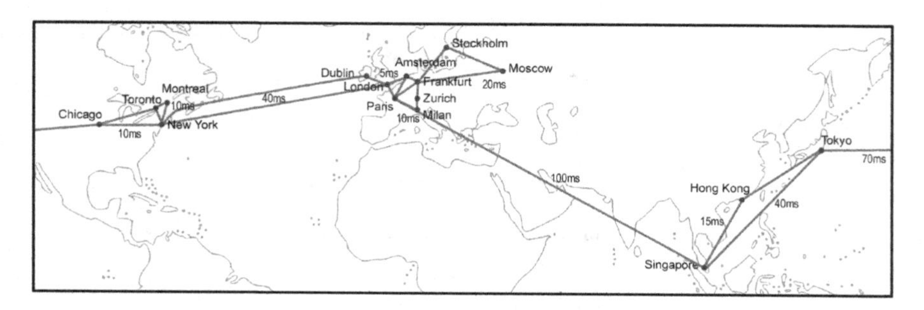

Figure 1.14. Qualitative values for worldwide latencies in 2012.

fit in with the market listeners, and the SOR has to be able to adjust its decisions with respect to feedback from the market.

Aggregate liquidity to minimize the impact of each order

Figure 1.15 shows that while the average trade size (ATS[8]) of an order has decreased overall since early 2007, the daily number of deals has increased regularly. This is a well-known consequence of the development of electronic trading. While the acceleration of the decrease of the ATS due to MiFID and the financial crisis can easily be seen, the slope of the increase of the daily number of deals did not change with MiFID. This probably stems from the fact that the current average trading size is conditioned on the size of passive orders. As long as the average size of aggressive orders is larger than the size of posted orders, any decrease in the size of aggressive orders has no impact on the ATS or on the number of deals. For instance, if an aggressive order of 150 consumes two posted orders of 100 and 50 at the same limit price (say 10.00), two deals will occur and the ATS for these two transactions will be 75, which is the average size of the two passive orders. Therefore, these charts have to be read as indicators of the behavior of passive orders: With market fragmentation, the ATS goes down, and moreover, passive orders are now spread over more trading destinations. Market feeds hence do only give information on the orderbook dynamics seen from liquidity providing orders. An SOR's main task is thus to be

[8]The Average Trade Size is often mistaken for an Alternative Trading System, since they share the same acronym: ATS.

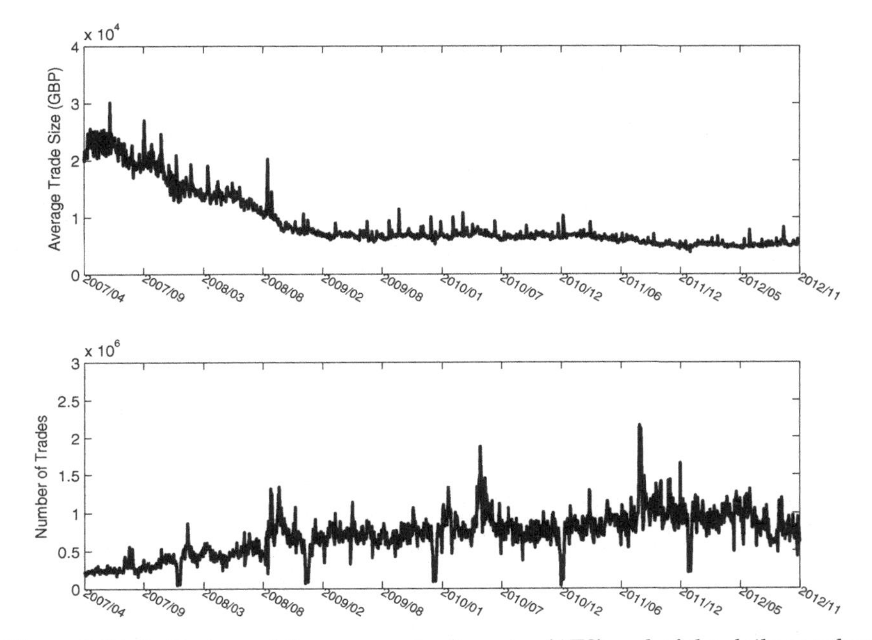

Figure 1.15. Indicators of the average trading size (ATS) and of the daily number of trades for the FTSE 100.

able to build a consolidated view of all these small quantities to avoid a dramatic decrease in execution quality. Going back to the previous example: If the two posted orders are no longer on the same trading venue, if the sender of the marketable order (say it is a buy) does not use an SOR, he will need to take quantity at a higher price after 100. Figure 1.16 shows how summing liquidity on two venues decreases the price impact of a market order.

Smart Order Routers or Smart Fee Savers?

Since the transaction fees are different from one venue to another, the logic of a SOR cannot ignore them when choosing where to send orders. Nevertheless the complexity of some fee schedules prevent the SOR from easily taking them into account. For instance:

- *Clearing and settlement fees* are often computed on netted transactions, meaning that the same order can cost or spare money depending on the net inventory of the trading member.
- *Conditional pricing*: On some venues the fees are computed conditional on the cumulated turnover traded at the end of the month, or

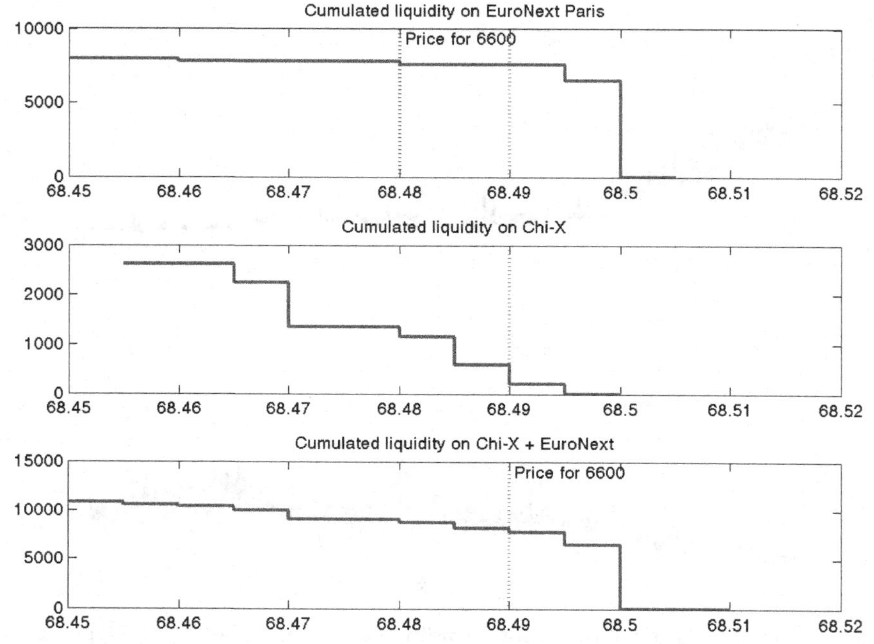

Figure 1.16. The aggregation of two orderbooks (Chi-X and Euronext) give access to more liquidity than only one of them. This is an example of a selling order of 660 shares.

they offer rebate with respect to volume traded on another venue (like Nyse-Euronext offering rebates conditioned on the amount traded on Nyse-Arca).

As a consequence, the marginal gain due to one order is far from obvious.

Some elements of SOR logic are detailed in Chapter 3, Section 3.3.2.

Beware of duplicate liquidity

High frequency market makers' behaviour has to be considered when designing a SOR, since they became heavily involved during the first years of MTFs. Their typical activity is to be present simultaneously at the bid and ask of the same security on several trading destinations. They agree to take on some market risk (because they maintain an inventory rather than immediately unwinding their positions), and are "rewarded" with a fraction of the market bid-ask spread. The maker/taker fee schedule of many MTFs helps high frequency traders be profitable. These HF traders invested substantially in technology, and each one generally focuses on a small subset of instruments whose behavior is compliant with their trading robots. Once market makers have posted liquidity on the same side of the orderbooks on several trading venues, their inventory-keeping strategies often imply that as soon as one of those orders is executed, all the remaining ones are immediately canceled. This leads to "duplicate" quantities in the orderbooks, which makes the SOR's task more complex. Adding pegged and iceberg orders, it is now clear that so-called "pre-trade transparency" is not very useful for guessing where liquidity really is. Post-trade transparency (i.e., trade reports) give far more information to investors. This makes small Dark Pools (with no pre-trade transparency but clear post-trade transparency) more attractive than they were in the early ages of fragmentation. Figure 1.17 gives keys to understanding how latency is an issue in such a context: It is a simplified view of an

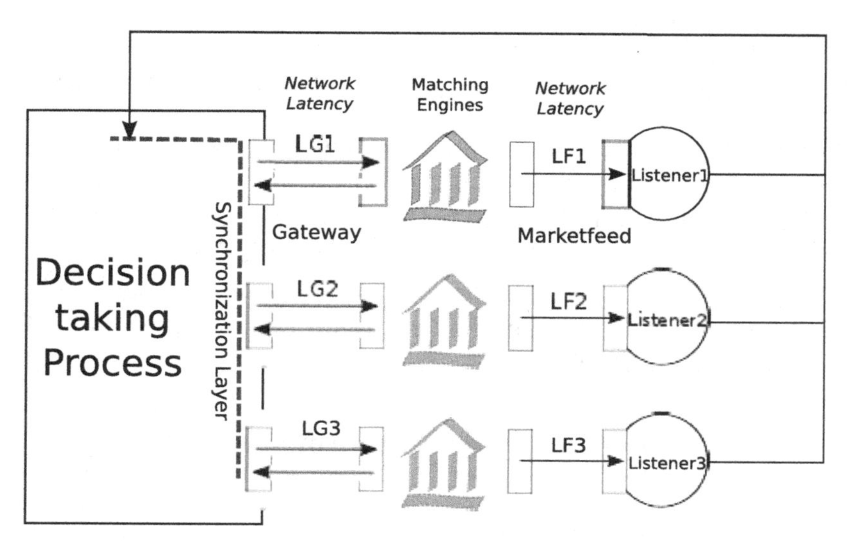

Figure 1.17. Simplified diagram of trajectories of messages.

order's trajectory. A SOR's goal is to obtain an execution that is in line with the information used to make its decision:

- The first step is to build an aggregated view of the market data. This view is usually built on the fly as updates come in from the markets ("synchronization layer" of Figure 1.11);
- Then the SOR has to compute its decision according to its tactic. This is usually very fast because the only limiting factor is the clock of the server it runs on ("decision taking process" of Figure 1.17).
- After that, the orders sent have to go from the SOR to the trading venues. If the trading venues are close to each other, the SOR can be positioned in the same area, but this is not always the case and physical distance cannot be crossed instantaneously.

For instance, it takes light around 1.14 ms to travel the 350 km distance between Paris and London; the Eurostar's route would take 1.6 ms at the speed of light, while in a standard network backbone (slower than light speed), a message needs around 4 ms to cover the same distance.

- Then the orders have to reach the matching engines of the trading destinations. Depending on its type, an order will not have the same priority (for instance, inserting a new order will have a better rank than a modified order).
- Finally, the execution reports have to be returned to the SOR.

All these steps give an idea of the different "latency arbitrages" that can occur during the life of an order. Nevertheless, the efficiency of an SOR cannot be stated in terms of latency but in terms of the results obtained: for well-defined orders and given that the price obtained is better than or equal to the one that could have been obtained on the main market only, the higher the quantities executed on MTFs, the more efficient the SOR.

1.2.2. *Fragmentation is a consequence of primary markets' variance*

The preceding sections analyzed the optimal split for aggressive orders, and have shown that a natural consequence of the availability of quantities at the best bid and offer on alternative venues was that the bigger the quantity sent to MTFs, the more efficient the execution. For passive orders, the question is more complex, because the prices and quantities of many of these are often reassessed. In such a context, it would be nonsensical to produce aggregated statistics for passive orders, because such data would mix orders that have overly divergent goals. Nevertheless, very interesting conclusions can be drawn from macroscopic simulations of a market with SORs. The assumptions used to illustrate this are that, considering one traded stock:

- Its primary venue has 76% of the flows;
- A main alternative venue has 17% of the flows;
- And another "small" alternative venue obtains 7% of the flows.

The illustrations come from large-scale simulations and are backed by theoretical calculations. The important point here is that the average size of the investor order we will study is lower than the average size traded on the market.

The mechanics of the model used here is that traders adjust their SORs dynamically to split an order across trading venues taking into account the historical performance of their executions. This means that when an SOR sent more quantity to one venue but did not get enough shares, the SOR will lower its expectations for this venue and send a smaller fraction of orders to it in the future.

The effect of the variance stems from: *The lower the level of randomness, the easier it is to guess to correct fraction of order to send to each venue.* The fraction of an order to send to a venue with a large variance will thus be minimized by a rational SOR.

On a longer time scale the market shares themselves evolve: if a venue is underweighted by SORs long enough, its market share will decrease.

Theoretical development: A dynamical model of fragmentation. See Appendix A.3 for more details.

Figure 1.18 shows simulations in two different contexts: a medium variance environment (top), and a large variance one

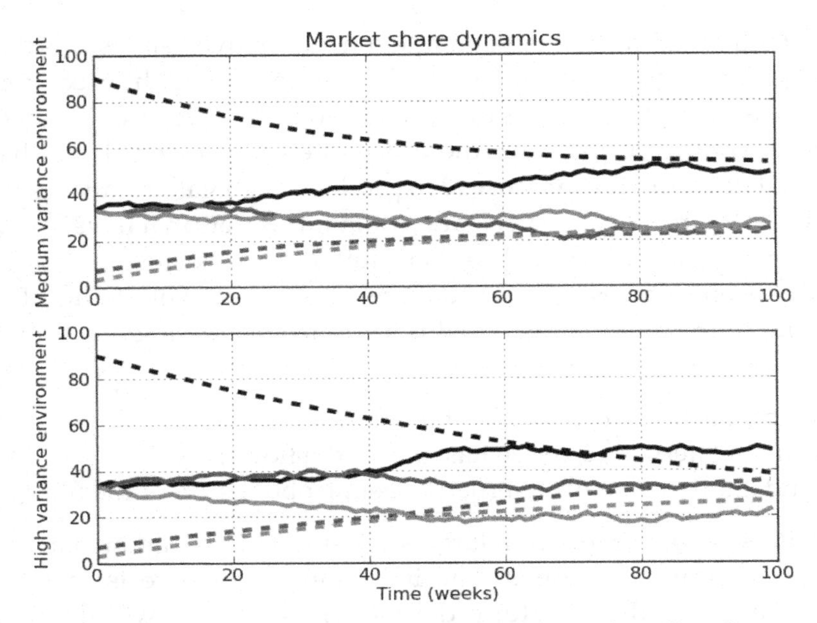

Figure 1.18. Simulation of the evolution of market shares when all trading venues have a medium variance (top) vs a high variance (bottom).

(bottom). The variance quantifies the regularity of the flow that a venue can guarantee. For instance, let's assume one venue can ensure you a flow of execution between 60 and 120 (with an average of 90), while the range of the flow for another lies between 20 and 25 (the average is 22.5). Given that the size of your orders is around 80, your best split is 60 for venue A and 20 for venue B and you are sure to have the order filled. This leads to a rate of 75% for venue A when its market share is 80%.

The upper chart stabilizes with a market share for the largest market that went from 87 to 56, while for a large variance simulated market it decreases to 40 (lower chart).

All studies have shown that variance is proportional with market share, so the main markets automatically have more variance than mid-players like Chi-X or Turquoise. As a result, most of the investors send to Chi-X more often than its market share would imply. An important remark is that given the shape of the distribution of the volumes going to the market, a significant percentage of investors have an average size lower than the overall market. The only situation where no investor has an average size lower than the overall average is when all investors have exactly the same order size. Another important point is that investors with an average size larger than the market have no reason to send more than their market share to primary markets: This automatically leads to a situation of eroding market share for the main players (some investors send less than their market share, others send the market share: The combination of these factors is a decrease in market share for the next month). This explanation fits perfectly with the observations: The main market loses market share each month, especially when the flow it provides is volatile (as is the case for the London Stock Exchange in Europe).

1.3. Still Looking for the Optimal Tick Size

1.3.1. *Why does tick size matter?*

Tick size defines the price grid on which a limit order must lie. That is to say: To be valid any price indicated in an order must be a multiple of the tick size. As a consequence it is also the minimal increment between the prices of two limit price orders. Depending on the market, it can be applicable to any stock whatever its price and liquidity (as in the US for stocks whose price is over US $1) or it can be dependent on the price range and the quotation group that the stocks belong to (as is mostly the case around the world except notably US, Australia, and India). The latter case is often referred to as a tick size regime (or dynamic tick size) and theoretically groups stocks according to their liquidity.

As tick size defines the grid of prices, it will set the degree of discreteness of traded prices. This can be an important consideration for some models, either simplifying the model with constant price increments, or complicating it by having to take into account this observed discreteness with an underlying continuous model. For instance, consider an asset with a big tick size (relative to spread, meaning the bid ask spread will stick to one tick), and a period of time on which the bid and ask will be constant. Without any further information, and if based only on traded prices, a measure of volatility on this period will merely be seen as a function of tick size. This measures indeed uncertainty on the next traded price, but this measure will probably not have the same meaning as the same one on a small tick asset.

The difference between large tick assets and small tick ones is for instance noted in [Wyart *et al.*, 2008] in which the authors measure that the relationship between spread and volatility found on small tick assets does not hold for big tick ones. An attempt to retrieve this relationship through explicit modeling of the discretization via the uncertainty zone model is found in [Dayri and Rosenbaum, 2012]. Thanks to their model, they claim to measure the implicit spread, the one that is related to volatility, and which would be observed if tick size was not a floor to the spread. Another model trying to measure this underlying spread is provided by [Harris, 1994], and we chose to present this model in our Annex A.5.

Theoretical development: Harris Model: Underlying Continuous spread Discretized by Tick. See Appendix A.5 for more details.

Nevertheless, the real difficulty and question of interest is to assess how tick affects the quality of the liquidity. The usual metrics for market liquidity and its quality are quoted/effective spreads, price impact, market impact, quoted sizes, depth of orderbook, trading sizes, resiliency, order exposure, quotes adverse selection, limit orders profitability taking into account waiting time to fill, ease of front running strategy and queue jumping, total transaction cost for institutional investors, etc.

Whereas these quantities are just components of liquidity quality, and not a direct answer to the question of interest, most of them are still not properly defined and there is no consensus on how to measure and synthesize them. We will therefore focus on the most easy ones to define and state how tick size affects them. The reader has to keep in mind that none of these measures really answers the most important questions which are:

1. How does tick size affect market quality?
2. How can tick size be used by trading venue to earn market share?

3. How does tick size change the profitability of the various participants in the market?

Obviously these questions are linked to each other, for instance it is not really relevant to study a stock's liquidity decrease in one market due to a tick change (question 1) if, the liquidity has in fact been transferred to another trading pool trading the stock (question 2). Going further on this example, if the market that earned market share in this change is mostly used by a category of actors (because its use requires sophisticated enough technology) then the third questions emerges. Furthermore, suppose we are able to answer this third question, then: When is the cost paid or rent earned by this category too much for the improvement they provide to the Price Formation Process (which pre-supposes they indeed enhance the quality of the market)?

The link we made between the two first questions is indeed faced by most of empirical studies that have tried to measure the effect of decimalization in the US. Furthermore, it would also make questionable any study of current European ones that would be based on orderbooks, as studying the orderbook of only one market would make little sense, yet it would not really make sense either to aggregate all trading venues' orderbook given the presence of mirroring orders that will be canceled when trades occur on the other destinations (a study on this subject can be found in [van Kervel, 2012]).

To get some insights on these tricky questions, we will first list the most used proxies of market quality. These proxies have been used in academic studies empirically studying the effect of tick size changes (generally reductions as this is the current trend) and we will recall what these studies found as significant changes.

We will then study the effect of tick size on the inter-market competition, because as we will see, it is a source of biases when studying one of these proxies, but more importantly it should be kept in mind that tick size can and has already been used as a leverage to gain some market share in these competitions, and not as a way to improve market quality.

Finally the proxies of market quality, though useful to understand the mechanisms by which tick size changes the market, are not a measure of the quality of the market for a given investor for two reasons. First, all these effects are mixed in real trading so that analyzing the change in these proxies separately does not give a real insight on the global effect. Second, because the transaction cost for a given investor depends on its investment and execution strategy, which would undoubtedly be changed to adapt to a new market design. Nevertheless technological or research investments needed to face a change of market design are obviously impossible to measure but often far from being negligible. We will try in the final part to give some insight on the benefits for different categories of market participants, which are the different voices that markets or regulators have to listen to in the debate about the optimal tick size.

1.3.2. *How tick size affects market quality*

Decreasing the tick size lowers spreads when tick size is a constraint

Being the minimal increment between two limit orders, the tick size will of course act as a minimal bound for the bid-ask spread. This intuitive idea motivates the model of an underlying continuous spread discretized by tick size which is exposed in the Appendix A.5 (p. 235).

Theoretical development: Harris Model: Underlying Continuous spread Discretized by Tick. See Appendix A.5 for more details.

The aim of the model is to quantify the decrease in spread that can be expected from a decrease in the minimal price variation. Obviously, the more the spread is constrained by the tick, the greater the expected decrease in spread for a small enough tick.

There exists simple measures of how much the tick size constrains the spread. The most widely used are:

- Binding probability: The percentage of trades or monetary value or duration of quotes with a bid-ask spread equal to one tick. This measure will obviously range from 0 to 1 and the greater it is, the higher the constraint of tick size.

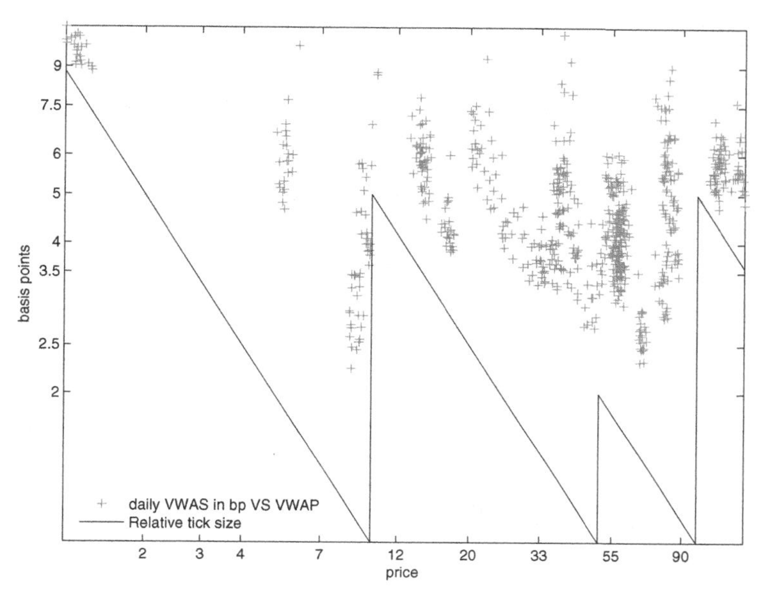

Figure 1.19. Average daily relative spread against stock price for DAX stocks on XETRA, July 2012.

- Spread Leeway: Spread expressed in tick unit, minus 1. The greater it is, the less constrained will be the stock. For some illustration purposes in what follows, we will simply use the spread expressed in tick.

These measures are simple to compute and effective to asses which stocks there have a decrease of spread associated with a smaller tick size.

On Figures 1.19 and 1.20 we used crosses to plot the volume-weighted average spread (over a day for one stock) of the S&P500 and DAX stocks, against the daily VWAP of this stock. This is a log-log scale. As the spread computed here is already relative to the price (bid-ask spread divided by mid-price) there is no reason for a relationship to appear between price and spread (which is the case of DAX stocks or S&P stocks priced above $150), except when tick size becomes an active lower bound for the spread.

It is really obvious that most of S&P500 stocks with a price below $20 will have a nominal spread equal to one tick most of the time.

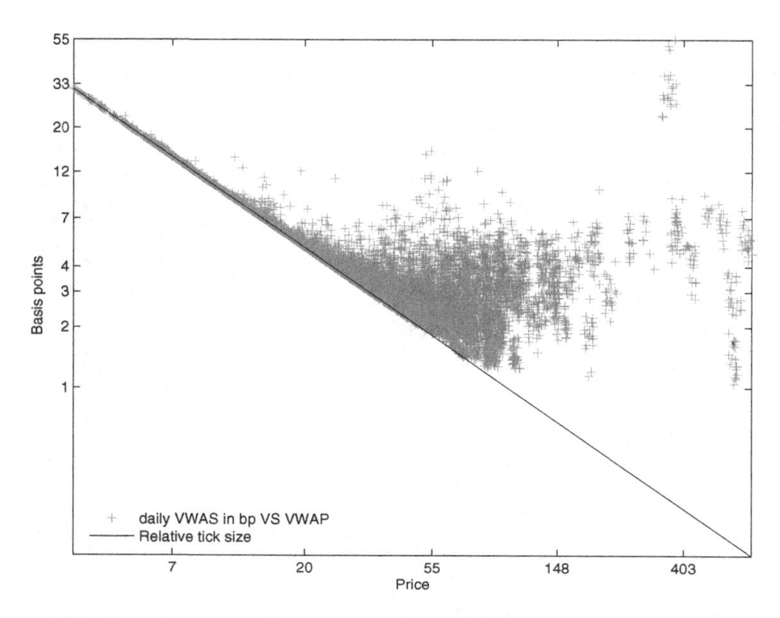

Figure 1.20. Relative spread against stock price for S&P 500 stocks on July 2012.

Conversely, the bid-ask spread of stocks priced above $150 clearly have no constraint at all. This policy of "one size fits all" offers the potential for empirical studies about the effects of tick size without a change in tick size. This can be done by finding two stocks with similar characteristics but different spread in tick, in order to measure the effect of tick size on a specific liquidity measure. We will indeed use this in the next section in order to illustrate the use of tick size in the competition between trading venues.

There is a long history of a policy of small tick sizes in France and especially in Germany, as we can see from Table 3 in [Angel, 1997]. In 1994 Germany already had a 2 basis points relative tick size (despite a 35 median basis point spread at this time). Consequently, the decreases of tick size that have been observed in post MiFID European trading has more affected UK, Italy and the Nordic countries. Nevertheless, these changes in the market design did not lead to academic studies on its effect. In order to expose the results of the 20 years of research on the effects of changing the minimum price variation, we will often have to refer to studies on the subject of "decimalization" which occurred in the US in the 90's that lead to a decrease from 1/8th of a dollar to one cent.

Indeed, the American Stock Exchange (AMEX) reduced the minimum price variation from eighths to sixteenths for stocks priced between $1 and $5 on September 3, 1992. [Ahn *et al.*, 1996] used this event to test the predictions of spread decrease provided by Harris' model. The result was that the direction of change in spread was right, but the magnitude of change was overestimated.

Among others, [Jones and Lipson, 2001], [Chakravarty *et al.*, 2005], [Wu *et al.*, 2011] used the US decreases in tick sizes, from eighths of a dollar in 1992 to a cent in 2001, to measure the changes in quoted and realized spreads. Like other studies, they found a decrease in these quantities for stocks that needed this change; more explicitly: Highly traded, low priced stocks which probably had a spread mostly equal to one tick.

But they also report at best no effect, and unfortunately even some increases in spreads for illiquid high priced stocks. Thus it seems that there is a threshold for tick size below which it is useless to go, as the main purpose of such reduction, explicitly: decreasing spread, will not be achieved (so the situation will be worse as measured by any liquidity proxy). Academic studies on other markets, such as [Aitken and Comerton-Forde, 2005] confirmed this result that there is a tick size below which a further decrease will increase the spread. When useful, decreasing tick size allows for a lower spread, so that at least for small volume traded the cost of market orders (the liquidity premium paid by liquidity taker) is decreased, but this comes with a decrease in quoted sizes.

Therefore, next question is: For a given volume does increasing the tick size increase the cost for a liquidity taker? We will first have a look at the effect of tick size on quoted sizes, as the sum of quoted sizes will be of interest when trying to measure the cost of a trade for a given volume.

Smaller and faster liquidity, does this means more unstable?

A smaller tick size will split limit orders over more price points. As a mechanical consequence, there is less quoted size at each of these limit prices. Moreover, as priority for a limit order can be earned with a small increment in price (queue jumping) there is less need to anticipate and post behind the queue, waiting for it to deplete, as it will always be possible to improve the best quote with a small increment. The quoted sizes on the best limits are therefore a lot smaller with a small tick size.

We can easily illustrate this with the same sample as the one used in Appendix A.5. We used data from the FTSE 100 and plotted the mean monetary value quoted on the best bid and ask against the spread expressed in tick. More precisely, we computed for one day one stock the VWAS (Volume Weighted Average Spread, in pence) and divided it by the tick. This will be our "spread in ticks". The sample was then divided into deciles of spread in ticks and we made for each of these deciles a boxplot of mean quoted sizes at the best limits for the sample lying in this decile.

As one can see from Figure 1.21, there is far less volume on the best limits with a smaller tick size. So that the smaller quoted spread

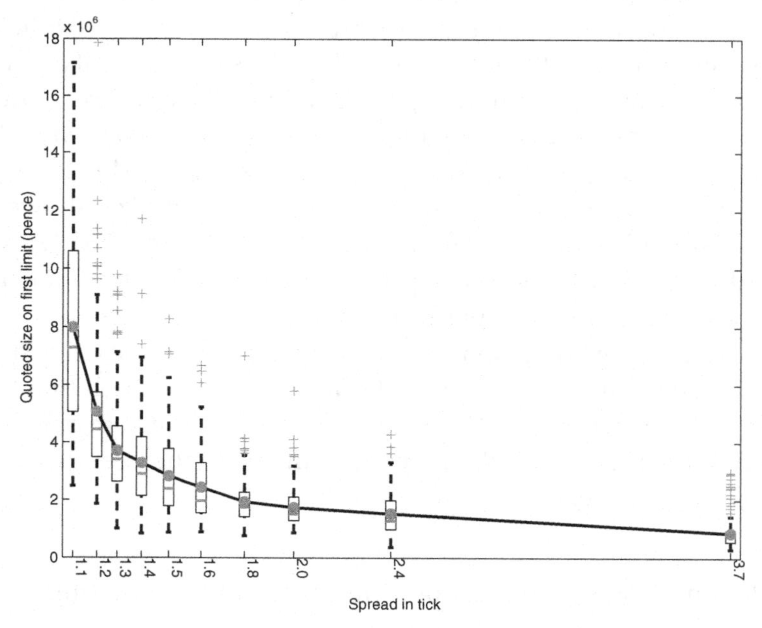

Figure 1.21. Quoted size (pence) on first limit against spread in ticks, FTSE 100 stocks, April 2012.

discussed earlier is in fact available for less volume than with a bigger tick, and it is unclear whether the cost of crossing the spread for a given volume exceeding this quoted size will be higher or lower. This simply illustrates that spreads are really not enough to assess market quality, at least regarding the question of optimal tick size.

But more than what can be seen as a mechanical consequence of having more price points to spread your order on, is the economic incentive to conceal the full size of any order. [Bacidore *et al.*, 2003] and [Goldstein and Kavajecz, 2000] among others indeed showed that there was not only less orders at each limit price but that these orders were also smaller. The reason is once again the easiness of stepping ahead of other orders with a small price improvement. Therefore market participants prefer to show less size in order to avoid being front run.

This effect can be shown with our FTSE 100 sample. On Figure 1.22 we represented with boxplots the distribution of daily

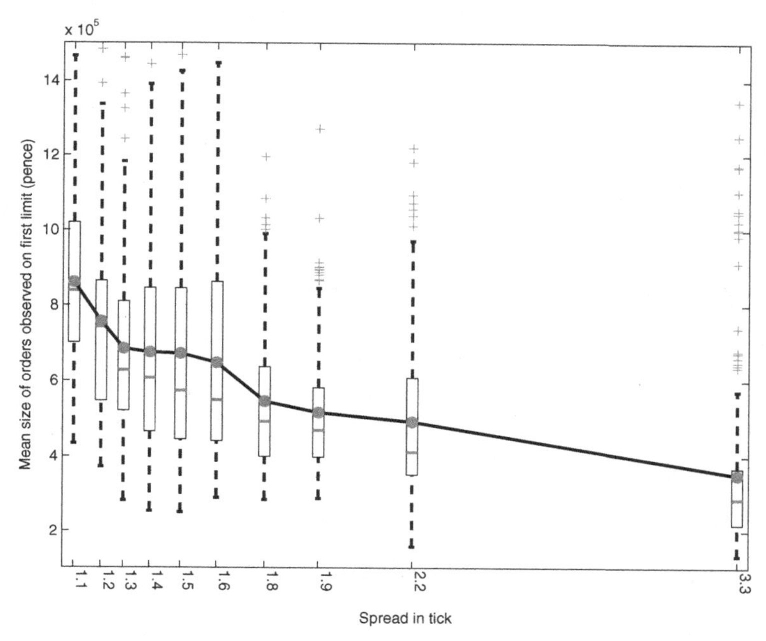

Figure 1.22. Mean size (pence) of each order on first limit against spread in ticks, FTSE 100 stocks, April 2012.

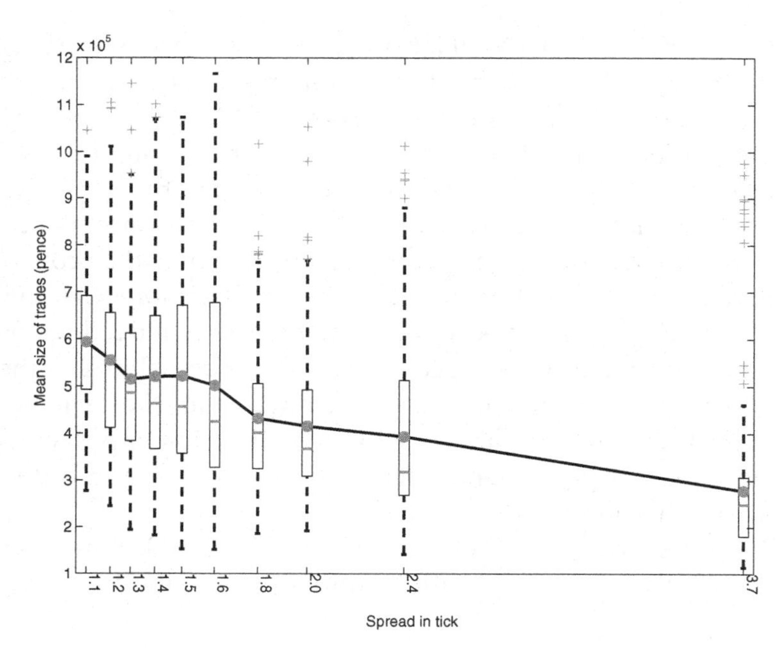

Figure 1.23. Average trade size (pence) against spread in ticks, FTSE 100 stocks, April 2012.

time weighted limit orders sizes conditional on the decile of spread expressed in tick. One can see that from the first to the last decile there is nearly a threefold decrease in the size of orders posted on the first limit. This shows that the disincentive to post large orders with a small tick size is very important. Obviously this will lead to a decrease in the average trade size as the size of trade is the minimum between the size of the liquidity provider and liquidity consumer order. This is illustrated on Figure 1.23, on which we represented the distribution of trade sizes conditional on spread in tick.

Almost any study on tick size change events concludes that there is no change in traded volume, which is quite surprising given that proponents of small tick sizes claim that spread decrease is a sign of reduced transaction costs, so that there should be more trades as the cost of trading is lowered. But this is not still our point here, as we said, traded volume does not change with tick size change, but trade sizes decreased, so there should be more trades. But what about the frequency of orderbook events?

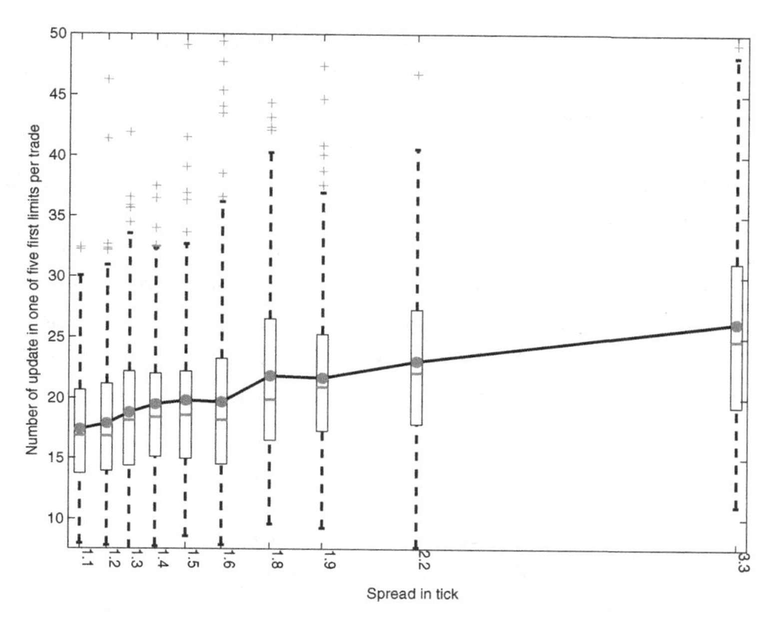

Figure 1.24. Order to trade ratio against spread in ticks, FTSE 100 stocks, April 2012.

On Figure 1.24, using the same sample as the previous figures, we plotted the distribution of the ratio of number of orderbook updates to the number of trades. This normalization aims at making a more homogeneous sample cross stock and not overweighting the measure with the most active stocks. This is also a meaningful measure in the sense that it values the informational content of a single orderbook update, the greater this ratio, the less important is a single orderbook update.

We can see an increase of 50% between the first and last decile of spread in tick. This means that with a smaller tick size, liquidity is not only becoming thinner, but also jumps more often from one price to another, and the value of quote decreases, both because of its smaller size and its shorter life.

The figures are explicit enough: The smaller the tick size, the less volume is found on a given limit. This is not a surprising result: the more limits available for posting liquidity, the less liquidity you will find on each of them. Nevertheless, one cannot help but recognize that a sound and deep orderbook is desirable.

We have seen that with smaller tick sizes, quoted sizes are smaller, and these quotations have to be refreshed more often (even relative to the frequency of trades which are themselves smaller hence more frequent); so we would need a dynamic model of orderbook to try to measure the influence of tick size on its quality. But as there still no such model which would have to take into account the resiliency of the orderbook (its ability to fill depleted quotes after a price impact), we will keep on observing the effect of tick size either on snapshots of quotes, or on the observed cost for a liquidity consuming order but for any size, and not just the smallest one as is done when looking at quoted spreads.

Cumulative depth and order exposure incentive

Trying to mix the effect of spread and quoted size in order to shed light on the execution cost of a given volume can be achieved by several measures. When the order-by-order database of an exchange is available, then it is possible, by rebuilding the limit orderbook, to measure the cost of immediate liquidity consumption for marketable orders of any size (called effective spreads or sometimes price impact). We can compare pre- and post-event cost for any volume and tell which orderbook is sounder.

This approach has the advantage that it takes into account hidden liquidity in this market, but there is a downside conditional on the behavior of liquidity consumers, so that if they had to decrease the size of their orders due to a decrease in tick size then it will not be possible to make any comparison. Furthermore, most academic studies using this measure were about the US decimalization event. As US was already a very fragmented market at that time, the potential change found in a given limit orderbook is not necessarily representative of what market participant really faced given that they were able to execute on another market (ECNs for instance).

This measure is used in [Bacidore *et al.*, 2003]. In this study, the authors had access to the NYSE orders database. They showed that for any given size the expected cost of a marketable order was lower after decimalization, so that NYSE limit orderbook, conditional on the timing of liquidity consuming orders as well as their size, was deeper than it was before the switch of tick size from sixteenths of dollars to cents. This result is confirmed by many other studies, including [Goldstein and Kavajecz, 2000] and [Jones and Lipson, 2001].

Nevertheless it is also interesting to have a look at the orderbook at any time and not only conditional on the occurrence of a trade. More than just de-conditioning on the behavior of liquidity consumer, this also gives a little insight about the resiliency of the orderbook that is to say its ability to replenish limit price queues with liquidity after a liquidity consumer left its footprint.

The same authors ([Bacidore *et al.*, 2003]) had a look at cumulated depth on the same sample and found that whereas liquidity was indeed sounder below a distance of 15 cents from the BBO, it was indeed worse after the tick size change for deeper limits. These results might seem contradictory, but are not, because marketable orders with a cost greater than 15 cents are almost non existent in their sample. Therefore the missing liquidity in the deepest layers of the orderbook cannot be seen in trades.

Nevertheless their methodology on the subject of depth measurement is questionable because the costs are not relative to the value being traded, relative meaning that if a consumer would feel the same with an additional cost of one dollar for buying a 1,000 dollar product or a 10 dollar one.

[Goldstein and Kavajecz, 2000] studied the same sample, using NYSE order data, then adding specialist's quotes, and finally looking at effective spreads in order to include hidden liquidity. They also measured costs in basis points, making them comparable for high and low priced stocks. Regarding the value traded, they unfortunately also use number of shares, but at least they split their sample into high and low price stock samples. This makes the meaning of share volume a bit more homogeneous between their samples. Finally they also split stocks into high and low volume stock samples, which can help to see the effect of tick size conditional on initial liquidity of the stock.

They found that the publicly available orderbook was less deep after decimalization, the cost of a virtual large trade for frequently traded stocks was greater, and for infrequently traded stocks the cost for any size was greater.

Nevertheless when adding specialist's liquidity (which is publicly available but cannot be seen pre-trade), the cost for small size orders of any stock's category is found to be better after decimalization (at least quoted spreads improved). Unfortunately, the cost of a large quantity remains more costly for any given stock's category.

Finally, their analysis of effective spreads reveals that the cost for small size orders had indeed decreased for all stocks, but there is no improvement for trading a large size on a high price frequently traded stock, and the cost of large order did improved significantly for infrequently traded stocks.

The authors of [Goldstein and Kavajecz, 2000] hence confirmed our previously stated danger of tick size reduction: applied without regards to the stock, the tick size reduction harms the liquidity by increasing costs. Moreover, the study gives some insight about orders' exposure incentive, as we saw that the public limit orderbook was indeed less furnished after the decimalization.

Indeed, [Harris, 1996] using data from the Toronto stock exchange, as well as Paris Bourse (no change in tick size but enough heterogeneity of spread in tick to measure its influence on order exposure), and [Bourghelle and Declerck, 2004] studying a tick size change (increases for some stocks and decreases for other) on the Paris Bourse both confirm the result that limit order exposure is discouraged with a smaller tick size, and market participants make more use of hidden liquidity in order to avoid being front run.

Aitken and Comerton-Forde's study [2005] of a tick size decrease on the Australian market in 1995 confirms the previously stated results about cheaper liquidity for stocks needing a smaller tick and a more expensive one for stocks that already have small relative tick sizes and low trading volume. Contrary to what we just said they claim that there is no effect on order exposure, nevertheless this is mainly because they refuse to interpret results due to statistical tests stating results are not significant whereas the magnitude of changes are important from a practitioner perspective. For instance, all their samples except one show an increase (statistically insignificant given their test) in the proportion of partly undisclosed orders, but this sample is a group of stocks in which the relative tick size remains really huge after the tick size reduction, with a minimal tick relative to price of 1%.

There are indeed potentially different forces when it comes to order exposures, and depending on the way we decide to measure it, results might be very different. Indeed as we will see in the section dedicated to trading venue competition, the off lit market trading in the US is greater for stocks which have the biggest relative tick size on the lit market. This is a consequence of the ability to trade on a finer grid than the tick size off lit markets, therefore allowing queue jumping with very small price improvements. As we will see later, the reasons for these strategies to be even more dominant for big tick size stocks in the US is two fold: First these big tick size stocks have a large spread (as a consequence of tick constraint) so that someone able to undercut limit order with a small price concession will just be able to make the market, earning a large spread rent. Second, almost all trading venues in the US have adopted the maker taker fees, i.e., paying a rebate to provider and taking a fee from the consumer. These fees are expressed in dollars per share, not relative to the value traded, so that, relative to the value traded, rebates paid to the liquidity consumer are far greater for low priced stocks. This second effect is an additional incentive to provide liquidity in low priced stocks, and using ECN to do so helps win the competition for liquidity provision with a small price improvement.

We will now have a look at what is felt to be the reason for order disincentive with a small tick size, namely: Queue jumping. This practice could, when not done by someone willing to trade in order to accumulate an inventory, be considered front running in the sense that the lost opportunity will force some of the patient market participants to become impatient, cross the spread and trade against the very same liquidity provider that previously took the opportunity. Apart from this intentionally excessive analogy (nevertheless used in academic literature, e.g., [Aitken and Comerton-Forde, 2005]), the problem of giving the ability to queue jump with a small tick size is that it makes time priority nearly meaningless and accentuates the current trend of quotations to become more and more fleeting.

Queue jumping and the profitability of limit orders relative to marketable ones

The spread may be lowered when tick size decreases, but we saw that the shape of the whole orderbook will change. Before a decrease in tick size, the volumes are very high on the BBO, and these large volumes will then be split on the first few limits. From an intra day trading point of view this will change many things, especially when the spread is generally equal to the tick size (which means that, for example, the best bid cannot be improved). With huge volume at the first limit and a spread equal to the tick size, someone who needs fairly fast execution will be forced to use a market order. A liquidity provider will have to take great care about the "queue", as it may take a long time for a limit buy at the best bid to be executed, whereas with a small tick size, someone who wants fairly fast execution can, for example, improve the best bid (if willing to buy), and a liquidity provider has much more space for its strategy. A small tick size (relative to latent spread) will therefore move the investor's attention from 'queuing issues' to 'limit price issues'.

It is often believed that reducing the tick size would make limit orders less profitable compared to marketable ones, the reasoning being that as the spread is reduced so is the liquidity premium received by limit orders. But on the other hand, waiting time for a limit order to be filled is also reduced, moreover some have argued that the adverse selection cost of limit orders is also decreased. Furthermore, if such a lack in liquidity provision was felt, liquidity traders would enter the market to make the market and earn the spread. All these effects are probably well balanced, hence the quantity of posted liquidity is unlikely to change, but some of its characteristics might, such as the size of orders or the increased use of hidden liquidity.

Some empirical studies (e.g. [Bacidore *et al.*, 2003]) examined the use of limit and market orders surrounding a change in the minimum price variation and did not find that one type of order was more used after the change. They nevertheless observe, as stated previously, that orders sizes decreased, and the frequency of cancellation also increased. The last observation is consistent with our illustration on

Figure 1.21 showing that the message traffic has increased relative to the true trading activity.

This belief of no change in the balance between market and limit order profitability is confirmed by [Wyart *et al.*, 2008], whose authors, through the relationship between volatility and spread, study the profitability of market making and market taking strategies. The paper concludes there is no evidence for an increase in market making profitability with a bigger minimum price variation.

Finally, [Coughenour and Harris, 2004] using the decimalization event, studied the profits of NYSE's official market makers: The specialists. They found that their overall profits did not change. Nevertheless, as spreads decreased, so did their profits per trade as well as the size of trades, hence their participation had to increase. To cope with the decrease in per trade profits, these specialist therefore had to be involved in a higher proportion of trade, hopefully for them they were able to do so thanks to the decrease in minimum price variation, which enable them to step ahead of other limit orders with a small price improvement.

Indeed [Bacidore *et al.*, 2003] and [Bourghelle and Declerck, 2004] stated that frequency of trading and quoting one tick better than prevailing quotes increases as the tick size decreases. This is a natural consequence when one desires to foster the competition for providing liquidity in order to lower spreads. Unfortunately this also has the effect of shifting the role of liquidity providers from the natural investors to professional market makers. The problem for natural unsophisticated (from an execution perspective) investors is that, even though spreads may be decreasing, they are paying the spread more often and as a result we cannot say that their transaction costs have decreased.

Moreover, as we will see, some trading venues specialized themselves as a niche for undercutting strategies, and made such features available even when the lit market has a big tick size (relative to spread). More than the fact that this creates unfair competition (or if allowed for the lit market creates a race to bottom for tick size), this makes the quotations observed on the lit markets (the only ones providing it) quite meaningless.

1.3.3. *How can tick size be used by trading venue to earn market share?*

We will see that poorly designed regulation in the US, and still no formal regulation in Europe can be exploited by trading venues in order to provide an edge to their members, hence earning more market share.

Though the question may be asked for stocks listed on foreign markets, the competition between markets for small price increments is obviously far greater when there is a full fungibility and the lowest possible latency between markets.

The question of interest here will therefore be more answerable where a certain degree of fragmentation have already been achieved, more explicitly in the US and in the post MIF European environment.

Tick size war in the US

To recount the history of the equity trading market in the US as a whole, and even a clear picture of how it is currently organized, would be a fairly hard task. Consequently, we will just focus on a short description of tick size regulation.

The rule 612 of Reg NMS establishes a minimum price increment for stocks above one dollar, the Sub-Penny Rule which "prohibits market participants from accepting, ranking, or displaying orders, quotations, or indications of interest in a pricing increment smaller than a penny, except for orders, quotations, or indications of interest that are priced at less than $1 per share."

Nevertheless, there is a long standing practice of payment for order flow from broker-dealers in the US. Through this mechanism the broker dealer gets the choice to either receive a small price improvement on an order or re-route it to public markets. By doing so, they can trade at prices forbidden on lit markets because they don't have to display an order whose price would be outlaw, they simply accept an economically insignificant price improvement and thanks to this have the power to step ahead of a public limit order for small to no cost.

Furthermore, ECN's have adapted to the changes in public markets, for instance when NYSE was trading with a minimum

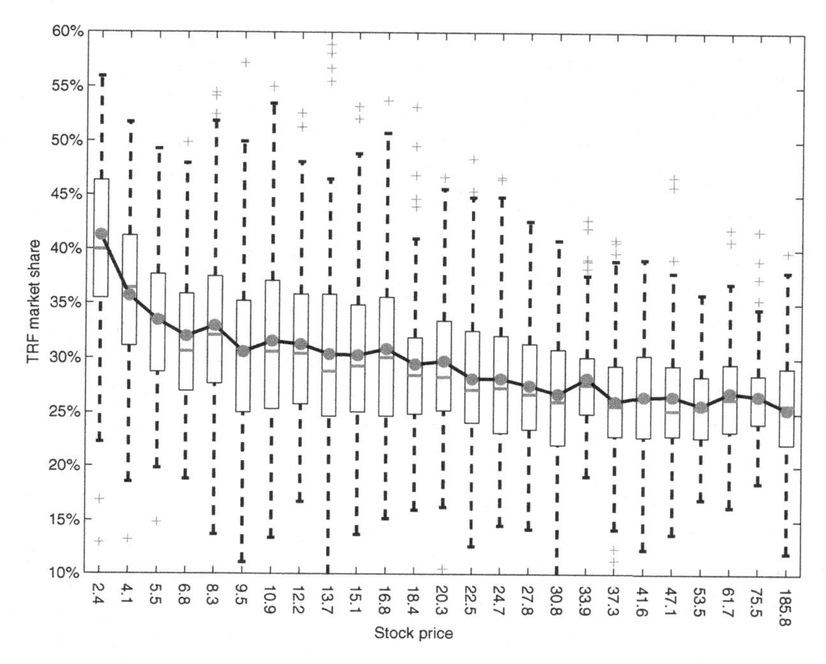

Figure 1.25. TRF Market share against stock price, Russel 3000, August 2012.

price variation of one eighth, the minimum price variation (MPV) on Island was already one cent, and when decimalization occurred Island reduced its MPV to $0.0001 so that its members could continue to undercut public prices.

This practice is currently far from being negligible, as according to [Delassus and Tyc, 2011] the value traded in March 2010 with negligible price improvement in stocks priced above but very close to $1 was 10% of the total value traded in all markets in these stocks. The value traded off lit market is enough to show this effect as can be seen on Figure 1.25.

The reason for the appetite for queue jumping in such low priced stocks is pretty clear: With an artificially wide spread of 1% there are considerable profits to make if you don't face the excessively long queue posted at best bid and ask prices on public markets.

On the other hand, some orders receive the best improvement they could receive (given public information) and are traded at the mid-point. But even for such orders, it could be argued that they should not be too important a proportion of the total traded value as they do not take part in the public price formation by contributing to public quotes. Furthermore it is worth noting that the Sub-Penny Rule of reg NMS (applied 01/31/2006) was designed with the aim of avoiding a tick size war between markets and to prevent queue jumping. It has indeed lead to an immediate a twofold decrease in the total proportion of sub-penny trading. But market participants (and trading venues) have adapted to this environment and there is now a greater proportion of sub-penny trading than before Reg NMS.

Given the appetite of some market participants for queue jumping, the benefits from this rule have now totally vanished, but the constraints still exist, making the spread artificially wide for low priced stocks.

These problems are a concern for anyone desiring fair and orderly markets, and this is reflected in the publicly released "Comments on Concept Release on Equity Market Structure", but also in a petition ([Bats *et al.*, 2010]) from public markets BATS Exchange, NASDAQ OMX, and NYSE Euronext, asking the SEC to approve a six-month pilot program permitting market participants to quote under a penny.

Tick size war in Europe

MiFID initially set no regulation over tick sizes, so that the different trading venues were free to set a tick size for each stock different from other trading venues.

This possibility was indeed used for instance by Chi-X, considering that some stocks did not have their optimal tick size. Chi-X reset the tick size for a few stocks, such as Alcatel-Lucent setting a tick size lower than the one of Euronext as early as 2007 and decreasing at the beginning of 2008. The convergence of Euronext's tick size in September 2008 to Chi-X's one showed that this was probably a bright move from Chi-X.

At the beginning of 2009, MTFs started working collaboratively in order to find a way to harmonize tick sizes in Europe. The LIBA (London Investment Banking Association) and the FESE (Federation of European Securities Exchanges) then joined these discussions.

This led to the FESE tables, a list of four different tick size regimes that should become the standards in European trading.

Nevertheless there was still no agreement on how these harmonized tables could be used, which stocks should use which table, or who should make these decisions.

At the beginning of June, Chi-X decided to implement smaller tick sizes for Danish, Norwegian, Spanish and Swedish stocks. There was still no agreement for the tick size harmonization. This move as well as the probable beginning of trading of a big market maker in these names, who is likely to have expressed its desire for more granular tick size in these stocks, lead to a huge increase of Chi-X's market share. As we can see, smaller tick size has consequences on an execution venue's market share if you have a good market maker and enough significant members connected to your venue with effective SORs. This is indeed the exact aim of SOR technologies to benefit from the better quotes enabled by this more granular tick size.

This obviously made other MTFs quite envious, and indeed, they too began to set their own tick sizes. These venues saw a need for a smaller tick size for some UK and Italian stocks. It is worth noting that UK and Italian stocks were traded with a relative tick size of 10 basis points while most liquid European stocks were trading with a spread smaller than that.

This move was viewed as a tick size war, as it gave the three main MTFs a significant market share gain for the short period of time when they had a different tick size from the primary market. Indeed, it enabled trading on MTFs with a smaller spread than the 10 basis point minimum imposed at the time by the rules of the LSE Group.

Here is the time line of this war: On 8th June, Turquoise chose to reduce the tick sizes for five UK blue chip stocks. One week later, Turquoise implemented smaller tick sizes for five more UK stocks and five Italian stocks, and the same day, BATS followed in the steps of Chi-X and Turquoise, and implemented the same tick sizes as Chi-X (for Danish, Norwegian, Spanish and Swedish stocks) and Turquoise (for the UK and Italian stocks). The consequences, in terms of market share, of the steps taken by Turquoise and BATS can easily

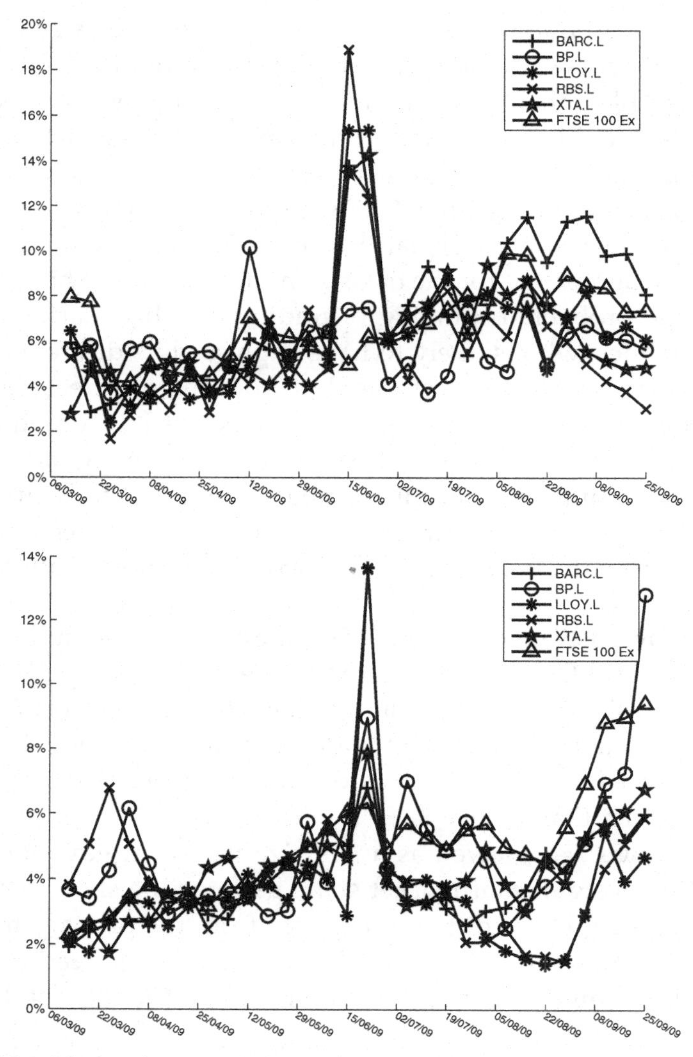

Figure 1.26. Market shares excluding fixing auction volume for Turquoise (top plot) and BATS (bottom plot) during the tick size war.

be seen in Figure 1.26: the venue that offers a tick size that best fits a stock is immediately rewarded with an increase in market share.

European primary markets were then compelled to act. LIBA and FESE organized a conference call on 16th June, during which MTFs and exchanges agreed not to implement smaller tick sizes until a meeting on June the 30th. On June the 22th, the LSE, Chi-X, Turquoise, BATS Europe and NASDAQ-OMX Europe standardized the tick sizes where differences had appeared.

This is an important step in the history of tick size regulation, as markets themselves agreed that they should not leave this choice to be used for market share competition. Instead, they had to find a rational way to determine the tick size for the sake of liquidity and not the interest of a select few. On 30th June, a FESE press release announced that the MTFs were now committed to adopting the same tables as the domestic venues, and to make no further moves in their tick size regimes outside the timetable agreed for each market to implement the chosen table.

When tick size may be used to gain market share the race to bottom has no reason to stop before tick size reaches an economically insignificant value, because front runners will push trading venues up to this point, generating extra traded volume by being a nearly mandatory intermediary, hence attracting the attention of venues. This race to bottom, would stop when tick size becomes economically meaningless and would lead to tick size below its optimal level, harming market quality.

Nevertheless, it is time for the regulator to take on its role in this process set in place by the financial industry. The "gentlemen's agreement" of the FESE members now has to be enforced: There is no need for a dozen tick size tables in Europe, and there is no need to allow a market to use its own tick size table if the standard ones are well designed. A tick size table should simply span all possible ranges of prices in Europe and set a tick size relative to price as constant as possible. Then it should be possible to choose an initial tick size table for each stock given its liquidity, and with a simple "trial and error" process, it should be possible to adjust the optimal table for each stock given its "spread in tick", spreads, and other market quality proxies already cited.

The situation looks hopeful, as it is highly probable that the newly formed regulator ESMA will take on this role and propose a rational process for the determination of the optimal tick size, taking into account trading venues' voices as they showed their good understanding of the issues underlying this choice of a market design.

1.3.4. *How does tick size change the profitability of the various participants in the market?*

Recently, the SEC examined the possibility of increasing the tick size with the aim of encouraging IPOs ([SEC, 2012]). Whereas the mechanism by which tick size would be able to have such an effect is not clear, the question is nevertheless interesting because one should not forget that the primary aim of stock markets is to provide capital to firms. The point of increasing market quality is then only a way to reduce investors transaction cost so that they can provide firms the needed capital while being able to manage the risk of their investments.

The question of how institutional investors' trading cost is affected by tick size is therefore essential as they are primarily providing this essential service to the society. Furthermore, it is argued that a spread decrease is important because it reduces the cost for retail investors but this cost is in fact not very significant compared to other costs they have to face. Indeed who can really argue that the few basis points in English and Italian stock that we have recently observed in Europe thanks to tick size decrease were an important burden for retail investors. Moreover, most investments from retail are handled by institutional investors and not directly managed by the individuals themselves, so they mainly face the costs to institutions.

Finally, the study of institutional trading cost is an important question, because more than revealing the cost for this particular category of market participant, it integrates market impact, information leakage, and easiness of front running for instance. More generally, it mixes all kind of transaction cost for large orders. These costs can therefore be considered as the most direct measure of liquidity quality, but obviously their analysis face the aforementioned problem of being conditional on institutional trading strategy.

Despite the importance of this question, there is not much academic literature on the subject. The reason is probably more the difficulty to get the necessary data for such research, and the difficulty of the question rather than lack of interest. All the available studies measuring institutional trading cost are based on the tick size changes in the US from eights to sixteenths and to cents.

Overall the results are rather mixed, while [Jones and Lipson, 2001] and [Bollen and Busse, 2006] find significant increases in institutional trading cost during these events, [Chakravarty *et al.*, 2005] claim there was no change in these costs during the decimalization, and [Werner, 2003] state there has been a decrease in these costs. The last study is to be taken with care as, contrary to other mentioned papers, the data used are not from the category of market participant we are interested in, but from a market, with an indirect inference on its origin, and no relationship with a parent order that would enable us to evaluate the cost for the whole inventory change desired by a portfolio manager.

Neither will we discuss [Bollen and Busse, 2006] in detail as they do not directly measure the cost of some orders but instead estimate trading costs by comparing a mutual fund's daily returns to the daily returns of a synthetic benchmark portfolio that matches the fund's holdings.

The remaining studies ([Jones and Lipson, 2001], [Chakravarty *et al.*, 2005]) would lead the reader to conclude that there might have been an increase in institutional cost at least in the reduction from eighths to sixteenths, and perhaps no change in the decimalization event but thanks to a change in the trading strategy and more efforts for a careful execution.

Indeed [Jones and Lipson, 2001], as well as [Chakravarty *et al.*, 2005] both used data from the Plexus Group. The Plexus Group is a widely recognized consulting firm that works with institutional investors to monitor and reduce their equity trading costs. At the time of the study, their clients managed over $1.5 trillion in equity assets, and the data to which those studies had access to accounted for approximately 25% of US marketplace volume. Nevertheless not all of these orders could be used for natural reasons, so finally the orders used for instance in [Jones and Lipson, 2001] represents 13% of US marketplace volume. The other interesting aspect of this data is that contrary to [Werner, 2003] the full inventory requested by the institution is known, before being split into blocks and several brokers.

The study [Jones and Lipson, 2001] show that during the change from eights to sixteenths, institutional trading cost did increase.

Not all orders were affected, and indeed the category of portfolio managers facing the worst increase were high liquidity consumers such as momentum traders using very large orders. The study also highlighted that the less the order was worked (high participation ratio) the more the cost increased.

On the other hand [Chakravarty *et al.*, 2005] studying the switch to decimals claims that overall trading cost decreased and that this decrease was more important for larger trades. Furthermore, they notice that costs declined for stocks in which tick size was more likely to have been binding whereas it increased for stocks in which tick size was not a constraint. Finally, they also insist on the fact that orders not worked (executed within a single day) saw their cost increase, and that compared to [Jones and Lipson, 2001] their sample contained a greater proportion of worked orders. This final remark is an indication that institutional traders might have learnt from the costs faced in the switch from eights to sixteenths that they should more carefully split their trade and take more time to execute it.

This is also one of the conclusions of [Garvey and Wu, 2007] which rather than studying the cost faced by institutional traders analyzed the changes in their trading strategies during these events. They found that larger orders take significantly longer and more trades to execute after decimal pricing. Traders had to adapt to the changing market design by submitting smaller order sizes, increasing their trading frequency and making more use of ECN in order to better manage their order exposure.

The vague, though most common, definition of a liquid asset is to be able to trade fast, at small cost, a large quantity. Therefore it's reasonable to consider that the increase in time and efforts needed for large executions in the aforementioned papers is a sign of decreased liquidity from an institutional viewpoint.

1.3.5. *The value of a quote*

There are concerns about the decreasing value of quotes. With smaller quote sizes, quotes existing for shorter times (often too short for anyone to trade against), and the shortcuts that exist off lit market with the sub penny increment, the value of quotes has drastically decreased over recent years.

This lead Maureen O'hara, a microstructure expert, to write an article to ask the question: "'What is a quote?" ([O'Hara, 2010]). We have seen that decreasing tick size lead to:

- Increased order to trade ratio,
- smallest sizes of each order posted on the best limit,
- less orders posted on the best limit.

Moreover, [Harris, 1996] and [Bourghelle and Declerck, 2004] showed that a reduction in tick size increases the use of hidden orders. Avellaneda, Reed, and Stoikov, in a paper trying to forecast price moves thanks to level I orderbook notice that it is harder to do with stocks that have a small tick size relative to spread. They capture this effect through a hidden liquidity parameter, but also admit that this could also be interpreted as the best limits have less informational content with a smaller tick size.

The value of quotes, and the informational content of Level I quote data undoubtedly has to be protected as only sophisticated market actors can pay the price for storing, processing, and doing research on full depth orderbook. For instance, the usefulness of a consolidated tape (desired in Europe by many actors), which will obviously at best contain the first limit of the limit orderbook, would be decreased by further tick-size lowering.

Going further in the process of tick decrease therefore has to at least be a balance between the small price improvement received by small orders and the value of what most investors can see from the orderbook.

Finally, the choice of an optimal tick size table for a given security is a tricky problem that has been studied, and there are some stylized facts that have emerged from academic literature, which help in designing a pragmatic way to choose the right tick size:

- There is no use in lowering the tick size past the point that enables a decrease in the spread.
- Even so, the liquidity of a stock is harmed even before reaching this point.

- Any decrease should always be implemented reasonably and smoothly to give time for market participants to adapt.

Despite the recent trend towards decreasing tick sizes in Europe, there is still room for a further decline for some well chosen stocks, but there are a lot more stocks (not necessarily in traded value but in number of stocks) that would need an increase in tick size.

For the sake of the European trading landscape, it is strongly believed that the regulator ESMA will be given the power to design tick sizes for European trading and set an upper limit for the order to trade ratio. This should hopefully preserve the integrity of the price formation process which could otherwise be jeopardized by the biggest market players dictating their interest to the trading venues.

1.4. Can We See in the Dark?

This section is a comprehensive study about role, evolution and specifics of Dark Pools in Europe. It also tries to give an overview of how Dark Pools work in general and their true impact in market microstructure. Dark Pool is the generic name given to an alternative exchange where the available liquidity is not visible to the public. The main interest of Dark Pools is to protect institutional investors willing to execute large blocks of orders from opportunistic traders that want to make profits on a short term horizon.

In Europe these Dark Pools became an important participant in the microstructure landscape as a result of the MiFID. This directive was intended to increase competition and consumer protection in investment services. As a result, different types of multilateral trading facilities were born, radically changing the way the price is formed. This new paradigm, were prices are no longer created in a single centralized orderbook but in different exchanges competing with each other, is known as market fragmentation. Understanding how this fragmentation impacts the way markets work and how the price is formed is key making the right decisions when optimizing the trading process.

1.4.1. *Mechanism of dark liquidity pools*

In 2007 the Market in Financial Instrument Directive (MiFID) became effective in the European Union. This directive has as its main objective the increase of competition and consumer production in investment services as well as the provision of harmonized regulation across the members of the European Economic Area.

Before MiFID, regulated markets and OTC concentrated all market activity. Markets were organized in a straightforward way going from investors to intermediaries to the trading platforms. Today investors have the choice between a large variety of exchanges such as MTFs, Crossing Networks, Dark Pools, etc. These new exchanges have each one their own rules when matching orders, making the price formation process way more complex than during the old days.

Dark pool is the generic name given to exchanges that do not publicly announce their available liquidity. Dark trading has existed as a practice for years, often by other names (internal crossing, upstairs trading, OTC). Dark pools in the way we know them today are just the electronic version of what was previously a manual telephone-based process. In practice there are different categories of dark liquidity pools, whose main types are listed below

- **Crossing Networks**: When we talk about Dark Pools at a generic level, we usually talk about these Crossing Networks. These pools of liquidity cross buy and sell orders for the same stock using prices (mid-price) derived from the primary market (NYSE Euronext).
- **Internalisation Pools**: These are dark liquidity pools where a Broker internalizes its own flow.
- **Electronic Market Makers**: These Dark Pools do not cross orders with the orders of other client but with the operators flow. The mechanism is different from internalization pools as Electronic Market Makers immediately accept or reject the incoming orders.
- **Exchange-based Pools**: These are not exactly dark exchanges but it is dark liquidity that is hidden on lit exchanges. These orders are executed when the counterpart is larger than a certain threshold.

- **Dark Aggregators**: Provide access to all the Dark Pools simultaneously and create a single point access to fragmented liquidity. They receive an order and split it between the various pools. As the algorithm gets filled, it adjusts the allocation to reflect the activity in the various pools.

The main MTFs with significant market shares in the "lit" world (namely Chi-X, BATS, Turquoise and NASDAQ-OMX) have launched their Dark Pools using the reference price waiver, which only permits orders to be crossed at the mid-point of the best bid and offer of a reliable source.

To be consistent with MiFID rules and the principle that the smaller the quantity of an order, the more the owner has to be protected, a model with two distinct orderbooks has been chosen:

- *An integrated book*: The integrated book accepts all visible orders and hidden orders that are Large In Scale (LIS). An order is considered to be large in scale compared with the normal market size if it is equal to or larger than the minimum order size specified in Table 2 in Annex II of the MiFID Implementing Regulation.
- *Dark or mid-point book*: This book accepts hidden orders smaller than the LIS, and matches only at the mid-point of the Primary Best Bid and Offer.

The basic principle of order routing depends on the order size: "dark" LIS orders participate in the price formation process (i.e., they interact with lit orders and LIS orders in the integrated book), whereas "small" dark orders (under the LIS size threshold) can only be matched in the mid-point book.

Adding to this standard, some Dark Pools follow specific rules in routing orders to each book, depending mainly on the order type. For instance, on Chi-X, LIS orders can also be routed to the dark (or mid-point) orderbook if the order is specified with a minimum quantity.

To conclude this overview, it is important to note that the four MTFs cited above only accept mid-peg dark orders, wherein limit price, minimum acceptable quantity, and IOC characteristics are allowed.

1.4.2. *In-depth analysis of dark liquidity*

European Dark Pool market share

In the overall European landscape, Dark Pools now represent approximately 5% of non-OTC trades. In the US (after Buti, Rindi and Werner, Zhu) Dark Pool activity is to be about 10–12% of share volume. The six biggest hidden liquidity pools in Europe are Chi-X, BATS, Turquoise, Liquidnet, Nomura and POSIT, and together they would represent more than 90% of dark traded volume. To illustrate how fast this market share has grown, let's take a look at the proportion of notional that is executed in the dark for Chi-X and BATS over the past few months:

Before 2005 Dark Pools had low market share. The main users of Dark Pools were institutions wanting to trade large blocks without revealing their intentions in order to avoid front running. After Reg NMS and MiFID the situation started to change. These regulations encouraged new electronic exchanges to compete with existing markets. Dark Pools took a fundamental place in market microstructure since.

Even if the average daily volume has not increased over the last years (in fact market share on the primary exchange has decreased) Dark Pool market share has experienced a continuous growth (see Figure 1.27).

It is worth noting that to achieve such market share growth, BATS typically uses aggressive pricing, and also offered a maker-taker fee schedule initially.

To summarise, the Dark Pool landscape in Europe is currently evolving very fast and the three main MTFs — CHI-X, BATS and Turquoise — together represent more than 60% of European Dark Pool trades. Therefore, the data we will use to give an idea of the characteristics of this liquidity is drawn from the first three weeks of March 2010 on these three Dark Pools.

Dark Pools and price discovery

Prices cannot be created in Dark Pools and they only serve as a liquidity reservoir. Transactions in the dark are made at the mid-price

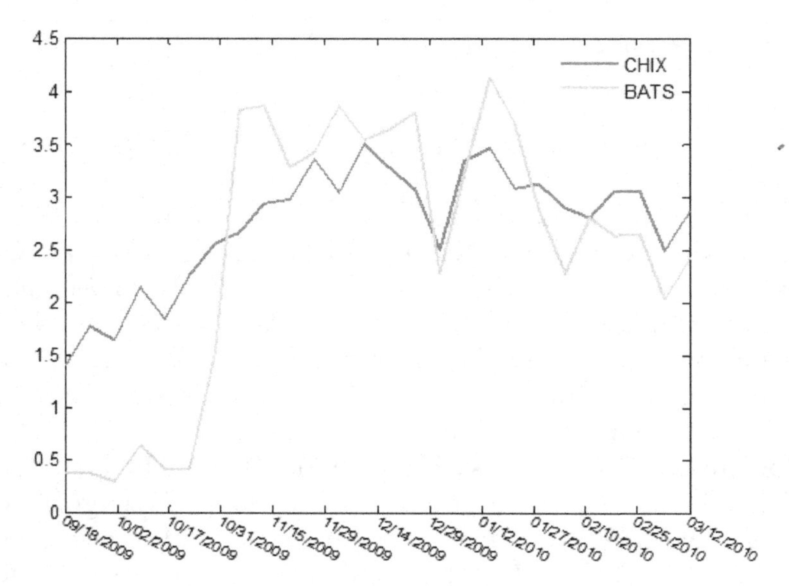

Figure 1.27. Percentage of dark trades on the two main Dark Pools.

of the primary market. Dark Pools then do not participate directly in the price formation process. However, Dark Pools attract an important piece of the market's activity and liquidity; consequently they play, in an indirect way, a very important role in the price formation process.

This question about their role in the price formation process especially concerns people in the SEC and in the European Commission who say that it is possible to argue that on some level Dark Pools are harming price discovery. There are different attempts in economic and financial literature to give an answer to this question, some with empirical studies (see e.g. [Buti *et al.*, 2010]) others with economic models (see e.g. [Zhu, 2010]). The answers varies from article to article. Some authors propose that Dark Pools reduce price discovery while others argue that Dark Pools improve the informativeness of exchanges.

The main aspects to consider when trying to answer this question are

- What are the types and what is the quality of information present in crossing networks?

- What are the factors that motivate someone to choose a Lit or Dark Pool?
- What are the relationship between Dark Pools activity and information on Lit Pools?
- How does information in Dark Pools affect Lit Pool liquidity?

One interesting viewpoint is in [Zhu, 2010] where the author argues that Dark Pools improve the trading process.

Now, we want to know what the determinants of Dark Pool activity are and how they can be linked to price discovery. Along these lines, the authors of [Buti *et al.*, 2010] studied US stock data to answer this question by studying the relationship between Dark Pool market share across different stocks and over different time frames, Dark Pool volume and its relationship with market quality, and Dark Pool volume and it relationships with market efficiency.

Some of the conclusions of their report include:

- Dark Pool Activity is concentrated in liquid stocks;
- For a given stock, activity is higher in days with high share volume, higher depth and lower intraday volatility;
- Dark Pool activity is lower in days with large order imbalances relative to share volume;
- Dark Pool activity improves market quality in terms of spread, depth and daily intraday volatility;
- Dark Pool activity is associated with short term overreaction (autocorrelation, volatility).

Main characteristics of dark liquidity

In the Dark Pools report of 2011 by Rosenblatt Securities Inc. [Rosenblatt Securities Inc, 2012], the authors pointed out the following characteristics for Dark Pools in Europe and the US (and Canada):

- Execution sizes decrease compared with preceding years,
- there is no clear relationships between market share and volatility,
- Broker-dealer pools dominate exchange based Dark Pools,
- there was modest Dark Pool market share growth in the US during 2012,
- impact of OTF designation of MiFID II on BCN/non-MTF pools.

To show some characteristics of dark liquidity, we first have to clarify the investor motivation to go to Dark Pools. When inquiring into the possible benefits of trading on Dark Pools, two obvious reasons come to mind. The first is suggested by the very name of such destinations: Being "in the dark", i.e. hidden, because revealing trading intentions is one of the greatest risks to any trading strategy. This factor motivates a growing demand for trading venues that make it possible for institutional traders to keep theirs orders secret, offer low rates, and allow them to be crossed against other institutions thereby receiving large trade sizes. Dark Pools are indeed one of the means to achieve this to the benefit of the final investor to reduce "information leakage" (avoiding being front run) and market impact. The second reason is that Dark Pools enable investors to be slightly more aggressive but without paying the whole spread, hence trading at the mid-point.

Therefore, the first question about the basic characteristics of Dark Pool liquidity would be whether investors are more likely to use Dark Pools in order to reduce market impact or to avoid paying at least half the spread. On the one hand, we know that market impact is driven by volume and volatility, so it would be interesting to look at the increase in Dark Pool volumes when volatility is high or when volumes are low. On the other hand, it should be possible to gauge the strength of the incentive of saving half the spread by observing the joint distribution of dark volumes and spread. Indeed, if investors tend to use Dark Pools more when spreads are high, then this would mean that this liquidity is mainly driven by the appeal of earning part of the spread.

Figures 1.28 and 1.29 show our initial attempt to look at such hypotheses. The methodology is simple: We gathered data (aggregated in one minutes slices) for the volume-weighted average spread (VWAS), volatility, and turnover traded in the dark. Then, for a single stock, we split the VWAS and the volatility into ten deciles and summed the turnover traded on Dark Pools according to the relevant deciles. Finally we summed these turnover on all stocks. Thus, we obtain a simple way to view the joint distribution of VWAS (or volatility) and Dark Pool turnover and the distribution of dark turnover conditional on VWAS or volatility.

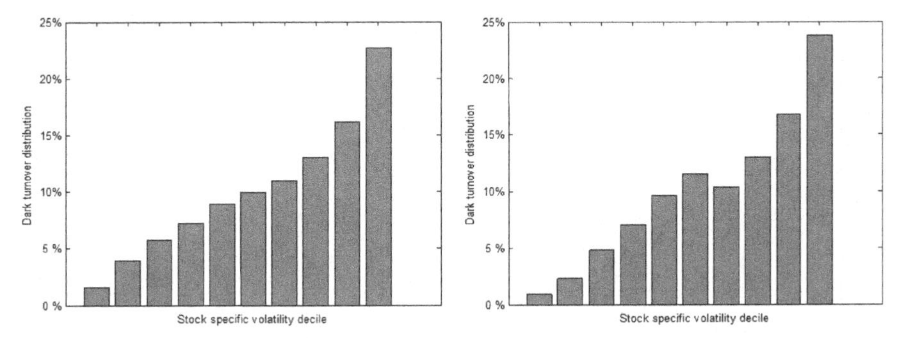

Figure 1.28. Distribution of mid-point turnover according to the deciles of volatility (CAC 40 stocks (left) and FTSE 100 stocks (right)).

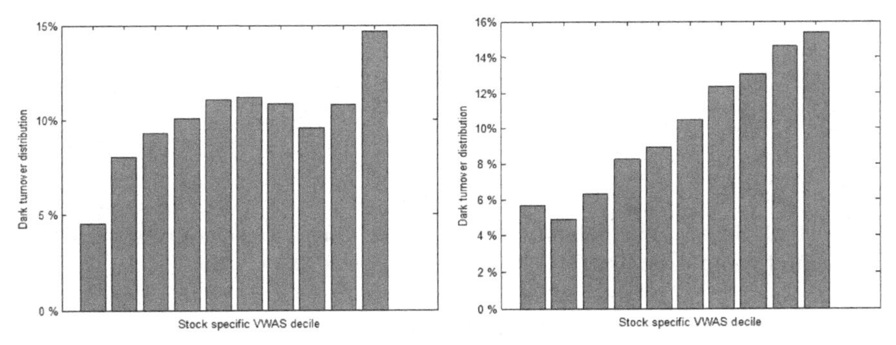

Figure 1.29. Distribution of mid-point turnover according to the deciles of spread (CAC 40 stocks (left) and FTSE 100 stocks (right)).

Obviously, either the spread or the volatility is related to the volume traded in Dark Pools: The higher the volatility, the higher the volume traded in Dark Pools, with nearly one-quarter of overall turnover being traded in the most volatile tenth of trading days. But the conclusion is the same for the spread, with 15% of dark turnover being traded in the last decile of the spread.

The conclusions that one might draw at this stage, with so few elements, would be that there seems to be a stronger relationship between volatility and dark turnover than between the spread and dark turnover.

Nevertheless, it is well known that there is also a stronger relationship between volume and volatility than between spread and volume. Indeed, there is also a strong relationship between spread

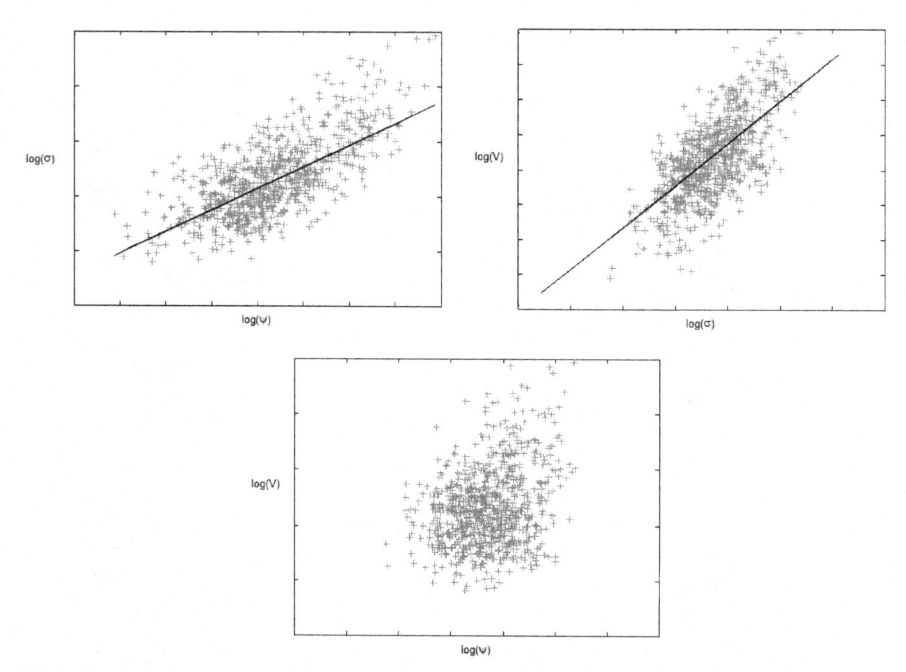

Figure 1.30. Spread and volatility (top left), Volume and volatility (top right), Spread and volume (bottom), TOTF.PA in February 2010.

and volatility. The causality and the real dynamics of these relations are still unclear, but they are easy to illustrate.

In Figure 1.30, we have data aggregated in 15-minute slices for Total SA (TOTF.PA) in February 2010 in order to chart some scatter plots illustrating these relationships.

Figure 1.30 (top left and right charts) show a strong relationship between spread and volatility on the one hand, and between volume and volatility on the other. But it is important to note that it does not imply such a clear link between spread and volume. Nevertheless, everyone knows that if an investor makes extensive use of market orders over a very short span of time, he will enlarge the spread. This can be seen in the extreme event circle. And indeed, there is a relationship between spread and volume, but mostly at these times.

Theoretical development: Clusters of liquidity: from Engle to Hawkes. See Appendix A.11 for more details.

Nevertheless, the fact that the link between volume and volatility is stronger than that between spread and volatility implies that we must moderate the conclusions we would draw from Figures 1.28 and 1.29. Indeed, with only an extreme event relationship between spread and volume, we would now question why we see a relationship between dark turnover and spreads. A different approach to the question is to focus on the relationship between Dark Pools' market share, and volatility or spread. This is especially interesting, because if this measure gives us information about the relative incentive for the market to use Dark Pools more under certain market conditions, it would also give a simple way to split volume across lit and dark venues.

In Figure 1.31, in order to illustrate the joint distribution of dark market share and volatility, we have proceeded as follows: We again used one minute data, and broke the volatility for a single stock into deciles. Then, for each stock of the index, we summed the dark turnover in each decile, as well as overall turnover, to obtain a dark market share for this stock in each volatility decile by dividing the former by the latter. One stock gives us one point in a decile of volatility. We repeated the computation for all the stocks of an index so that the following boxplots comprise as many points as stocks in the index. We have added green points linked by a dark line to the boxplot, these are simply the average of the dark market share in the decile of volatility on the whole index.

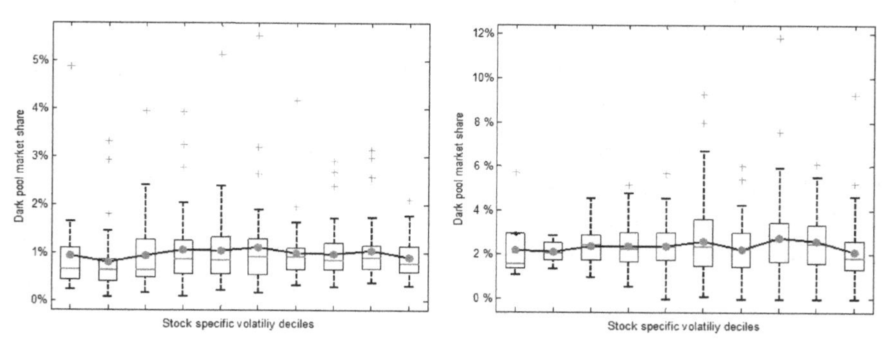

Figure 1.31. Relation between Dark Pool market share and volatility on CAC 40 stocks (left) and on FTSE 100 stocks (right).

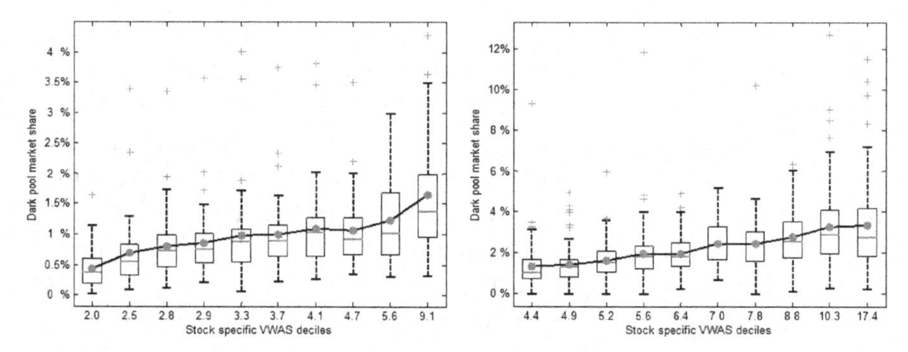

Figure 1.32. Relation between Dark Pool market share and spread on CAC 40 stocks (left) and on FTSE 100 stocks (right).

The conclusion is clear: Currently volatility is not yet the strongest incentive for investors to use Dark Pools more.

In Figure 1.32, we have followed exactly the same methodology, but instead of looking at volatility deciles we used VWAS deciles for the stocks. We also added the cross-stock median of the VWAS in basis points. This median is made across stocks and has no kind of weighting by the turnover of the stock, so these figures should be used with care as VWAS is very different for liquid and illiquid stocks; this is especially true when looking at the FTSE 100, which contains some very illiquid stocks.

In contrast to volatility, the relationship between Dark Pool market share and spread is high. The median Dark Pool market share is indeed three times as high in the last decile of the spread as in the first decile. It is obvious from these figures that the higher the spread, the easier it will be to find liquidity in Dark Pools.

This is particularly true when looking at Figure 1.33, which was built using the same methodology but using less liquid stocks from the SBF 120 (excluding CAC 40 stocks) and the FTSE 250. It is very easy to understand such behavior by looking at the median spread of the last decile on the FTSE 250, which is as high as 77bp. Indeed, when an investor really needs to trade a stock that has a high spread and needs to trade fast, it is easily understandable that he will look to use Dark Pools before sending a market order.

There are many other good reasons for using Dark Pools than just using them before sending a market order. But we should agree

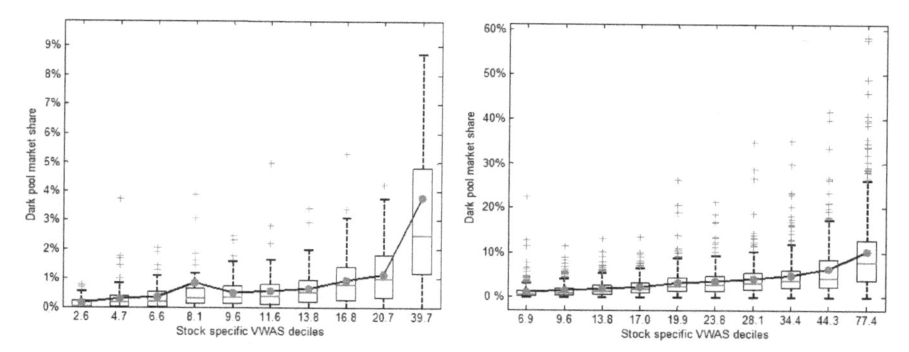

Figure 1.33. Relation between Dark Pool market share and spread on SBF 120 stocks excluding CAC 40 (left), and on FTSE 250 stocks (right).

that this is the most obvious one: Earning half a spread when the spread is consequential.

Nevertheless, Dark Pool trading has many other advantages such as reducing the market impact. As the benefit of reducing market impact is more difficult to measure, it is not still clear that Dark Pools are being used in this way.

Another incentive for using Dark Pools is a situation where there are very few trades on Lit Pools, in which case Dark Pools are simply an additional liquidity pool; if the Lit Pools cannot provide enough liquidity, you have to try the dark ones. Such an effect can currently be observed only on the FTSE 100, which has always been the fastest to take advantage of new liquidity pools. This can be seen in Figure 1.34 (below), which is built using the same methodology as the previous charts, but the dark market share is conditional on overall turnover. This simply shows (by looking at the left of the figure) that when the turnover on stocks is very low (first decile), there are relatively more trades being carried out in Dark Pools.

This could be a first sign of the advantage of using Dark Pools for reducing market impact (or at least the price impact), as there is no doubt that in such market conditions the market depth is very thin.

This intra-stock analysis is confirmed by Figure 1.34 (right). On this figure, one point stands for one stock over the first three weeks of March 2010. We have represented the dark market share according to the liquidity of the stock. The stock liquidity indicator chosen here

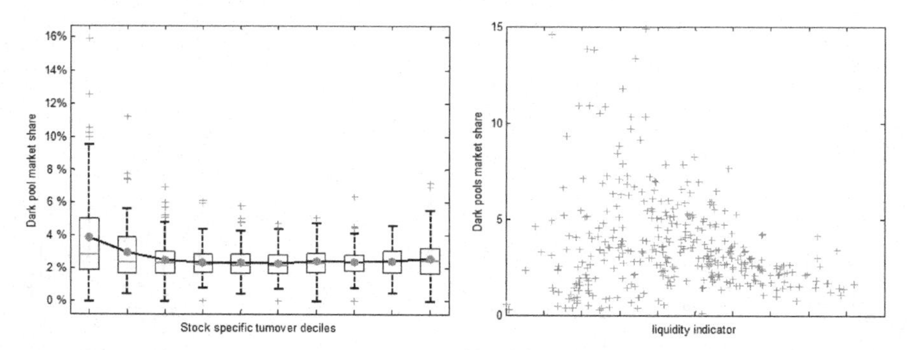

Figure 1.34. Dark market share conditional on overall turnover: FTSE 100 March 2010 intra-stock analysis (left) and FTSE 100 and FTSE 250 stocks March 2010, cross stocks analysis (right).

is the log of the turnover traded for this stock over the full period. There is obviously a variance effect, that is to say, when there is more variance in the dark market share when the turnover is low. Nevertheless, we can also see that the lower a stock's liquidity, the more investors are likely to use Dark Pools in order to find liquidity.

Dark Pools risks and toxic liquidity

The main purpose of Dark Pools is to reduce costs and protect investors willing to execute large orders in the market by not displaying the available liquidity. However in practice there exists some gaming tactics performed by some high frequency traders allowing them to detect large volumes inside Dark Pools and, by modifying the price on the primary market, taking advantage of the institutional investor. The main risks institutions face when executing orders in a Dark Pool are information leakage, adverse selection and gaming.

Adverse selection occurs when an investor gets executed after an adverse move on prices (the other side of the execution having a better alpha model). High frequency traders can detect dark orders by sending small orders or by sending orders on they opposite side they are interested. To protect large investors from gaming and toxic liquidity some Dark Pools implement policies that prevent bad practices, for example enforcing large minimum quantities, restricting access and limiting participants, tracking participants that behave like gaming HFTs practicing gaming, statistical analysis to detect participants that are consistently making money.

Information leakage is when a trader can detect liquidity in a Dark Pool that cannot be observed explicitly from the market. One of the methods used by gamers is fishing, which means sending smaller orders to detect if there is a large order sitting in that pool. Another form of information leakage comes through IOIs or any other exchanges share information with one of their clients.

Chapter 2

Understanding the Stakes and the Roots of Fragmentation

2.1. From Intraday Market Share to Volume Curves: Some Stationarity Issues

MiFID enabled MTFs to start businesses as secondary markets in cash equities, leading to a fragmentation of liquidity and spreading volumes over the new trading venues. But as not all market participants trade for the same reasons, they were not equally affected by this fragmentation and do not make the same use of these new venues. Whereas some market participants, generally acting as liquidity providers, do create bridges among these pools of liquidity, we will see that part of this liquidity remains highly concentrated.

This spatial distribution will therefore not be independent from the long studied intraday time conditioned volume distribution initiated by [Jain and Joh, 1988] and [Admati and Pfleiderer, 1988], whose fundamental reasons according to [Admati and Pfleiderer, 1988] lie in the intentions and patterns of different investors. We do not think as partly stated in [Jain and Joh, 1988] that these patterns are different from one day of the week to another. To be more explicit, a specific pattern will not emerge every Friday, but some important events such as the release of the US monthly Employment Report or the derivatives expiries always happen on Friday. We will therefore present some of the most significant events provoking these specific patterns.

In the case of the release of macroeconomic news, there is no reason for an investor trading because of this new information to have a preference for a particular trading venue where he will catch its liquidity. Nevertheless when it comes to catching and being part of a reference price, we will see that primary markets will be preferred for a natural reason: They create these reference prices, as only the trades done in these markets will be taken into account to set such prices.

Indeed, closing auction prices, which are used to compute the Net Asset Value of funds in Europe are still a primary market monopoly. This is the case for historical reasons, as obviously one unique price is needed for the valuation of portfolio and as nothing has forced competition on this field, such a reference price is still defined as pre-MIFID. With the market share lost during continuous auctions, this niche is an increasingly important part of primary market trading revenues, since, as can be seen in Table 2.1 the volume traded in auctions represents a fifth of the total volume traded on primary markets. We will therefore give more insight on the mechanisms and market participant order dynamics in Section 2.1.1.

Primary markets maintain a monopoly on the flow of a different set of actors through another reference price effect, namely the

Table 2.1. Primary markets' proportion of volume traded during fixing auctions, August 2012.

Primary market	Percentage of volume traded during fixing auctions	Considerered index
London Stock Exchange	24%	FTSE 100
Borsa Italiana	11%	FTSE MIB INDEX
Euronext	22%	CAC40
	16%	AEX
	20%	BEL20
Deutsche Börse	26%	DAX
SWX Europe	23%	SWISS LEADER PR INDEX
Nasdaq OMX	15%	OMX STOCKHOLM 30
	14%	OMX COPENHAGEN 20
	14%	OMX HELSINKI 25
Oslo Borse	17%	OBX

EDSP ("Exchange Delivery Settlement Price"), that is to say the reference price that will be used for the valuation of derivatives at their expiry. As these derivatives are listed on the primary markets, they obviously kept the rules stating that the prices traded on their markets are the ones used to set these references prices.

We will first have a look in Section 2.1.2 at the importance of trading volume linked to the expiration of the derivatives, and use this methodology to illustrate some other events inducing specific patterns in the traded volumes.

We will then in Section 2.1.3 have a look at how these patterns have different effects on each trading destination's market share, highlighting again that investors may have different uses of trading venues and are not necessarily only looking for the best price.

Fixing auctions are still a primary market monopoly, and, as we will see in Section 2.1.3, market share patterns emerged and have evolved since the birth of MTF's. We highlight in this part that market share is indeed conditional on the time of day and some important events.

2.1.1. *Inventory-driven investors need fixing auctions*

Worldwide equity trading contains two types of trading sequences: A continuous phase and a fixing auction phase. The number of fixing auctions depends on the market. Having no fixing auction at all is an exception, as it is generally accepted that it is important to have an opening auction in order to fill the orderbook. One can have as many as four fixing auctions can take place as is the case on the Japanese primary market at the beginning an end of morning and afternoon continuous trading session. Some market even have no continuous auction, only periodic fixings throughout the whole trading session. Some of these specifics will be detailed in the next section, which focuses on volume curves around the trading world. While all types of platforms ushered in by MiFID are available during the continuous phase of trading, call auctions only take place on primary markets as yet, except for Equiduct which had on 2012 August a market share for CAC 40 stocks of 0.4%.

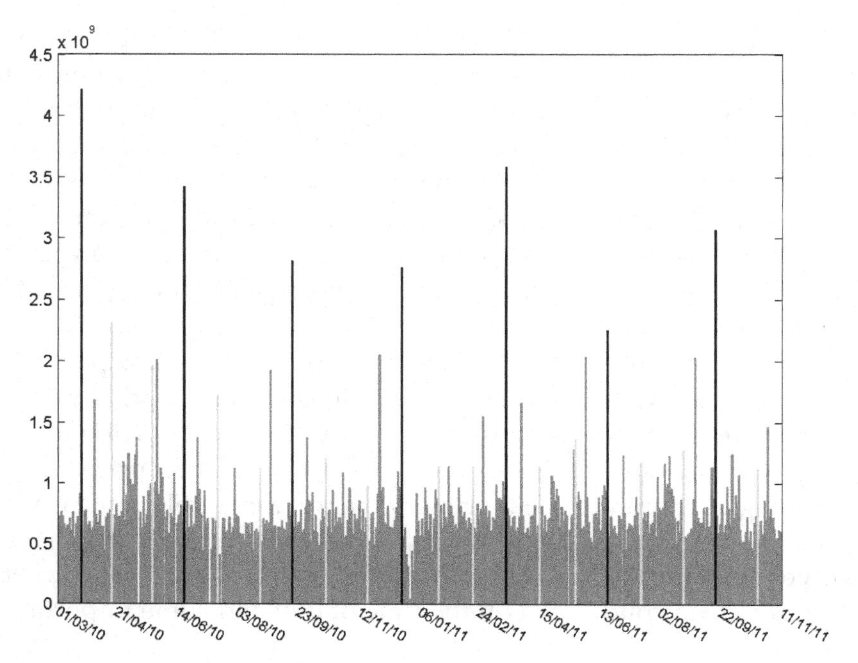

Figure 2.1. Daily turnover during fixing auctions on CAC40 stocks.

Fixing auctions: What's at stake

Fixing auctions are useful thanks to the consensual price and the huge volume necessary to unwind large positions. Figure 2.1 represents the daily turnover (in Euros) on CAC40 stocks during fixing auctions. Black lines stand for turnover on triple witching days, while the light grey ones stand for derivatives monthly expiry witching days. In fact, fixing turnover appears extremely high during witching days, especially triple ones, as would be expected. Positions in combination with derivative products that expire during these days are taken or closed during these auctions, benefiting from the same price. The total volume traded on such days during the fixing auctions indeed represents half the traded volume during the continuous auction.

The London Stock Exchange has specifically created an intraday fixing auction phase on the third Friday of each month, where high turnover is also noted, in the same manner as in Figure 2.1. This suggests that fixing auctions are useful to deal with this specific type of volume days, as this helps to gather different trading interests for these settlements around a single reference price, as opposed to the huge volume traded at different prices during a continuous phase for the CAC40 stocks (see Figure 2.9 (bottom) for an example).

Whether they happen for opening auctions, intraday auctions, closing auctions, or a volatility interruption auction, fixing auctions serve one main purpose: concentrating more agents, hence forming a more 'consensual' price for the whole volume traded. This feature is useful when the price is used as a reference for many valuations, as closing prices often are, but also for building orderbooks before opening the market.

Another illustration that order concentration during fixing auctions allows for a more thorough price formation process can be made with trading halts triggered when a stock's volatility is too high. Academic studies have been carried out on the subject, such as in [Kandel *et al.*, 2008]. According to the authors, "In the call auction, consolidation of order flows may reduce the price impact of a trade. Furthermore, the enhancement of information revelation could improve the price discovery process and, by reducing intraday volatility, result in increased price stability."

Basic matching rules during call auctions

Fixing rules differ slightly from market to market. However, they basically follow the same principles. On most markets the fixing price is determined by a four-step approach based on conditional decision rules. If a rule does not lead to a clear auction price from the overlapping buy and sell orders, the next rule is applied, and so on. If orders are not executable against one another, no fixing price can be determined.

- **Rule 1 — Maximum Executable Volume:** Establish the price(s) at which the highest quantity will be executed.
- **Rule 2 — Minimum Surplus:** Determine the eligible auction price(s) at which the quantity left in the market at the fixing price is minimum. The word surplus will be used several times in this

part and will always refer to the quantity not matched and thus left in the market, at the fixing price.

- **Rule 3 — Market Pressure:** If the surplus for all potential auction prices is on the same side, it is used to determine the auction price. If the whole surplus lies on the buy side, the highest potential auction price is designated as the fixing price. If the whole surplus lies on the sell side, the lowest potential auction price becomes the fixing price. If the surplus is zero for all potential prices, or if there exist at least two potential prices with a surplus on opposite sides, the next rule is applied.
- **Rule 4 — Reference Price:** If none of the preceding rules leads to a decision, a reference price is consulted. The reference price is generally the last price traded (either on the same day, or on the day before if no trade has yet occurred). Potential prices determined by the minimum surplus rule are examined according to their relative position to the reference price.

Differences in methodology are noticeable, notably the end time for the fixing auction. Some markets use a random time after the theoretical end during which orders can still be sent. Table 2.2 is a recap of these maximum random durations (in seconds) for the trading destinations considered. Note that these durations can apply randomly on brackets of stocks.

Table 2.2. Maximum random durations after the theoretical end of fixing auctions (in seconds).

Trading destination	Opening auction	Closing auction	Index/stocks considered
London Stock Exchange	0	0	FTSE100
Borsa Italiana	60	60	FTSE MIB
Euronext Paris	0	0	SBF120
Deutsche Börse	30	30	DAX
Nasdaq OMX Stockholm	0	30	OMXS30
US Markets	300	300	NYSE stocks
Australian Stock Exchange	30	30	All

While the London Stock Exchange (LSE) and NYSE Euronext do not apply any random durations after the theoretical end of the fixing auction, Deutsche Börse, for example, enables orders to be sent from 0 to 30 seconds after the theoretical time. This additional time can vary by day and by stock. Moreover, Xetra fixing auctions can be subject to an extended time before the price determination, in the case of volatility interruption or market order interruptions (if market orders or market-to-limit orders could not be executed at the end of the fixing auction). As we will see later on in this section, these are not the only specific features of German auctions.

Some countries outside Europe also apply very specific rules. In the United States, for example, trading in stocks quoted on the NYSE is opened by specialists on the floor that are in charge of each particular stock somewhere between 09:30 and 09:35. However, orders cannot be sent after 09:30. Closing auctions work the same way. In Asia as well, the Australian Stock Exchange indicates a theoretical open time for five separate groups of stocks (depending on their code). The open time can happen in a range of 15 seconds around the indicated time. The closing auction starts at 16:00 for all stocks and matches somewhere between 16:10 and 16:11. Japan does not have any randomness in its fixing auctions but applies a specific calculation method — the Itayose method — and the opening of a stock happens as soon as this calculation is over. Other Asian exchanges use fixed times for fixing auctions.

Pre-fixing dynamics demystified

Theoretical matching curves. The composition of market participants is different at the opening auction and at the closing auction. This translates into two different approaches to the fixing volume.

We studied market feeds during auctions for stocks on the FTSE100, FTSE MIB, SBF120, DAX and OMXS30 from 1 January, 2011 to 30 March, 2011. The data are messages sent by the exchanges which indicate for each given instant the volume that would be matched if the fixing auction had ended, the related price, the surplus (defined above), and depending on the market, the full orderbook, some limits, or nothing further (German case).

For the rest of this section, we will refer to the relative difference between the volume that would be matched at time t if the auction ended at time t with the final volume matched at the real fixing, for each time t: these will be called "matching curves". Thus, if a point of the matching curve equals zero, this means that total end volume has been sent to the market, indicating that every participant revealed its desire to trade.

Figure 2.2a presents the median matching curve during the opening auction, with the inter-quartile range (grey) and a sample day (black). The figure has been built on CAGR.PA during our dataset period. The x-axis represents time passed since the beginning of the auction call (in minutes). Figure 2.2b presents the same data for the closing period.

During the pre-opening period, book building accelerates as time goes on, and theoretical matched volume only reaches its final level in the last few moments: The curve is convex. During the closing call, matched volume rapidly increases to its final level, as agents are already present on the market and many must participate in the fixing in order to unwind their positions: The curve is concave. Participants take longer to intervene in the opening session than they do in the closing one. This reveals less uncertainty but also less patience at the end of the day. In fact, participants face more constraints in the closing session, as it is the last time they can open or close a position that day.

The opaque German orderbook is tested. Interestingly, one fixing stands out from the crowd, as it is the only one where a significant portion of the matching curve reaches a bigger value than the final fixing volume and then decreases towards it. For closing call matching curves on other markets, more than 90% of the distribution remains below the final value. This phenomenon can be seen in Figure 2.3a and Figure 2.3b (p. 116). They show the UK and German volume curves, respectively. Figure 2.3a shows that only the max volume curves (less probable situations) go above the zero threshold. On the contrary, the median curve of Figure 2.3b already reaches the zero threshold. This means that, 50% of the time, the final volume will be reached before the end of the fixing auction. Moreover, the upper

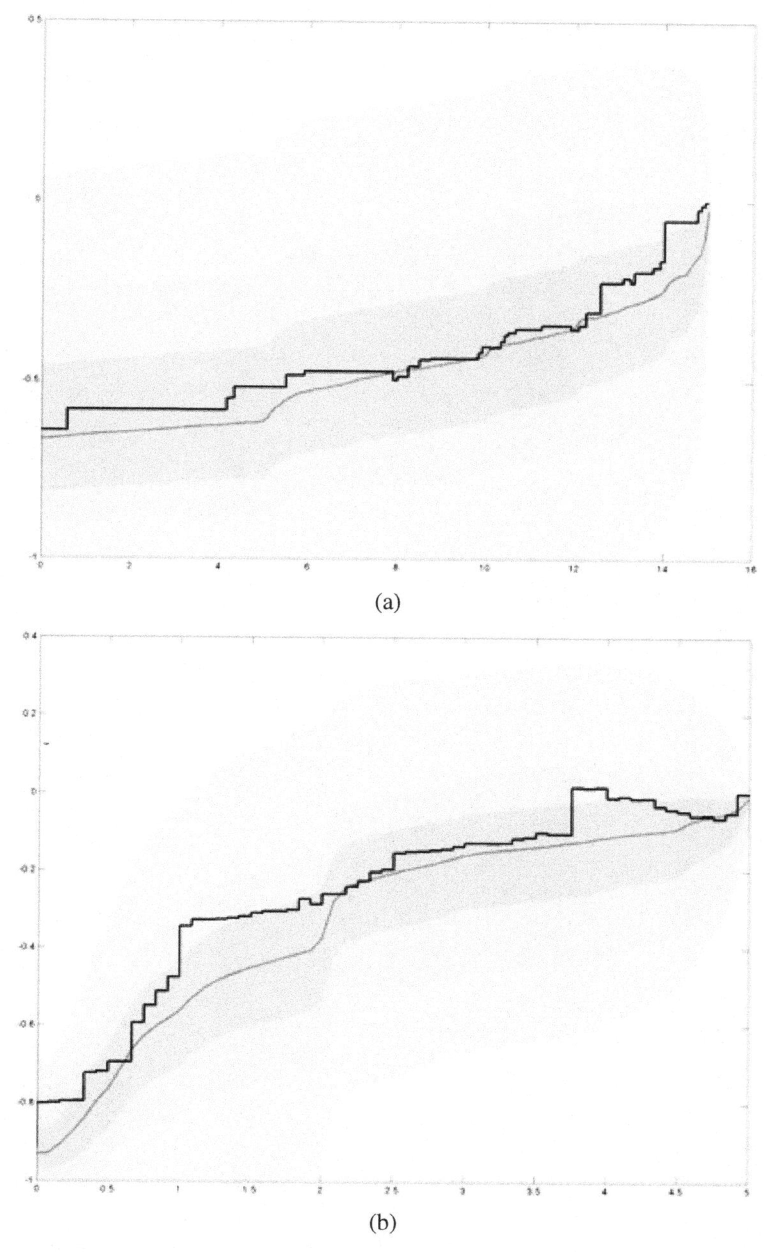

(a)

(b)

Figure 2.2. Matching curves (convergence of theoretical fixing volume to its final value) for Crédit Agricole during opening auctions (top) and closing auctions (bottom).

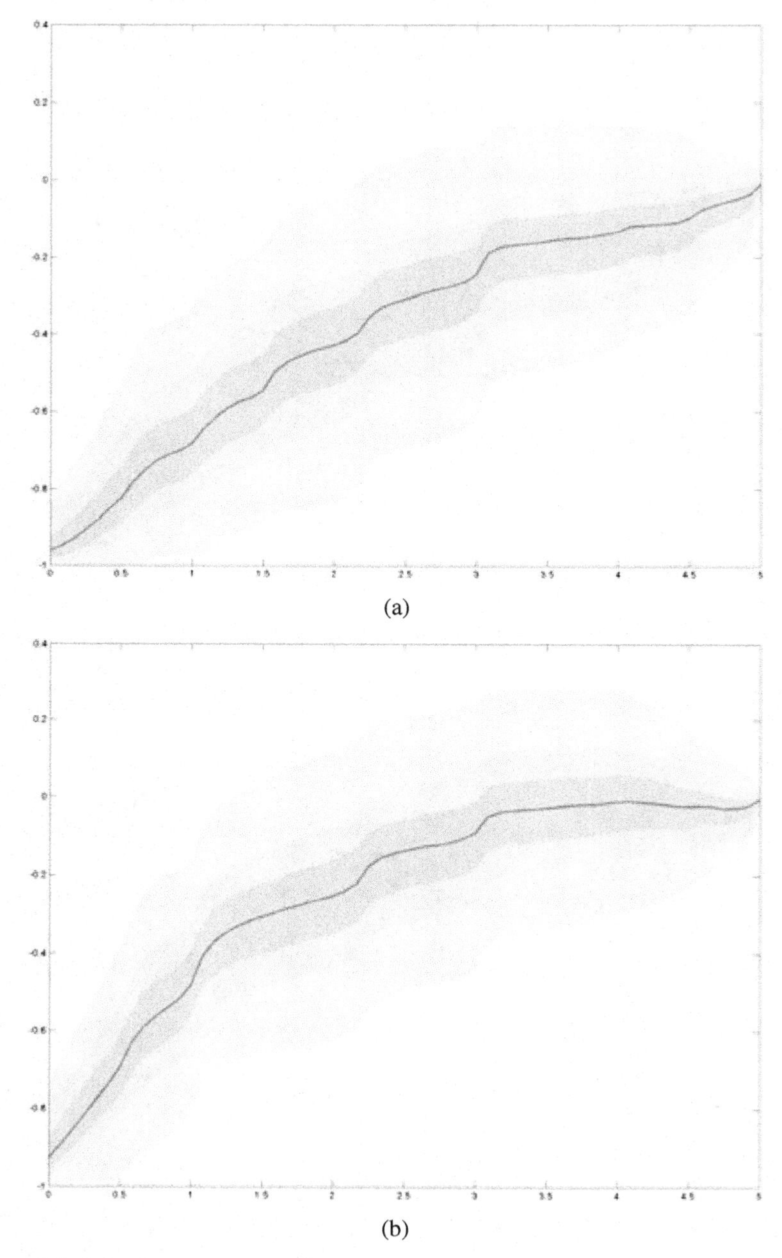

Figure 2.3. Matching curve on closing auction on FTSE 100 stocks (top) and DAX stocks (bottom).

quartile goes higher than this zero threshold. Since one fixing rule is the maximisation of volume, going over the zero threshold implies that a certain amount of orders have to be cancelled or modified before the end, and that this occurs in 25% of situations studied.

One specific feature of German auctions is that the orderbook is not revealed to participants during the fixing auctions. This phenomenon may be a sign that players are trying to get information on volumes and price by sending orders that they would then cancel, thus testing the orderbook due to a lack of transparency and getting information from the new theoretical price, volume and surplus of a theoretical fixing that their order has settled. This lack of transparency forces them to optimize the exploitation/exploration tradeoff in order to get the best price for their order without a full information on the orderbook.

Informational peaks. Delving more into the dynamics of pre-fixing periods, one can see that, although the global approach to final volumes differs for opening and closing auctions, the pace at which the information arrives follows a similar pattern. Indeed, there are informational peaks that are common across all stocks and European markets. Almost every stock every day has an important number of updates around a particular time. These updates tend to make the matched volume closer to its final value, therefore one can see these peaks as informational peaks.

To visualize these peaks, Figure 2.4a presents the probability that an update during the closing auction happens in a 5-second range. The stems stand for informational peaks. The x-axis is once again time passed since the beginning. DAX30 opening auction data are used.

Peaks are seen at 10 min, 5 min, 3 min and 2 min 30 s, 1 min, 30 s and 10 s. Although our figure represents German data, these times are fairly common across all opening auction data.

Times differ when focusing on opening or closing auctions. When concentrating on the last minute before theoretical end t, peaks are located around t-10s for opening auctions, while they are around t-30s and t-5s for closing auctions.

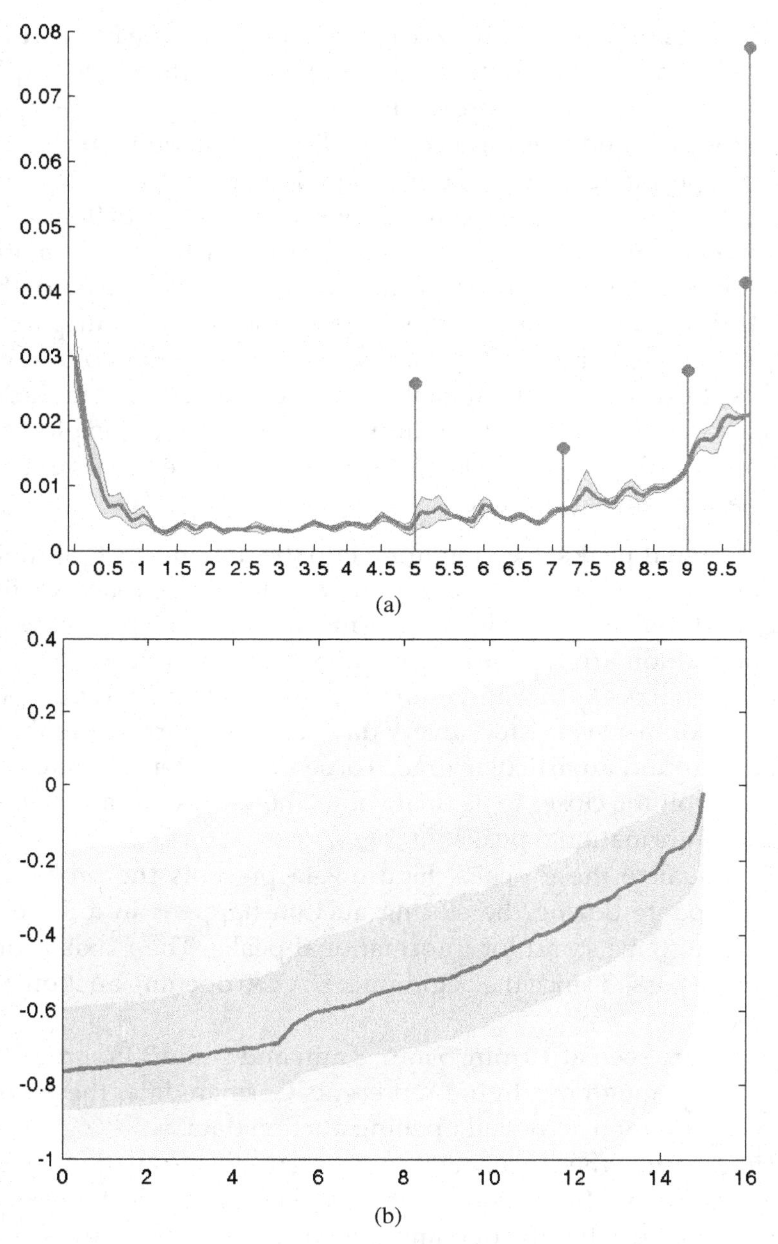

Figure 2.4. Probability that an update during the closing auction happens on a 5-sec range (top). Matching curve on DAX stocks during the closing auction (bottom).

Fixing auctions have demonstrated their usefulness, particularly when dealing with large positions. They are thus dedicated to inventory-driven investors, as opposed to relative-valuation investors, whose price formation process needs continuous auctions. Opening auctions and closing auctions have shown their own specifics in terms of participants' behavior, suggesting that they offer different services and attract different types of traders. In the next section, we will take a step back to look at the timespan of the day and study the overall behavior of participants, to finally concentrate on specific players in the markets.

2.1.2. *Timing is money: Investors need to trade accordingly*

Market design and information flow timing imply liquidity patterns

Intraday volume patterns are important, not only because they are critical for execution to a benchmark such as VWAP, but also because the concentration of trading in a specific time span during the day often reflects how informative the traded prices during this interval are.

More than 20 years ago, Admati and Pfleiderer [Admati and Pfleiderer, 1988] demonstrated the very intuitive result that there is an incentive, for both informed traders and liquidity traders, to time their trades to occur simultaneously. Furthermore, there are meeting points in terms of information, such as the opening or closing of some markets, that influence trading on other markets, or the release of important macroeconomic news at a predetermined time of day. Such meeting points create specific patterns.

In Figure 2.5, we have represented the intraday volume patterns of the some important markets. More specifically, we have used 15-minute bins in order to accumulate the traded turnover on a specific market, and plotted these accumulated volumes with green bars. The fixing auctions have been plotted with a dark line ending with a point, in order to highlight these specific market phases. The timings represented here in Coordinated Universal Time are obviously dependent on the period of the year, as many of these countries are subject to daylight savings time, which will change

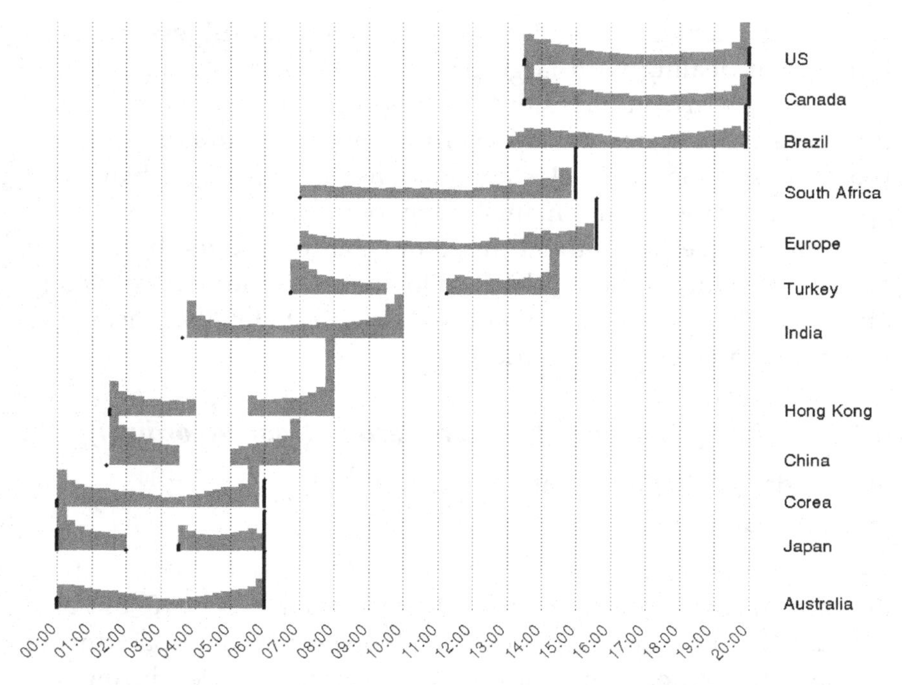

Figure 2.5. Intraday volume patterns across the globe.

their position on this axis. Even the relative position would be different, as not all the countries use daylight savings time, and the ones that do, do not enact the change on the same day. Finally, some markets have variable trading times, even in their own time zone, depending on the day of the week (Indonesia), during Ramadan (Pakistan), or to have closer trading times to a linked market that is subject to daylight savings time (the Brazilian market is an example of such a market; it has summer and winter trading times).

The classical U-shaped or J-shaped patterns observed for US stocks can become a much more complex pattern when several effects are introduced into the mix. These specific patterns are often induced by one of the following causes:

1. The opening of another linked market;
2. The release of news at a predetermined time of day on a regular basis (e.g. macroeconomic news or earnings announcements, which are often released before the opening);

3. The way reference prices are computed, and whether a specific fixing phase is used especially for this purpose.

Before going into an in-depth analysis of these effects, let's clarify the third driver. The reference price in Europe for many funds' NAV computations or equity derivatives' margin computations is the price of the closing auction, which makes it a very important source of liquidity. The effect of the increased importance of the closing auction when its price is used as a reference has been shown in [Kandel *et al.*, 2008] by comparing the reallocation effect caused by the introduction of a closing call auction to the markets of Paris (1998, with the reference price set to the price of this call auction) and Milan (2001, when the reference price remained computed as a VWAP over the continuous phase).

Conversely, India has no closing fixing, and the reference price is computed as the VWAP over the last half-hour of trading, hence the two huge green bars at the end of India's trading day (see Figure 2.5). We focused on this in Figure 2.6a by plotting the volume pattern during the last 40 minutes of trading on a specific stock. This shows that there is a substantial shift in the level of volume during the last 30 minutes.

A striking example of the reference price effect in Figure 2.6b is Hong Kong, with 17% of the traded volume falling in the last 15-minute bucket and a quarter of this volume being concentrated in the very last minute. The reference price for this market is indeed the median of five prices observed every 15 seconds during the last minute of trading, which undoubtedly explains the very pronounced J-shaped pattern for this market. Figure 2.6b focuses on this effect and shows that inside the very last minute of trading in Hong Kong, the volume pattern is clearly driven by the specific way the reference price is computed on this market. As we can see, there is an increase in the level of volume traded for the last minute, but also four spikes in volume at 15:59:00, 15:59:15, 15:59:30 and 15:59:45, the exact times of the four first snapshot prices used for reference price computation. The absence of the fifth spike is probably due to the risk of not being able to complete the order if trying to get the price at the exact time of the close of the market.

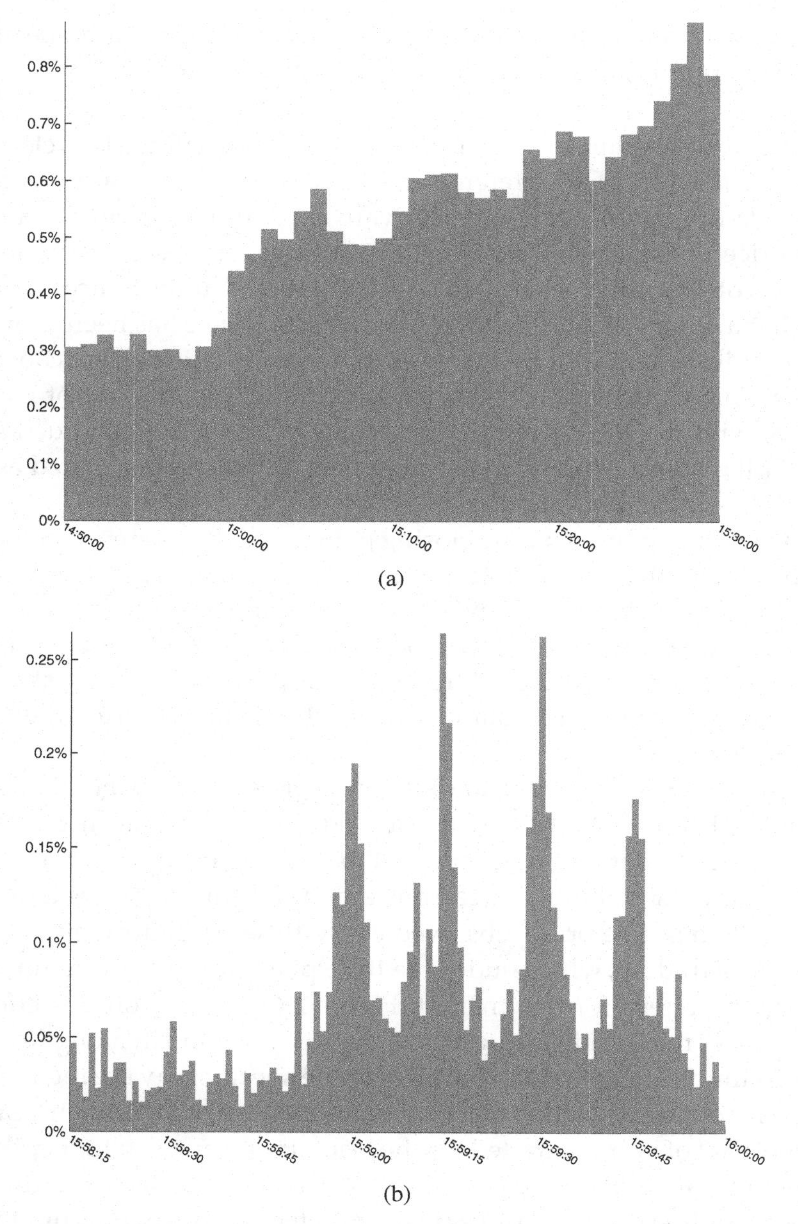

Figure 2.6. *Top plot*: Reliance Industries Ltd's volume pattern in India during the last 40 minutes of trading (1-minute bins). *Bottom plot*: CNOOC Ltd's volume pattern on Hong Kong during the last two minutes of trading (1-second bins).

The Hong Kong stock exchange made an attempt to change this closing price determination by introducing a closing call auction in May 2008, but suspicions of manipulation of the closing price made it reverse the change on 23 March 2009.

Regarding the effect of the opening of one market on another one, an example can be seen in Figure 2.5, on Brazil's volume pattern. The influence of the US market even causes the volume to increase at the very beginning of the day, creating a very special shape compared to all the other markets across the world. It has the effect of delaying the "real opening" of the Brazilian market. That is to say that it is effectively possible to trade at the opening of the market, but the real price formation process will only take place half an hour later, when the US market opens.

This strong dependence on the US market also explains why Brazil has summer and winter trading times, with the aim of being more closely matched to US business hours.

Another clear illustration of such a phenomenon is given on Figure 2.7, which represents the volume pattern in South Africa. As can be seen in Figure 2.5, this country is not subject to daylight savings time, so during the summer, the South African market opens at the same time as most European ones, but opens one hour earlier than European ones during the winter. This leads to a change in the shape that can be seen at the beginning of the curves. As is the case for Brazil, the dependence is strong enough to make the volume increase at the very beginning of the day.

Examples of mixed effects

We will now take a more in-depth look into the effect of the aforementioned causes of volume patterns. Consider the case of Total SA (the largest market cap on the CAC40) on Figure 2.6a, which is a clear example of a mix of all these effects. In these charts, we show the traded turnover in 10-minute buckets using data from 1st January 2006 to July 2011. In light green we added the same computation made on the days when the US stock market is closed, i.e. 36 days in our sample. Note that unlike the previous charts, we plot the mean traded turnover (in 10-minute buckets) and not the proportion of

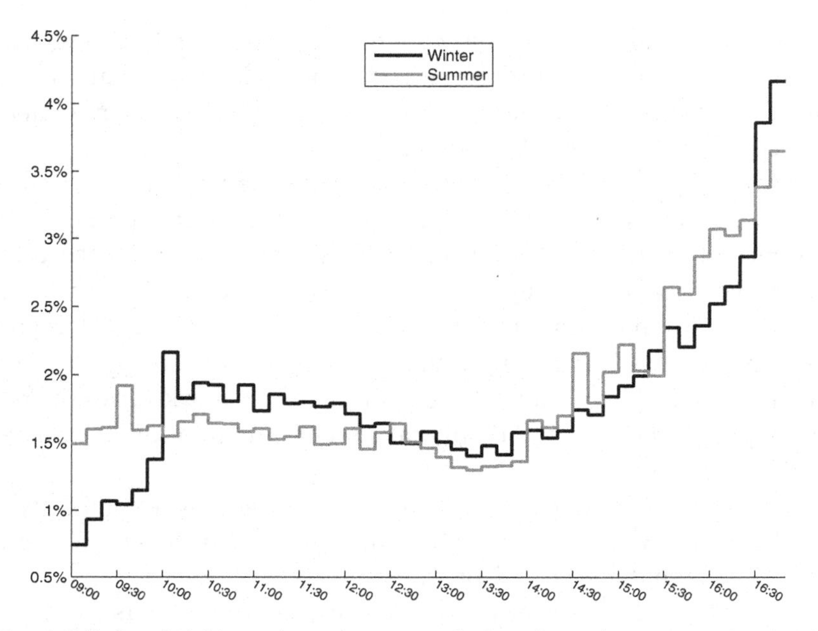

Figure 2.7. South Africa volume pattern excluding fixing (10-minutes buckets).

volume that is traded in the bucket. This will therefore enable us to observe the effect on activity during the whole day, and not only the distribution of volume in a day.

1) Opening of the US market

On Figure 2.8, we have plotted the volume pattern over our full sample (which appears on all four figures from Figure 2.8 to Figure 2.9b in order to facilitate comparisons of the different patterns), as well as the NY "shift" volume pattern and the NY closed volume pattern.

The NY "shift" volume pattern has been computed using the days when there is only a five-hour difference between French time and US time. This usually happens during two weeks in March and one week in November, and is due to the fact that daylight savings time starts earlier in the US than in Europe, and lasts longer.

The effect during this particular period of time is fairly clear, and the change in the shape of the volume pattern matches what intuition suggests, i.e., the increase in volume occurring at the time

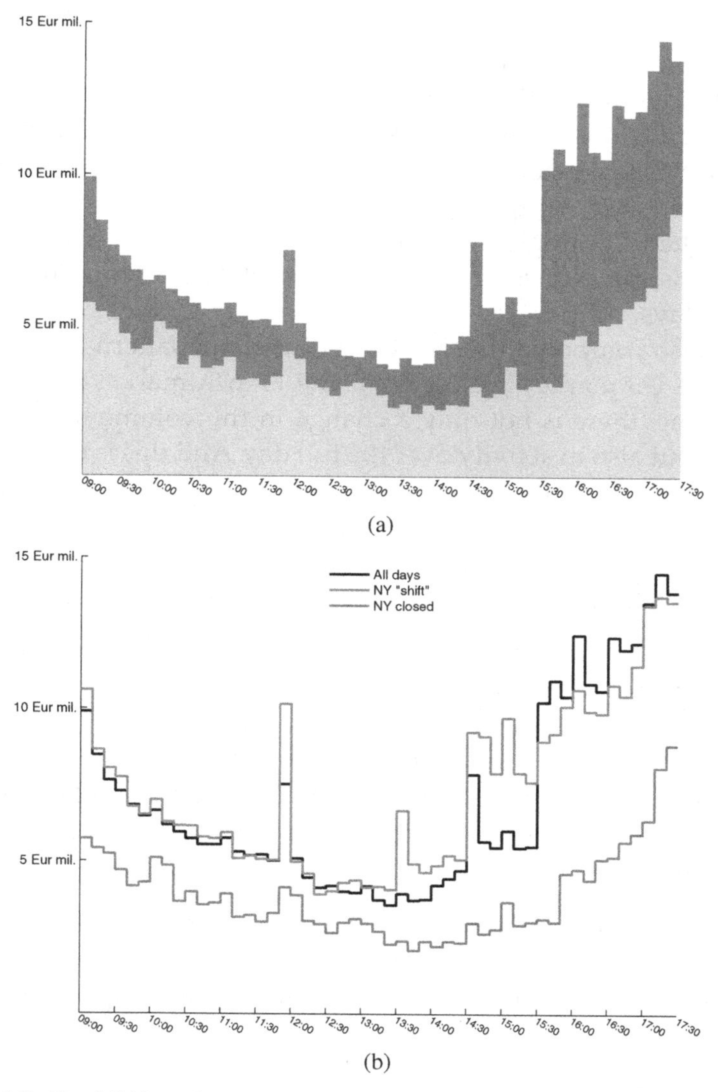

Figure 2.8. Total SA's volume pattern on the French market during continuous auction. Top graph: The effect induced by days where NY only has a five hours offset to Paris.

the US markets open is one hour earlier than usual. The spike due to macroeconomic news releases (which will be discussed later) is naturally also one hour earlier (13:30 CET instead of 14:30 CET usually).

It is also worth noting the exaggerated spike in volume at 12:00 CET is a consequence of the computation period; the time period includes March, and therefore the third Friday of March: The expiry of futures and options on the Eurostoxx 50. These expiry days are the cause of this spike (as we will see later), the consequence being that in this NY "shift" sample, the proportion of witching days is higher than in the full sample, hence the exaggerated spike. On a regular day of this sample, volume is no higher at 12 pm than on the full sample days.

We also computed the 'NY Closed' volume pattern on the days when the US market is closed but the French market is open. As we can see, there is not only a change in the volume distribution pattern, but also in activity over the full day. And this is true even in the morning when the US market would not be open anyway. This shows the reluctance of investors to trade on such days when no information will come from the leading US market.

The opening of a linked market can have an impact in three ways:

- Investors trading on the markets that have just opened decide to invest in the other market, thus generating extra volume traded;
- Information from the opening prices leads to an increase in the volume traded, as new information is digested and leads to a correction in the evaluation of the fundamental price of the stocks;
- Arbitrages can be made between the two markets, generating extra volume.

The third reason is not fundamentally different from the first two but is not caused by the same pool of investors. We are thinking more of systematic arbitragers in the third case, as opposed to asset managers in the previous two.

2) US macroeconomic news

On Figure 2.9a, we have plotted the volume pattern over our full sample, as well as the "US employment situation" and "ISM manufacturing", which are the volume patterns computed on the days when these economic reports are published.

The Bureau of Labor Statistics releases a report on the employment situation in the United States usually on the first Friday of

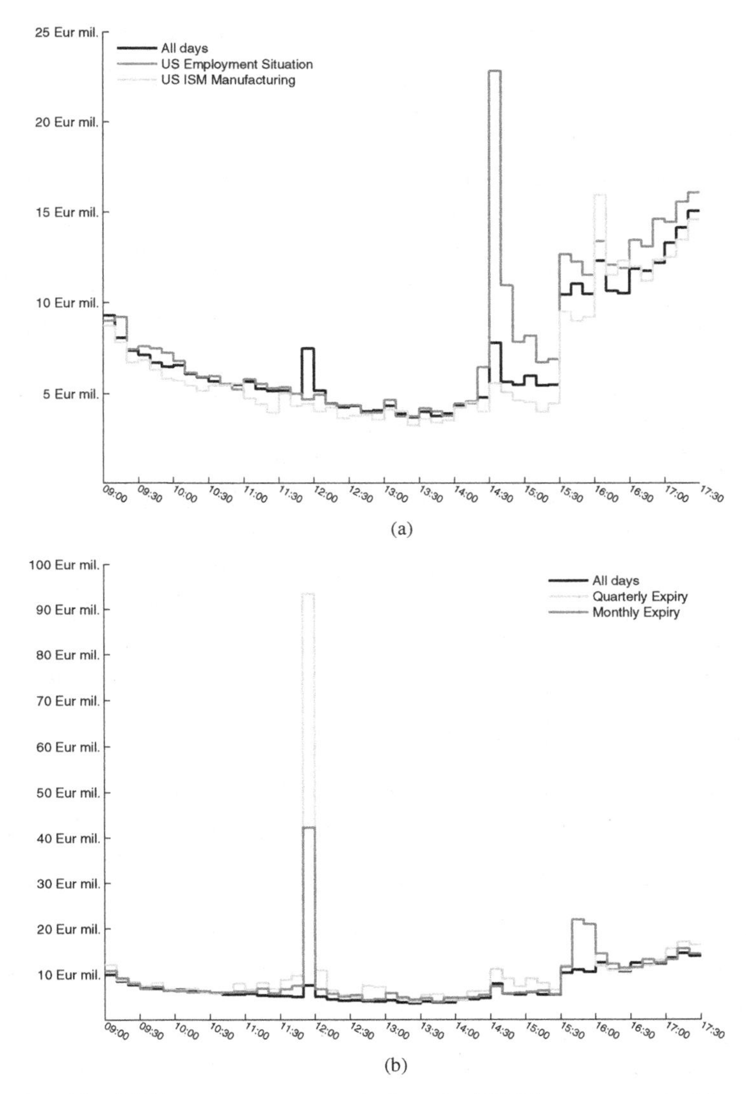

Figure 2.9. Total SA's volume pattern induce by US Macroeconomic News (top) and derivatives expiry (bottom).

the month at 08:30 (US eastern time, which converts into 14:30 on the chart). The "US employment situation" volume pattern has been computed exclusively with days on which this report has been released. The most popular indicator in this survey is the change in non-farm payroll employment, which is meant to represent the number of jobs added or lost in the economy over the past month, not including jobs related to the farming sector. As shown in Figure 2.9a, the volume traded just after the release of the report can be impressive, reflecting the information content of this report on the general health of the worldwide economy. The other pattern, "ISM manufacturing", refers to the report usually released at 10 am (US eastern time, which converts into 16:00 on the chart) on the first business day of the month. The ISM manufacturing composite index indicates whether manufacturing and the overall economy are growing or declining. We can see on Figure 2.8a (p. 125) that the effect of this indicator is more mitigated than the previous one, but this is not surprising as only a portion of the economy is concerned.

Obviously, the immediate effect of the release of any economic indicator on the volume traded will depend on how surprising it is for the market (generally measured by its distance from the consensus range). But we can also see that even without any further information the volume pattern is different on these days, especially in the case of major releases such as the employment situation.

3) Equity derivatives expiries

In Figure 2.8b (p. 125), we have plotted the volume pattern of Total SA on 'witching' days. These are the dates that equity derivatives expire. The name "witching" comes from the historically erratic behavior shown by cash markets on these days, due to the unwinding of hedge positions or the need to deliver physical settlement. Nowadays, this still generates considerable activity on the cash market, as shown in Figure 2.8b, but the effect on price is somewhat mitigated.

In the case illustrated here, the expiries happen on the third Friday. The derivatives with an expiry here are futures and options on the Eurostoxx 50 as well as the CAC40. The EDSP ("Exchange Delivery Settlement Price") for derivatives on the Eurostoxx 50 is the arithmetic mean of the index price disseminated between 11:50 and 12:00 CET. So if you have a position in this future, hedged by stocks, and do not want to roll the position over, then you have to unwind your cash position, preferably at the same value your position in the future will have, that is to say the one computed on the EDSP.

As a result, you would target the unwinding of your cash position between 11:50 and 12:00, generating the huge volume as shown in 2.8b. The smaller effect seen in Figure 2.7 is just the consequence of averaging; the impact of monthly expiries is divided by a factor greater than 20 and the one of quarterly expiries by more than 60. It obviously makes little sense to incorporate this into a trading profile used for VWAP execution during a non expiry day, so both a more robust statistical methodology and outlier filtering should be used in an estimation dedicated to execution algorithms.

The extra volume between 15:40 and 16:00 that can be observed in Figure 2.8b is due to CAC40 derivatives, whose EDSP are computed on prices observed in this specific span of time.

We have already shown in the previous section that equity derivatives expiries also have an effect on the volume traded at the closing fixing. We have not shown it here, as it would have made the plot even harder to read as this effect is very high on a stock such as Total SA. The cause of this effect is that the EDSP for single-stock futures and options is the closing call auction price.

2.1.3. *Fragmentation and the evolution of intraday volume patterns*

We will now have a look at the intraday market shares of the different trading destination that have been successful up to now. The illustration we give here is made only from the CAC40, but the effects we show here also exist on other major European indexes. In Figure 2.10 we have represented the intraday market share of Euronext, Chi-X, Bats and Turquoise for two different periods on five minute buckets. The first period used is January and February 2009, while the second period used is made from the same months but for 2012.

Looking at Euronext's market share, two observations can be made. First, we note that on both periods, the market share of Euronext is more important at the very beginning and end of the day. At the beginning of the day the price formation process is taking place on the primary market because it is the only trading venue at that time to have a sound orderbook filled thanks to the orders

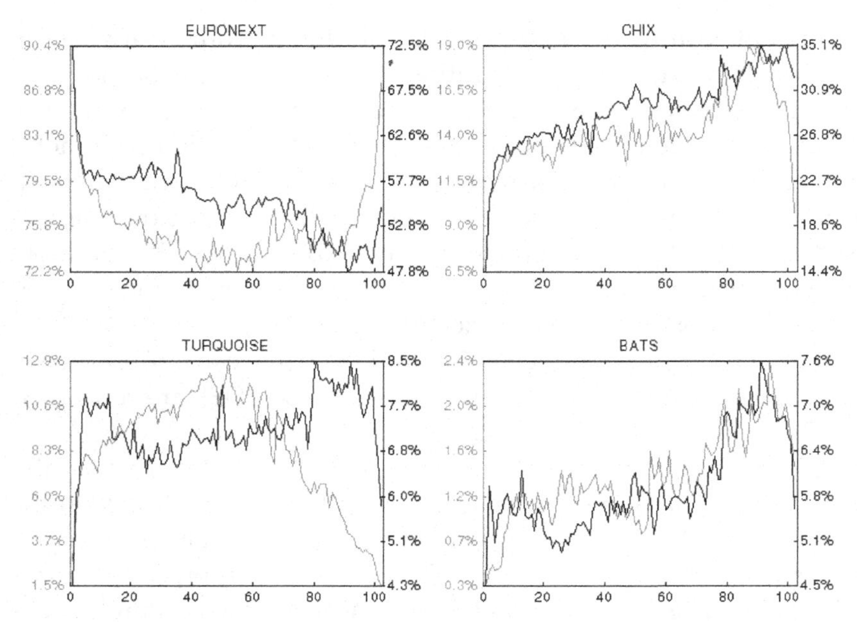

Figure 2.10. Intraday market share on CAC40 stocks (January and February 2009 in grey, January and February 2012 in black).

not matched during the opening fixing. But there is another reason, shared with what is happening at the end of the day. Indeed many players have timers to start and stop their smart order routers in order to be sure that some orders will not be sent to the MTF's at a time (fixing auctions) when it would be useless to do so, and would instead expose them to the risk of not being executed. It can also be observed that with the increased maturity of market participants and MTF's the duration of these periods without SOR technology seem to have decreased.

Second, the intraday market share on January–February 2012 is decreasing during the day and even goes below the symbolic threshold of 50% at the end of the day. This monotonicity is indeed the inverse of Chi-X market share which is constantly increasing during the day. There is no explanation for this characteristic of Chi-X's intraday market share, but the fact is that this pattern can be found on all European indices and has been quite significant for two years now. There might nevertheless be a link between the higher proportion of professional liquidity providers in Chi-X than on primary markets, the monotone decreasing of bid-ask spread as the day progresses (except for news release), and the need for these liquidity providers to increase their activity towards the end of the day.

Another observation could have been made about Euronext market share, but this is indeed a Turquoise specificity: The U-shape pattern of Euronext intraday market share in 2009 is the inverse of Turquoise's. Furthermore we can see from Turquoise's intraday market share that it had an important market share, but a very atypical profile. Indeed its volume curve at that time was nearly flat (not shown here), executing nearly the same volume at any time of the day.

The explanation for these strange characteristics is simple: Turquoise had market-making agreements among its founding members, which aimed at supplying liquidity. This activity was clearly not run by professional market makers having an interest in supplying liquidity, but market participants which probably had either static constraints in terms of spread, making them not competitive at the end of the day, or in terms of frequency of traded volume which would be a more direct explanation. Anyway, these agreements expired in mid-March 2009 and this led to a sharp drop in activity, halving Turquoise's market share in one week; even though it had already reached more than 10% on some european indices. The end of these probably highly binding agreements, explains why, even nowadays, Turquoise has not reached its previous levels of market share.

In contrast, BATS's has not evolved much and is rather flat except for when the US market opens, when it significantly increases. Chi-X in 2009 had the same pattern as can be observed.

Finally, there is another significant intraday market share pattern that we have already mentioned. As we said, the stocks traded price used in the computation of the Exchange Delivery Settlement Price, that is to say the final price for the expiry of derivatives, is the one traded on Euronext. Market participants need to unwind their cash hedging position at a price as close as possible to this EDSP on the expiry day, and by trading on the market on which the price will be observed they not only target these reference prices (which would

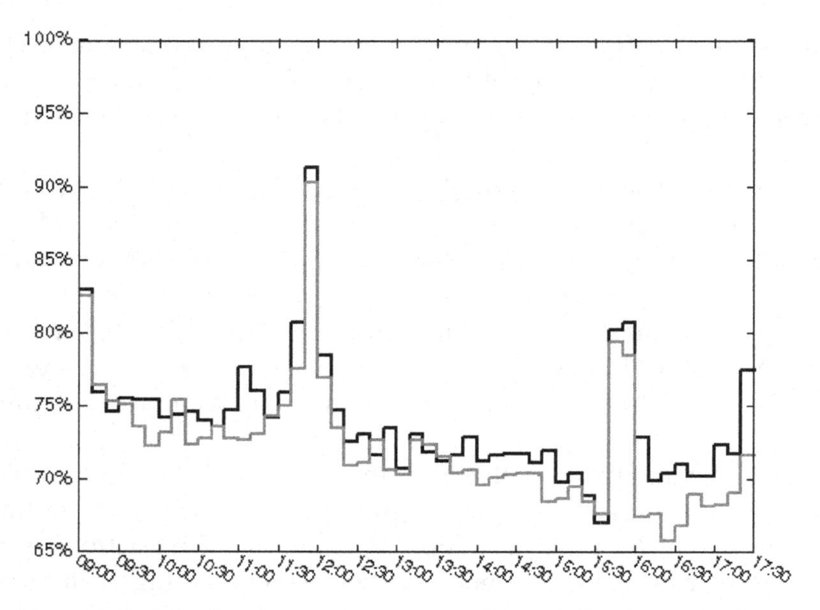

Figure 2.11. Intraday market share on total SA on derivative expiry days.

not be very far anyway on MTF) but participate directly in its fixing with their own execution prices.

In Figure 2.11 one can see the intraday market share of Euronext on TOTAL SA on quarterly derivative expiry (black) and monthly ones (grey, sample excluding the quarterly as in Section 2.1.2) on ten-minute buckets.

The effect on Euronext market share is pretty clear, the spikes of Euronext market share are timed at 11:50 to 12:00 the time at which the EDSP of derivatives on Eurostoxx 50 is computed and 15:40 to 16, the time at which the EDSP of derivatives on CAC 40 is computed. Looking at Figure 2.8b and making a simple computation should be enough to be convinced that almost all the volume traded to unwind these cash hedging positions is done on Euronext.

2.2. Does More Liquidity Guarantee a Better Market Share? A Little Story About the European Bid-Ask Spread

Before MiFID was introduced in European markets, transactions took place on single national exchanges. There were liquidity providers (Market Makers) and investors mandated to interact at the same place. Investors needed market makers, while exchanges only had to technically satisfy offer and demand as much as possible. At that time, the latter did not have any incentive to improve the liquidity provided. Since exchanges started facing competition, neither the presence of Market Makers nor the presence of investors on a specific trading venue is established (despite during fixing auctions which are discussed in the previous section and only take place on Primary Markets). As for continuous trading, exchanges now have to attract and keep Market Makers and to transform investors into "connected members".

Attracting Market Makers can be achieved through maker/taker fees, i.e., by giving a rebate to market makers who provide liquidity and charging a fee to members who take liquidity. Attracting members can be done by refunding connection costs — this was the strategy of several trading venues at the beginning of fragmentation — even though it implies selling at a loss. For example, Chi-X and others applied these promotions in Spain to try to get a head start in the fragmented landscape.

We can link this to the theoretical model constructed by Foucault, Kadan and Kandel which is described in the Mathematical Appendix ("Information seeking and price discovery"). By expressing the gain of each participant in terms of costs and fees, the paper concludes that a lack of High Frequency Market Makers can generate negative efficient maker fees (i.e. rebate for High Frequency Market Makers), while having too many High Frequency Market Makers can generate negative efficient taker fees (i.e. rebate for investors).

Theoretical development: Information seeking and price discovery. See Appendix A.2 for more details.

The number of connected members, and the satisfaction of Market Makers, is then conditioned on the liquidity on the exchange. The three main liquidity features are volume, volatility and bid-ask spread. High volume combined with low volatility and a tight bid-ask spread characterize a liquid stock. On the other hand, high volatility with a wide bid-ask spread indicates a lack of liquidity in a stock. Mechanically, the higher the volume on a trading venue, the more its market share. Volatility can not be considered as an element of market design choices for an exchange, but bid-ask spreads can.

The bid-ask spread represents the reward given to Market Makers for the risk they are taking when providing liquidity to the markets. At the same time, as a liquidity feature, the bid-ask spread is a way for exchanges to grab market share: via Best Execution policy and Smart Order Routing, a better bid-ask spread increases the chances for a trading venue to host transactions. Note that the situation is quite different in the United States. In Europe, the Best Execution Policy compels brokers to find the best price available (combining several criteria), while the American Trade Through Rule mandates that exchanges execute orders at prices given by the Consolidated Tape.

Creating and maintaining a trading venue thus requires three qualities: liquidity providers (Market Makers), competitive bid-ask spreads, and connected members. With competition, a business relationship appeared between exchanges and Market Makers, with both having common interests they did not have before. Determining the link between a trading venue's bid-ask spread and its market share is a key to the understanding of fragmentation.

2.2.1. *The bid-ask spread and volatility move accordingly*

The daily bid-ask spread increases with daily volatility, as shown in Figure 2.12. In fact, as mentioned earlier, it rewards the risk taken by market makers. The higher the volatility, the higher market makers ask for to compensate for their possible losses. For that matter, the market context determines an incompressible value of the bid-ask spread. Note that Figure 2.12b is an illustration of the role played by the tick-size in this relationship. The importance of tick-size when several venues are competing against each other is developed in Section 1.3, Chapter 1.

Periods of extremely high volatility, or, on the other hand, periods when markets were relatively quiet are highlighted in Figure 2.12a via symbols. The dots represent the 2008 crisis when volatility broke

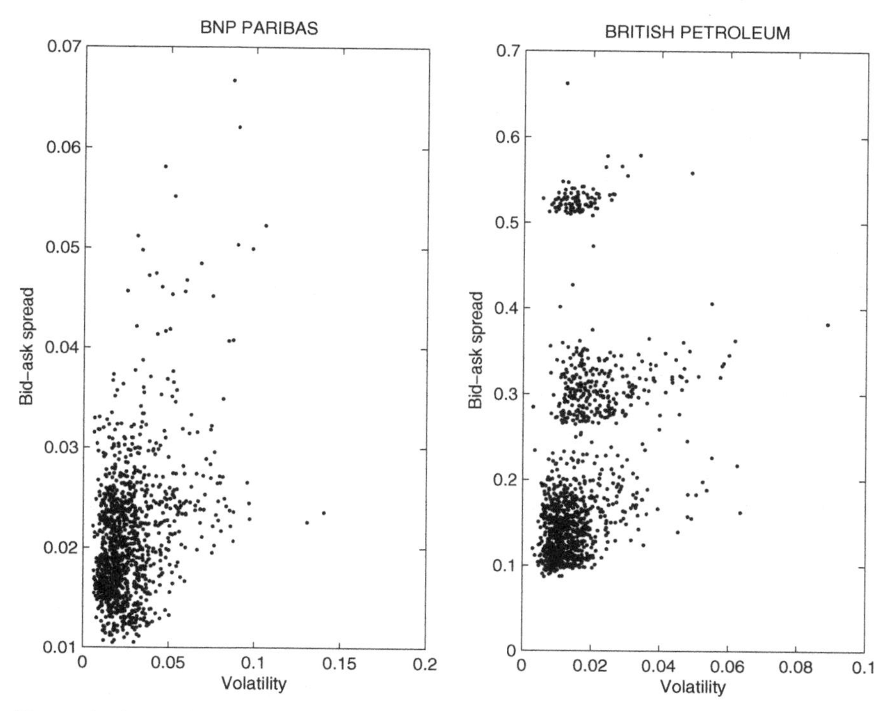

Figure 2.12. Daily bid-ask spread and daily volatility on BNP PARIBAS (left) and BRITISH PETROLEUM (right).
Note: Data from January 2008 to July 2012 on the primary market.

a record unequaled since, and squares represent values in the quiet month of March, 2012. Some dots are off-centered, they identify the August 2011 crisis, when the short selling ban prevented market makers from fulfilling their engagements on financial stocks, and the bid-ask spread therefore overweighted market risk.

The intuitive relationship between volatility and bid-ask spreads can be studied thanks to a Simple Linear Regression Model. This is described in the Mathematical Appendix, which also highlights the fact that it should be applied on the logarithm of these variables.

Theoretical development: Linear regression. See Appendix A.9 for more details.

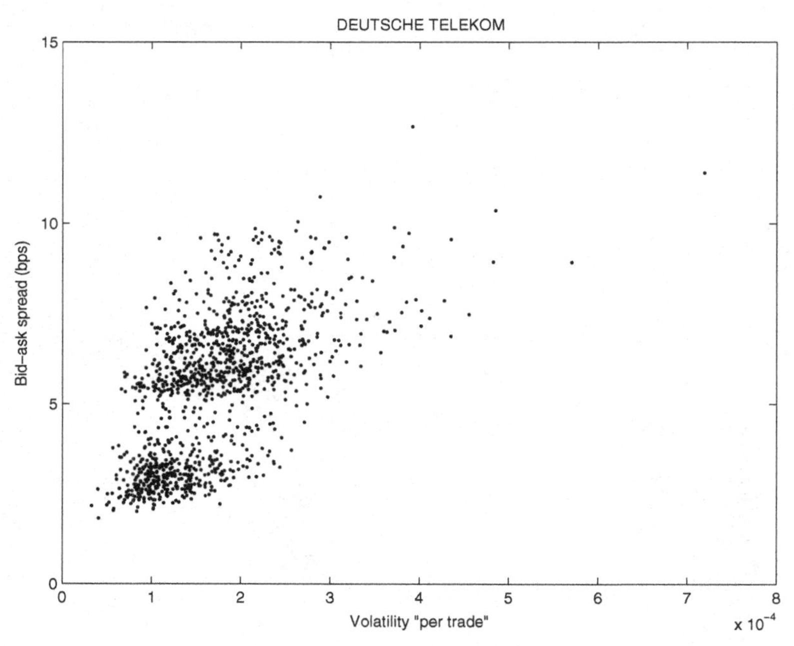

Figure 2.13. Bid-ask spread and volatility per trade on DEUTSCHE TELEKOM. *Note*: Data from January 2008 to July 2012 on the primary market.

The relationship between bid-ask spread and volatility can also be adjusted by considering the level of volatility per trade. Figure 2.13 illustrates how the daily bid-ask spread evolves as function of the daily volatility divided by the number of trades during the day.

Studying the bid-ask spread contribution to microstructure requires more detailed analysis than daily values. Short-term intervals should be taken into account, e.g. 5-min intervals during the day. Going from daily to intraday analysis highlights three trading patterns. As shown on Figure 2.14, the beginning and the end of the day behave very differently from the rest of the day. After the opening auction, the market suffers from a lot of noise: bid-ask spreads and volatility are particularly high. This is due to uncertainty, with prices taking into account overnight moves, and due to the time needed for people to start their Smart Order Router (the randomness of some opening auctions, such as in Germany as seen in Section 2.1.2,

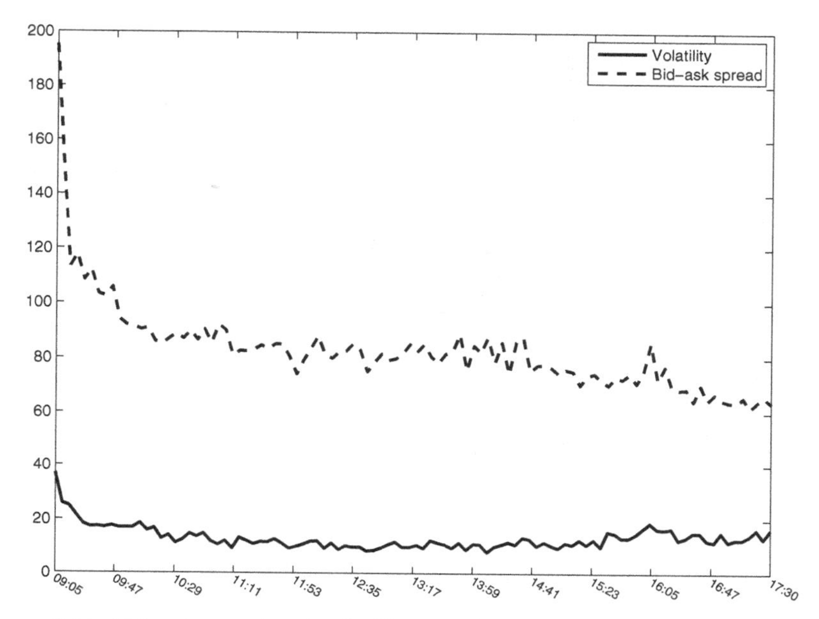

Figure 2.14. Bid-ask spread and volatility intraday curves on SBM OFFSHORE NV.

intensifies this waiting time). At the end of the day, High Frequency market makers need to flatten their residual inventory. This makes them accept tighter bid-ask spreads regardless of the relative risk. The middle period hosts the price formation process without these two specific patterns, and fragmentation is fully available, therefore the following study of the relationship between short-term market share and bid-ask spreads shall concentrate on this time-frame.

2.2.2. *Bid-ask spread and market share are deeply linked*

Table 2.3 and Table 2.4 quantify the absolute evolution of bid-ask spreads, and corresponding market shares for FTSE 100 constituents.

It attests to a long-term decreasing trend in bid-ask spreads which was common to all venues and indexes in Europe. However, bid-ask spreads stayed wider for less liquid stocks as they are a proxy of stocks' liquidity. Again, Market Makers' activity is more risky on less traded stocks, hence their reward is higher. The above-mentioned historical trend in bid-ask spreads, as well as its dependence on market context (e.g. volatility) or tick-size, requires us to study the

Table 2.3. The yearly evolution of market shares on FTSE 100 constituents since 2008.

Index	Primary market	CHI-X	Turquoise	BATS
2008	85.0%	13.6%	1.3%	0.1%
2009	65.4%	22.3%	6.8%	5.6%
2010	53.2%	30.4%	5.5%	10.9%
2011	48.6%	32.8%	8.4%	10.2%
2012	50.8%	33.6%	8.3%	7.3%

Table 2.4. The yearly evolution of bid-ask spreads on FTSE 100 constituents since 2008.

Index	Primary market	CHI-X	Turquoise	BATS
2008	11.4	16.3	32.7	20.2
2009	13.7	12.7	26.8	19.8
2010	6.8	6.3	16.6	9.5
2011	6.7	6.0	7.9	6.8
2012	6.4	5.8	7.2	7.3

relative values of bid-ask spreads among trading venues at each point when comparing it to market shares.

The market share of each trading venue moves according to the quality of its bid-ask spread, in relative terms. A first insight into this conclusion is given by Figure 2.15 where Turquoise (Continuous line) and Chi-X (dotted line) market shares seem to depend on their bid-ask spread relative to the primary market's. The efficiency of Chi-X is noticeable, with bid-ask spreads becoming tighter than the primary market's. Turquoise's trajectory shows a bump corresponding to the lapse of the agreement we describe below:

Turquoise's change of behavior came after market makers stopped their agreements. A drastic fall in Turquoise's market share is visible in 2009. This phenomenon comes from the end of agreements that eight market makers had initially taken to trade on Turquoise. They all had the duty to provide constant liquidity on this new trading venue. Therefore, Turquoise's intraday market share was

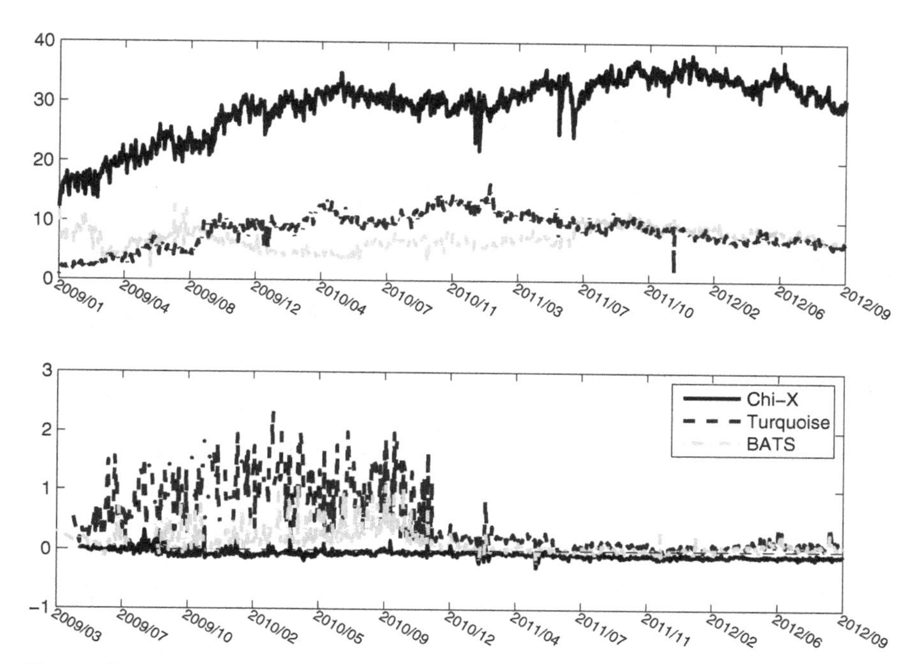

Figure 2.15. Market shares (high) and relative bid-ask spreads (low) on DAX30 stocks since 2007.

very high during low volume intervals (typically between 12:00pm and 2:00pm, Paris time). Due to this unprofitable business model, the agreement came to an end and Turquoise had to adopt a new market model in order to grab market share. One reason why a tight relative bid-ask spread implies an increasing market share is that Smart Order Routers are mandated to generate transactions on the venue providing the best price. This is especially true on average variables: the venue offers a better bid-ask spread more often than others. We will check this phenomenon on shorter time frames.

Figure 2.16a highlights the decrease in market share when the relative quality of the bid-ask spread becomes poorer. This is not due to a consistent pattern in intraday market share which can change significantly in real time, as shown by Figure 2.16b. In conclusion, the Best Execution Policy works well: at the level of microstructure, exchanges providing better liquidity are favored.

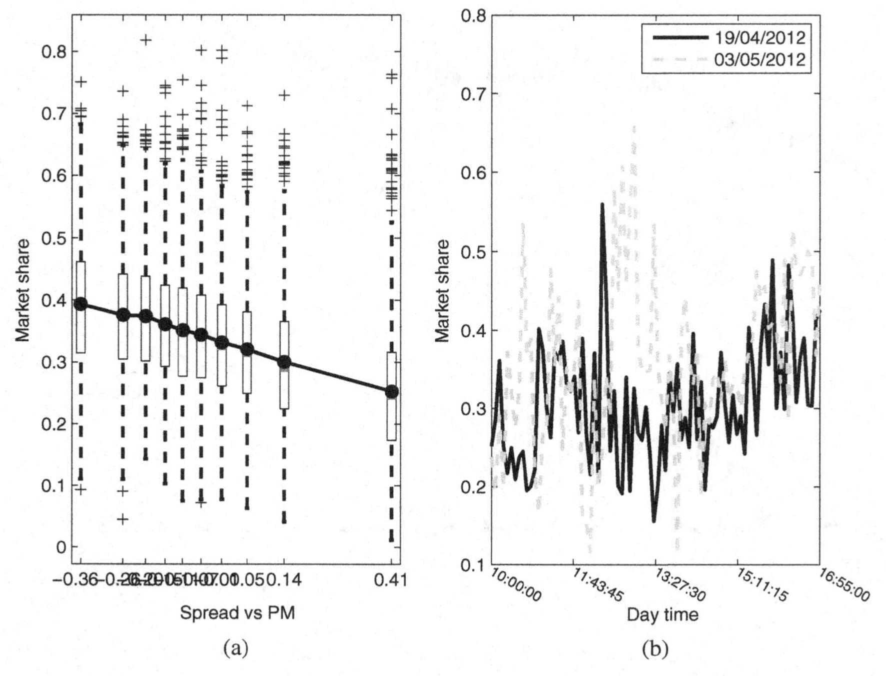

Figure 2.16. Chi-X market share on SCHNEIDER ELECTRIC versus its relative bid-ask spread (left), and intraday trajectory of Chi-X market share over two days in 2012 (right).

Note: 5-minute data intervals between 9:30am and 5:00pm from January to July, 2012.

2.2.3. *Exchanges need to show volatility-resistance*

The dependence of the bid-ask spread on volatility mentioned in the previous section must be taken into account since it has an impact on Market Makers. Whatever the variations and uncertainty coming from transactions that shift prices, Market Makers have the duty to provide liquidity to other participants. Therefore they will chose markets that are resilient to relatively high levels of volatility: liquidity should not vanish with growing uncertainty. This resilience can be studied thanks to the relationship between the number of trades on a trading venue and its price volatility.

Figure 2.17, where the High Frequency volatility is on the horizontal axis (in basis points per 10 minutes) and the number of trades is on the vertical line, shows the evolution of these dependencies.

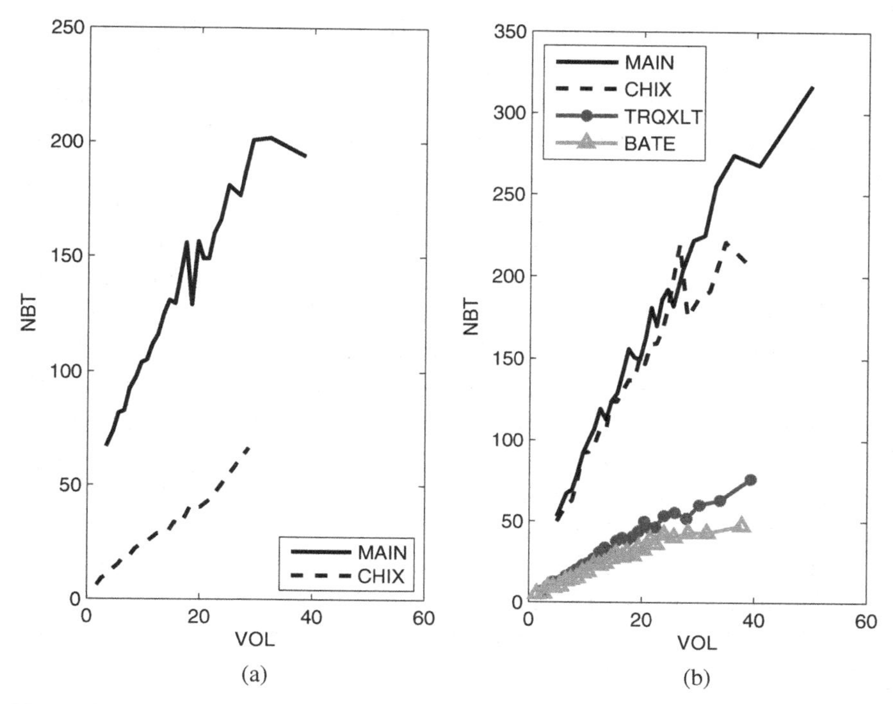

Figure 2.17. Median number of trades over quantiles of High Frequency volatility for TOTAL in 2008 (left) and 2012 (right).
Note: 15-minute data.

They appear as curves with different slopes for each market. In 2008 Figure 2.17a, the primary market had the highest slope, meaning that it offered a far higher relative number of trades during volatile periods than other markets. In 2012, Chi-X has gained a very similar pattern. Turquoise and BATS, consistent with their market share, have not improved to that extent. More precisely, the price formation process tends to occur where transactions have the most resilience to volatility and so Chi-X takes a greater part in the Price Formation Process.

Note that the behavior differs from liquid to illiquid stocks. For example, TOTAL will not show the same pattern as GEMALTO.

Indexes and trading venues can be compared thanks to a single measure of this resilience: The correlation between the number of trades and High Frequency volatility. This indicator can be called

"Flow Reactivity". Among main European indexes, the BEL20 is clearly one of the indexes where the number of trades is less correlated to the level of activity. The hierarchy of trading destinations with respect to the Flow Reactivity metric will nevertheless be the same as on other market places. The primary market appears in the best position, closely followed by Chi-X. This is proof of the maturity of the flow offered by this trading destination. BATS held the last place position for several years, meaning that when market activity increases, High Frequency Market Makers stop offering as much liquidity as they do during calmer periods.

The most important facts remain: There is a strong relationship between the quality of a trading venue, its success, and the High Frequency Market Makers that operate on it. Trading venues have the obligation to keep market makers active in order to improve their market share through competitive bid-ask spreads and resilience to volatility, hence better liquidity. Low latency trading systems and collocation are ways for trading venues to look after these clients, especially since the lower the latency the smaller the inventory risk.

2.3. The Agenda of High Frequency Traders: How Do They Extend their Universe?

As seen in the previous section, High Frequency Market Makers play a significant role in fragmentation. In fact, they conduct arbitrage between available trading venues and prevent prices from experiencing inversions. One simple example outside of financial markets could be vegetable markets: Two of them in the same town, separated by a few streets. There is no fundamental reason for the tomatoes to be cheaper in one of these two markets. If there was a difference of price, a traveling salesman could go back and forth between the two markets and cause the tomatoes prices to match. In real-time financial markets, High Frequency Market Makers do this job.

The question is: "Does this market design enabling competition between several markets have negative externalities?" The main reason for regulators to create fragmentation in financial markets was that monopoles had to be broken, so that prices would decrease and trading quality would increase. Did fragmentation live up to expectations, and was it as efficient for all European stocks? Practically, did the traveling salesman do his job as well for carrots as for tomatoes?

2.3.1. *Metrics for the balance in liquidity among indexes*

In order to answer this question, a measure has to be chosen to quantify the heterogeneity of liquidity among stocks. First, the appropriate proxy of liquidity for this purpose is the turnover. Among the components of any index, how well is the total turnover dispatched? Are only a few stocks responsible for the activity on one index, or do all components contribute equally to it? The coverage liquidity metric and the Gini coefficient both evaluate the level of inequality among a universe of stocks. The former indicates which percentage of the number of stocks is needed to realize 80% of the total turnover. As such, it is a static viewpoint that does not take into account the shape of the repartition of turnover across stocks. For a perfectly balanced index, the coverage liquidity metric would be 80%. On the other hand, the Gini coefficient uses the whole repartition curve to estimate the degree of inequality among stocks. Its calculation is fully described in the Mathematical Appendix (see Section A.8), but for now just remember that a value of zero corresponds to perfect equality while a value of one represents total inequality among stocks. Practically, the repartition curve of turnover is obtained by summing the intra-day turnover on each component after the components have been sorted in decreasing order, and dividing it by its sum (to obtain a maximum of 100%).

Theoretical development: Gini index and measuring discrepancies. See Appendix A.8 for more details.

The higher the coverage liquidity metric or the lower the Gini index, the more an investor can find an equivalent quality of liquidity on every stock of the index for a specific exchange. The discrepancy (i.e. the imbalance between the components of an index) would naturally be high for indexes with too many components (because it

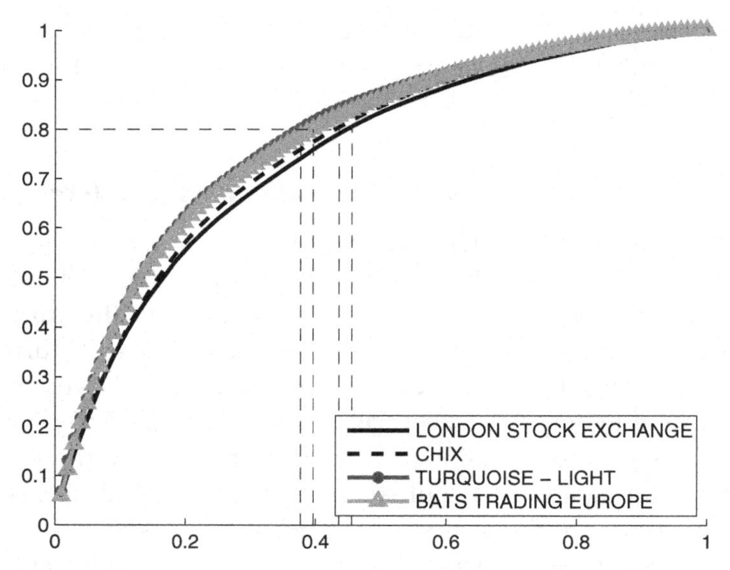

Figure 2.18. Repartition of turnover among FTSE 100 stocks on the four main trading venues: The Primary Market, Chi-X, Turquoise and BATS. The dotted lines show how the coverage liquidity metric is built: Trace an horizontal line at a level of 80%, and read the value on the horizontal axis when it crosses the repartition function. The Gini index equals two times the area between the repartition curve and the bisector line.
Note: Data from January 2012 to June 2012.

is more difficult for a large set of stocks to be equivalent than it is for a small set of stocks).

For instance, as shown on Figure 2.18, turnover on 45 FTSE 100 stocks equates to 80% of the total turnover of the entire index on the LSE. Therefore, the LSE's coverage liquidity metric on the FTSE 100 is $45/101 = 45\%$. More precisely, its Gini Index, indicating how far the repartition of turnover is from a uniform repartition, is equal to 0.99.

The obtained coverage liquidity metrics are: 45% for the FTSE 100, 52% for the AEX, 55% for the CAC 40, and 56% for the DAX. Corresponding Gini values are 0.99, 0.96, and 0.97 for both CAC40 and DAX indices.

The coverage liquidity metric shows that when considering its primary market, the DAX is the most balanced index in terms of liquidity. The CAC40 comes in second position, but it was the other way around a few years ago. With respect to the ratio between the highest and the lowest turnover within each of those indexes, the CAC 40 and the DAX are quite similar (with a ratio of around 24). This comparison between indexes helps comparing, for each index, the coverage liquidity metric of available trading venues.

2.3.2. *A history of coverage*

From 2009 to 2012, coverage values increased for all trading venues and indexes, and the previous huge discrepancies between trading venues have disappeared. This positive homogeneity is seen for both very liquid and illiquid stocks. However, the coverage value remained weaker on less liquid stocks. This implies that High Frequency Market Makers could not increase their activity on illiquid stocks. In fact, there exists a barrier that prevents them from being present in less liquid stocks: hedging and short selling are far more expensive. As professionals, they can not practice their profession on stocks that would generate unrewarded risk.

We can link this effect with the evolution of MTFs' (Multilateral Trading Facilities) market shares depending on stocks' liquidity. MTFs' market share increased faster on liquid stocks than on illiquid ones, as highlighted in Chapter 1. Fragmentation appeared more slowly for the same hedging and short selling reasons that prevent High Frequency Market Makers from being more active. Still, the situation has improved, meaning that market makers started getting more interested in these stocks. This is due to strategies carrying over: Once a market maker has constructed a hedging strategy for the most liquid stocks, including the closest less liquid one does not represent a huge cost. They can gradually extend their hedging. Moreover, the technological investments that they had made in order to trade in the first place represent a fixed cost and so extending stock coverage is an easy way to improve profitability. Finally, the growing competition between all High Frequency Market Makers has forced them to diversify their sources of revenue. Still, there is a liquidity threshold below which High Frequency Market Makers can not trade a stock.

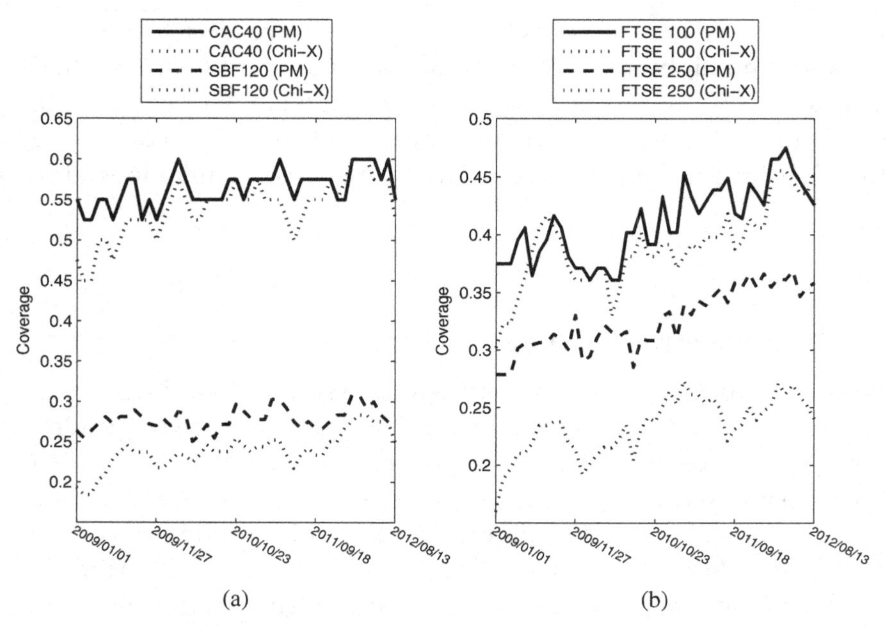

Figure 2.19. Coverage on CAC40 and SBF120 constituents (left), FTSE 100 and FTSE 250 constituents (right) since 2009, for the Primary Markets and Chi-X.

High Frequency Market Makers extending their activity to less liquid stocks justifies the increase in coverage for MTFs for wide indexes such as SBF120 and FTSE 250 seen in Figure 2.19, both in the Primary Markets and Chi-X.

Thus, High Frequency Market Makers have a strategy to extend their perimeter of action. MTFs step in to help them because they need to in order to remain competitive, as highlighted in the previous section. Following these statements, High Frequency Market Makers appear only as positive for financial markets: They increase the uniformity among indexes' constituents (coverage) and insure the contribution of MTFs to the Price Formation Process by arbitrage. However, other participants kept complaining about their activity, accusing them of increasing volatility, and gaming real investors. Do these complaints come from a fear of the unknown, or gini indo these improvements generate hidden costs?

2.3.3. *High-frequency traders do not impact all investors equally*

With the advent of competition between trading platforms, some arbitrageurs began to specialize in arbitraging liquidity imbalances between several pools quoting the same stock. Thanks to the maker/taker fee schedule on MTFs, platforms may reward such trading strategies in order to provide liquidity. The intensive use of technology allows these arbitrageurs to lower their inventory risk by trading very small orders, very frequently. These arbitrageurs are called HFTs (High-Frequency Traders). They are said to be a counterpart in more than 80% of the deals in the US, 40% in Europe, and 35% in Japan.

High-frequency trading (HFT) is defined by the US financial regulator (SEC) as follows:

1. The use of extraordinarily high-speed and sophisticated computer programs for generating, routing and executing orders;
2. Use of co-location services and individual data feeds offered by exchanges and MTFs to minimize network and other types of latencies;
3. Very short timeframes for establishing and liquidating positions;
4. Submission of numerous orders that are canceled shortly after submission;
5. Ending the trading day in as close to a flat position as possible (that is, not carrying significant, unhedged positions overnight).

This type of trading can be specific to certain traders of funds or embedded in larger strategies or management of client orders.

HFT is an important component of a market that seeks competition between pools. In brief, it is the "price to pay" to support competition. The question that has increasingly been raised and which remains unanswered is: "Is the value they extract from the market worth the service they provide?" This led the European Commission to try to address HFT in its review of MiFID, but things are extremely complex. The first element is to define exactly what service HFTs are providing to the markets.

How could HFT lower the spread without changing execution costs?

One major argument given by HFT proponents is that they have decreased bid-ask spreads. In order to visualize how HFT can intervene in the market and decrease spreads, one strategy is detailed here. The conclusion will be that the effective spread is reduced on an overall basis, but that costs for other participants are unchanged or slightly increased, contrary to popular belief.

Considering a market with two participants interacting with each other (players A and B), it is interesting to see the impact of the introduction of a HFT into this market.

When the first two players are alone, they are present in the first limit of the orderbook, and waiting to be able to trade. In Figure 2.20a, player A becomes impatient and hits player B's price in order to trade. His cost is the effective bid-ask spread, noted ψ. The next time (Figure 2.20b), since player A has already crossed the spread, it is player B's turn to become impatient. Player B thus hits player A's price in order to trade. His cost is, as for player A, the effective bid-ask spread: ψ. If the situation remains unchanged, both player A and player B will bear the same cost on average: $\frac{\psi}{2}$.

Concentrating on Figure 2.20c, where a HFT intervenes on the market, he (or she) takes a position just on the inside of player B and becomes the first limit against player A. Player A becomes impatient and hits the HFT's price. His cost is slightly more than half the former effective bid-ask spread: $\frac{\psi}{2} + \epsilon$. For the moment, it seems that both the bid-ask spread and the cost for player A have been lowered.

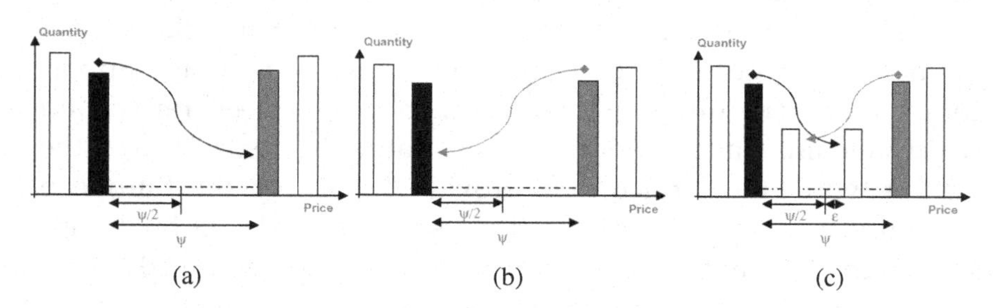

Figure 2.20. Three cases of orderbook: without HFT (first player is aggressive, left), without HFT (second player is aggressive, middle) and with a HFT (right).

The HFT takes a new position very rapidly in front of player B. Since player B's order has not been matched, he needs to hit the HFT's new price. His cost is the same as player A's: $\frac{\psi}{2} + \epsilon$.

The final effective bid-ask spread is genuinely reduced, since it represents slightly more than half the former bid-ask spread. However, the average execution cost for player A and player B is still $\frac{\psi}{2} + \epsilon$, since they are forced to become aggressive for each trade. On the other hand, the execution cost for the HFT player is nil.

In addition, note that HFTs prefer smaller trade sizes, which prompt other actors to fraction their trades and thus to pay more and report more often to clients or authorities. These reporting costs, which only non-proprietary trading firms face, are on the rise, in addition to the technological cost. These fixed losses are unevenly distributed and lead to a deterioration in the trading conditions for final investors.

Bid-ask spread: Cost and uncertainty for investors

Let us consider whether bid-ask spreads for investors would have been unchanged since 2007 if high-frequency traders had not appeared among financial players. This bid-ask spread is denoted by ψ_B, with B as "Before". As we saw in the previous subpart, HFT players lower the effective bid-ask spreads. However, the spread paid by other investors when hitting a HFT's price is a little wider: $\frac{\psi_B}{2} + \epsilon$, where ϵ is the additional part due to HFT, and corresponds to half the new tighter spread: $\psi_{HFT}/2$.

If we consider that HFTs are involved in $q\%$ of trades, the new bid-ask spread for investors is expected to be ψ_N (N as "new"), with:

$$\psi_N = q\psi_{HFT} + (1-q)\psi_B.$$

In practice, if the proportion of HFTs among trades is assumed to be 40% ($q = 40\%$ in our previous formula), ψ_B and ψ_N take the following values:

$$\psi_B = 5.41bp, \qquad \psi_N = 4.73bp.$$

These were obtained by considering a "before" period from April to November 2007, and a "new" period from April to November 2011, on CAC40 stocks. Note that only primary market data (Euronext Paris) are taken into account.

Now having a look at the real cost this implies for investors is possible when considering one investor looking at posting one order. He has a probability r to meet a HFT. His cost C will depend on the situation that occurs:

- If he meets a HFT, he has to become aggressive (with regard to our previous subpart), and pays $C = \frac{\psi_{HFT}}{2} + \frac{\psi_B}{2}$ This case corresponds to the upper line of Figure 2.21.
- If he does not but is aggressive for other reasons: he pays $C = \psi_B$ This case corresponds to the middle line of Figure 2.21.
- If he does not and is passive: he pays $C = 0$. This case corresponds to the lower line of Figure 2.21.

Figure 2.22 represents the cost C for an investor and the uncertainty that relates to this cost C. The y-axis is thus the expected

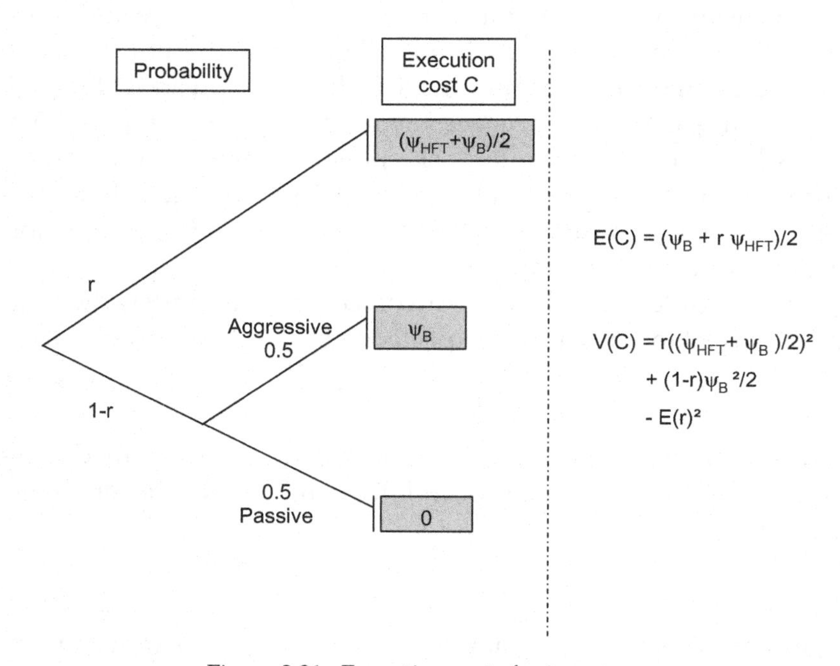

Figure 2.21. Execution costs for investors.

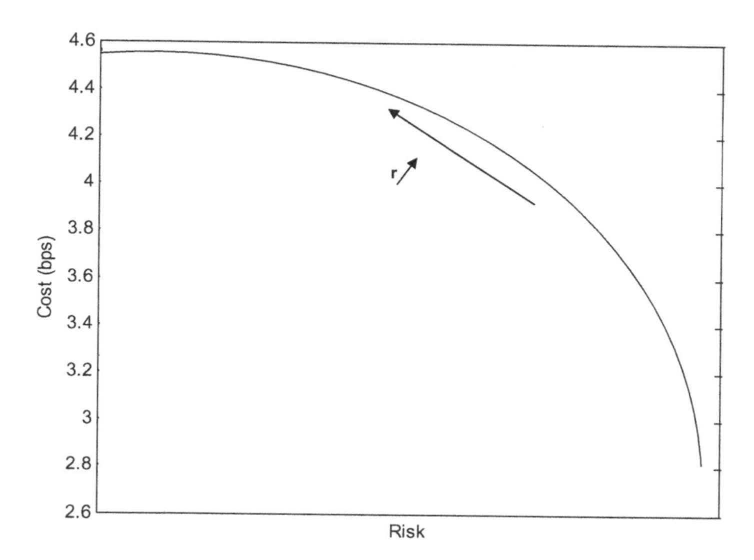

Figure 2.22. Execution cost (y-axis) and its uncertainty (x-axis).

cost $\mathbb{E}[C]$ mentioned in Figure 2.21, and the x-axis is the uncertainty seen as the standard deviation of the cost C (the square root of variance $\mathrm{Var}(C)$ in Figure 2.21).

This highlights the fact that the smaller the cost the higher the uncertainty about it, just as in an efficient frontier for portfolio management: One cannot increase one's expected gain without increasing the risk one takes. Secondly, the points of the line vary depending on the probability of meeting a HFT. As shown by the long arrow, increasing the probability to meet a HFT increases the cost (by $\epsilon = \frac{\psi_{HFT}}{2}$), but reduces the uncertainty (i.e., "risk") of the cost.

Above, the expectation and uncertainty are studied for an investor involved in one trade in the market. However, the situation is different for investors that are involved in a large number of trades. From now on, the number of trades will be denoted by N and $C_1, \ldots, C_N$ the cost of its trades. The Central Limit Theorem indicates that the variance we are looking at decreases in $\frac{1}{N}$.

$$\mathbb{E}\left[\frac{1}{N}\sum_{i=1}^{N} C_i\right] = \mathbb{E}[C] \quad \text{and} \quad \mathrm{Var}\left(\frac{1}{N}\sum_{i=1}^{N} C_i\right) = \frac{\mathrm{Var}(C)}{N}.$$

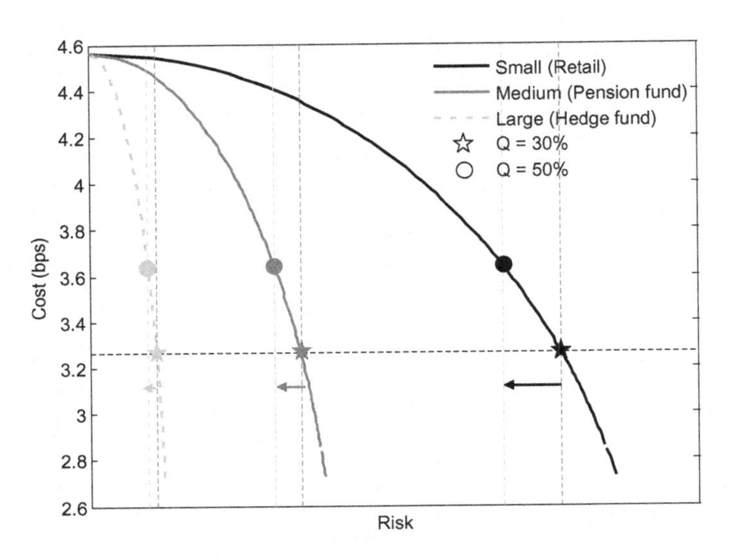

Figure 2.23. Which uncertainty (i.e. "risk") for which investor?

Consequently, the standard deviation that is seen in various figures decreases in $\frac{1}{\sqrt{N}}$. The uncertainty is already lower for any investor that has a larger number of trades, all else being equal.

When increasing the number of trades, the line plotted in Figure 2.22 is shifted to the left by homothety: For the same probability of meeting a HFT, the expectation of the cost remains stable, but the uncertainty already decreases. This is highlighted in Figure 2.23, where the curves for three types of investors are presented.

Increasing the number of HFT (and thus the probability of meeting one) by 20% (from 30% to 50%) increases the expected cost by approximately 0.5bp, for any type of investor (from the star to the circle in Figure 2.23). It also decreases uncertainty, but not for everyone: retail investors benefit from a large decrease of uncertainty on their cost, while the uncertainty on the cost of a pension fund cannot be reduced much further (it was already minimised by the large number of trades).

To summarize, bid-ask spread is a source of cost for investors in the market. Both the expected value of this cost, and the uncertainty it is subject to are key figures for them. Depending on the number of trades and the probability they have of meeting a HFT actor, expectations will not vary, but uncertainty will, and significantly.

2.4. The Link Between Fragmentation and Systemic Risk

Diversification is a common way to reduce risks. It consists of buying and selling financial instruments to hedge risks which the trader does not want to be exposed to. The systemic risk can be seen as the residual risk that is left in a portfolio when all the other risks have been hedged through all possible financial instrument. Since MiFID went into force and with the rise of HFT, microstructure specialists have been asking if volatility (intraday or extraday) and systemic risk have increased. The supporters of high frequency trading promoted the fact that high frequency activity lowers the volatility as it increases market liquidity. On the other hand opponents to high frequency trading argued that since MiFID and the advent of high frequency trading systemic risk increased. As an example they often refer to May 6th, 2010's Flash Crash on the US equity market.

This question raises other questions about the relation between extraday and intraday volatility. Actually it is of importance to differentiate those two types of volatility. Investors, as they have extraday constraints are impacted by the extraday volatility but not directly by the intraday volatility. But to what extent does the intraday scale impact the extraday one? Put it differently did the changes in the PFP (price formation process) following MiFID produce visible effects at the extraday scale? This section presents an extensive reflexion about the link between the two scales going from the impact of MiFID on the intraday volatility considered from the Spanish market perspective, then through a discussion about correlations between components of an index and index volatility, then through the Flash Crash that occurred on the US equity market on May 6 2010 and outages on the European market.

2.4.1. *The Spanish experiment*

Theoretically, MiFID appeared in Spain at the same time as in any other European countries: On 1 November 2007. However, due to the legislative complexity of the Spanish market, MTFs appeared very late on and their market shares still remained at a low level at the beginning of 2010. For example, Chi-X's market share on the IBEX 35 only exceeded 0.5% for the first time in August 2009. At the beginning of 2010 its market share was still limited, with a peak at 1.43%. Turquoise and BATS were in the exact same situation, with even weaker market shares.

This situation resulted from the legislative context which make the clearing and settlement of trades done on MTFs difficult to carry out. The only authorized clearing house, before the passage of Titulo V in June 2011, was Iberclear whose holder was exclusively BME, the Spanish primary trading destination. Until June 2011 this fact prevented MTFs from setting up themselves up in Spain. Indeed, the issuance of registration code was the privilege of Iberclear which charged high prices for that. Since Titulo V, MTF held clearinghouses are entitled to issue this code thereby relaxing the clearing and settlement fees for MTFs.

Until June 2011, the MTFs had found a way to bypass this problem. At the end of the day they crossed transactions involving all their volumes with BME brokers. This trick did not entirely solve the problem of clearing and settlement costs because MTFs still had to pay extra fees to BME in addition to clearing and settlement ones. In particular MTFs remained much less competitive than they could have been and were still disadvantaged for entering into direct competition with BME. This explains the very low market share of MTFs during the 2007–2011 period.

During the November 2007–January 2010 period Spain remained unaffected by the fragmentation that should have arisen from MiFID implementation. This specific feature makes the Spanish market a relevant frame to study the behavior of other European markets that applied the European directive properly.

Figure 2.24 shows the average number of trades per day across the components of indices CAC 40, FTSE 100 and IBEX 35. The number of trades per day is a good proxy to get an idea of how intense high frequency activity is on a stock. We can see on this chart that the average number of trades per day on stocks from FTSE 100 and CAC 40 is constantly increasing on the studied period indicating an increase in high-frequency traders' activity, especially on the FTSE.

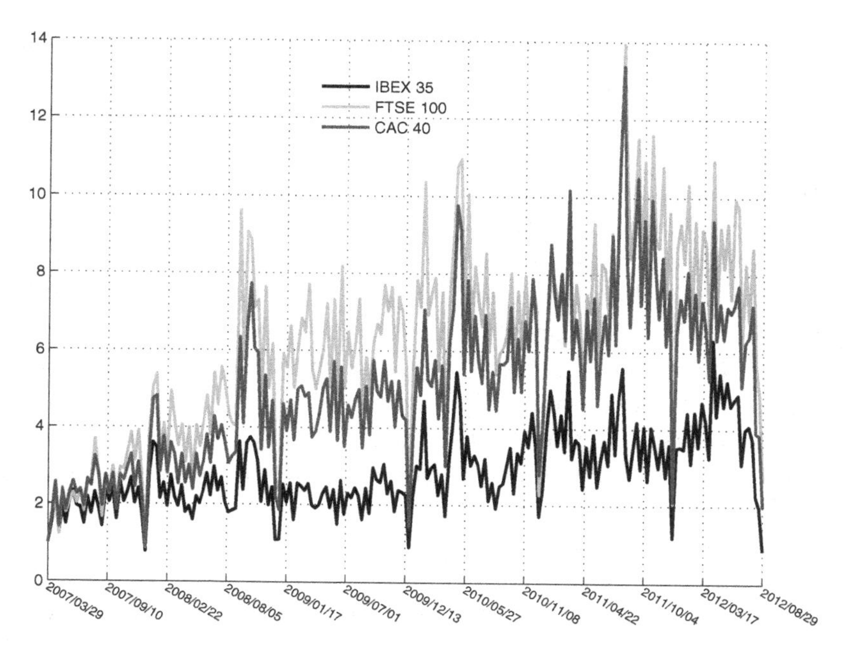

Figure 2.24. Daily number of trades (based at 1).

Conversely the average number of trades per day remained quite stable for stocks of IBEX 35.

The question of concern is: What is the impact of fragmentation and high frequency trading on the volatility of the markets? To put things in context, as explained before Figure 2.24 indicates the significant increase in high-frequency traders' activity since the introduction of MiFID. Does this change in market microstructure actually reduce volatility as assumed by a number of market participants? Volatility is one important point of market behavior, as it is the random (i.e. unexpected) component of the PFP (price formation process). It stems from business uncertainty on the listed firm, which becomes market uncertainty via the asset structure of the company. Thus, daily volatility represents the amount of risk taken by the investor. To attract investors, a stock with more volatility should offer a higher return.

Microstructure gives us a link between the market price and the fundamentals of a stock, via the PFP. The more efficient the microstructure is, the lower the intraday volatility of a stock. Intraday volatility is a proxy for intraday market risk and it is also part of the implicit costs of trading as a significant parameter in the market impact caused by a trade. Moreover, this link between intraday volatility and trading costs is emphasized by the economically-founded relationship between volatility and the bid-ask spread. We would therefore expect that a decreasing spread would imply decreasing volatility. However, while we have effectively noted a narrowing of bid-ask spreads after MiFID (mainly due to tick size changes), the decrease in volatility is less obvious. This is also partly due to the 2008–2010 financial crisis.

A comparison is thus only significant between two markets that have faced similar market contexts. We will focus on the UK and Spain. On the period studied the former was clearly impacted by fragmentation while the latter more or less kept its pre-MiFID operating model.

Figure 2.25a shows the difference between the 20-day moving average of 15-minute Garman-Klass volatility averaged over day across the components of FTSE 100 and of IBEX 35. The definition of Garman-Klass volatility (denoted by Vol_{GK}) is the following,

$$\text{15-minutes Vol}_{GK} = \frac{\sqrt{\frac{1}{2}(\text{high} - \text{low})^2 - (2\log(2) - 1)(\text{close} - \text{open})^2}}{\text{Average Price over the period}},$$

where open, high, low and close are computed over 15 minutes intervals. The difference is based at 0 on 6 June 2007. From June 2007 to February 2010 the difference remains positive, that is to say the intraday volatility of FTSE 100 stocks is higher over that period. From February 2010 to September 2012 the difference tends to stay around 0 with some negative spikes. Over that period the difference between the intraday volatility of the Spanish and of the British indexes is significantly lower than over the period before. This regime change is due to the intensification of the European sovereign debt crisis, to which Spain is more exposed to than the UK, in the beginning of 2010.

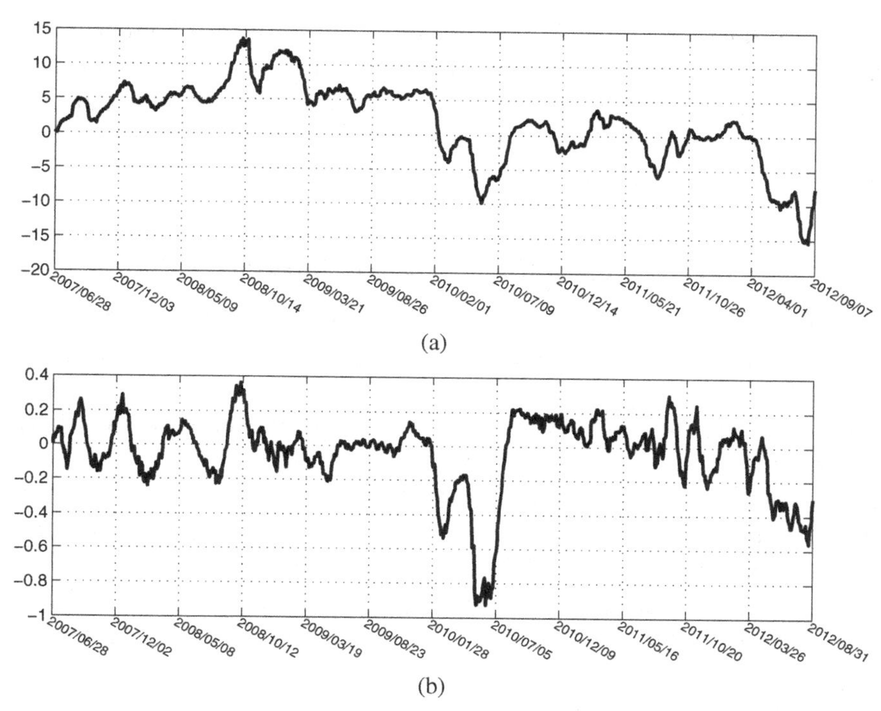

Figure 2.25. (a) Difference between 20 days moving averages of intraday volatilities for FTSE 100 and for IBEX 35 (base: 0). (b) Difference between 20 days moving average of intraday to daily volatility ratios for FTSE 100 and for IBEX 35 (base: 0).

Although British and Spanish stocks have both been exposed to the crisis, their respective exposure has not occurred at the same pace or with the same amplitude. To compensate for this effect, we used the differences between the intraday volatility to daily volatility ratios (Figure 2.25b where the difference between ratio for FTSE 100 and for IBEX 35 has been plotted). The difference is based at 0 on 28 June 2007. Over a period going from June 2007 to February 2010 the difference remains around 0. A shock incurs during the first six months of year 2010. This shock is due to the European sovereign-debt crisis. In August 2010 starts a trending period which goes until September 2012. Over that last period the intraday volatility compared to the daily volatility for IBEX 35 components grows more rapidly than for FTSE 100 components.

Both charts on Figure 2.25 do not show any significant effect of the increase of British market fragmentation after the implementation of MiFID (1 November 2007) on the intraday volatility. Neither can we say whether the intraday volatility increased or decreased when the British market grew fragmented.

2.4.2. *Volatility, cross-stock correlation, intraday, extraday*

Usually in periods of high market risk, as for instance during the months following Lehman Brothers' fall, the correlations between stocks increases. This is due to a natural reaction: When market risk is high people run away from stock market, as it is considered risky, and prefer to invest in less risky assets. This overall move creates co-movement among stocks and consequently the correlation level rises. Meanwhile, as diversification opportunities are less numerous, the systemic risk increases. The question of interest is about the link between co-movement among stocks and HFT activities: Could the rise of HFT be a factor that would increase co-movement and thus the systemic risk?

The arrival of fragmented markets following the implementation of MiFID has seen the attendant appearance of HFT. This activity consists of a significant amount in providing "liquidity bridges" to "natural" sellers or buyers (i.e. investors who will keep their positions for more than few days). In a concentrated market those investors are each other's counterparties. In the current fragmented markets, a natural seller's counterparty is often a high-frequency trader, who will sell the position back to a natural buyer few minutes or seconds later. The high-frequency trader will assume a risk proportional to the product of the volatility and the square root of the time between its buy and sell orders. In return she will be rewarded by a fraction of the bid-ask spread and potentially by rebates if she succeeds in being a liquidity provider during the trades. This is the way high-frequency traders and market makers provide "liquidity bridges" between the available trading pools. They are said to be counterparties in around 70% of the US deals ([Sussman *et al.*, 2009]) and 40% of the European ones.

In a highly-correlated and low-volatility market, the high-frequency trader will find it easy to provide such liquidity bridges: Firstly because the risk (proportional to the volatility) is low, and also because the trader will be able to hedge his market risk using indexes and correlated stocks. Each of his deals will be doubled by a buy or sell of an index for hedging purposes. This will automatically increase the correlations in the market. Therefore, the more correlated the stocks are, the more high-frequency trading will increase the correlations.

The volatility of an index depends on the correlations among its components

The volatility of an index does not equal the square root of the average component's squared volatility. For instance in the basic case where the stock volatilities are all equal, index volatility remains strongly dependent on the correlation between stocks. Let us illustrate this through the example of a 2 stock index, A and B, with same weights, where A_t and B_t denote the returns of those two stocks at time t, then

$$\begin{aligned}\sigma_{\frac{A_t+B_t}{2}} &= \text{std}\left(\frac{A_t+B_t}{2}\right)\\ &= \sqrt{\frac{\text{Var}(A_t)}{4}+\frac{\text{Var}(B_t)}{4}+\frac{1}{2}\text{Cov}(A_t,B_t)}.\end{aligned}$$

Based on the inequality $\text{Cov}(A_t, B_t) \leq \sqrt{\text{Var}(A_t)\text{Var}(B_t)}$

$$\text{std}\left(\frac{A_t+B_t}{2}\right) \leq \frac{\sqrt{\text{Var}(A_t)}+\sqrt{\text{Var}(B_t)}}{2}.$$

In the same way, as $\text{Cov}(A_t, B_t) \geq -\sqrt{\text{Var}(A_t)\text{Var}(B_t)}$

$$\text{std}\left(\frac{A_t+B_t}{2}\right) \geq \frac{\left|\sqrt{\text{Var}(A_t)}-\sqrt{\text{Var}(B_t)}\right|}{2}.$$

If the volatilities of both stocks are the same ($\text{std}(A_t) \sim \text{std}(B_t)$) one sees that the volatility of the index depends greatly on the correlation ρ

$$\text{std}\left(\frac{A_t + B_t}{2}\right) \sim \frac{\text{std}(A_t)}{\sqrt{2}}\sqrt{1+\rho},$$

where $\rho \in [-1, 1]$. Let us consider an index with a slightly larger number of components N. Let σ be the average volatility across all the components and ρ be the average pairwise correlation. We can then approximate the volatility of this index by

$$\sigma_{I_t} = \text{std}(I_t) \sim \sigma\sqrt{\frac{1}{N} + \frac{\rho(N-1)}{N}}.$$

Again we see the importance of the correlation. The volatility of an index depends on the two, the average volatility and the average cross-stock correlations.

The cross-stock correlation and the volatility at short time scales

Dealing with intraday creates a major difficulty to which analysts have to pay attention to: Microstructure noise. At very short time scales, usually lower than one minute, the two measured quantities, the volatility and the correlation suffer respectively an increase and a decrease. Microstructure noise appears because stock prices are not known with the highest precision. There is an uncertainty zone where the price has the highest probability to stay. This uncertainty range keeps the same size, what ever the time scale. Thus shrinking the time scale makes the range grow larger, so much so that at very short time scales the range starts to be wider than the volatility itself. This is known as signature plot. This phenomenon also results in decreasing measured correlations with decreasing time scale. This second fact is called the Epps effect.

Theoretical development: Signature plot and Epps effects on intraday volatility. See Appendix A.12 for more details.

Stylized fact: High correlation, high volatility

In the next paragraphs we will go through the data to see the link between correlations and volatility. We will first comment on the aforementioned stylized fact and then discuss the events that occurred over the May–November 2010 period, which saw high correlations with simultaneous low levels of volatility.

For the purpose of our analysis we have built two in-house indices, namely CLES 60 and the NASDAQ 100 + DJIA. The CLES 60 includes the UK stocks of the DJ Stoxx ex Euro Large, and the NASDAQ 100 + DJIA (Dow Jones Industrial Average) is made up of the combination of both indexes' components. We designed two metrics to assess the degree of correlation and the volatility of any given universe. By volatility, we mean the average volatility across all stocks, and by correlation, the average of correlations between each possible pair of the considered universe within a six-month window.

Figure 2.28 and Figure 2.29 represent the joint distribution of the correlations and volatility of the NASDAQ 100 + DJIA, and CLES 60, respectively over September 1991 — August 2012. The two solid gray profiles beside and below the scatter plot show the marginal distributions of correlation and volatility. The value of the correlation and volatility at the end of October 2010 is indicated by a diamond inside the scatter plot (at the junction of the dashed lines). Moreover, we used these dashed lines to show the positions of the correlation and the volatility on their respective marginal distributions. As can be seen on both representations, the line inside the volatility distribution profile corresponds approximately to the median distribution, showing that volatility on October 2010 was at a medium level. Conversely, the line crossing the correlation distribution shows that the value of the correlation on October 2010 was fairly high compared to its usual level.

If we take a closer look at Figure 2.28 and Figure 2.29 (p. 164 and p. 165 respectively), we see that the previous correlation spike, in March 2009 (upper right on both charts), occurred during a period of high volatility. Indeed, when uncertainty spreads in the market, volatility tends to increase, reflecting the fact that the market players lack a clear vision. Reacting to the augmentation of market risk, investors become keener to hold portfolios tracking the performances of the market. In this way they hedge themselves against the risk of being wrong compared to everybody else. Such a reaction results in correlation increasing in line with volatility.

High correlations during summer 2010

During the summer 2010 all index correlations over the world were showing high readings of the cross-stock correlations while paradoxically having low volatility levels. See for example Figures 2.26 and 2.27 which show correlation and volatility trends on both CLES 60 and NASDAQ 100 + DJIA indexes since September 1991. From July 2010, correlations between components of those indexes began to soar, while volatility remained low after the recovery from the 2009 spike following Lehman Brothers' fall.

Two explanations were put forward: (1) increased trading on index derivatives and on ETFs (Exchange-Traded Funds); and (2) the

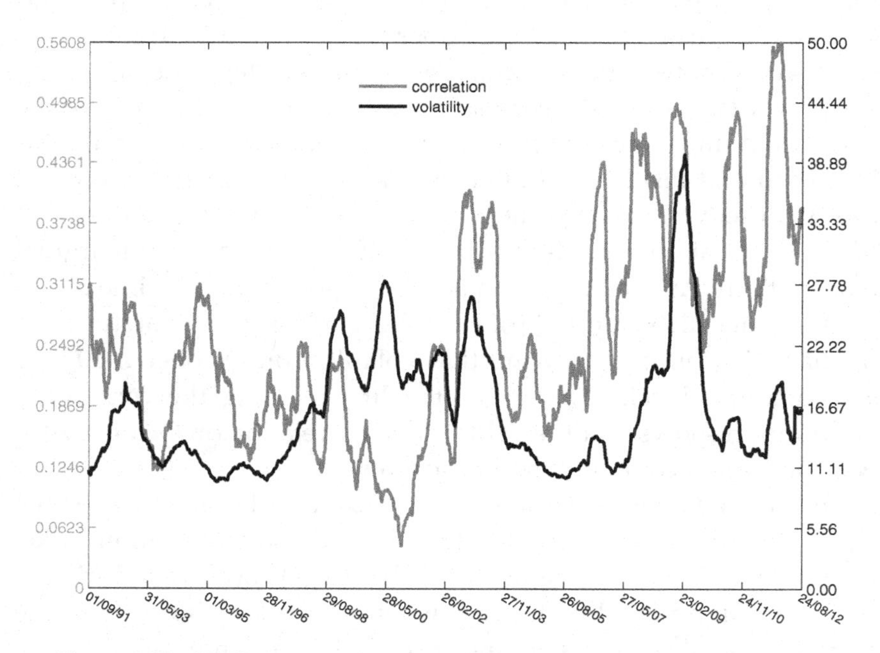

Figure 2.26. CLES 60 average pairwise correlation and average volatility.

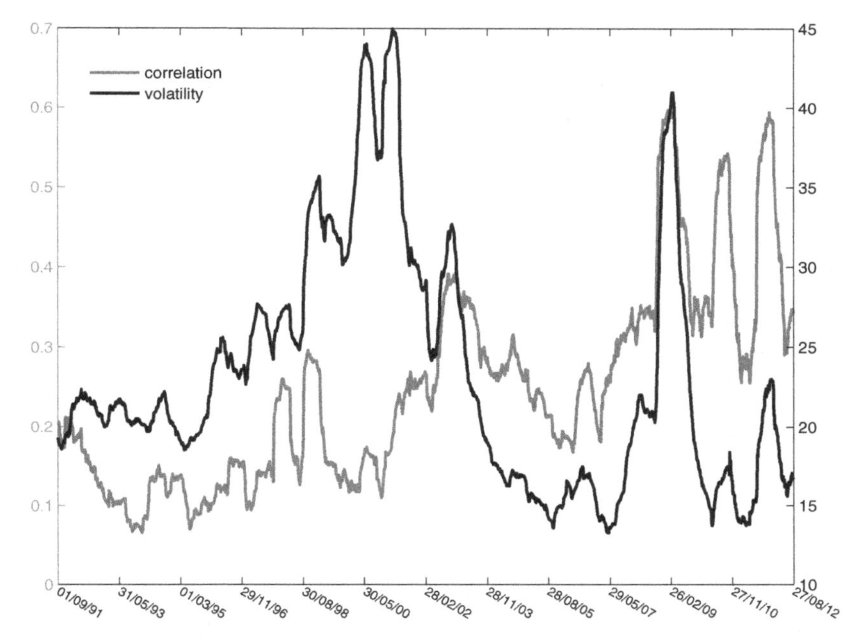

Figure 2.27. NASDAQ 100 + DJIA average pairwise correlation and average volatility.

rise in HFT — and their combined effect is likely to have caused this phenomenon.

In fact, in a market where investors are more exposed to indexes by holding positions on index derivatives, everybody's positions tend to be like everybody else's. As a result of this behavior, links between the returns of each stock increase as does, subsequently, the correlation across the stocks.

The second explanation concerns HFT. HFT players try to make a maximum gain out of liquidity arbitrages. Put a different way, they try to make money out of the mispricing of an instrument due to the liquidity needs of other players on the market. If, for example, a mutual fund comes to the market and decides to sell a large quantity of XYZ stock in a fairly aggressive manner, this sell order will push down the share price of XYZ driving it to a lower level compared to its peers, leading to an arbitrage opportunity. The action of the HFT player, by taking on the role of the counterparty of the deal,

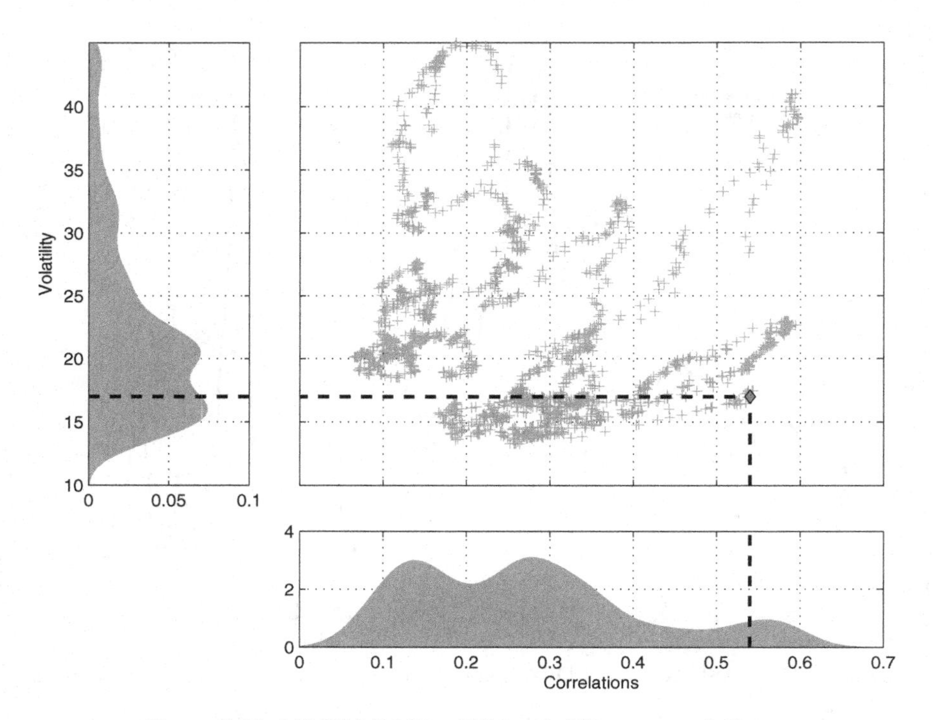

Figure 2.28. NASDAQ 100 + DJIA volatility vs. correlations.

will increase the link between the stock and its peers. There are two main reasons for this:

- The HFT player will limit the market impact incurred by XYZ by increasing the liquidity available; and
- Simultaneously it will exert selling pressure similar to that incurred by XYZ on peers, leading to a price adjustment of those stocks.

Increasing intraday correlation

During summer 2010 the surge in correlations across components of the major indexes was visible on both extraday and intraday correlations.

We calculated the correlation numbers as the correlations of the 5-minute returns over a 6-month window and averaged across all the possible pairs of components of the studied indexes. The volatility

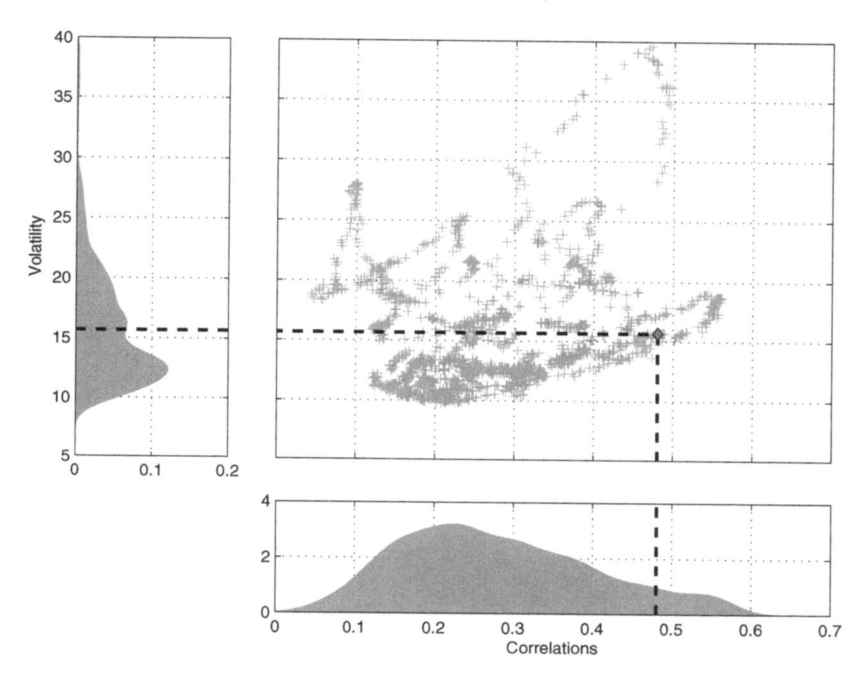

Figure 2.29. CLES 60 volatility vs. correlations.

is calculated as the standard deviation of those returns averaged the same way. We used historical datasets going back to January 2009. Figure 2.30 plots the correlation to volatility ratio for intraday (black curve) and extraday (gray curve) horizons on CLES 60 stocks. For comparison purposes these ratios have been based at 100. The trend of intraday correlation compared to intraday volatility, over the July 2009 — October 2010 period, is roughly the same at the extraday scale. Nevertheless the intraday values spiked three months before the extraday ones on 24 October 2010. From that date both ratios decline until end of January 2011. The subsequent increase is caused by the sovereign debt crisis in August 2011.

Figure 2.31 represents the ratio of intraday correlation to extraday correlation. It gives a more precise idea of the trend in intraday correlation compared to extraday correlation. In fact we see that during the summer 2010 surge in correlation, the intraday part of the extraday correlation tends to decrease. The intraday correlation

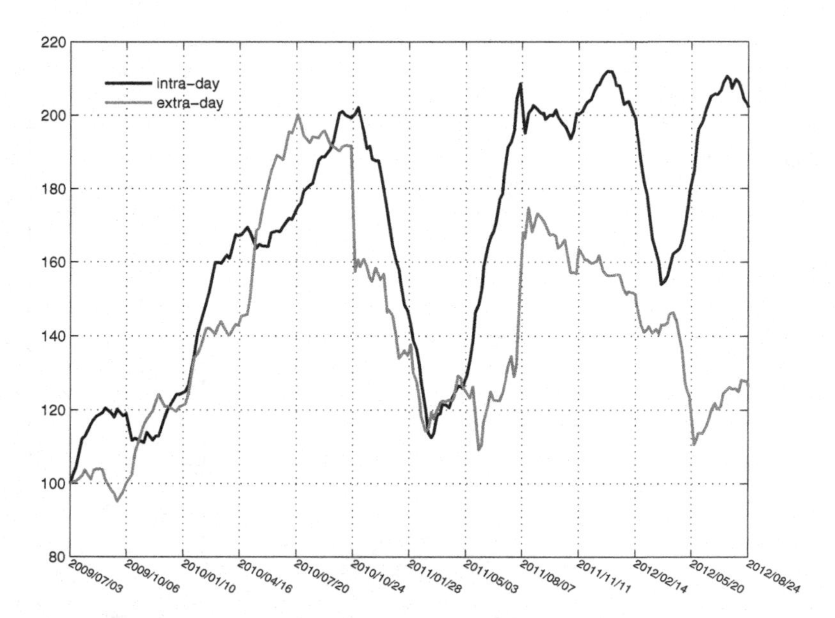

Figure 2.30. CLES 60 correlation to volatility ratio, intraday vs. extraday.

reaches 57% of the extraday one in August 2010, 23% lower than its level 4 months before.

The preceding observations, which relate the appearance of growing correlations could be interpreted in two different ways. But before we look at these interpretations in more depth, let us go off on a tangent for a minute and talk about a few facts from signal theory.

Let us consider two series of data, in this case the price time series of two stocks. We can model these series as the sum of a fundamental component, which bears the information (called 'signal'), and a noise component (denoted 'noise'), as follows[1]

$$\text{Price}_t = \text{Signal}_t + \text{Noise}_t. \tag{2.1}$$

The values of the noise are not related to the signals or to each other but to the nature of the system (as it happens, the market), which drives the information going to the observer. The noises of

[1]The "signal" component can be seen as the systematic moves of the price, and the "noise" one as the idiosynchratic ones.

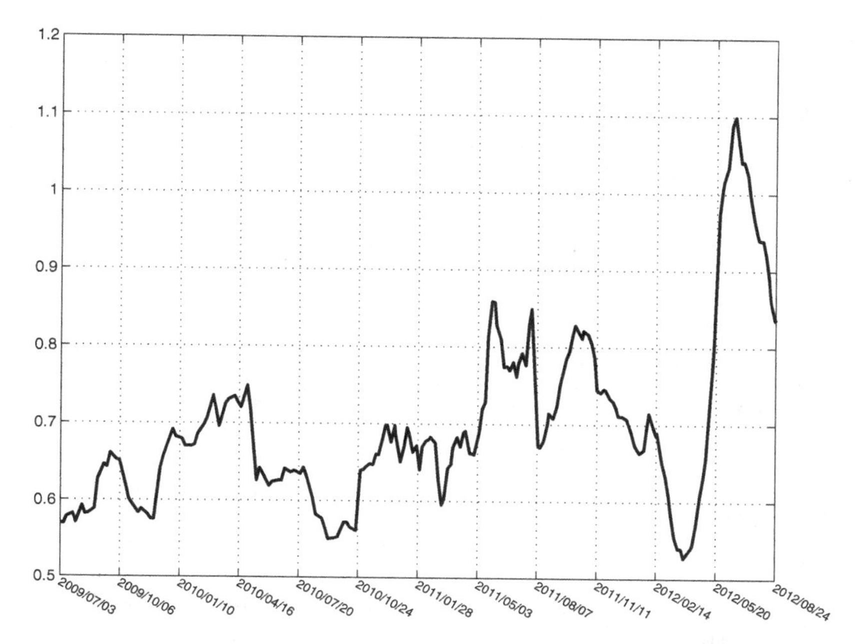

Figure 2.31. CLES 60, ratio of intraday to extraday correlation.

the two price series are therefore not correlated. In fact, the noisier the data, the less correlation there is. Conversely, the stronger the signal is relative to the noise, the stronger the correlation. For the time series of a share price, the signal and the noise are hidden. The only accessible variable is the combination of both ('Price' in (2.1)). In market data the noise comes from the microstructure of the market. This means that the price of a stock depends on both the Walrasian equilibrium between the supply and demand, and the way the stock is traded (is it a continuous double auction or auction fixing?) One stylized fact of high-frequency finance is the smaller the sampling-time scale, the noisier the data (see the discussion above about Epps effect and signature plot). Thus when looking at ever smaller scales, we might find decreasing correlations.

We explore the consequences of this in the equations. Let A, B be two stocks and P^A, P^B their prices,

$$P_t^A = S_t^A + N_t^A, \quad P_t^B = S_t^B + N_t^B.$$

The correlation between those two stocks is

$$\mathrm{Corr}(P_t^A, P_t^A) = \frac{\mathrm{Cov}(S_t^A, S_t^B)}{\sqrt{\mathrm{Var}(P_t^A)\mathrm{Var}(P_t^B)}}$$

$$= \frac{\mathrm{Cov}(S_t^A, S_t^B)}{\sqrt{\mathrm{Var}(S_t^A) + \mathrm{Var}(N_t^A)}\sqrt{\mathrm{Var}(S_t^B) + \mathrm{Var}(N_t^B)}}.$$

Let us assume that both price series P^A and P^B have the same volatility and the same amount of noise, thus $\mathrm{Var}(P_t^A) = \mathrm{Var}(P_t^B)$ and $\mathrm{Var}(N_t^A) = \mathrm{Var}(N_t^A)$. Then $\frac{\mathrm{Var}(S_t^A)}{\mathrm{Var}(N_t^A)} = \frac{\mathrm{Var}(S_t^B)}{\mathrm{Var}(N_t^B)}$, and $\mathrm{Corr}(P_t^A, P_t^A)$ becomes

$$\mathrm{Corr}(P_t^A, P_t^A) = \frac{\mathrm{Var}(S_t)\mathrm{Corr}(S_t^A, S_t^B)}{\mathrm{Var}(N_t)\left(\frac{\mathrm{Var}(S_t)}{\mathrm{Var}(N_t)} + 1\right)} = \frac{\mathrm{Corr}(S_t^A, S_t^B)}{1 + \frac{\mathrm{Var}(N_t)}{\mathrm{Var}(S_t)}}.$$

Let us go back to the interpretation of growing correlations. Based on the explanation above, we can view the increase in correlations as the result of two possible phenomena:

- The Signal components of the share prices are more correlated, that is to say $\mathrm{Corr}(S_t^A, S_t^B)$ increases in equation (2.2);
- The Noise components of the share prices are diminishing. $\frac{\mathrm{Var}(N_t)}{\mathrm{Var}(S_t)}$ is decreasing in equation (2.2)

Of course both phenomena could happen at the same time and, in fact, this is what we believe is happening.

Overnight versus overday correlation

This paragraph examines the trends of the average overday and overnight correlations among components of an index. The correlation spikes are often well explained by overnight ones. During the summer 2010 high correlation episode, the overday correlation spiked as well. This overday spike was the highest recorded so far. Since the summer of 2010 there has been another period of high correlation, namely in August 2011, when the correlation looked like summer 2010's one from an overday overnight comparison

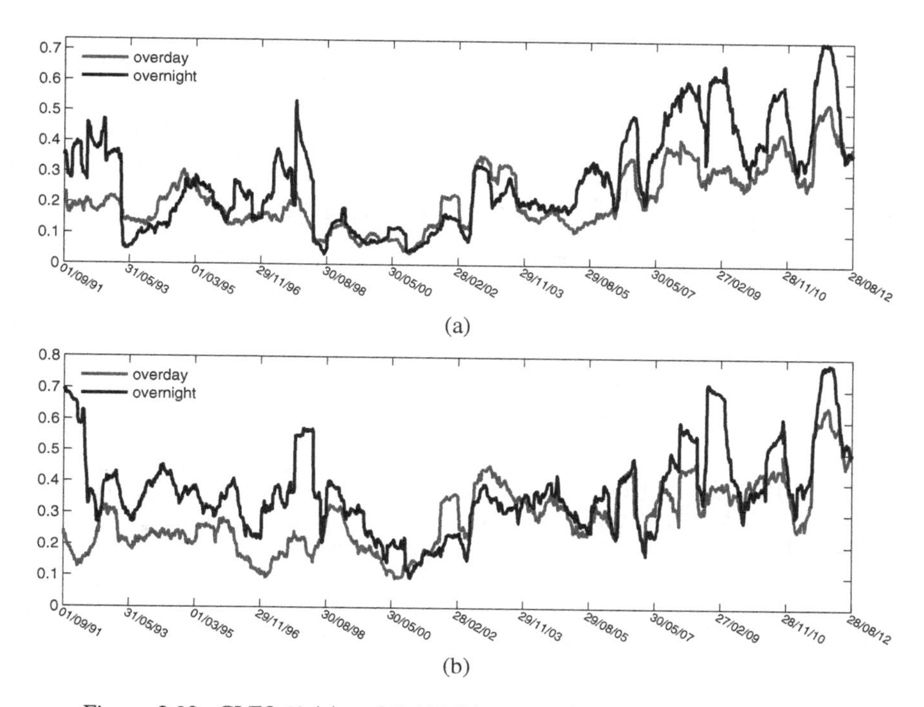

Figure 2.32. CLES 60 (a) and DAX (b) overnight vs. overday correlation.

perspective. It is during that spike that overday correlation reached its highest value. The overday correlation reflects to some extent the amount of co-movement between securities at intraday scale. This is an intermediary marker in the contagion process which leads microscopic causes to create macroscopic effects. The next paragraph will examine how the summer 2010 high correlations could have been strengthened by trading activities at intraday scale.

Figure 2.32 and Figure 2.33 show the average pairwise correlation on CLES 60, DAX, CAC 40 and IBEX 35 components on both overnight and overday data. Calculation of the overnight correlation is much the same as that for extraday values (see equations (2.2) and (2.3)). Instead of looking at returns between the close of two consecutive days, we take the returns between the close of the previous day and the opening of the subsequent day. As in the case for extraday correlation, we computed these metrics on a six-month

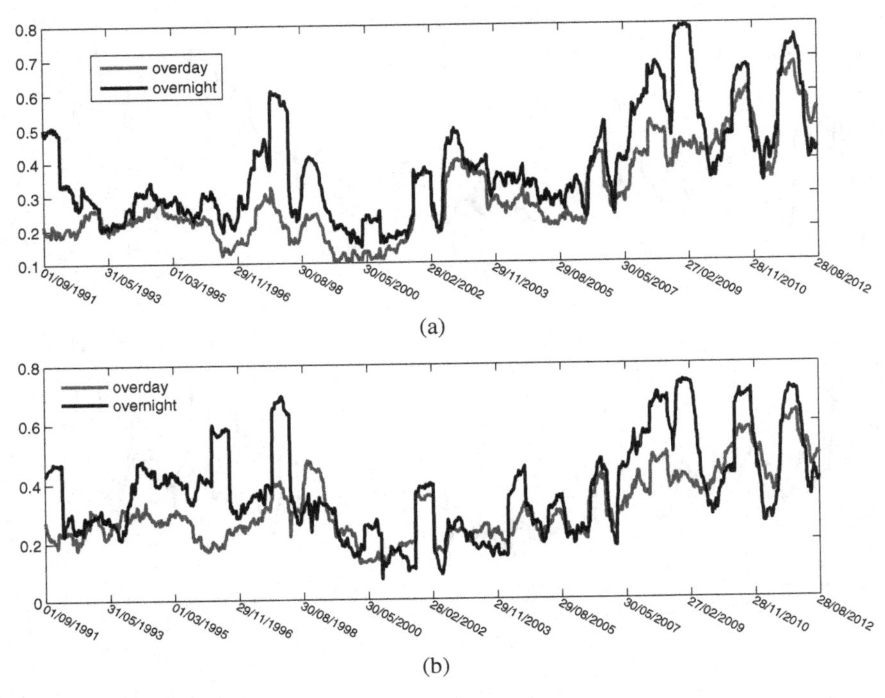

Figure 2.33. CAC 40 (a) and IBEX 35 (b) overnight vs. overday correlation.

sliding window. The calculation of overday correlation follows the same methodology as its overnight version.

$$\text{overday correlation} = \text{Corr}(\text{overday return}^A, \text{overday return}^B) \tag{2.2}$$

$$\text{overnight correlation} = \text{Corr}(\text{overnight return}^A, \text{overnight return}^B) \tag{2.3}$$

where

$$\text{overday return}_t = \log(\text{close}_t) - \log(\text{open}_t)$$
$$\text{overnight return}_t = \log(\text{open}_t) - \log(\text{close}_{t-1}).$$

The overday correlation on October 2010 was lower than the overnight one. This remark has been valid since the start of the surge in June 2010. When looking at Figure 2.32 and Figure 2.33 we see that the overday correlation plays the role of a baseline for the overnight correlation, which keeps bouncing above it.

On the CLES 60, DAX, CAC 40, and IBEX 35, the increase in correlation is mainly driven by the overnight side, as Figures 2.32 and 2.33 show clearly. What is also noticeable from these figures is that the overnight correlation explains well the spikes in extraday correlations. Further examination of these four figures reveals that for three indices (the CAC 40, CLES 60, and IBEX 35) their overday correlation was in October 2010 at its highest level since 1991. In fact, the last overnight correlation spikes in 2008 and 2009 were pretty much as high as the current ones. This is not the case for the overnight correlation. This observation can be related to the above-mentioned comment about growing intraday correlation and the impact of HFT on this correlation.

In fact these discrepancies result from two different microstructures. We wrote above that the value of the price was largely dependent on a microstructural parameter. Figure 2.32 and Figure 2.33 present a good example of that assertion. During the night the market is organized as an auction fixing and during the day it is a continuous double auction. In fact the opening fixing is less liable to become contaminated by loud microstructure noise and thus tends to better reflect the investors' consensus on the price of an asset than the closing fixing does. As a matter of fact, the overnight correlations are closer to the extraday correlation. Based on the above explanation of the discrepancies between overnight and overday correlations, it can be said that the spike of extraday correlation from March to October 2010 is in part due to increasing overday correlation, which itself is the consequence of a less noisy PFP (price formation process). The growing level of HFT activity could be one explanation for this.

2.4.3. *The Flash Crash (May 6th, 2010) in NY: How far are we from systemic risk?*

Is the Flash Crash an indication that systemic risk has increased since the markets became fragmented? In any case there is no doubt that the changes the market has been subject to for seven years are responsible for it. Even if the Flash Crash is bad news for the market it is not evidence of an increase in systemic risk. However, some troubling questions remain: what would have happened if the Flash Crash occurred just before the trading session close? No doubt the consequences would have been more serious. Markets would have swept the valuations of some funds in their wake and would probably have been disrupted over a longer period.

Theoretical development: Small dynamical model of the Flash Crash. See Appendix A.4 for more details.

On 6 May 2010, the US stock market suffered a sudden and rapid drop followed by a rapid recovery. The S&P 500, which was already on a downtrend since the beginning of the day, saw its slide start to accelerate at 14:30. Within minutes, the equity and futures markets suffered a decline of 5%. The high volatility on the markets at the beginning of the day suggests that this Flash Crash might have been caused by a temporary and significant drop in liquidity.

At 09:00 this day the S&P 500 opened not far from its last closing price. The economic background in Europe was causing some concern. The debt crisis seemed to be worsening as sovereign CDS spreads were widening. In particular, there were mounting concerns about the sustainability of the Greek economy. In this context of unsettling political and economic news, the market was already down at 11:00 and volatility (Figure 2.34) was reaching higher levels than in the previous days. At noon the S&P 500 had lost 1%. At 13:55 the S&P 500's slide was accelerating and volatility increased dramatically. The Flash Crash itself happened at 14:46 when the S&P 500 was showing a 7% loss compared to its level 50 minutes previously. It quickly went back up to 1,123.5. This rapid recovery saw the S&P 500 rebuild 5.85% of its value compared to the low of the day.

Example of the Flash Crash impact: Procter & Gamble

This decline impacted all stocks on the major US indexes. Stocks such as Procter & Gamble lost 36% in seven minutes. At 14:40, Procter &

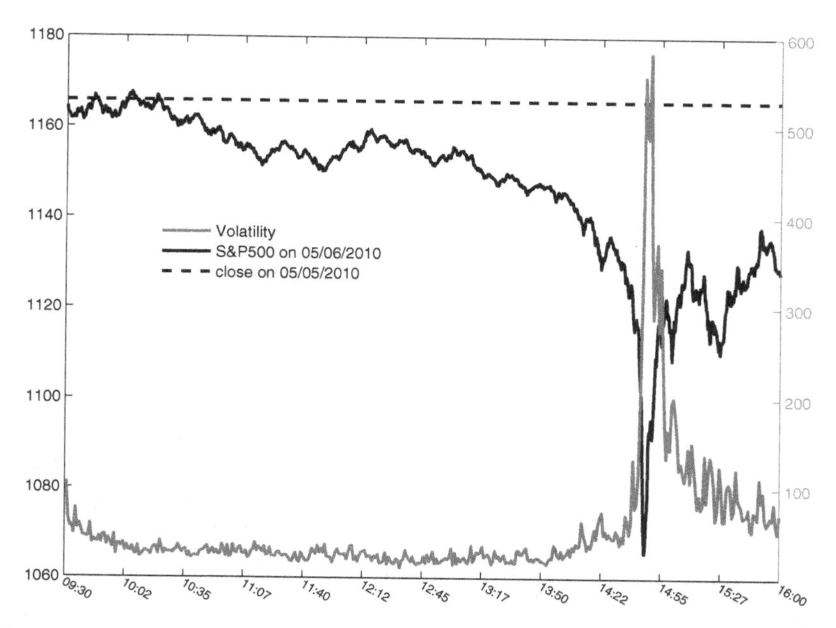

Figure 2.34. S&P 500 and volatility among S&P 500 components on 6 May 2010.

Gamble was trading at USD61.50 (chart (a) on Figure 2.35). At 14:47 it was worth USD39.37.

Figure 2.35 shows various metrics which provide a better understanding of what happened to the PG (Procter & Gamble) share on 6 May. Chart (b) on Figure 2.35 shows the volumes (grey curve) and number of trades (black curve) on PG during one-minute intervals throughout the day. Chart (a) on Figure 2.35 presents the trend in the average bid-ask spread weighted by volumes over one-minute time intervals (gray curve).

Volumes traded on Procter & Gamble began to increase significantly at 13:30 (Figure 2.35). This movement continued until 14:44, which is when the price of PG stock was dislocated. In line with the trend observed for volumes, the number of trades increased dramatically at around 13:50 to reach 600 trades per minute at 14:22. Trading rates did not fall below this barrier until the end of the day. In Figure 2.35 we can see the volume-weighted average bid-ask spread, which spiked at above USD2 at 14:40. After this shock the spread

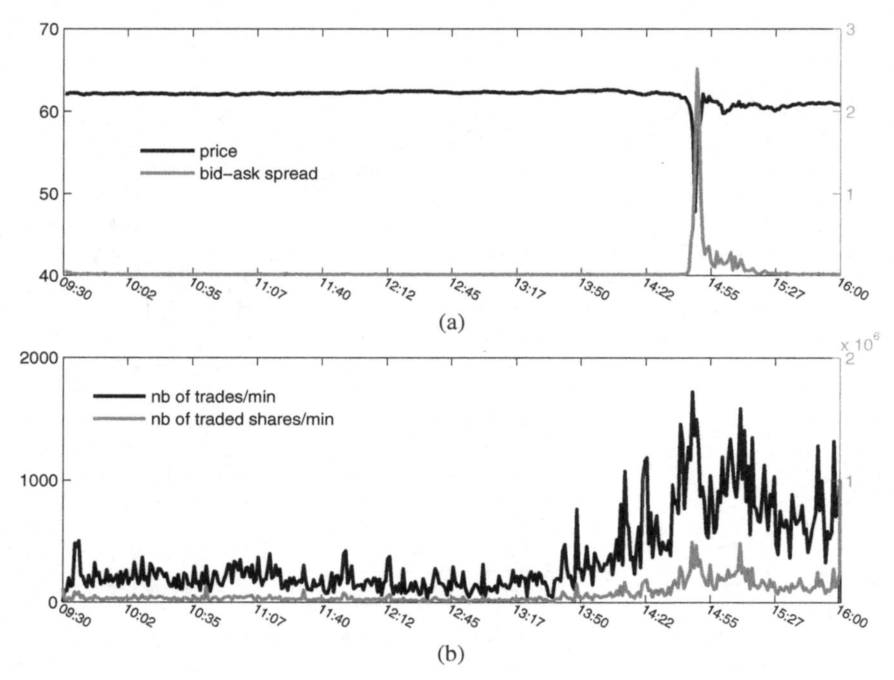

Figure 2.35. (a) Price and bid-ask spread of Procter & Gamble, (b) Number of trades and number of shares traded during one-minute intervals, 6 May 2010.

declined rapidly back to 30 cents and then gradually reverted to a typical level of around 1.5 cents, until 20 minutes before the close.

A large order initiated by a fundamental trader lighted the Flash Crash

In a joint report [cit, 2010b] ("Findings Regarding the Market Events of May 6, 2010") the SEC and the CFTC suggested several reasons that could explain these rapid movements on futures and stock markets on 6 May 2010. The sale of a large amount of US index futures (E-mini contracts) initiated by a fundamental trader at 14:32 may have been the event that triggered the Flash Crash. The trader was trading using an automated execution algorithm aimed at tracking the market volume; she did not put a limit price on the algorithmic order.

At the moment of the sale, volatility was already high and liquidity was low on the futures market. The counterparties of the trade, which have been identified as High Frequency players, then moved rapidly to the equity market to hedge themselves in this context of high market risk. The excess of volume thus brought to the equity market then, for the same reasons, brought players in these markets to hedge their positions on the futures market. This game of hot potato, which was transmitted step by step until it returned to its starting point, caused the escalation of volumes exchanged while the liquidity offered remained unchanged. This artificially increased volume caused the trader to increase his flow sent to the market and thus fed the vicious circle that was starting.

The jump in volume incurred by the market was followed by a large number of HFT players liquidating their positions, further increasing the imbalance between the demand and supply of liquidity.

The E-mini and SPY, which is the ETF tracking the performances of the S&P 500, were both declining slightly ahead of the stock market. In fact the E-mini was leading the general fall. The fact that the E-mini and SPY were showing worrisome desynchronization, plus the high volatility on both derivatives, caused an interruption in the number of orders. This is the mechanism that transmitted the shock to the stock market. While an increasing number of orders were being paused, the aggressive pressure was rising. The stock market quickly followed the derivatives market.

Furthermore, as most of the brokers paused their orders, the retail flow that is usually executed OTC by internal matching engines was routed to the market, thus increasing pressure on the aggressive side of the orderbooks.

Another mechanism may have played a role that might have worsened the situation. This is the Liquidity Replenishment Point (LRP). LRP is a NYSE-specific system that slackens the market for a period of time in order to let liquidity return. It is possible that such a mechanism could have exacerbated the imbalance between the supply and demand of liquidity. When an LRP is triggered all aggressive orders are rerouted to other exchanges. Such a mechanism has the immediate effect of removing from the market the passive liquidity present inside the NYSE while retaining the aggressive liquidity.

In addition to all the reasons highlighted above, the SEC also mentioned the fact that the absence of a stock-specific circuit breaker mechanism may have been one of the aggravating factors in the Flash Crash. On 10 June, 2010 the SEC decided to remedy this problem by introducing a mechanism that places a five-minute hold on stocks with a movement of more than 10% during the previous five minutes.

The package of measures under examination or adopted by the SEC in the Flash Crash aftermath

Following the Flash Crash observers have pointed out the lack of single-stock circuit breakers. In fact on May 6 only market-wide circuit breakers were operational. Those circuit breakers halt trading during a severe market decline as measured by a single-day decrease in the DJIA (Dow Jones Industrial Average). Those did not trigger on May 6, 2010.

In a period starting September 2011, markets filed proposals to SEC in order to revise the existing market-wide circuit breakers. The SEC reviewed these contributions in April 2012. Among other things the following suggestions have been made: Reduce the market decline percentage thresholds necessary to trigger a circuit breaker; shorten the duration of the resulting trading halts; change the reference index used to measure a market decline (from the Dow Jones Industrial Average to the S&P 500 Index).

In June 2010, the US stock markets adopted procedures for single-stock circuit breakers. Trading pauses for five minutes if a stock price moves up or down sharply in a five-minute window. These circuit breaker rules were initially applied only to stocks in the S&P 500 Index but were extended to all National Market System (NMS) securities in June 2011. For most traded stocks and ETFs, a 10% price move would trigger a five-minute pause. For less traded stocks and ETFs priced at or above USD1, a price move of 30% would trigger a pause, and 50% price move will trigger a pause for securities trading below USD1.

In addition to single-stock circuit breakers, the SEC is examining the opportunity to apply a limit-up or limit-down mechanism. Because circuit breakers are triggered only after a trade occurs outside of the applicable percentage threshold, there has been a propensity for the circuit breakers to be triggered by erroneous trades. In contrast, a limit up-limit down mechanism is intended to help to prevent erroneous trades from occurring in the first place by preventing trades in individual securities from occurring outside of a specified price band, and would be coupled with a trading pause mechanism to accommodate more fundamental price moves.

Following the Flash Crash, the SEC had a large amount of data to process. It took almost five months to rebuild a few hours of trading. In July 11, 2012 the SEC approved a new rule to create a so-called consolidated audit trail. The purpose of such a system is to collect trading data to help the agency track trading orders across the market. Originally, the SEC required the implementation of a real time reporting but finally decided to go for a repository that the brokers and exchanges will have to provide information to before 8am the next day.

On November 8, 2010 the SEC approved a proposal aimed at prohibiting market-makers stub quotes. A stub quote is an offer to buy or sell a stock at a price so far away from the prevailing market that it is not intended to be executed, such as an order to buy at a penny or an offer to sell at USD100,000. A market maker may enter stub quotes to nominally comply with its obligation to maintain a two-sided quotation at those times when it does not wish to actively provide liquidity. Executions against stub quotes represented a significant proportion of the trades that were executed at extreme prices on May 6, and subsequently broken. The market makers are now bound to maintain continuous two-sided quotations within a certain percentage of the national best bid and offer.

On November 3, 2010 the SEC voted to ban naked access to the market. This rule prohibits brokers from granting unfiltered access to the exchanges and the Alternative Trading Facilities and now have to fulfill a minimum level of risk control.

This event has shown that the concerns raised by the SEC in January 2010, when it issued its Concept Release "Seeking Comment on the Structure of Equity Markets" [cit, 2010a] were well-founded. The components of this Flash Crash are enlightening: an investor selling without taking into account the liquidity risk, a trader blindly using an algorithm, high-frequency market makers hedging their positions among themselves (with one leg on the futures market and the other on the equity market), the pause in internalizing retail orders exacerbating the phenomenon, and the trading destinations doing nothing to preserve the integrity of the price formation process. Every layer of the market contributed to the crash.

Outages in Europe

Outages, that is to say when an exchange or a MTF is put on hold, can be placed alongside the May 6th event in the US.

At 16:42 CET on 13 October, 2010, the NYSE Euronext cash markets (consisting of the Paris, Amsterdam, Brussels, and Lisbon exchanges) were halted due to human error. No more trades occurred on the venue until 17:20, when NYSE Euronext reported that quotation resumed, but without any market data being distributed.

For 40 minutes, Euronext offered trading conditions that were very similar to those of a Dark Pool (no pre-trade visibility). In the end, members were able to request cancellation of their trades ex post.

As a preliminary remark, concerns arose about the fact that European primary markets, claiming that they primarily host the price formation process, continue to suffer from outages and similar "bugs" or technical issues. Euronext is not an isolated case. The LSE announced on 2 November, 2010 its decision to postpone, for several months, the upgrade of its trading engine following an outage of around 2 hours on Turquoise. The migration was finally done on February 14, 2011. Fragmentation can also be viewed as a solution to avoid relying on them providing a microstructure for equity trading in Europe. Even if Chi-X and BATS have been putting competitive pressure on historical exchanges for years now, the result is not as good as could have been expected.

Nevertheless, these events are rare market phases during which it is possible to examine the price formation process without a "subjective reference price". Bear in mind that without a trade-through rule, most MTFs decided to import the price of primary exchanges rather than that of a "consolidated European Best Bid and Offer" (BBO). During such periods, mid-points stop trading and all orders previously "pegged" to the primary BBO are canceled or paused (depending on the trading rules of each platform).

The amount traded during the outage on most stocks was close to that usually traded off Euronext: Some mid caps stopped trading, but not all of them, and most large caps continued trading on MTFs. For most of the latter, the trading price was close to the last traded price on Euronext. When the VWAP from the opening to the outage was close to the last traded price on Euronext, prices barely moved. Nevertheless, we observed deviations of around 2% on some stocks during the outage. As shown in Figure 2.36 and Figure 2.37, even

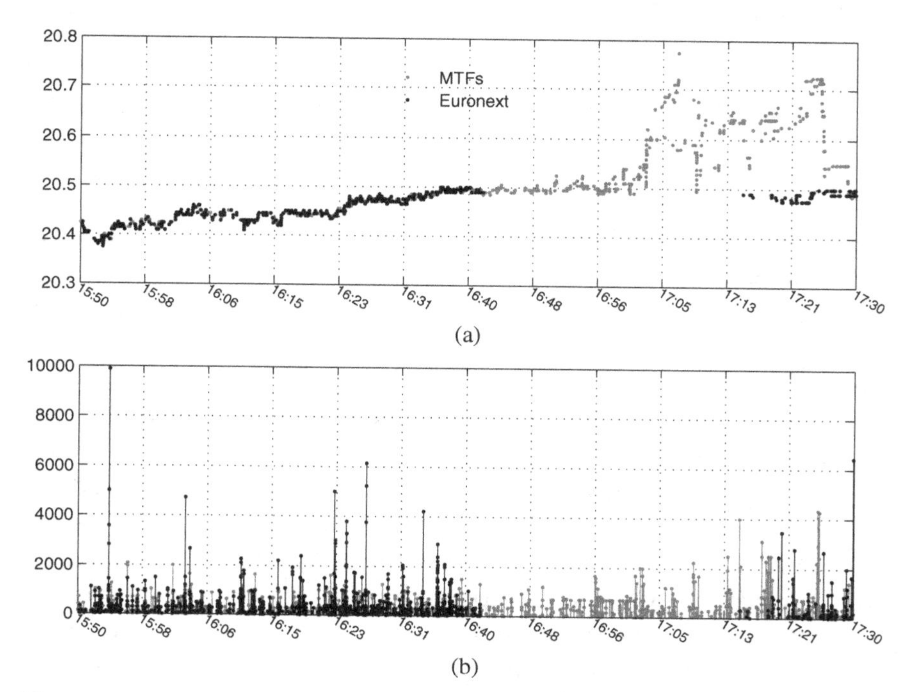

Figure 2.36. VIV FP on 10 October 2010 between 3.50 pm and 5.30 pm CET: (a) Stock price and (b) traded volumes in number of shares.

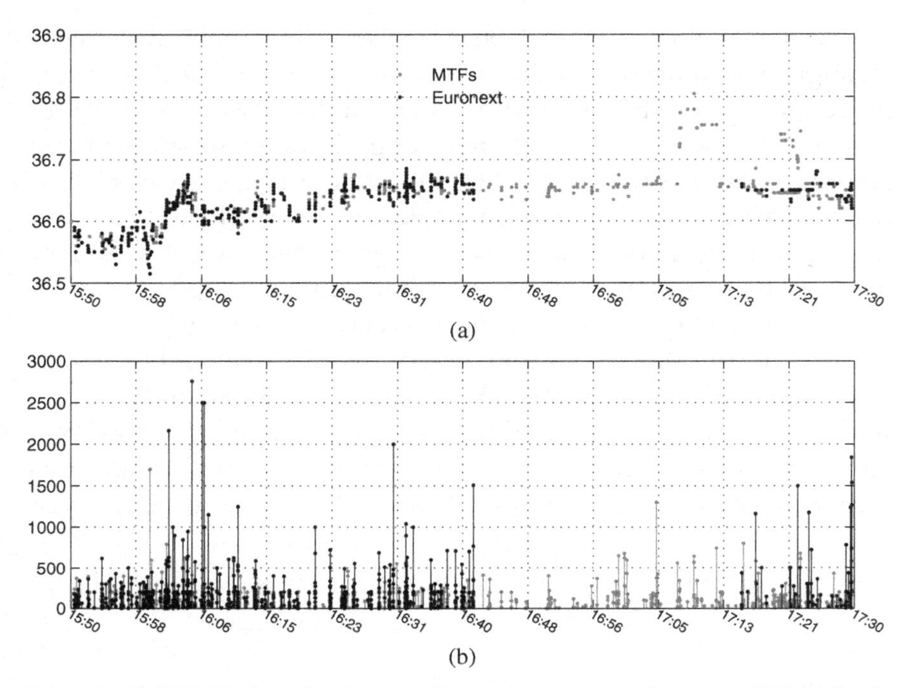

Figure 2.37. PUB FP on 10 October 2010 between 3.50 pm and 5.30 pm CET: (a) Stock price and (b) traded volumes in number of shares.

stocks on the EuroStoxx 50 and the CAC 40 were subject to such price changes.

Moreover, the post publication of market data by Euronext shows the differences between the price on MTFs and Euronext. For such stocks, it was as if two price formation processes took place in parallel. We can never know exactly the number of trades but we can nevertheless comment on what happened in real-time.

On Vivendi, for instance (Figure 2.36), we can clearly see trading on BATS and Chi-X at higher prices than on Euronext, even when "anonymous trades" occurred on Euronext. Moreover, this disjunction of prices proves that the primary markets do not inherently own the price formation process. Without any consolidated tape, and as MTFs decided to peg most of their trading activity to primary markets, they decided to index exploration of prices on their pools to the primary BBOs. The fact that the price on the primary markets leads that of MTFs stems from the fact that most agents (brokers, investors and MTFs themselves) decided that most of their decisions should be tied to the state of the primary markets.

We hope that if a consolidated post-trade tape is asked for by regulators, it will suffice for information-sharing among pools and traders so that the kind of instability of the price formation process, as seen on Euronext on 13 October, 2010, will not happen again.

To conclude with regard to this outage, we can say that the price formation process is not specifically in the hands of one trading destination or another, but that it comes out of the mix of information about traded prices and bids and offers. A consolidated post-trade tape in Europe, where deals under a given size would have to be reported almost immediately, including dark orders, would be the easiest and most robust means of guaranteeing the emergence of a European price formation process, rather than adding liquidity around prices displayed by historical markets.

Chapter 3

Optimal Organisations for Optimal Trading

3.1. Organising a Trading Structure to Answer to a Fragmented Landscape

The more the asset management industry matures, the more it controls its risks and lower its costs. Trading costs (explicit and implicit) are a source of expense, especially for actively managed portfolios. Large asset managers thus concentrated the tasks of mounting and unwinding positions to dealing desks, which take care of:

- The relationships with intermediaries;
- Measuring the trading costs and comparing broker performances thanks to TCA (Transaction Cost Analysis);
- Choosing the benchmark to target (VWAP, TWAP, Implementation shortfall, Target Close, etc) according to the investment style that generated the trade (see Section 3.2).

Hence, the dealing desks demand accuracy in the trading process and in its monitoring. Exchanges are also providing more and more services around "best execution" (Smart Order Routers (SORs), even some trading algorithms). And last but not least, software vendors include in their standard offers advanced monitoring tools and standard performance measurements and comparison features. These put pressure on brokers to build efficient trading services, as innovative and as close to their client needs as possible.

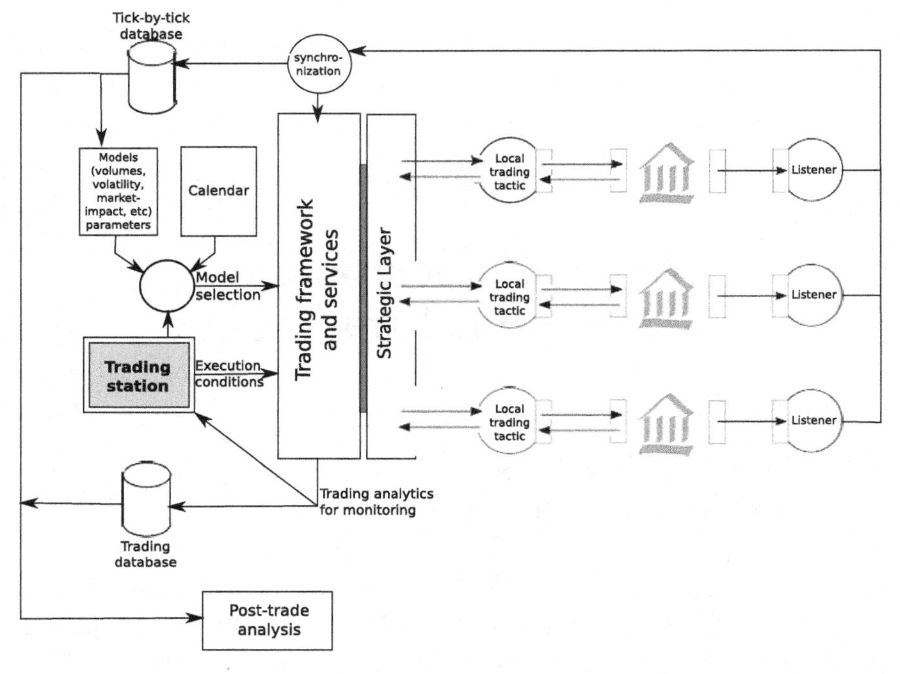

Figure 3.1. Stylized blueprint of a trading architecture.

Such suites of services have to rely on a proper organization (i.e. architecture) of the main components needed to offer automated trading features. Figure 3.1 sketches the main components of a trading architecture.

3.1.1. *Main inputs of trading tools*

The market data

Real time market data feeds are the eyes of any trading algorithm. Within a fragmented market, a consolidation of all available market data is needed. Some vendors are providing an already consolidated tape, otherwise the real time consolidation has to be built. This consolidated source should be able to be disaggregated as fast as possible: It is one thing to be able to identify that a good price is available somewhere, but in practice it is necessary to know which trading venue is currently offering this price.

Market data contains:

- Market trades, described by a price, a quantity and a timestamp (not always precise enough),
- Limit orderbooks (bid and ask prices, quantities available at each of these prices, and the number of different market participants contributing at each price level), or sequences of modifications of the orderbook (in the latter case the limit orderbook of the venue has to be built on the fly).

These data have to be *enriched with analytics*, some very simple, like computing the bid-ask spread (subtracting the best bid price to the best ask price) or qualifying the observed market trades (are they initiated by a buyer or a seller?), and more sophisticated ones, like intraday volatility, *efficient bid-ask spread*,[1] or estimates of the hidden quantities in the book.

Formally there is no difference between analytics and raw market data since they are simultaneously needed to make decisions, which is why the sooner they are computed, the better. Ideally, very fast computers (like hardware based calculators [Leber *et al.*, 2011]) can be in charge of computing such indicators as soon as raw data is available.

The connection to venues

To be able to trade, trading algorithms need to be connected to exchanges. These connections are not natively synchronized with market data (they are usually faster) and are two-way:

- One to send messages to the trading venue: creation of a new order, cancellation or modification of another order, etc.
- The other to receive messages from the trading venue about the orders of the trading algorithm: acknowledgments of messages sent by the algo, rejections (if the message is ill-formed), cancellations, partial fills, etc.

[1] The *efficient* bid-ask spread is often defined as a measure of the spread over a time interval, or the difference in price to buy and sell immediately a given quantity.

Another kind of analytics can be computed using the incoming messages. For instance, since Dark Pools are not to provide any orderbook data (they are disseminating information on trades they host), the orders sent by the algo can be used as *probes* coming back with information about the state of the dark orderbook. Typically, when a dark buy order is fully filled at a given price, it means that the orderbook of the Dark Pool contains resting sell quantity at this price or better.[2]

Historical data

Optimal trading relies on views on intraday risk control and the usual rhythms and behaviors of market features (like traded volumes or price volatility), that are captured by *models* whose parameters need to be estimated on a stock-by-stock or sector-by-sector basis. Historical data are needed for that, and should contain:

- Market data (usually named tick-by-tick or order-by-order data);
- Analytics that have been computed in real time, so they will not need to be recomputed;
- Recordings of the messages sent and received by the algorithms of the firm (to study the performance of the past occurrences of the trading algorithms);
- Context-related information like news, corporate events, activation of circuit breakers, outages of trading venues, etc. (to do comparisons and statistics on a per context basis and thus discriminate influence of contexts on market data and trading performances).

Models

Models are mathematical formulas (like the market impact formula — see Section 3.2 —, the market risk one, etc.). They are implemented using a programming language and stored into libraries. Practically, a model is made of three components:

- *The formula* itself, taking as inputs parameters and variables. In the following formula of the market impact: $\kappa \cdot \sigma \cdot (v/V)^\gamma$, the

[2]This can be used to build optimally trading algorithms [Laruelle *et al.*, 2011].

parameters are κ and γ that can be tuned on a stock-by-stock basis, and the variables are σ (the current volatility of the stock to trade), V (the market volume during the trading) and v (the volume to be traded by the algorithm). The parameters can be estimated once per day and stored, the variables are known in real time and have to be plugged in the formula on the fly.

- *Estimation* that is a mathematical procedure taking as input historical data on a given universe and a given horizon and computing *estimated values* for the parameters of the model. In the example of the market impact model, any formula to estimate κ and γ using historical data is such an estimating procedure.
- *The accuracy computation* is another mathematical procedure to qualify the quality of the model and its parameters according to the immediate past or in real time. It is indeed crucial to be able to activate or deactivate a model if the likelihood that it is adequate to use it in the current context is low.

3.1.2. *Components of trading algorithms*

Trading algorithms are implemented using a programming language and stored in libraries; they are usually instantiated on the fly when a user *launches* an algo of a given class (like VWAP, TWAP, Implementation Shortfall, Target Close, or Liquidity seeking). Very often trading algorithms can themselves launch other algorithms.

A trading algorithm is made of different components:

- *The execution parameters* defining the execution conditions that apply to the algorithm, typically the side and quantity, the benchmark (VWAP, TWAP, percent of Volume, Entry price, Close price, etc.), the start and end time, some trading rate bounds (maximum and minimum percent), aggressivity level, access to Dark Pools, etc.
- *The risk control layer* in charge of computing reasonable maximum and minimum trading rates to target during the trading. This is usually called the *trading curve* of the algorithm (see Appendix A.6). This layer uses models (market impact, market risk, alpha signals, etc.) and "expected market contexts" to produce a minimum and maximum trading envelope to follow

in order to make the balance between two main sources of risk: The market impact and the market risk (and the associated adverse selection risk).
- *Trading robots* or *liquidity seeking tactics* like a SOR (Smart Order Router) or any more sophisticated opportunistic tactic dedicated to navigate inside the trading envelope defined by the risk control layer. These robots have to take into account the immediate state of the liquidity to extract as much value as possible from the trading venues under the risk constraints.

The communication between the two lower layers (risk control and tactics) is controlled by the risk control layer sending messages to tactics to assign them short term goals. In case of a fragmented market, some autonomous tactics can be located as close as possible to the trading venue they address and the risk control layer has to be located at equal distance to all its robots.

Figure 3.2 shows a trajectory of a trading algo; the envelope can be seen and the real trajectory of the algo (in grey) is realized by trading robots launched by the risk control layer.

3.1.3. *Main outputs of an automated trading system*

Pre-trade analytics

The historical data, the models, and their parameters have to be used to provide decision support before the effective launch of a trading algorithm. Such a pre-trade analytics is very useful on portfolios since it can check the consistency of the portfolio and generate automated directives to speedup some lines and slow down others according to a pre-computation of the balance between expected market risk and expected market impact.

Typical measurements included in pre-trade analysis are:

- Estimation and comparison of expected trading cost components (bid-ask spread, usual traded volume, usual quantities *on the book,*[3] etc.);

[3]Quantity on the book is an estimate of the quantity that is usually available on first limits of the Limit Orderbooks.

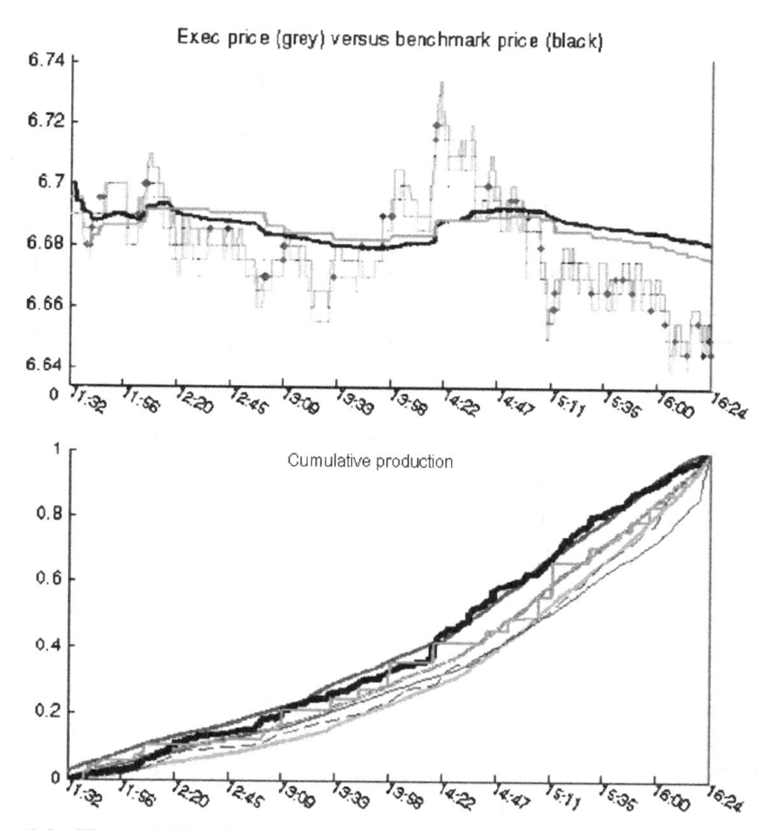

Figure 3.2. The real life of a trading algorithm; on top: the price and the obtained trades (dots); on bottom: The cumulated traded quantity by the algo (grey), by the market (dark), the envelope can be seen in red and green.

- Expected trading profiles;
- Expected context (including news, volatility levels, etc.);
- Breakdown by sector, currency, country, etc.

Thanks to the information provided by the pre-trade analytics, the user of the trading algorithm can adjust its execution parameters to reduce its footprint in the market and to avoid exposure to specific events. In the case of a portfolio, some synchronization measures can be taken if its different lines have common constraints (like the same end time, or a constant exposure to a given market factor, etc.).

Monitoring indicators

Once the trading algorithm is launched, it has to be monitored by traders. One trader usually monitors several hundreds of working algorithms. The monitoring indicators are an essential element of decision support; they allow the trader to build an on the fly diagnosis of the algorithms. Typically a trader has to be able to identify as fast as possible that the trading algorithms with bad performances are concentrated on one sector, or that the associated stocks are affected by a specific news event or currently have a greater volatility than usual.

Since they are part of a decision support process, these indicators have to be built to enable a human user to make decisions, i.e. to make concrete decisions to improve the quality of execution, like on the fly modifications of execution parameters. Moreover, monitoring indicators can be used by models to autonomously identify potential causes of bad performances [Azencott *et al.*, 2013].

Performance indicators

A specific subset of monitoring indicators are direct measures of what the performance would be if the trading should stop now and others are estimates of the performance of the trading when it will end, *seen from now* if the market conditions do not change. The other monitoring indicators are to be put in perspective with the performance ones, to try to understand what is currently affecting the trading process in a negative way.

Typical performance indicators come from the decomposition of the average price of the trading algorithm according to different effects. Following Appendix A.6, one can for instance use the decomposition of formula (A.26):

$$\text{AVG Price} = \text{Immediate Price} + \text{Market Moves} + \text{Market Impact}.$$

On a benchmark by benchmark basis, such a decomposition can be refined towards:

$$\begin{aligned}\text{AVG Price} = {} & \text{Immediate Price} + \text{Planned Price} \\ & + \text{Unexpected Market Moves} + \text{Trading Efficiency} \\ & + \text{Market Impact},\end{aligned}$$

where the *"Planned price"* is what the risk control part of the trading algorithm expected on average, and the *"Trading efficiency"* rates the success of the liquidity seeking tactics used by the trading algorithm. As explained in Section 3.2, the market impact itself is very difficult to estimate, and has to be considered with respect to the timing of the trades.

Each of these components can be estimated or computed separately to understand the root of over or under performance.

'What if' scenarios?

During the trading process, it is useful to have real time clues about what the performance would be under some changes of execution conditions. *What if* I finish the order just now by aggressively capturing all the needed liquidity in the visible orderbooks? *What if* I convert my Implementation Shortfall benchmarked algo to a percentage of volume one? etc.

The outcome of some "what if" scenarios can be computed, others involve estimations. They allow a human user to make rapid decisions while being informed of their probable consequences, hence they are an important component of a suite of decision support tools.

Where to produce real time indicators?

Since it is of paramount importance that the users share indicator values with the trading algorithms, a natural solution is that the algorithms themselves produce the indicators to publish. They are thus *indicator publishers*. This is compatible with the fact that trading algorithms can be modeled as *stateless agents*, and should have introspection capabilities (see [Batali, 1983]); publishing views on their own state in real time to share with final users or companion algos is an important component of modern trading algorithms.

Post-trade analysis

The post-trade report rounds out the suite of tools composed of pre-trade, monitoring and post-trade. These three components should be compatible — for example considering one like the bid-ask spread:

- The pre-trade analysis gives an *expected average value;*
- The monitoring gives: the *current value*, the *updated expected average value*, the *likelihood of the current value* (i.e. scoring the pre-trade value) with respect to what happened so far. It also give the ability to quantify the relationship between the current trading performances and the trajectory of the bid-ask spread.
- The post-trade analysis gives an *assessment of the value of the bid-ask spread* during the trading and its influence on trading performance.

This viewpoint can be extended to all indicators used in pre-trade, monitoring and post-trade analysis. Some meaningful breakdowns are usually added to these visualizations: by sector, by currency, by country, by side (buy or sell), etc. In terms of graphical representations, the ones used in statistics apply to this suite of tools (see for instance the early work of Tukey [Cleveland, 1988] and the more recent and design-oriented work of Tufte [Tufte, 2001]).

Transaction Cost Analysis (TCA)

The TCA is the tool used by users of different algo providers to compare the efficiency of their tools. The datasets involved in TCA (several weeks of data) are larger than the ones used during the post-trade analysis (usually one day of data). The latter aims to understand what happened *because of the market context* while the former seeks to explain what part of the performance *comes from the design of the trading algorithms.* TCA hence relies on averaging using huge datasets to cancel most of the market effects, while post-trade analysis requires a fine grained analysis of market behavior.

The outcome of a proper TCA is to associate a given trading algorithm with a given market context or trading style, so that the user of the algorithms will then send flow to the proper algo provider given the market conditions. TCA thus involves breakdowns[4] according to characteristics of the market (like volatility, jumps, liquidity, occurrence of news, etc).

---

[4]The statistical methods used to identify *clusters* of market conditions associated with good or bad performance are called *statistical clustering*. See for instance Biau,

One important characteristic of the traded stocks to be taken into account during the TCA assessment is its liquidity since it is useless to compare the efficiency of an execution on a very liquid stock with one on a very illiquid one. Typical indicators used to quantify liquidity are: Bid-ask spread, tick size in basis points, *quantity on the books* (i.e. number of shares usually available "around" the first limits), daily turnover, average trade size, free float, trading rate (i.e. number of shares usually traded by minute), etc.

3.2. Market Impact Measurements: Understanding the Price Formation Process from the Viewpoint of One Investor

Several different factors could drive the market impact. Among others there are the liquidity of the traded stock, the quantity which is executed relative to the overall quantity traded by the other participants, the aggressiveness of the trading algorithm, the duration of the execution. Those elements are of importance when dealing with market impact, but they do not explain it entirely. There is another determining factor, timing (if one leaves aside liquidity tracking considerations). Trade timing describes how an order is being traded compared to what happens in the market. Let us illustrate that with the following consideration. Some executions are triggered by a signal. For instance the detection of the formation of a trend or the arrival of a signal indicating that the price is about to rise, or the rebalancing of a portfolio following an index rebalancing, or an indication that the price is about to revert back to a mean historical position. Timing tells you if you are a trend follower or a mean reverter. Timing also tells you if the way you trade makes you visible to HFT eyes. Each of the above mentioned situation will lead to a different impact on the market.

This section is a reflection on market impact at different time scales while relating to market conditions and execution parameters. We will then develop a more qualitative discussion on market impact considered from the perspective of timing. In the first part we study

---

Devroye, and Lugosi [Biau *et al.*, 2008] for theoretical aspects, or Bertrand [Bertrand, 2010] for a modern perspective of original Benzecri's work [Benzécri, 1973].

intraday market impact. We will see how market impact moves stock prices while an order is being traded. We will also see a few facts about the dependency between participation rate, duration and market impact. In the second part we will focus on market impact and investment style.

3.2.1. *Better understanding on what impacts the price*

We study the market impact on two different scales: Intraday and extraday. On the intraday scale, we see that the impact of an order being executed increases over time. It also appears that at the end of the execution the price of the traded stock tends to revert back to its level before the execution. On the extraday scale, we study the evolution of prices over a period of several days before and after the execution day. We adapt the CAPM (Capital asset pricing model) framework, which breaks down the price of assets into two components, a market component (also called systematic) and an idiosyncratic component, to the exploration of market impact. We can then separate a "market" market impact from an idiosyncratic market impact. The analysis of these two types of impacts enables us to emphasize different types of investor behavior. There are investors who have a higher impact on the market component and those who mainly affect the idiosyncratic component. These types of investors are not expected to trade the same way.

In a CAPM perspective, the price of a stock is mainly driven by two forces: a market or systematic component, and an idiosyncratic component based on information specific to the stock.

$$\text{Price} = \text{Systematic Component} + \text{Idiosyncratic Component}.$$

Market impact measures how the price of a stock moved away from its past level due to the presence of an order being executed. As in the CAPM framework, this movement could be a market-wide one or could be specific to the stock traded. In order to disentangle this combination of two different impacts, we developed a specific framework inspired by the CAPM.

$$\begin{aligned}\text{Market Impact} = {} & \text{Systematic Market Impact}\\ & + \text{Idiosyncratic Market Impact}.\end{aligned}$$

3.2.2. *Market impact over the trading period*

Theoretical development: Averaging effects. See Appendix A.13 for more details.

The major benefit of an intraday analysis of market impact is to quantify the changes in the market impact as an order is being executed and the dilution of this impact after the end of an execution. However, this requires a huge amount of execution data and the ability to process it. The difference between the price at any given time and the arrival price is a good and often used measure of market impact. Figure 3.3 shows the trend in the return of a stock according to the arrival price in units of spread over time. For this study, we used Crédit Agricole Cheuvreux executions during 2010 on components of the French CAC40 stock index.

Figure 3.3 shows the changes of the price of a stock while an order is being executed. We chose to look at the returns of the stock from

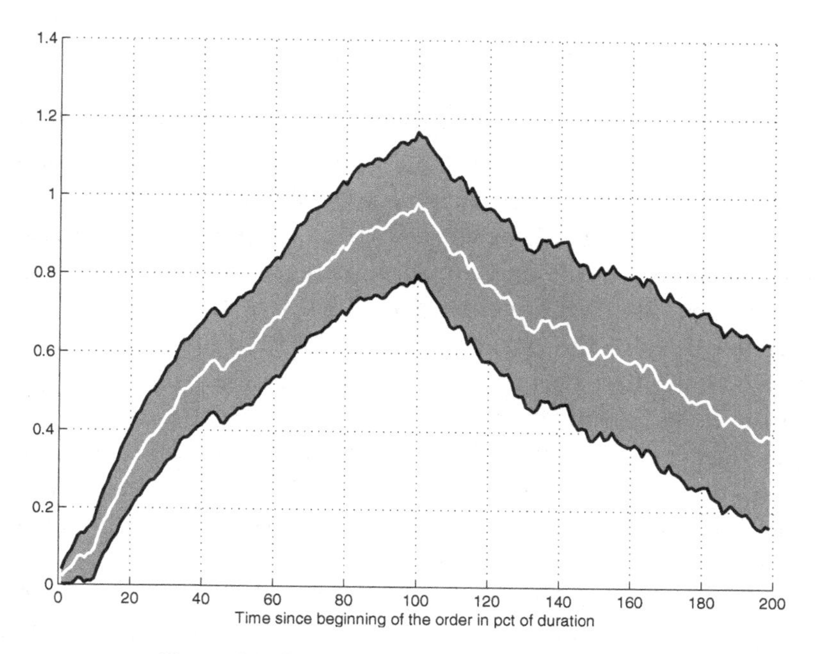

Figure 3.3. Intraday market impact in spreads.

the perspective of a buy order. This means that if the price change is above 0 at any given time, the investor will pay more to purchase a share or will get paid less to sell a share at this time versus the beginning of the execution. The x-axis is graduated in percentage of execution time. That is to say each execution starts at 0 and terminates at 100. The white curve shows the average of stock returns according to arrival price in units of spread across all the orders executed. The grey area is the 95% confidence interval of that average. The shape of the impact curve, when an order is being executed (from 0 to 100) is concave over time, or to put it another way, a slice executed at the beginning of the order has more impact than one executed at the end of an order. This kind of result is exactly the same as those found in academic studies. See for example [Moro *et al.*, 2009].

The second part of the chart in Figure 3.3, that is to say from 100 to 200, shows the stock returns after the end of the execution. The price reverts back after the execution to a level lower than that reached at the end of execution.

Market impact may depend on several parameters. There are stock-specific characteristics: Liquidity of the stock, volatility, spread size; and there are order-specific ones: Aggressiveness of the execution, quantity to execute, expected duration.

In what comes next, we focus on the structure of the dependency between market impact and different parameters, namely the participation rate (or participation liquidity ratio, PLR) and the duration of an order. We observe that the market impact increases when participation rate and duration increase, even independently.

In Figure 3.4, we have plotted curves of market impact for different values of the participation rate. These are the same kind of curve as the first part of the curve in Figure 3.3 (from 0 to 100). The grey level bar on the right of the chart indicates for each level of grey the corresponding value of the participation rate. The lowest participation rate stays near the bottom. It increases as gray gets darker. It is quite obvious that the market impact curves get steeper as the participation rate increases.

In Figure 3.5, we have indicated impact curves for different participation rates and duration values. The components of both figures are the same as those in Figure 3.4, but instead we have plotted a surface where x-axis gives the percentage of order duration,

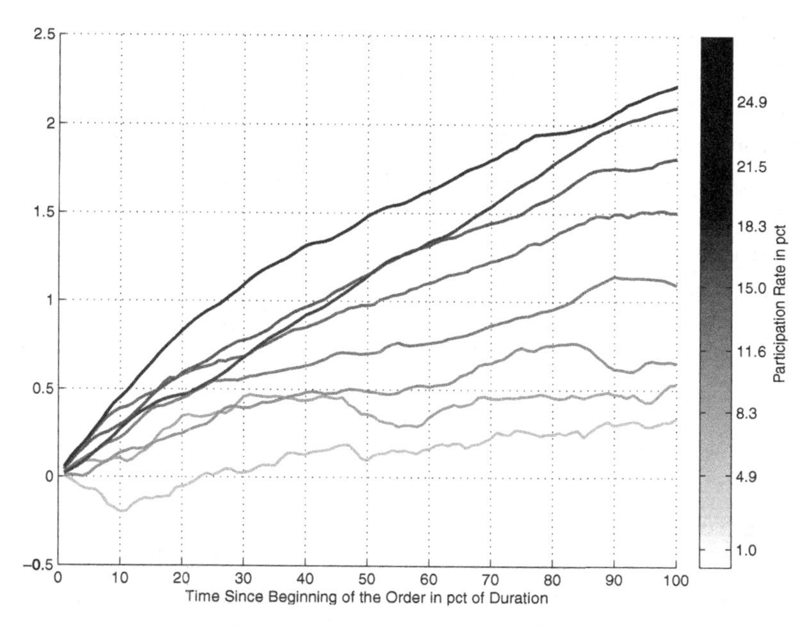

Figure 3.4. Intraday market impact in spreads depending on the participation rate.

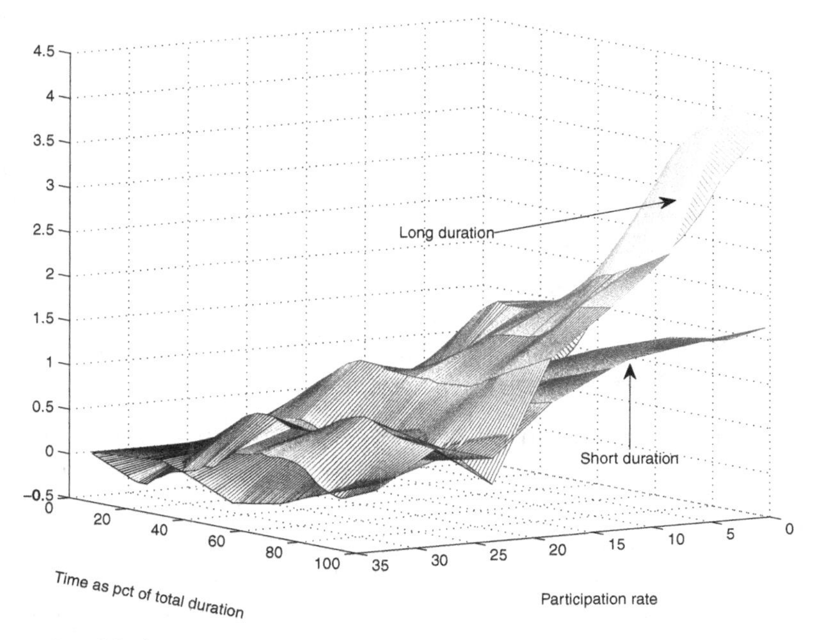

Figure 3.5. Market impact vs. participation rate for two different sets of durations.

y-axis the participation rate in percentage and z-axis the impact in number of spreads. The two surfaces correspond to two different duration sets. The short duration set gathers the executions whose duration is shorter than 25 minutes and the longer duration set the executions whose durations stay between 25 and 50 minutes. We see on this figure that the surface corresponding to the long duration set is always above the other surface indicating that the longer the duration the bigger the impact.

Based on those observations we have built a market impact model which takes into account the participation and the duration factors:

$$\text{Market Impact} \propto \text{Duration}^{\alpha} \times \text{Participation}^{\gamma}.$$

The two 3D charts in Figure 3.6 show how market impact depends on duration and on the participation rate. The dots are the average values of the market impact across buckets of duration and participation rate. The surface shows our model's prediction for the corresponding value. The duration in number of 5-minutes interval reads on the y-axis and participation rate on the x-axis. Charts (a) and (b) represent the same surface but seen from two angles. We see on those charts that the dependency of market impact on the two parameters separately is concave. This means, for instance, that the impact of one additional percent of participation rate for an order of a given duration is lower for high participation rate orders than for low participation rate orders. Moreover, the calibration of the model gave us a gamma (the scale parameter of market impact according to participation rate) approximately equal to 0.5.

3.2.3. *Market impact on a longer horizon: Different patterns for different investment styles*

The previous subsection allowed us to highlight different things about the intraday market impact. In this subsection, we will consider the problem of market impact from a slightly wider perspective. We will zoom out from 5-minute sample data to daily data.

Data analysis at this scale, using the analytical toolbox of the CAPM, will allow us to distinguish different types of investor

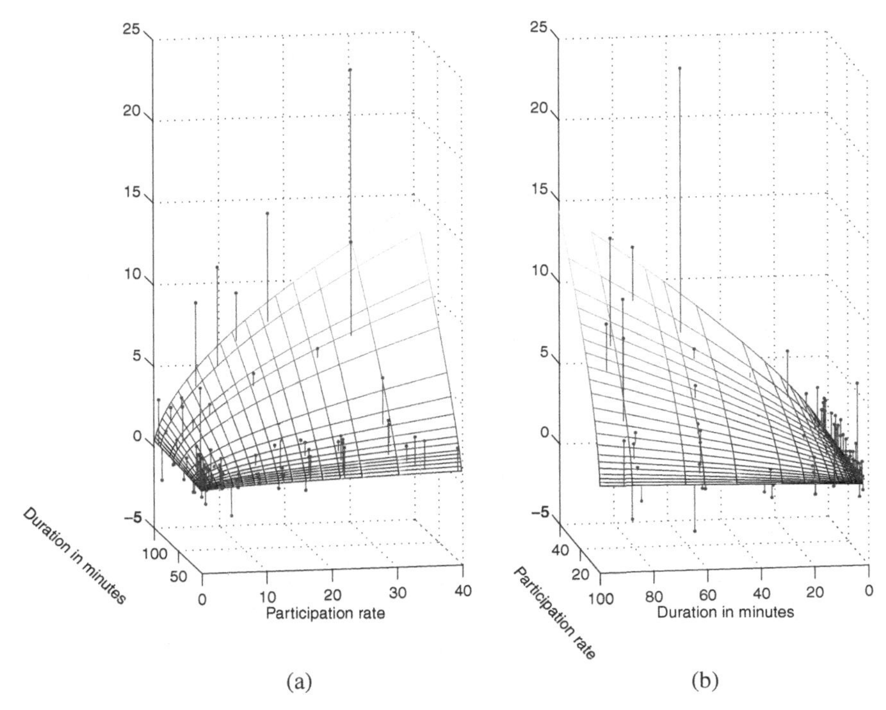

Figure 3.6. (a) Modelling of the market impact; (b) Dependence of market impact on duration and participation rate from two angles.

behavior. For instance, some investors are more keen to trade baskets of index components, thus impacting the market widely, while others trade only a few stocks: Some are trend followers, while others bet on mean reversion. The following analysis will allow us to rank the behavior and especially to show that for each of these types, there is a best type of execution. Taking into account these different types of behavior and using the recommended execution is the best way to minimize its market impact.

From now on, we will study the changes of the daily closing price of a stock over a period of several days before and after the execution date. The black curve in Figure 3.7 shows the average of price moves each day. We decided to look at closing price moves according to the closing price on the day before the execution date (date -1 in Figure 3.7). Each point of the black curve is the average of these price moves across all orders posted in 2010 by Crédit Agricole

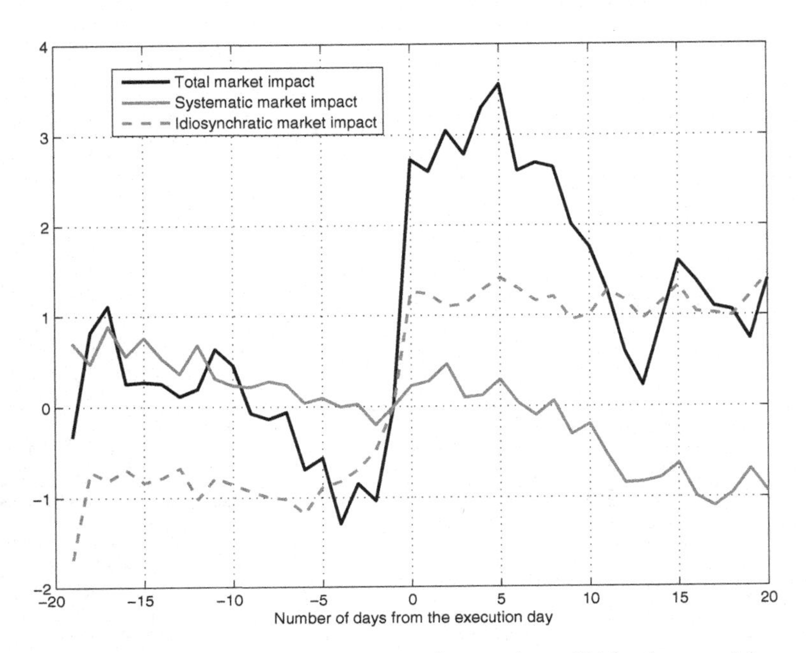

Figure 3.7. Extraday market impact (in number of bid-ask spreads).

Cheuvreux[5] depending on the distance from the execution day. Thus the point on date 0 is the average of closing price moves on the execution day and the point on date -10 the average of closing price moves ten days before the execution day. These moves are measured in number of spreads. We took the perspective of a buyer. This means that if the curve is above 0 on any given date *d*, the cost to acquire one share on *d* (or the amount received to sell one share) will be higher (or lower, if this is a sell order) than on 0. We see that the average execution day closing price is (in the case of a buy order) two or three spreads higher than the previous day's closing price.

To apply a CAPM-like approach to market impact, we broke down stock prices into systematic and idiosyncratic components. Figure 3.7 shows the average of these two components as the two grey curves. We can see in this chart that the jump present on the execution day (date 0 in Figure 3.7) is almost completely

[5]The brokerage arm of the Crédit Agricole Corporate Investment Bank.

integrated into the idiosyncratic component, indicating that, on average, investors are more likely to impact the stock price than the market.

3.2.4. *Dependence between investment style and market impact on a monthly horizon*

Let us extend the above methodological framework for the purposes of analyzing the specifics of extraday market impact according to investor behavior. The same interpretative framework can be usefully applied here to link the shape of the extraday market impact curve to investor behavior. Figure 3.8 and Figure 3.9 show curves of extraday market impact (similar to Figure 3.7) for two types of investor behavior. Note that in the first case (Figure 3.8), the black curve increases after the execution day showing that prices increase (or decrease if it is a sell order) for several days. Those investors are interested in stocks whose prices follow a trend. We call them trend-followers. In the second case (Figure 3.9), the price (black curve) of

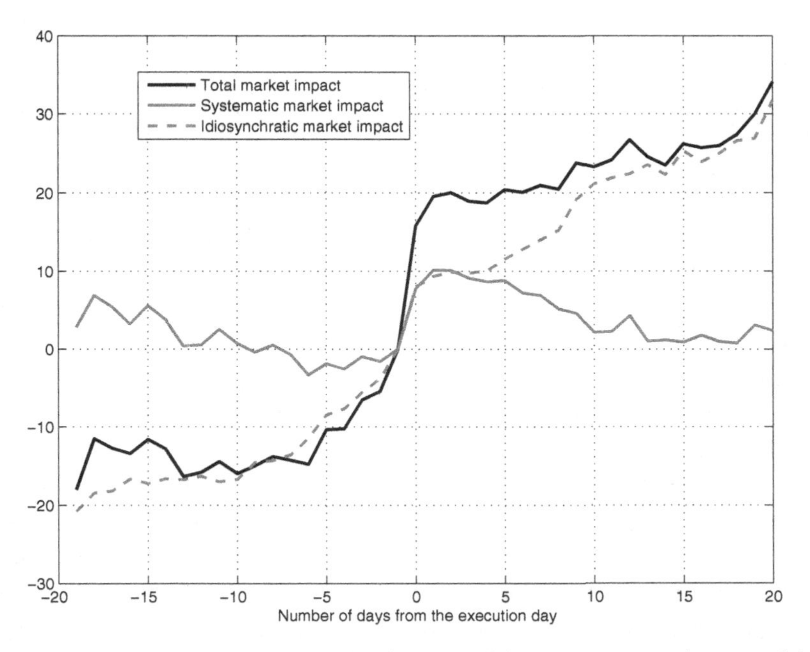

Figure 3.8. Market impact extraday for trend-follower investors (in spreads).

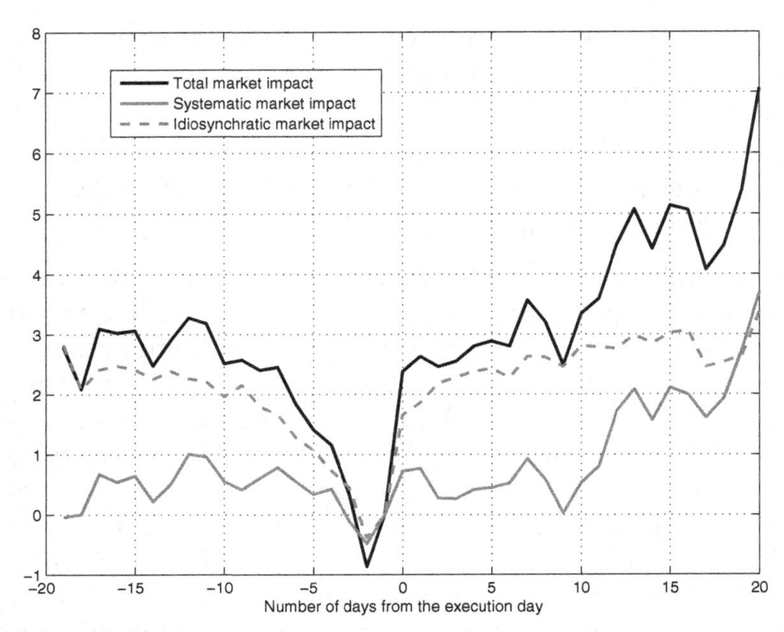

Figure 3.9. Market impact extraday for investors playing mean reversion (in spreads).

the stock after having taken a plunge recovers quickly on execution day back to its level a few days earlier. This phenomenon is a sign that we are in the presence of investors whose preferred strategy is mean reversion.

On those same figures are also plotted the breakdown of the market impact curve (black curves) into systematic (solid grey curves) and idiosyncratic (dashed grey curves) components. One can observe that the impact of the market component in Figure 3.8 is greater than in Figure 3.9. So investors who are more trend followers are more likely to impact the market than investors who are more mean reverters.

The two types of behavior presented here are very normal. The first type characterizes the trend followers, who buy exposure to the market and play long-term trends. The second type encompasses all the investors betting on mean reversion and who practice stock picking. Their market impact on the overall market is weaker than those of the first type.

3.3. Optimal Trading Methods

3.3.1. *Algorithmic trading: Adapting trading style to investors' needs*

Each trading feature has its own benchmark

Comparing the main needs in electronic execution from investors in the three main regions, it can been said that:

- In the US, where HF traders are almost everywhere, stealth trading is the main point to focus on.
- In Asia, the comparison between the efficiency of trading in each local market is very important, since it is crucial to take into account the discrepancies from one market to the next.
- In Europe, the need is a mix between avoiding being detected by HF traders, and understanding the efficiency of interacting with a set of orderbooks, to adjust order routing policies as fast as possible.

In terms of benchmarks, this implies that on paper European investors should target Implementation Shortfall (IS) benchmarks, Asian ones VWAP or Percentage of Volume (PoV), and US ones liquidity seekers. Of course, the size of the order and market conditions have to be taken into account to adjust these drastic rules: liquidity seekers are more suitable to trading orders without minimum participation rate constraints, IS are for small orders, VWAP for larger ones and PoV for very large ones.

Table 3.1 summarizes these remarks, adding information on typical market conditions naturally associated with each benchmark. The "type of hedged risk" column of this table is of importance, because a trading algorithm is always performing a "risk-reward" arbitrage. As soon as the risk it has to take care of is under control, it has the freedom to adjust the prices and quantities of orders sent to obtain good prices. Optimal execution is therefore the proper combination of risk control (via the following of an "optimal" trading rate) and price and liquidity opportunity capture. This table should not be read as "all conditions in the columns have to be fulfilled to justify the choice of the associated benchmark", but it gives information on all potential good reasons to use a given benchmark.

In terms of trading style, other characteristics have to be linked with each benchmark: The liquidity of the stock traded and the type of investment style that motivated the trade. As we have underlined in previous sections of this issue of Navigating Liquidity: Each stock has its specificities because of market design, and each investment style conditions the type of market impact that the trade will be exposed to (hedging trades are more exposed to "execution idiosyncratic impact" than long-term position-building trades that are more exposed to "systemic impact" against which trading algos cannot fight that much).

Table 3.1 is a summary of the typical stock features that are suited for such or such benchmark; the typical investment reason related to the trade; and the main expected feature of each benchmark. Table 3.2 gives the typical features of trading algorithms.

Table 3.1. Typical uses of benchmarks for trading algorithms.

Benchmark	Region of preference	Order characteristics	Market context	Type of hedged risk
PoV	Asia	Large order size (more than 10% of ADV: Average daily consolidated volume)	Possible negative news	Do not miss the rapid propagation of an unexpected news event (especially if I have the information)
VWAP/ TWAP	Asia and Europe	Medium size (from 5 to 15% of ADV)	Any "unusual" volume is negligible	Do not miss the slow propagation of information in the market
Implementation Shortfall (IS)	Europe and US	Small size (0 to 6% of ADV)	Possible price opportunities	Do not miss an unexpected price move in the stock
Liquidity Seeker	US	Any size	The stock is expected to "oscillate" around its "fair value"	Do not miss a liquidity burst or a relative price move on the stock

Table 3.2. Typical features of trading algorithms.

Benchmark	Type of stock	Type of trade	Main feature
PoV	Medium to large market depth	(1) Long duration position	(1) Follows current market flow, (2) Very reactive, can be very aggressive, (3) More price opportunity driven if the range between the max percent and min percent is large
VWAP/TWAP	Any market depth	(1) Hedging order, (2) Long duration position, (3) Unwind tracking error (delta hedging of a fast evolving inventory)	(1) Follows the "usual" market flow, (2) Good if market moves with unexpected volumes in the same direction as the order (up for a buy order), (3) Can be passive
Implementation Shortfall (IS)	Medium liquidity depth	(1) Alpha extraction, (2) Hedge of a non-linear position (typically Gamma hedging), (3) Inventory-driven trade	(1) Will finish very fast if the price is good and enough liquidity is available, (2) Will "cut losses" if the price goes too far away
Liquidity Seeker	Poor a fragmented market depth	(1) Alpha extraction, (2) Opportunistic position mounting, (3) Already split / scheduled order	(1) Relative price oriented (from one liquidity pool to another, or from one security to another), (2) Capture liquidity everywhere, (3) Stealth (minimum information leakage using fragmentation)

Theoretical development: Optimal trade scheduling. See Appendix A.6 for more details.

Customization offers multi-feature trading styles

From a practical standpoint, the benchmarks can be combined: You can add minimum or maximum participation rates to an algo to make it behave like a PoV in case of really high or low market volume during the trading; you can use a "limit price" and a "would level" to make an algo behave like an IS. You can also plug a Smart Order Router (SOR) into an algo to tweak its behavior to resemble that of a liquidity seeker.

Thanks to this you can match sophisticated benchmarks like "follow market flows if there is high volume, finish fast if the price is really low, and use as much liquidity as possible" using a VWAP or TWAP backbone with a minimum participation rate, a limit price and a SOR to send orders to trading pools (including Dark Pools).

Figure 3.10 gives an example of the combination of a VWAP and a minimum participation rate. Such "hard" combinations are what people in stochastic control call "bang-bang control": 100% of a zero or one policy is applied when a threshold is crossed. It can be gamed (if the threshold is detected, for instance) or be adversely selected (finish too early because of the constraints such as participation rates and limit prices) if the execution conditions are not chosen with enough accuracy, and are not sufficiently adapted to market conditions. A better solution to be able to merge the desired features of different benchmarks in the same trading algorithm is to base the trading logic on trading envelopes. It is first worthwhile to remark that the market data needed to build a benchmark-based policy are noisy: Because of high-frequency activity in the orderbook and uncertainty on some important parameters (of a market impact model or a volume curve, for instance). From a practical standpoint, the "optimal trading curve" to follow is expressed as a trade rate that has to be respected by the algorithm: If it obtains trades too fast with respect to this curve, it has to stop posting; if it does not obtain enough, it needs to obtain trades aggressively, paying the spread.

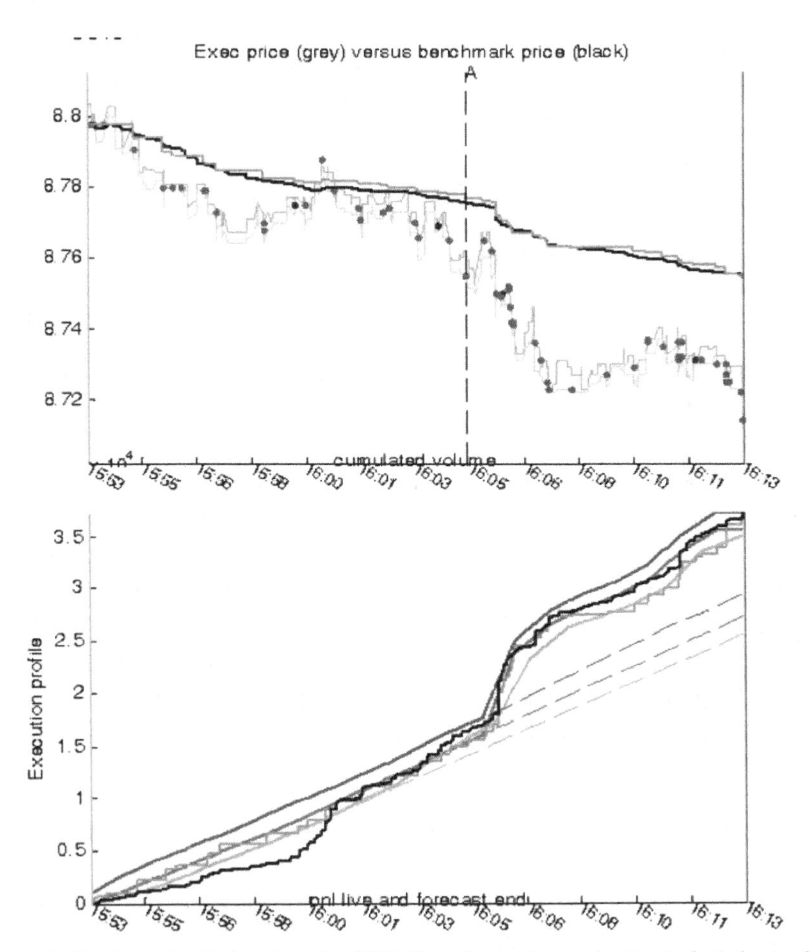

Figure 3.10. Intraday behavior of a VWAP with a min pct (activated at the end of the trading period). Top chart is for the market price (grey and dark lines are for the avg. price and the VWAP, dots for algo trades), bottom chart: The trading envelopes (upper in red, lower in green) and the trading curve (in grey) vs. the market curve (in dark).

Because of the uncertainty and noise around the analytics used, the "curve" is not a thin line at all; it is a thick one, thick enough to define in fact a "trading envelope" (see Figures 3.10 and 3.11 for such envelopes for a VWAP and an IS). Inside such an envelope, any trading trajectory cannot a priori be said to be more efficient than another from a risk-control perspective.

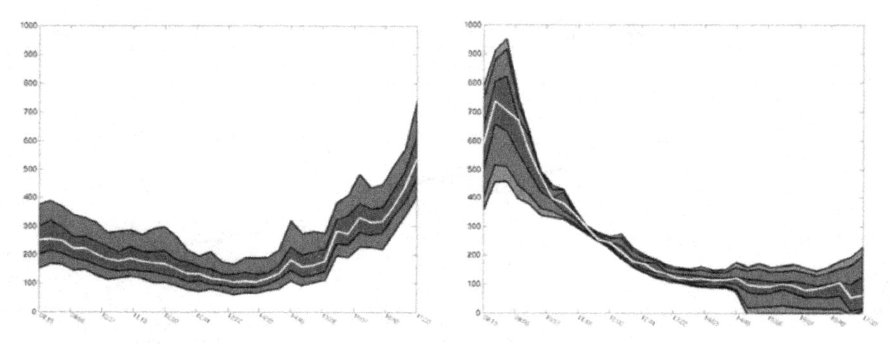

Figure 3.11. Trading envelopes at different risk levels for a VWAP (left) or an (right) trading algorithm.

Inside a trading envelope, any combination of liquidity capturing tactics can be plugged in without harming the optimality of the risk control layer (that will be called a "strategic" layer). Now that equations to build optimal trading envelopes are widely known (see, for instance [Bouchard *et al.*, 2011], [Lehalle, 2012], or [Guéant-Lehalle-Fernandez Tapia, 2012]), it is also possible to inject any volume or price-driven constraints, if needed, into the way they are built. Customization of a trading algorithm thus follows a two-step process:

1. Understanding the desired risk profile and injecting the needed constraints into the trading envelope building process.
2. Understanding the mix of liquidity adapted to the investment style and plugging the associated tactics into the envelopes with respect to properly-defined market conditions (to implement behaviors such as "go into Dark Pools if volatility increases").

3.3.2. *Liquidity seeking algorithms are no longer nice to have*

From Smart Order Routing to liquidity seeking

The multitude of trading venues can implement real competition only if there is a way to ensure the dissemination of the prices (and quotes): Any market participant should be able to evenly access all of the trading venue quoting a given instrument. Any investor should be able to access all the available liquidity at a given *marketable price*. The definition of *marketable price* itself is no longer obvious as soon as more than one trading venue exists: If destination D_1 hosts sell orders at 10.00 Euros for 50 shares, destination D_2 at 11.00 Euros for 150 shares and a trader wants to buy 50 shares up to 10.50 Euros, such a limit order is marketable on D_1 but not on D_2.

In the US the *"trade-through rule"* (see [Jickling, 2005]) demands that trading venues themselves re-route orders that are marketable at a better price elsewhere. In Europe the executing broker is in charge of the kind of re-routing; he has to disclose to his clients a *"best execution policy"* explaining his re-routing methodology.

The difference is of paramount importance:

- In the US the trading venues have to be able to access to an official *consolidated orderbook* (or consolidated pre-trade tape). Moreover the clearing and settlement fees/costs have to be the same for all trading venues, otherwise a market participant could direct a marketable order on a venue that seems to offer a cheaper price than another but at the end of the day the market participant will pay more (all costs included).
- In Europe the executing brokers are in charge to select themselves the way they offer a consolidated access to liquidity, and have to prove it. It increases the cost of fragmentation for the intermediaries and demands that the investors are able to understand the stakes of these "consolidation services".

A typical example of smart routing

Let us assume that Table 3.3 (Figure 3.12 for a graphical representation of this orderbook) is the state of the orderbooks on the ask side (resting sell orders) on Chi-X, Euronext, and Turquoise on a given stock. Suppose further that a trader wants to buy 500 shares at *any price* (i.e. using a market order).

Add to this example three executing brokers:

- Broker B_1's best execution policy includes Euronext and Chi-X only, and he uses a smart order router splitting an order to obtain the best average price;

Table 3.3. An example of European orderbook on the ask side.

Price	Euronext	Chi-X	Turquoise
104.00	300	200	200
103.00	125	175	100
102.00	100	200	150
101.00	100	100	100
100.00	50	25	50
99.00	25		

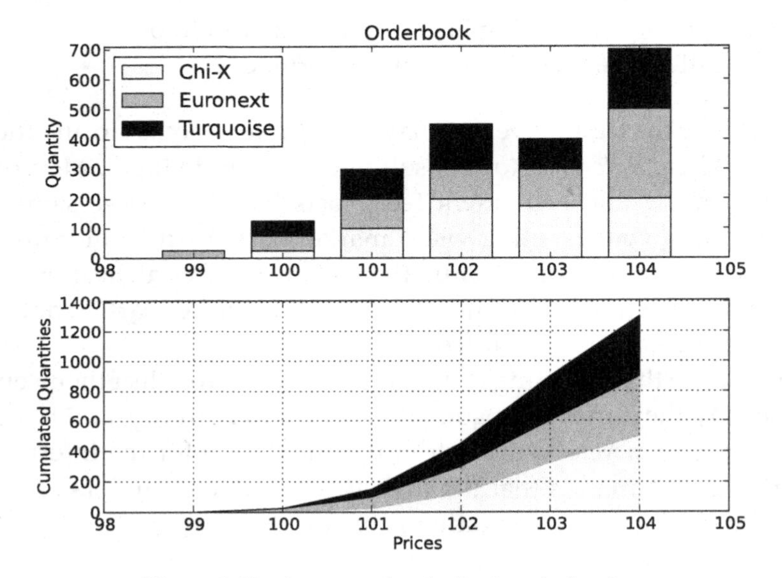

Figure 3.12. An example of a limit orderbooks.

- Broker B_2's best execution policy gives access to Euronext, Chi-X, and Turquoise, and he uses a smart order router choosing the venue offering the best price;
- Broker B_3's best execution policy gives access to Euronext, Chi-X, and Turquoise, and he uses a smart order router splitting an order to obtain the best average price.

It is easy to compute the outcome for the trader if he chooses each broker (given that there is no latency issue; the brokers are below the Nyquist-Shannon latency bound, cf. introduction):

- Broker B_1 obtains an average price of 101.15 Euros, consuming up to 4 limits of the books of Euronext $(25+50+100+100)$ and Chi-X $(0 + 25 + 100 + 200)$;
- Broker B_2 obtains a price of 102.50, on Chi-X only which is the cheapest venue;
- Broker B_3 obtains an average price of 100.75, consuming up to 4 limits in the three books $(25+50+100$ on Euronext, $0+25+100$ on Chi-X and $0 + 50 + 100$ on Turquoise; the remaining 50 on any of the three venues).

It is worthwhile to note that broker B_3 has a choice: He can buy the 50 shares at 102.00 on any of the three venues; surely he will use the cheapest one in terms of trading costs/fees.

Impact of trading costs/fees

One can question if a difference in trading fees can have such an importance that instead of removing liquidity on venue V at price P with fees f, it could be cheaper to remove liquidity on another venue V' at an higher price (for a buy order) $P(1+\delta)$ (where $P\delta$ is a tick size in Euro) because of cheaper fees (say the fees on V' are f' and on V they are f such that $f' = f - \phi$).

Having a better price on venue V' than on V (for a quantity Q) reads

$$P\,(1+\delta)\,(1+f-\phi)\,Q < P\,(1+f)\,Q$$

that is equivalent to having the tick size (in basis points) small enough:

$$\delta < \left(1 - \frac{\phi}{1+f}\right)^{-1} - 1 \simeq \phi.$$

This means that the tick size should be as small as the fee difference (for instance if the value of one share in 100 Euros and the fees are cheaper by 0.1 bp on one venue compared to the other, the tick should be smaller than 0.1 cent so that this kind of arbitrage occurs). Figure 3.13 shows this relationship with $\rho = \phi/f$. It can be read that the tick size up to which it is worthwhile to use a "worse price but better fees" increases with the relative difference of fees ρ.

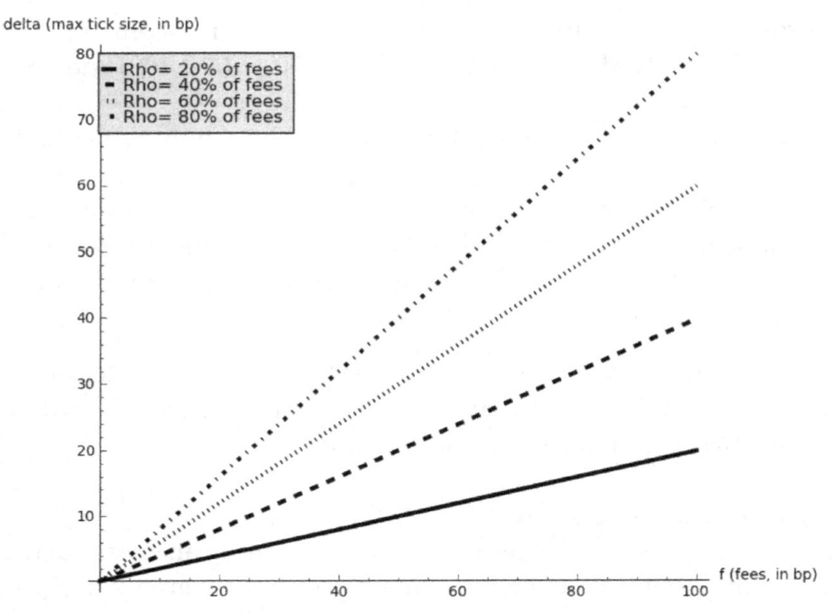

Figure 3.13. Relation between the fees on two venues and the corresponding critical tick size value. For a given value of fees on one venue (x-axis), the y-value is the maximum tick size giving advantage to another venue improving the fees by ρ percent (cf legend).

Impact of latency

Coming back to our example with three brokers, we have seen that broker B_3 seems to offer the best average price, but what if the orderbooks are read with latency or if mirrored liquidity existed in the orderbook?

For instance assume that the 50 shares offered at 100.00 Euros on Turquoise are a duplication (i.e. mirror) of the 100 shares at the same price on Euronext and the 100 at 101.00 (on Turquoise again) are duplicated on Chi-X. Assume also:

- The brokers B_1, B_2 and B_3 have the same latencies to all three venues: 1 ms (millisecond) to Euronext, 1.5 ms to Chi-X Europe and 3 ms to Turquoise,
- the "high frequency trader" who duplicated these 150 shares is co-located in the Euronext and Chi-X datacenters ($\sim$0 ms) and has a latency of 1 ms to Turquoise.

Hence the orders sent by any of the brokers will reach Euronext 2 ms (and Chi-X 1.5 ms) before Turquoise, the HFT will notice it and cancel his 150 (i.e. $100 + 50$) shares on Turquoise *before* the order of the broker reaches Turquoise.

Broker B_3, even if on paper his split is optimal, will see 150 shares not executed on Turquoise. The next question is: What will be the state of the orderbook when he finds out that he has 150 shares remaining to buy? He will know that $6 = 2 \times 3$ ms later; who knows what will be the state of the orderbook then? If the price is rising one can bet that orders above 102.00 Euros will have been canceled.... Thus the price he will finally obtain will be worse than the one offered by broker B_1.

As a conclusion to this example, it can be said that what is important is not the liquidity that can be seen in the orderbooks, but the *probability that you will be able to obtain liquidity at a given price level when your order reaches the orderbooks, taking into account the latency discrepancies between venues, the mirrored orders and hidden liquidity*.

Seeking an optimal liquidity capturing scheme

We have just underlined that liquidity seeking should take place at high frequency to compensate the effect of fragmentation. Moreover the previous example, dealing with a marketable order (i.e. a buy market order or a buy order with a limit price higher than the best ask price on at least one trading venue), has shown that effects to take into account are:

- The probability of hidden liquidity in the orderbooks,
- the probability that, when the latency to all venues is not the same, a high frequency trader took advantage of the information conveyed by a market order reaching one venue to cancel his liquidity providing orders.

For a limit order (i.e. a buy order with a limit price strictly lower than the best ask price), a lot of other phenomena have to be taken into account.

Table 3.4. An example of European orderbook on the bid side.

	Price	Euronext	Chi-X	Turquoise
	101.00	50	100	75
(Ask)	100.00	75		25
	...	...	...	...
(Bid)	97.00	50		25
	96.00	75	20	75
	95.00	325	80	100

Example of a passive split

Let's say that a market participant wants to buy 500 shares at a price of 95.00 Euros, but the best ask on available venues is 100.00 Euros or more. Moreover, assume that on the bid side, the state of the orderbook is described in Table 3.4.

This means that any order inserted:

- In Euronext orderbook at 95.00 will see 450 shares before it in the waiting queue,
- in Chi-X at the same price will see 100 shares with a better priority,
- in Turquoise at 95.00 again will have to wait 200 shares to be sold before being consumed.

Looking at these figures only, one can expect an optimal split to allocate less quantity on venues with more shares with a better position in the queue. With respect to this criterion, the priority should be: *More on Chi-X, then on Turquoise, and the remaining on Euronext.*

But looking at the ask side, one should conclude that market participants are *more aggressive on Euronext, then on Turquoise, and finally on Chi-X*. This is clearly not the same ordering as looking just on the bid side.

Last but not least, the *immediate selling flow* on each venue could be taken into account. Let's say that according to recent trades:

- On Euronext buy orders hit the 95.00 price level at a rate of 100 shares per 10 seconds,
- on Chi-X the selling rate at 95.00 is 50 shares per 10 seconds,
- on Turquoise it is 50 shares per 10 seconds.

Table 3.5. Some results for the passive posting example.

Variable	Euronext	Chi-X	Turquoise
$\tau(500)$	95 sec	120 sec	140 sec
τ^*	62.5 sec	62.5 sec	62.5 sec
f_n	35.0%	42.5%	22.5%
$f_n \cdot D$	175	212	113

With respect to the trading rate: *Euronext is number one then Chi-X and Turquoise have the same rank.*

From a quantitative viewpoint, combining a sell rate r_n and the number of shares with a better priority Q_n (on trading destination number n) is not very difficult since the time to consume an order of size D (on average) is:

$$\tau_n(D) = \frac{D + Q_n}{r_n}. \tag{3.1}$$

This quantity for each venue can be read on Table 3.5: According to this measure *Euronext is better than Chi-X which is better than Turquoise.*

But a trader could do more than this: He can split the order to minimize the average time to completion of the whole order. This means that an order of 500 shares can be split in $500 \times f_1, 500 \times f_2, 500 \times f_3$ (such that all the order is split: i.e. $\sum_{n=1}^{3} f_n = 1$) and such that $\tau_n(D f_n)$ is the same (and minimum) on all venues.

It is not very difficult to check[6] that this *minimum resting time* τ^* of an order of size D satisfies:

$$\tau^* = \frac{D - \sum_n Q_n}{\sum_n r_n}. \tag{3.2}$$

It is then easy to deduce any f_n using the formula:

$$f_n = \frac{\tau^* r_n - Q_n}{D}.$$

[6]Using classical results of linear constraint optimization (i.e. Lagrangian multipliers [Bellman, 1956]), there should exist a constant τ^* such that for any n: $(f_n D - Q_n)/r_n = \tau^*$. It reads $f_n D = \tau^* r_n + Q_n$. Summing over n and taking into account the constraint (i.e. $\sum_n f_n = 1$) we obtain $D = \tau^* \sum_n r_n - \sum_n Q_n$. Equation (3.2) is then straightforward.

Table 3.6. Summary of the examples.

Criterion	1st venue	2nd venue	3rd venue
Rank in the queue	Chi-X	Turquoise	Euronext
Distance to the best	Euronext	Turquoise	Chi-X
Trading rate	Euronext	Chi-X or Turquoise	
Minimum resting time	Chi-X	Euronext	Turquoise

The associated results are in Table 3.5. It can be seen that *with respect to the minimum average resting time criterion: 212 shares have to be sent to Chi-X, 175 to Euronext and 113 to Turquoise.*

Table 3.6 summarizes the ranking of the venue for each possible criterion. The last row has the advantage to give exact numbers for the split. More detailed (and accurate) splitting methods can be derived from the *stochastic algorithm theory* (see [Laruelle *et al.*, 2011]).

Building a liquidity seeker

From a practical standpoint, a liquidity seeker has to take care of:

- Removing liquidity optimally using estimates of the hidden liquidity (including any potentially available in Dark Pools), the mirrored orders, and the latency to each venue open to trading;
- Posting limit orders optimally to end an order as fast as possible.

Note that:

- The specifics of Dark Pools have been described in Section 1.4 in Chapter 1 and have to be handled by liquidity seekers,
- the potential adverse selection that could be generated by ending an order *as fast as possible* should be solved by an optimal trading scheme at an higher time scale (10 minutes to few hours); Appendix A.6 gives elements to answer to this.

Such a liquidity seeking robot can be seen as an enhanced limit order. The typical duration of such a robot should be 10 minutes for very liquid stocks to few hours for highly illiquid ones.

This does not mean that liquidity should not been captured by similar means during longer periods, but in such a case adverse selection is of first order. Hence an optimal trading scheme should be put in place to avoid going too fast with respect to the expected price range (i.e. driven by intraday volatility).

Once either the expected fill rate or liquidity in the orderbook is known, and on the other hand the liquidity to be found in the orderbooks is known too, it is not that hard to choose a criterion and to derive from it a liquidity seeking scheme (see [Laruelle *et al.*, 2011] and [Laruelle *et al.*, 2013]); the hardest part is to obtain accurate estimates of the fill rate and real liquidity.

Like in Dark Pools (see Chapter 1, Section 1.4), liquidity in any pool is *clustered*, meaning that once a trade has occurred, the probability of observing another one increases.

Theoretical development: Clusters of liquidity. See Appendix A.11 for more details.

Using such estimates, it is possible to allocate a quantity to trade across different trading venues. Figure 3.14 gives typical "fill rate

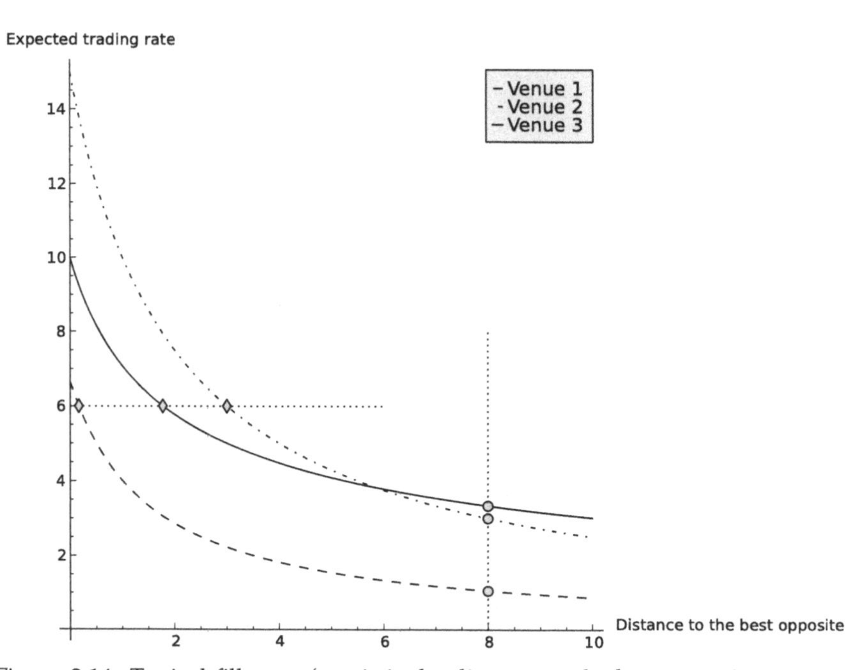

Figure 3.14. Typical fill rates (x-axis is the distance to the best opposite, y-axis is the expected fill rate) for three arbitrary trading venues.

curves": On the x-axis, the distance to the best opposite (zero means that the order is aggressive, obtaining a fill immediately), and on the y-axis the "expected fill rate" (named in applied maths the "intensity of the trading point process"). Each line decreases when the distance to the best opposite (best bid for a sell order, best ask for a buy order) increases (to the right of the x-axis) and each line is different because at a given time, the liquidity provided by each pool at different depths varies.

It is therefore possible to allocate fractions of an order on these lines (Figure 3.14):

- To obtain price improvement (horizontal line — i.e. diamonds — in the figure), allocate more quantity to the pool providing the same fill rate as others but at a better price;
- To obtain fast completion (vertical line — i.e. circles — in the figure), allocate more quantity to the pool, providing higher fill rates at the same price.

Appendix A

Quantitative Appendix

A.1. From Entropy to FEI (Fragmentation Efficiency Index)

Entropy is used in physics to measure the disorder level of matter (see [Feynman *et al.*, 1989]): the second law of thermodynamics states that the entropy of an isolated system always increases or remains constant. For instance if you lock a gas in a room, it is first in a disorganized state (particles can be accumulated in some places), as time passes, the gas tend to organise itself more uniformly. During this type of relaxation, the entropy is a physical measurement that changes: It increases.

Entropy has been used in mathematics and information theory to measure the order of any mapping or message (see [Arnold, 2011] or [Shannon, 1948]). It is now used in statistics ([Billingsley, 1978]) to discover relationships between variables, using the fact when you associate one variable X to a variable Y, the system (Y, X) is less disorganized than Y alone meaning that X can be used to explain Y (for instance in a regression, see Section A.9).

The analogy between gas in a room and liquidity in a market is not very difficult to explain: If the microstructure would follow the law of matter, the liquidity, like the gas, would naturally spread over all available venues and uniformly fill a room. Comparing the entropy of the liquidity now to the maximum it could give clues about how far from a 100% relaxed state the microstructure is.

The formula for entropy used to define the FEI (Fragmentation Efficiency Index) models the microstructure by N trading venues $\mathcal{T}(1), \ldots, \mathcal{T}(N)$, assuming that in a relaxed state the liquidity could find its way to any of them at the same cost. The "ideal" repartition of liquidity over such N pools should be $1/N$ of it in each of them.

Once the repartition of liquidity is measured in each trading venue by quantities q_n summing to one, for instance using the market share $\mathfrak{M}(n)$ defined in Section 1.1.1, the formula of entropy of the configuration $(q_1, \ldots, q_N)$ can be applied:

$$H(q_1, \ldots, q_N) = -\sum_{1 \le n \le N} q_n \log q_n \tag{A.1}$$

(by convention we will take $0 \cdot \log 0 = 0$).

It can be easily seen that:

- When only one liquidity pool is available, the entropy of the system is zero;
- When all the liquidity is concentrated into one pool only (i.e. for some n, $q_n = 1$ and for the others $q_{n'} = 0$) then the entropy of the system is zero;
- When the same amount of liquidity is in each pool (i.e. for any n, $q_n = 1/N$) then

$$H(1/N, \ldots, 1/N) = -N \times \frac{1}{N} \log \frac{1}{N} = \log N. \tag{A.2}$$

The repartition maximizing the entropy can also be found, for instance, by solving the following maximization program:

$$\left\| \begin{array}{ll} \text{Maximize} & -\sum_{1 \le n \le N} q_n \log q_n \\ \text{Variable} & (q_1, \ldots, q_N) \\ \text{Constraint} & \sum_n q_n = 1 \end{array} \right.$$

using a Lagrangian multiplier λ to express the fact that at the extremum, the slope of the criterion to maximize is tangent to the constraint, it gives $\forall n$, $\log q_n - 1 = \lambda$. All the q_n being equal implies that their value is $q_n = 1/N$ for all of them. Added to this, equation (A.2) says that **the maximum possible entropy** is $\log(N)$. This allows us to define the FEI:

Definition 1 (FEI (Fragmentation Efficiency Index)). *The FEI (Fragmentation Efficiency Index) of a distribution of liquidity* $q_1, \ldots, q_N$ *for*

N liquidity pools is the ratio of the entropy $H(q_1, \ldots, q_N)$ divided by the maximum possible entropy over N pools (i.e. $\log(N)$*):*

$$\mathfrak{F}(q_1, \ldots, q_N) = \frac{H(q_1, \ldots, q_N)}{\log N} = \frac{-\sum_{1 \le n \le N} q_n \log q_n}{\log N}. \tag{A.3}$$

The FEI value is in $[0, 1]$*, with a minimum value of* 0 *when the liquidity is highly concentrated on few pools, and* 1 *when it is uniformly spread.*

Some comments have to be made about this measurement of liquidity:

- The FEI measures the *efficiency* of the repartition across liquidity pools comparing it to a uniform one;
- The closer to 0, the more concentrated is the liquidity, in this sense it can be said that the microstructure is *inefficient*, since each pool does not provide the same amount of liquidity. In terms of **optimal trading**, this means that a trader will have to pay a lot of attention before spraying its order in a low FEI market.
- The closer to 1, the less concentrated is the liquidity. It means that all liquidity sources are *equal* (taking into account all the criteria implicitly valued by market participants): In this sense the fragmentation is *efficient*. From a trading perspective, this also means that **in a high FEI microstructure, a trader does not need to pay much attention to smart routing**, since all sources are valued equivalently by the participants.
- The FEI is very useful to monitor fragmentation through time: Instead of following N market shares $q_1(t), \ldots, q_N(t)$, it is enough (and easier to read) to follow one scalar: $F(t) = \mathfrak{F}(q_1(t), \ldots, q_N(t))$.
- The reference number of considered trading venues N is of importance, since if from one day t to the next $t+1$, a new trading venue opens trading, changing N to $N+1$, then if this venue is empty on day one, the FEI will go from $\mathfrak{F}(t) = H(q_1(t), \ldots, q_N(t))/\log N$ to $\mathfrak{F}(t+1) = H(q_1(t), \ldots, q_N(t), 0)/\log(N+1)$. This means that in this specific case:

$$\mathfrak{F}(t+1) = \frac{\log N}{\log(N+1)} \cdot \mathfrak{F}(t).$$

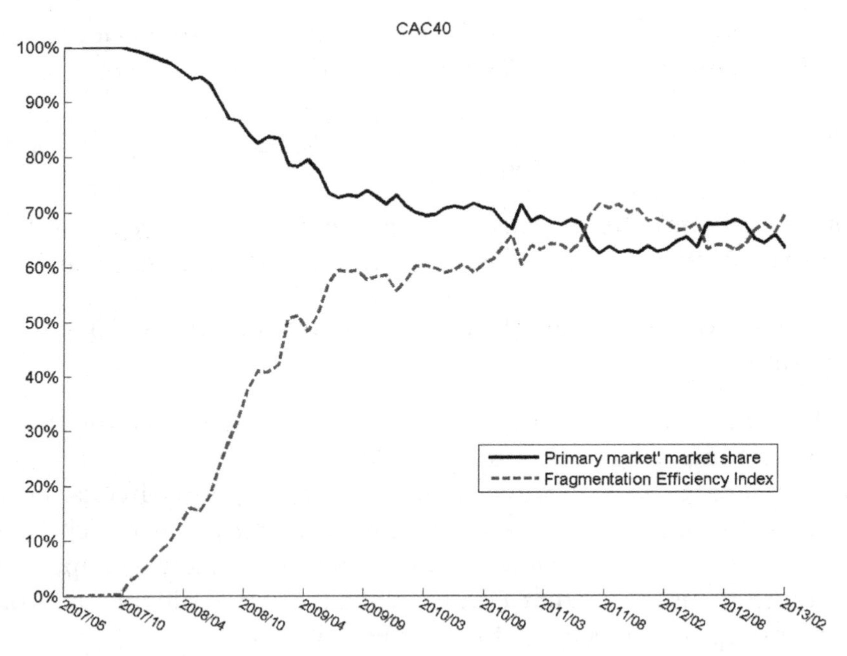

Figure A.1. (a) Market shares and (b) FEI on the CAC40 during MiFID 1.

An empirical rule can be used to smooth this kind of effect, for instance including a venue in the FEI only if it gathers at least 1% of market share (just note that for $N = 3$, $\log N / \log(N+1) \simeq 80\%$ and for $N = 6$ it is around 90%).

Figure A.1 visually compares the FEI and the market shares on the components of the CAC40 during a few years. All the information contained in the market shares can be seen on the FEI.

A.2. Information Seeking and Price Discovery

The market structure implied by MiFID in Europe raised a lot of questions, among them:

- The relative roles of "HFMM (High Frequency Market Makers)",
- the possible negative externalities linked to their activity (especially because they use more technology than other market participants),
- the impact of the fee schedules on the efficiency of the PFP (Price Formation Process).

In 2009 in [Foucault *et al.*, 2009], Foucault, Kadan and Kandel provided a theoretical model allowing us to understand all these effects. This section contains a summary of this model and some comments about it.

In this model the market participants are split into two groups: One containing M high frequency market makers (HFMM) and the other containing N *market takers* who could be called *longer term investors*. The paper only describes a model for buying investors, but it can easily be extend to selling ones. From the viewpoint of investors: They buy if the current market price of a security is v_0 and they valuate it at $v_0 + \Gamma$. On the other side the HFMM will agree to sell them at $v_0 + s \cdot \Delta$ (where s is the *liquidity premium* they ask to provide liquidity expressed in the tick size Δ). The two of them pay trading fees to the trading venue that are c_t for market takers (liquidity removing orders) and c_m for market makers (liquidity adding orders).

When a trade occurs, each type of market participant has its own earning:

- The HFMM earns $\pi_M = s \cdot \Delta - c_M$,
- the investor earns $\pi_T = \Gamma - s \cdot \Delta - c_T$,
- the trading venue consequently earns $\bar{c} = c_T + c_M$.

The model is interesting because it takes into account the *time to reach the orderbook* of each participant. It will allow us to understand how technological investments change the dynamics of the market microstructure. The mth market maker has an average time to market of $1/\mu_m$ and the nth investor (using brokerage trading algorithms) has an average time to market of $1/\tau_n$. The exact model of time to market is a Poisson process (see [Bremaud, 1981] for more details), that will allow us to obtain closed form formula. On average the time to market of market makers $1/\bar{\mu}$ and the ones of investors $1/\bar{\tau}$ satisfy:

$$\bar{\mu} = \sum_{m=1}^{M} \mu_m, \quad \bar{\tau} = \sum_{m=1}^{M} \tau_m.$$

Market makers are competing among themselves; the one who can come first will have the trade against an investor. Similarly investors are competing among themselves — the fastest will obtain the liquidity offered by the market maker. In this model there is no direct competition between market makers and investors. According to the model the duration between two trades is on average: $(\bar{\mu} + \bar{\tau})/(\bar{\mu} \cdot \bar{\tau})$. This means that the average number of trades per unit of time is $\mathcal{R} = (\bar{\mu} \cdot \bar{\tau})/(\bar{\mu} + \bar{\tau})$.

The race to low latency is not free, we will assume that the cost borne by HFMMs C_m and investors C_t is not the same, taking into account that the level of requirement and regulatory constraints is for instance greater for an investor than for a high frequency trader. To reach a time to market parameter $1/t$ (i.e. μ_m for an HFMM and τ_n for an investor) the costs will be, respectively:

$$C_M(1/t) = \frac{1}{2}\beta\frac{\mathbf{T}}{t^2} \quad \text{and} \quad C_T(1/t) = \frac{1}{2}\gamma\frac{\mathbf{T}}{t^2},$$

where $\mathbf{T}$ is the typical duration of one trading day. The cost differentiators to access low latency are thus β for the HFMM and γ for the investor.

All this allows to write the average gain of each participant:

- The mth HFMM will gain

$$\Pi_M(m) = \underbrace{\frac{\mu_m}{\bar{\mu}}}_{\text{own participation}} \cdot \underbrace{\pi_M}_{\text{gain}} \cdot \underbrace{\mathcal{R}}_{\text{nbe of trades}} - \underbrace{\frac{1}{2}\beta\mu_m^2}_{\text{technological costs}}$$

- Similarly, a given investor n will gain:

$$\Pi_T(n) = \frac{\tau_n}{\bar{\tau}} \cdot \pi_T \cdot \mathcal{R} - \frac{1}{2}\gamma\, \tau_m^2$$

- The operator of the trading destination earns:

$$\Pi_E = \bar{c} \cdot \mathcal{R} = (c_M + c_T) \cdot \mathcal{R}.$$

One of the interesting results of the paper is that, once each market participant optimized its technological investment, the imbalance between the taker fees c_T^* and the maker fees c_M^* are known thank to this formula:

$$c_M^* = s \cdot \Delta - \frac{\Gamma - \bar{c}}{1 + \left(\frac{M}{N} \cdot \frac{\gamma}{\beta}\right)^{1/3}}, \text{ given that } \bar{c} = c_T^* + c_M^*. \tag{A.4}$$

This interesting formula can be interpreted as follows:

- $\Gamma - \bar{c}$ (the investor gain minus the fees) is obviously larger than $s \cdot \Delta$ (the market maker gain/premium);
- when there are few market makers (M is small), *the efficient maker fees can be negative* (i.e. rebate for high frequency market makers);
- when there are a lot of market makers (M is large compared to the number of investors N) or when the technological costs borne by investors are larger than the one for HFMM, *the efficient taker fees can be negative* (i.e. rebate for investors).

Figure A.2 shows how the efficient maker fees can range from negative (rebate) to positive with respect to the imbalance between the HFMM and the investors on the one hand, and between the technological costs of these two type of market participants on the other hand.

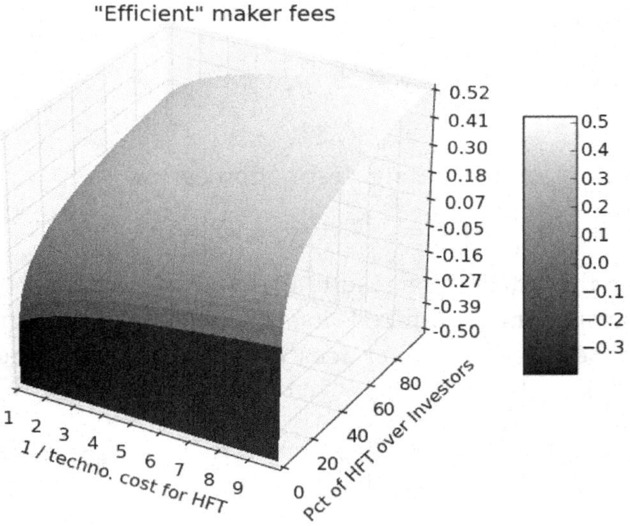

"Efficient" maker fees

Figure A.2. Variation of the maker fees with respect to the proportion of high frequency market makers and the relative technological costs borne by investors vs HFMM. It can be seen that when the number of HFT increases, the fees are no longer a rebate (it become positive), and that when the technological costs of the HFT decreases, the fees should become positive again too.

A.3. A Simple Model Explaining the Natural Fragmentation of Market Microstructure

Some academic papers (like [Foucault and Menkveld, 2008]) study in detail the influence of the use of SORs (Smart Order Routers) on the fragmentation of the market and on the information shared by market participants of a PFP (Price Formation Process) hosted by a double auction mechanism. Others present ways to optimize the trading from the viewpoint of one trader using one smart order router (see [Laruelle *et al.*, 2011] for smart order routing across Dark Pools). The model presented here does not target an in depth understanding of final equilibrium that would be attained, but on the components of the dynamics driving a monopolistic "meta-market" to a fragmented one.

Let's say that once a monopoly is broken (like it has been by MiFID in Europe), some new competitors appear quickly (think about Chi-X, Turquoise and NASDAQ-OMX) so that the initial state of the fragmentation across the K available trading venues is $p(0) = (p_1(0), \ldots, p_K(0))'$ (for instance $p(0) = (80\%, 15\%, 2\%, 3\%)'$). This list of probabilities captures the initial capability of each venue to attract transactions. As widely discussed in this book, this capability comes from a combination of fee schedules (see Appendix A.2), market making agreements (see Section 2.3 of Chapter 2), connections of market participants (see Section 3.1 of Chapter 3), etc.

Some market participants are equipped with a SOR (i.e. the device allowing them to automate the split of a limit or market order across different trading venues according to home-made analytics, the first of them being snapshots of available orderbooks and short term history of where trades took place). Such SORs will be considered to be "optimal" in the sense that they aim to maximize the amount of liquidity they capture.

A.3.1. *A toy model of SOR dynamics*

Say that at any time the liquidity available in the kth trading venue when asked is $D_k(\omega)$, including any arbitrary increase or decrease in the near future. The variable ω represents the stochastic aspect of liquidity. ω changes from one request to the next, potentially leading to a different value for each D_k.

Any SOR receiving an order of size $V(\omega)$ will split it according to a current repartition key $r(t) = (r_1(t), \ldots, r_K(t))'$. As stated before, r is built to maximize the captured liquidity, i.e. to maximize this criterion:

$$\mathcal{C}(r(t), \omega) = \sum_{k=1}^{K} \min\left(r_k(t) \cdot V(\omega), D_k(\omega)\right)$$

on average. The "average" comes from the fact that through time, each SOR will be confronted with various configurations of liquidity, represented by $(V(\omega), D_1(\omega), \ldots, D_K(\omega))'$.

It can be shown (see Appendix A.2), that an optimal solution to:

$$\left|\begin{array}{ll} \text{Minimize} & \mathbb{E}_\omega\left(\sum_{k=1}^{K} \min\left(r_k \cdot V(\omega), D_k(\omega)\right)\right) \\ \text{Variables} & r_1, \ldots, r_K \\ \text{Constraint} & \sum_k r_k = 1 \end{array}\right. \tag{A.5}$$

where $\mathbb{E}(\,\cdot\,)$ means "expectation" (i.e. "on average") satisfies for any k:

$$\mathbb{E}\left(\frac{1}{K}\sum_{\ell=1}^{K} \mathbf{1}_{r_\ell \cdot V_\ell < D_\ell} - \mathbf{1}_{r_k \cdot V_k < D_k}\right) = 0 \tag{A.6}$$

meaning that the average efficiencies of each venue are equal when a fraction r_k of the order is asked to the kth.

The most an SOR can do, because of the randomness of liquidity available on each pool (incarnated by the ω here), is implement a "trial and error" or "learn by trading" process. This process will be close to a progressive reassessment of the value of r close to this one:

$$r_k(\omega + 1) = r_k(\omega) + \gamma_\omega\left(\frac{1}{K}\sum_{\ell=1}^{K} \mathbf{1}_{r_\ell \cdot V_\ell < D_\ell} - \mathbf{1}_{r_k \cdot V_k < D_k}\right) \tag{A.7}$$

where ω is used as an "iterator" since the SOR sees sequential requests to split $V(1), V(2), \ldots, V(\omega), \ldots$ and readjusts its repartition key r.

This is a reinforcement learning procedure that will naturally conduct a partition satisfying equality (A.6) so long as an average through time is roughly equivalent to an ensemble average on r (technically it means that the law governing the randomness of $(V, D_1, \ldots, D_k)$ is i.i.d. or ergodic).

Using this process on r is a good way to compute an "optimal" r since looking closely at (A.7): If one venue is giving less liquidity than average, it is punished (next time less volume will be allocated to this venue) and if it gives more than others it is rewarded.

Once we have this generic model of optimal allocation dynamics by an SOR, we need to take into account the feedback of the activity of the SORs on the distribution of liquidity over the trading venues.

A.3.2. *A toy model of the impact of SOR activity on the market shares*

It is obvious that if no market participant is equipped with an SOR, meaning that all liquidity removing orders will be systematically sent to one venue only (the oldest one for instance), then the capability to attract liquidity of a new trading venue is useless.

On the other hand, if all SORs are blindly sending 5% of their orders to one venue, regardless of its fill rate, this venue will probably obtain around 5% of market share very soon.

Naming a the fraction of market participants equipped with SORs, the dynamics of the market shares of the kth venue can be modeled by

$$p_k(1+1) = (1-a) \cdot p_k(t) + a \cdot r_k(t). \tag{A.8}$$

This means that from one period to the other, the liquidity traded in each venue will evolve following the effective portion of the flow that is sent by the SORs trying to capture it efficiently.

A.3.3. *A coupled model of SOR-market shares dynamics*

Put together and translated in continuous terms, the dynamics (A.7) and (A.8) can be combined in:

$$\forall 1 \leq k \leq K : \begin{cases} \dfrac{dr_k}{dt} = \gamma \left(\frac{1}{K} \sum_{\ell=1}^{K} \mathbf{1}_{r_\ell \cdot V_\ell < D_\ell} - \mathbf{1}_{r_k \cdot V_k < D_k} \right), \\ \dfrac{dp_k}{dt} = a \cdot (r_k - p_k) \end{cases} \tag{A.9}$$

provided that at any point

$$\forall 1 \leq k \leq K : \mathbb{E}(D_k / \sum_{\ell=1}^{K} D_\ell) = p_k. \tag{A.10}$$

For equilibrium reasons, we will also ask of the model that the flow to route to the market is of the same order of magnitude than the tradeable liquidity: $\mathbb{E}(V) \simeq \sum_{k=1}^{K} \mathbb{E}(D_k)$.

The system of differential equations is stochastic in the sense that each time $(V, D_1, \ldots, D_K)$ are needed, they are chosen randomly according to a law. For this model we will choose to model them by independent log-normal laws (as is common when a positive random variable is needed in quantitative finance). The K equalities (A.10) give a constraint on their expectation, to which we add the fundamental assumption that *"the standard deviation of the liquidity provided by a venue is proportional to its quantity"*. This adds one parameter to our model, ν to fully define it.

A.3.4. *Simulations*

Figure A.3 shows a typical realization of this coupled model with:

- Three trading venues,
- an initial fragmentation of 95%, 3% and 2%,
- the market participants knowing nothing about the state of fragmentation, starting with no belief (a split of 1/3, 1/3, 1/3).

The upper chart shows that the fragmentation evolves to another state with one large trading venue (50% of market share) and two smaller ones (25% each). The lower chart plots the mean satisfaction

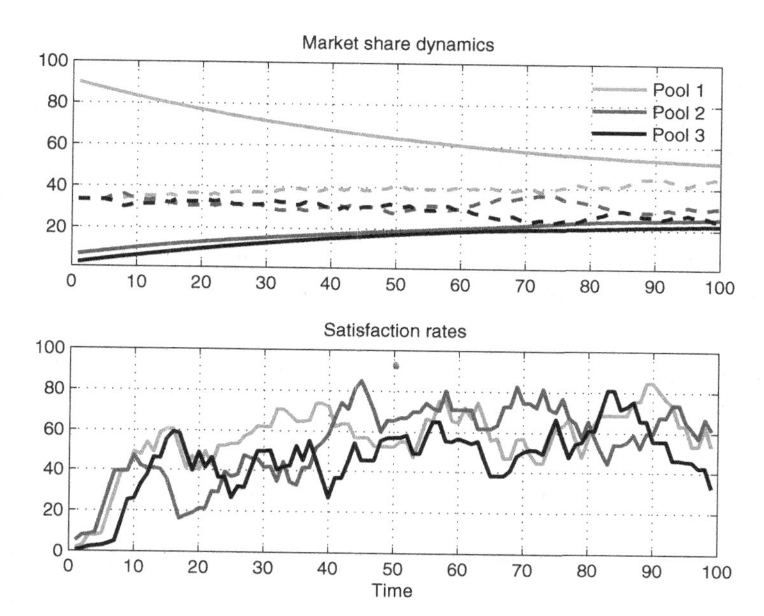

Figure A.3. An example of dynamics when the reassessment time of SOR strategies is low.

of the market participant on each venue (i.e. the fraction of the orders they send to one venue that is effectively filled and does not need to be re-routed).

The satisfaction rate evolves slowly but is kept low because of the random nature of the liquidity flow.

A.3.5. *Qualitative analysis*

First note that the dynamics of this simple model are fully compatible with the observation of fragmentation in European equity markets.

Its dynamics can be understood in the following way: In the short term the SORs aim to capture the available liquidity. But this is blurred by randomness, the vanishing nature of liquidity, its duplication, hidden orders, etc. At the end of the day the SORs will only be able to take into account the imbalance between the venues that are above a given signal to noise threshold: If a venue cannot be regular enough (i.e. low standard deviation) compared to the amount of liquidity it provides, it will take more time for the SORs to take advantage of its liquidity.

While the dynamics of r drives it slowly to p, depending on the noise level of each venue, the dynamics of p take into account the change of flows across the venue because of the action of the SORs.

At equilibrium, $p(\infty)$ will equal $r(\infty)$, and the faster this equilibrium is reached, the closer $p(\infty)$ is to $p(0)$. When r moves slowly, $p(\infty)$ can be very different from $p(0)$.

In short, considering that on average, the initial weights of SORs $r(0)$ are between $p(0)$ and an uniform repartition r^u where $r_k^u(0) = 1/K$ for any k:

- $p(\infty)$ will be close to $p(0)$ if (1) the variance of D is small and (2) $r(0)$ is closer to $p(0)$ than to r^u;
- $p(\infty)$ will be closer to r^u when (1) the variance of D is large and (2) $r(0)$ is closer to r^u than to $p(0)$.

The reality is that if the variance of the liquidity is large enough and the initial weights of the SORs are close enough to $p(0)$ then, in the obtained market dynamics, orders are split somewhat evenly across three large operators when two of them in reality only provide enough liquidity to be niche trading pools.

Going beyond this toy model, it can be said that the quality (i.e., modeled here by the variance) of the liquidity is more difficult to maintain by huge historical market operators than newcomers; significant fragmentation will occur, lowering the market share of the leader below 60%. It is nevertheless possible for small operators to survive if the nature of the liquidity they provide can be clearly labelled (since in our model the initial allocations of the SORs will be closer to the $p(0)$ for these venues, compensating the variance of their flows).

A.4. A Toy Model of the Flash Crash

The mechanism of the "Flash Crash" that is modeled here is the following (see [Madhavan, 2011, Kirilenko *et al.*, 2010] or [Menkveld and Yueshen, 2013] for more details):

- The usual trading rate at the bid or at the ask is close to an equilibrium value;
- the market depth is usually able to "renew" this consumption rate;
- during the Flash Crash an agent put pressure on the trading rate in one direction, consuming far more than the market depth can usually renew;
- it emptied the orderbooks fast on one side, so that the price moved down very fast;
- moreover this agent tries to keep its trading rate proportional to the market traded volume.

A.4.1. *A market depth-oriented model*

We first model the price dynamics on one side of the orderbook. For a more detailed model see [Menkveld and Yueshen, 2012]. Say that the trading flow of market orders on one side (for instance on the bid side) for a given stock is F_t (i.e. the rate of arrival of sell market orders). Consequently the traded volume is:

$$dV = F_t \cdot dt. \tag{A.11}$$

Moreover assume that the orderbook refills at a rate $\bar{F}$, meaning that limit orders are inserted on the same side of the book at this rate.

The "overflow" is modelled via variable R such that $dR = (F_t - \bar{F}) \cdot dt$ and with $r_t := F_t - \bar{F}$ this allows us to rewrite the traded volume:

$$dV = r_t \, dt + \bar{F} \, dt.$$

The "*market depth*" D is modeled thanks to the dynamics of the "*impact*" $I := 1/D$ (i.e. the *impact* is the inverse of the depth: less depth, more impact, and the reverse), whose dynamics are modeled as:

$$\frac{dI}{I} = \sigma_I\, dW_t + r_t\, dt. \tag{A.12}$$

This means that when more volume is traded than expected, R is large, thus the impact I is large and the market depth, being equal to the inverse of I, is very small. The stochastic component of the market depth is represented by dW. As usual in such an approach, the randomness models how information flow arrives in the market. Here we will have information coming from the trading participants, contributing to the market depth (in the upper equation), and information coming from the decision processes at a largest time scale, contributing directly to the price, in equation A.13. Randomness models all that is not endogenous to the model: All that comes from the outside of the model.

This is true for the volume traded at the bid V^- and at the ask V^+, giving rise to variables $F^{\pm}, r^{\pm}, R^{\pm}, I^{\pm}$ and finally to the price dynamics:

$$dP = \sigma^P\, dW_t^P + I^+\, dR^+ - I^-\, dR^-, \tag{A.13}$$

so that the price has an endogenous (random[1]) component $\sigma^P\, dW_t^P$ and a component coming from the pressure put by the trading rates on the depth at the bid $I^-\, dR^-$ (pushing the price down) and at the ask $I^+\, dR^+$ (pushing prices up).

Figure A.4 shows that the price simulated according to this model is realistic, even if for our convenience the model could allow the price to be negative. Replacing dP in (A.13) by dP/P could be possible but obtaining closed form formulas would be far more difficult. Moreover it is not rare in intraday models of the price to use arithmetic Brownian motions instead geometric ones.

[1]The randomness of this part of the PFP (Price Formation Process) comes from the fact that it does not come from the dynamics of the orderbooks themselves but from any "external" factor.

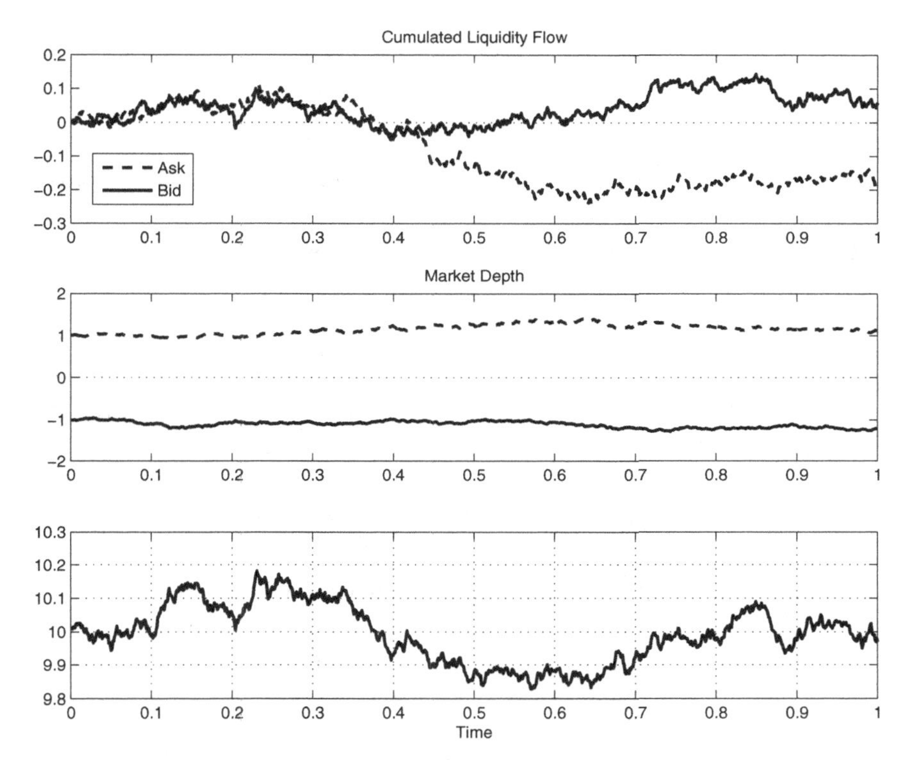

Figure A.4. One trajectory of price simulated by the model; top: R, middle: Market Depth $D = 1/I$, bottom: Price.

A.4.2. *Impact of the Flash Crash on our model*

The "hot potato game" played by the high frequency market makers on the futures and equity markets (see Section 2.4.3, Chapter 2 for more details) has the following impact on the model:

- When a large investor sells rdt at time t, a large proportion of its trade has high-frequency market makers as counterpart. They hedge themselves on the futures market, having high frequency market makers as counterpart too. Because these HFMM hedge themselves on the equity market too, the original investor, who wants to "follow the market volume" at a constant rate, immediately has to trade more;

- This leads to a trading rate close to:

$$r_t \simeq \frac{1-\rho^t}{1-\rho} r_0$$

where ρ is the proportion of traders playing this "hot potato game".
- This gives an "overflow" at the bid R_t^-, close to

$$R_t \simeq \frac{t}{1-\rho} r_0.$$

- The "impact" equation (A.12) can be solved explicitly thanks to stochastic calculus [Karatzas and Shreve, 1991], giving:

$$I_t^- = I_0 \exp\left(\frac{t^2}{1-\rho}\frac{r_0}{2} - \frac{1}{2}\sigma_I^2 t + \sigma_I W_t^-\right). \tag{A.14}$$

Hence the market depth is known at any time by

$$D_t^- = D_0 \exp\left(-\frac{t^2}{1-\rho}\frac{r_0}{2} + \frac{1}{2}\sigma_I^2 t - \sigma_I W_t^-\right).$$

- For the price dynamics, given that there is exactly no pressure on the ask (i.e. $F_t^+ = \bar{F}^+$ at any time), we get:

$$P_t = P_0 - I_0 \int_{\tau=0}^{t} \frac{r_0}{1-\rho} e^{\tau^2 r_0/(2-2\rho) - \sigma_I^2 \tau/2 + \sigma_I W_\tau^-} d\tau + \sigma^P W_t^P. \tag{A.15}$$

The dominating part of the value of the price P_t during the Flash Crash seen via this model is $P_0 - c\int_t \exp(t^2/u)dt$, which is highly explosive, driving the price to zero faster than an exponential decay.

Figure A.5 shows Flash Crash trajectories seen by the model, the speed of the decay is compatible with what was observed during the May 6 event on the US equity markets.

This model has the following components:

- The market depth is consumed by a trading rate above a given threshold $\bar{F}$ and refilled when the trading rate is below this threshold (since it can be refilled by the usual behavior of market participants),

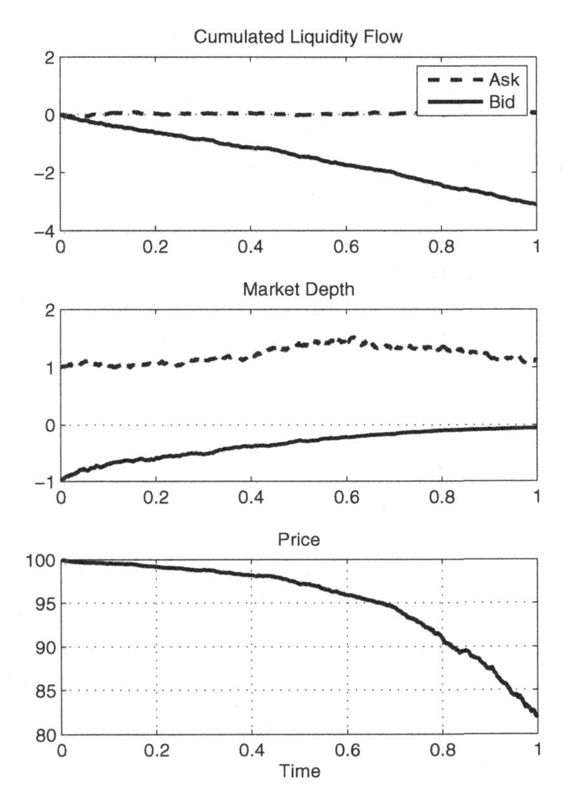

Figure A.5. Typical trajectories of the Flash Crash generated by the model; top: R, middle: Market Depth $D = 1/I$, bottom: Price.

- the impact of the trading flow is proportional to the trading rate and amplified by the inverse of the market depth.

The model shows that the mechanism of the Flash Crash can be theoretically explained by a rapidly decreasing market depth because of a trading algo blindly following the volume is in a "hot potato game" situation.

Two simple elements could prevent such an event:

- An *obligation* for market makers to refill the market depth quickly enough;
- a *circuit breaker* not only on price levels but on market depth break events.

A.5. Harris Model: Underlying Continuous Spread Discretized by Tick

This model was first introduced by Harris ([Harris, 1994]) in order to forecast the potential decrease of bid-ask spread induced by decimalization. It has been used recently, as James McCulloch quantified the potential decrease of bid ask spread induced by a proposed change of tick size for low priced stocks on the ASX, and Sirodom *et al.* ran the same kind of analysis for the Thailand Stock Exchange.

Motivation and notations

We will be trying to fit the relationship between spread, volatility, and a proxy of stock's liquidity, such as traded turnover. The intuition for this modelling is as follows. Turnover is a determinant of spreads because it is a proxy for stock liquidity. Volatility is a determinant of spread because of the extra risk taken by limit order traders when providing liquidity for a volatile stock. But price is not a determinant of relative spreads because liquidity providers and consumers are indifferent about the nominal stock price at which liquidity is supplied. Nevertheless some misspecified regression can lead to the erroneous conclusion that there is a link with the stock price. Indeed the price of the stock may appear as a determinant variable for spread because of the tick size acting as a minimum spread. Therefore, in a market for which the tick size is the same whatever the price of the stock, the lower the price everything else equal, the higher the spread.

Let's first have a look at some FTSE 100 components, using the same tick size regime (see Figure A.6). On this graph, there is one point per stock per day, for all stocks of the FTSE 100 using the FESE table 2 as a tick size regime. On the x-axis we have the mean price of the stock over the day, giving an idea of the tick size active this day, given the price range in which traded prices were, whereas on the yaxis we plotted the mean relative spread in basis points. Both axes are on a log scale. We added as a black solid line the tick size relative to price according to FESE table 2, in order to make obvious where the tick size acts as minimum spread.

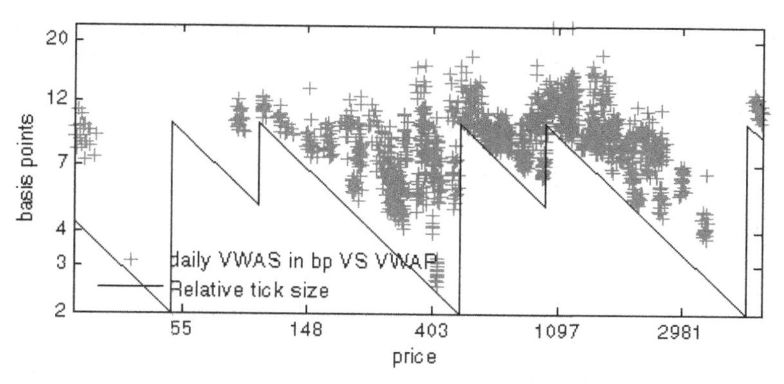

Figure A.6. Relationship between relative bid-ask spread and stock price for FTSE 100 stocks using the FESE table II.

It is clear from this graph that tick size acts as a lower bound, especially for those stock in the 500–1000 price range, where it would seem more natural if the spread values were lower. With the methodology presented here, we will try to take into account this tick size effect which makes the spread greater than what would be expected according to the liquidity and volatility of the stock.

We will proceed as follows. Let us consider $\tilde{f}_{s,\theta}$ the density of the underlying continuous spread, which would be the distribution of spreads if it were possible to choose any price for limit orders and not just multiples of tick size. s is the expectation of this distribution, while theta is the vector of other parameters of the distribution.

Let us denote $\Psi_{j,t} = \frac{\text{Ask}_{j,t}-\text{Bid}_{j,t}}{\text{tick}_{j,d}}$ the observed spread in ticks for stock j on the t-th trade which occurred on day d. We will use only stock's data for which there is only one active tick size in the day: $\text{tick}_{j,d}$ in order to avoid mixing different spreads distributions in a day. Let us denote T_j the mean turnover traded on stock j, $\sigma_{j,d}$ a measure of the volatility for stock j on day d and $D_{j,d}$ the set of indexes of trades occurring in day d for stock j. We will also note $P_{j,d}$ the mean traded price for stock j on day d, which will enable us to convert from spread expressed in tick size to relative spreads expressed in basis points.

Finally we need the tick size discretization function Φ, which gives the nearest integer for an input greater than 1.5 and gives 1 otherwise. We will assume that there exists an underlying continuous spread $\tilde{\Psi}$, such that:

$$\Psi_{j,t} = \Phi(\tilde{\Psi}_{j,t}) \quad \text{and} \quad \forall t \in D_{j,d} \;\; \tilde{\Psi}_{j,t} \sim \tilde{f}_{g(Tj,\sigma_{j,d})\times \frac{P_{j,d}}{\text{tick}_{j,d}},\theta},$$

consequently we have

$$\mathbb{E}\left[\tilde{\Psi}_{j,t}|T_j,\sigma_{j,d}\right] = g(T_j,\sigma_{j,d}) \times \frac{P_{j,d}}{\text{tick}_{j,d}}.$$

Our model is then consistent with the discreteness of observed spread, and will quantify the increase of expected spread from a continuous to a discrete distribution. Let us illustrate this on Figure A.7. The black solid line stands for the underlying spreads continuous density, denoted by $\tilde{f}_{s,\theta}$ previously. The discretized distribution $f_{s,\theta}$ is made of Dirac densities whose values are $\forall i \geq 2 f_{s,\theta}(i) = \int_{i-0.5}^{i+0.5} \tilde{f}_{s,\theta}$ and $f_{s,\theta}(1) = \int_0^{1.5} \tilde{f}_{s,\theta}$ for the probability of observing a one tick spread. We have also plotted the expectation of the two distributions

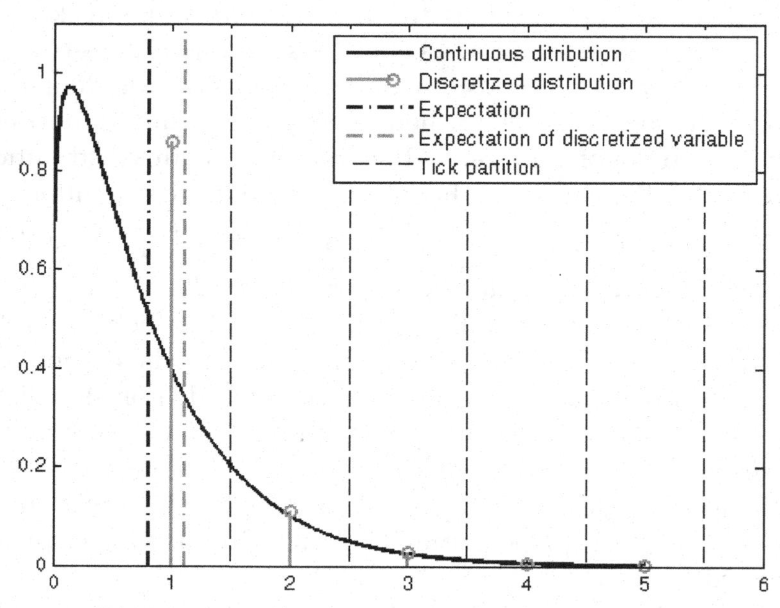

Figure A.7. Illustration of the relation between the underlying continuous distribution and the observable discrete distribution in the Harris model.

with vertical lines in order to show on this example the increase in expectation induced by the discretization.

We will then specify the function g which is the expectation of uncensored spreads given turnover and volatility, as a log-log linear relationship:

$$\forall j, \forall t \in D_{j,d} \;\; \mathbb{E}[\tilde{\Psi}_{j,t}|T_j, \sigma_{j,d})] = \alpha \times T_j^{\beta} \times \sigma_{j,d}^{\gamma} \times \frac{P_{j,d}}{\text{tick}_{j,d}}.$$

After the choice of a distribution for continuous spreads, namely the choice of the density $\tilde{f}$, one would be able to compute the likelihood. We need to define $N(j,d,k)$ the frequency of k tick spreads observed in the data of stock j on day d. The log-likelihood is then:

$$l(\alpha, \beta, \gamma, \theta) = \sum_j \sum_d \sum_k \ln (f_{\alpha \times T_j^{\beta} \times \sigma_{j,d}^{\gamma} \times \frac{P_{j,d}}{\text{tick}_{j,d}}, \theta}(k)) \times N(j,d,k).$$

We can then maximize it with regards to parameter $\lambda = (\alpha, \beta, \gamma, \theta)$ to get a maximum likelihood estimator, $\hat{\lambda} = \text{argmax}_{\lambda} l(\lambda)$.

Numerical application

In what follows, we will consider as data for our application the 60 most liquid stocks of the FTSE, the period used here will be April 2012, and we will use the gamma distribution as the continuous spread distribution. Everything being specified, we can maximize our likelihood to get our estimated parameters.

The value of the parameters will be highly dependent on the unit (e.g. pence for turnover) we will then rather give the standardized parameters, that is to say: $\frac{\beta}{\sqrt{\text{Var}(\ln(T))}} = -0.46$, $\frac{\gamma}{\sqrt{\text{Var}(\ln(\sigma))}} = 2.62$. The sign of these parameters is as expected: the more liquid the stock is, the lower the spread, and the higher the volatility, the higher the spread.

We can derive a plug-in estimator for expected relative spread given volatility, turnover and tick size, as:

$$\begin{aligned}\widehat{\mathbb{E}(\Psi Rel_{j,d}|T_j, \sigma_{j,d})} &= \frac{10^4 \times \text{tick}_{j,d}}{P_{j,d}} \times \widehat{\mathbb{E}(\Psi_{j,t \in D_{j,d}}|T_j, \sigma_{j,d})} \\ &= \frac{10^4 \times \text{tick}_{j,d}}{P_{j,d}} \times \sum_k k \times f_{\hat{\alpha} \times T_j^{\hat{\beta}} \times \sigma_{j,d}^{\hat{\gamma}} \times \frac{P_{j,d}}{\text{tick}_{j,d}}, \hat{\theta}}(k)\end{aligned}$$

To assess the goodness of fit between observed relative spread, we compute

$$\Psi Rel_{j,d} = 10^4 * \frac{\sum_{t \in D_{j,d}} \Psi_{j,t} \times \text{tick}_{j,d}}{P_{j,d} \times \sharp(D_{j,d})}$$

and the expected relative spread given volatility, turnover and tick size we can plot one against the other, as on the following graph:

It is quite clear from Figure A.8 that there is indeed a good fit between observed spread and its expectation given turnover, volatility and tick. To quantify this, we can compute a 'pseudo R-square': $1 - \frac{\overline{(\widehat{\mathbb{E}(\Psi Rel|T,\sigma)} - \Psi Rel)^2}}{\mathrm{Var}(\Psi Rel)}$. Its value for the fit plotted here is 0.8 which is pretty good and reveals the strong relationship between spread, volatility and traded turnover.

We will now have a look at the estimated increase in spread due to the discretization of the spread. On Figure A.9, we plotted $\widehat{\mathbb{E}(\Psi|T,\sigma)}$ against $\widehat{\mathbb{E}(\tilde{\Psi}|T,\sigma)}$ and added as a black solid line the first bisector. The vertical distance between this line and a point $(\widehat{\mathbb{E}(\tilde{\Psi}|T,\sigma)}, \widehat{\mathbb{E}(\Psi|T,\sigma)})$ is equal to the relative decrease in spread we would have with a theoretical zero tick size.

We see that obviously, the lower the spread expressed in tick, the higher would be the decrease in spread we can expect from a decrease in tick.

We can go further and estimate (again with a plug-in estimator) the decrease in expected spread we would get from a given decrease of tick size (see Figure A.10). Let us define δ the multiplier of tick size which would give the 'new tick': new tick $= \frac{\text{old tick}}{\delta}$. To do so, we need to generalize the definition of the discretized spread distribution:

$$f_{s,\theta,\delta} : k \in \mathbb{N} \setminus \{0\} \mapsto \begin{cases} \text{if } k = 1 : \displaystyle\int_0^{\frac{1.5}{\delta}} \tilde{f}_{s,\theta} \\ \text{if } k > 1 : \displaystyle\int_{\frac{k-0.5}{\delta}}^{\frac{k+0.5}{\delta}} \tilde{f}_{s,\theta} \end{cases}$$

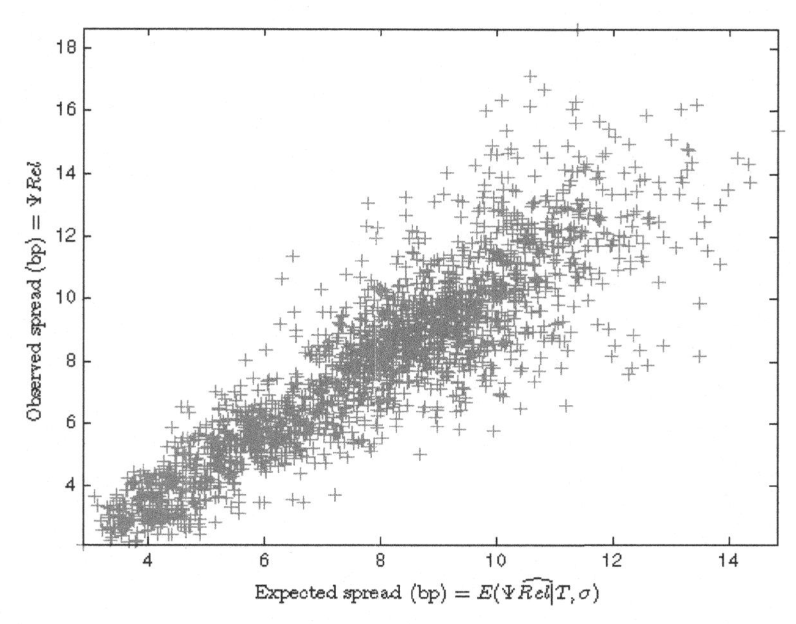

Figure A.8. Scatter plot of observed spread and the expectation of the estimated discrete distribution of spreads.

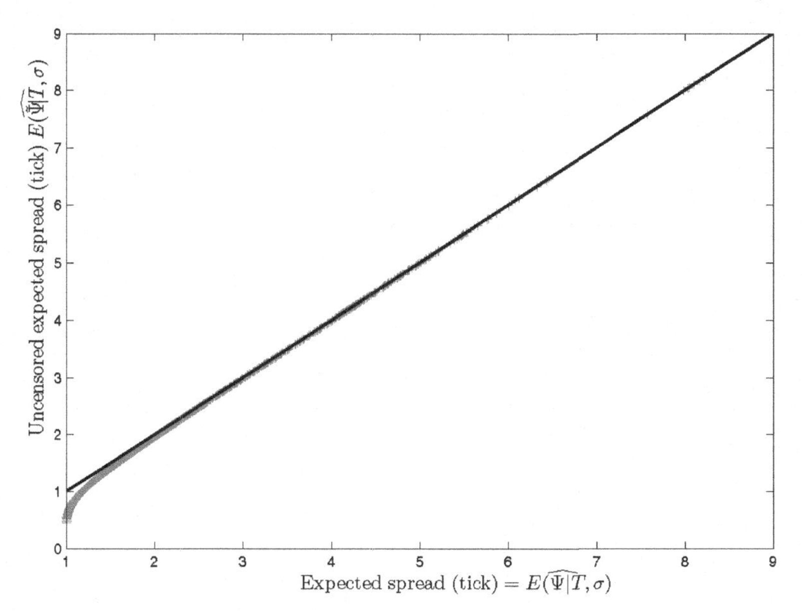

Figure A.9. Relation between the estimation of the expectation of the spread and its value if the tick size was not acting as a minimal bound.

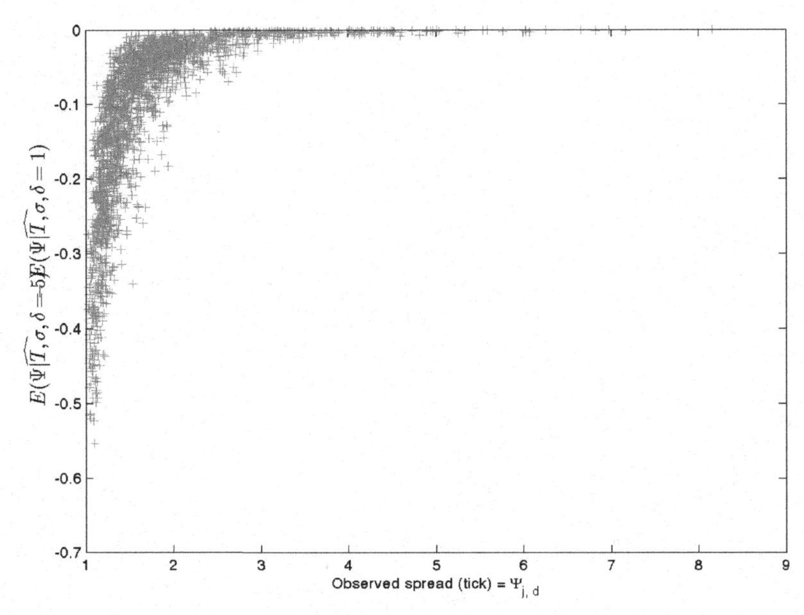

Figure A.10. Expected variation (in old ticks unit) of the spread for a fivefold decrease of the tick against the current spread in tick.

Then the expected spread given volatility, turnover and the new tick size would be:

$$\widehat{\mathbb{E}(\Psi_{j,d}|T_j,\sigma_{j,d},\delta)} = \sum_k \frac{k}{\delta} \times f_{\hat{\alpha}\times T_j^{\hat{\beta}}\times\sigma_{j,d}^{\hat{\gamma}}\times\frac{P_{j,d}}{\text{tick}_{j,d}},\hat{\theta},\delta}(k).$$

Figure A.10 represents the relative decrease in spread one can expect by dividing the tick by a factor of 5.

A.6. Optimal Trade Scheduling

With the emergence of trading platforms using intensively electronic and automated means, brokers have to offer trading algorithms for a large universe of traded instruments. It is consequently impossible to manually tune each trading algo on a stock-by-stock or instrument-by-instrument basis. The only way to simultaneously address a huge number of traded instruments (around 8,000 in Europe; 20,000 in the US) is to capture their main features (bid-ask spread, volatility, market depths, etc.) using models and to implement software solving the models, using the parameters and features associated to one instrument to generate a trading strategy adapted on the fly to the chosen instrument.

The parameters of the models are usually estimated on a daily or weekly basis, ready to be used by optimizers each morning. Moreover, some real-time analytics, computed on the fly, are ready for use by trading algorithms (see [Johnson, 2010] and Chapter 3, Section 3.1).

A trading algorithm can be formalized by two cooperating layers:

- One dedicated to "risk control" to avoid trading too fast or too slow with respect to expected properties of the traded stock or sector. This avoids both adverse selection and excessive market impact. The time scale of this layer is around 10 minutes (can be 1 minute for very liquid stocks or 30 minutes for illiquid ones). This puts maximum and minimum boundaries on the trading rate that the algo will have in the market.
- Another layer is dedicated to reacting opportunistically to short term liquidity and price variations. It has the freedom to choose its participation rate as far as it maintains it inside the bounds pre-computed by the upper layer. SORs (Smart Order Routers) are the simplest "trading robots" of this kind. Others are usually called "liquidity seekers"; they can react to alpha-generating signals.

This Appendix focuses on the first layer, which has been progressively identified and formalized during the nineties. It is built on top of models rendering two main effects:

- The market impact, putting the emphasis on trading as slow as possible;
- The market risk, pushing the algo to trade as fast as possible.

Initial academic proposals put these two effects face to face, first focused on market impact [Bertsimas and Lo, 1998], then using a mean-variance approach [Almgren and Chriss, 2000], close to the one commonly used for quantitative asset allocation [Markowitz, 1952]. For optimal trade scheduling the purpose is not to allocate quantities to components of a portfolio but to time intervals through the day. It gives a natural "time schedule" for a large trade to be optimally split through time. A simplified and commented version of the original Almgren-Chriss paper is presented there.

A.6.1. *The trading model*

A buy order of size v^* has to be planned over N consecutive time intervals, each of them having a duration of δt. During the nth time slice (from $(n-1)\delta t$ to $n\delta t$) the volume traded by the other market participants is expected to be V_n, and the intraday volatility of the price is expected to the σ_n (expressed in local currency and not in percent, as usual). The "fair price" diffuses according to a discretized arithmetic Brownian motion (i.e. a Markov process):

$$S_{n+1} = S_n + \sigma_{n+1}\xi_{n+1} \tag{A.16}$$

where $\xi_.$ is a standard Gaussian random variable.

During the nth slice, the price $\tilde{S}_n(v)$ to buy v shares is the sum of the fair price and a market impact:

$$\tilde{S}_n(v) = S_n + \underbrace{\kappa\,\sigma_n\left(\frac{v}{V_n}\right)^{\gamma}}_{\text{market impact}} \tag{A.17}$$

where γ and κ are stock-dependent constant, σ_n the volatility during the trading (reflecting that in a period of high uncertainty on the price — i.e. high volatility — the market impact is larger than usual) and V_n is the volume traded by the market during the trading period (the larger the volume usually traded, the smaller the impact of a given volume v, meaning that the trading rate v/V_n is the parameter of interest to estimate the market impact).

The volume to buy v^* has to be fully allocated on the N time slices (v_n on the nth slice), i.e.,

$$\sum_{n=1}^{N} v_n = v^*. \tag{A.18}$$

The cost of buying v^* shares is thus:

$$W = \sum_{n=1}^{N} v_n \cdot \left(S_n + \kappa\, \sigma_n \left(\frac{v_n}{V_n} \right)^{\gamma} \right). \tag{A.19}$$

A.6.2. *Towards a mean-variance optimal trade scheduling*

A minimum expectation criteria

Before going to a mean-variance criteria, one can consider first a pure expectation minimization one. The expectation of cost W can be written:

$$\mathbb{E}(W|V_1,\ldots,V_N,\sigma_1,\ldots,\sigma_N) = S_0 \cdot v^* + \kappa \sum_{n=1}^{N} \sigma_n \frac{v_n^{\gamma+1}}{V_n^{\gamma}} \tag{A.20}$$

where the conditioning by $V_1,\ldots,V_N,\sigma_1,\ldots,\sigma_N$ means that we assume that we are able to guess the traded volume and the volatility during the nth slice (for more, see [Lehalle, 2012]). This extensive writing of the conditioning will be omitted in the other equations of this Appendix for the sake of the notations.

Minimizing (A.20) under the constraint (A.18) can be naturally solved thanks to a Lagrangian multiplier (see [Bellman, 1956]), which says that λ exists such that for any n:

$$v_n = \left(\frac{\lambda}{\sigma_n(\gamma+1)} \right)^{1/\gamma} \cdot V_n.$$

Summing this relation over n and taking into account that the v_n sum to 1, we obtain the only possible value of the Lagrange multiplier:

$$\left(\frac{\lambda}{\gamma+1}\right)^{1/\gamma} = \left(\sum_{n=1}^{N} \frac{V_n}{\sigma_n^{1/\gamma}}\right)^{-1}. \tag{A.21}$$

This allows us to obtain the optimal trading rate:

Proposition 1 (Optimal trading rate for expectation minimization) *The only possible trade scheduling for an expectation-minimization criterion is linear in* $V_n/\sigma_n^{1/\gamma}$:

$$v_n^{\text{exp}} = \frac{V_n/\sigma_n^{1/\gamma}}{\sum_{\ell=1}^{N} V_\ell/\sigma_\ell^{1/\gamma}} v^*. \tag{A.22}$$

This result stems from the martingality[2] of the price: the only effect to be "protected from" is the market impact. Hence the linearity of the optimal schedule comes from the sensitivity of the market impact to the market traded volume and the volatility (power $1/\gamma$ because of the non linearity of the market impact model).

It is worthwhile to notice that:

Proposition 2 (Optimal trading rate for expectation minimization during a constant market context) *When the market context does not change during trading (i.e. for any* $n : \sigma_n = \sigma$ *and* $V_n = V$*), the optimal trading schedule is uniform:*

$$v_n^{\text{exp cst}} = \frac{1}{N} \cdot v^*. \tag{A.23}$$

This is the trading rate usually taken by proprietary traders to get rid of their tracking error. It can be considered as adapted to their situation since they are less sensitive to the risk (it is *their risk*, and they can count on it averaging out over one month).

A pure risk adverse trade schedule

The above results do not take into account that the more you wait to trade a given quantity, the more you are exposed to adverse market

[2] No view is taken on the trend of the price during the trading process.

moves. The natural way to take this effect into account is to minimize the variance of the buying cost W.

A change of variable (corresponding to an integration by parts) is needed to easily compute the variance of W: naming x_n the quantity remaining to trade from n to N (i.e. $x_n = \sum_{\ell \geq n} v_\ell$), we can write:

$$\begin{aligned}\sum_{n=1}^{N} v_n S_n &= v_1(S_0 + \sigma_1 S_1) \\ &\quad + v_2(S_0 + \sigma_1 S_1 + \sigma_2 S_2) \\ &\quad + \cdots \\ &\quad + v_N(S_0 + \sigma_1 S_1 + \cdots + \sigma_N S_N) \\ &= v^* \cdot S_0 + \sum_{n=1}^{N} x_n \sigma_n \xi_n\end{aligned}$$

under this change of variable it is straightforward to express the variance of the cost:

$$\mathrm{Var}(W) = \sum_{n=1}^{N} \sigma_n^2 x_n^2 \tag{A.24}$$

under the constraint (A.18) that is now just two terminal conditions: $x_0 = v^*$ (i.e. at the beginning, the remaining quantity to trade is v^*) and $x_N = 0$ (i.e. nothing remains to trade at the end).

The solution of this variance-minimization scheme is obtained by forcing to zero the partial derivative of $\mathrm{Var}(W)$ with respect to any x_n. Hence:

Proposition 3 (Optimal trading rate for variance minimization) *The only possible trade scheduling for an variance-minimization criterion is:*

$$v_1^{\mathrm{var}} = v^*, \ \forall n > 1 : v_n^{\mathrm{var}} = 0 \tag{A.25}$$

meaning that all shares have to be bought as soon as possible, since the market impact has no influence on this strategy.

Combining market impact and risk: The mean-variance criterion

The mean-variance criterion combines the expectation part (see Proposition 1) and the variance part (see Proposition 3) thanks to a risk aversion parameter λ, which is homogeneous with our previous Lagrange multiplier (see equation (A.21)). This ad hoc criterion is thus:

$$\begin{aligned} C &= \mathbb{E}(W) + \lambda \cdot \mathrm{Var}(W) \qquad \text{(A.26)} \\ &= \underbrace{v^* \cdot S_0}_{\text{immediate buy}} \underbrace{+\kappa \sum_{n=1}^{N} \sigma_n \frac{v_n^{\gamma+1}}{V_n^{\gamma}}}_{\text{market impact}} \underbrace{+\lambda \sum_{n=1}^{N} x_n^2 \sigma_n^2}_{\text{market risk}} . \end{aligned}$$

The two last components of this cost function reflect what we want to take into account:

- The market impact, which will demand us trade as slowly as linearly in $V_n/\sigma_n^{1/\gamma}$;
- The market risk, which will pressure us to trade as fast as possible.

It is easy to guess that the balance between these two effects will give a sub-linear (i.e. convex) trading curve in x_n.

In the special case of a linear market impact (i.e. $\gamma = 1$) it is possible formally to go a little further, writing C as a function of x (using the fact that $v_n = x_n - x_{n+1}$):

$$C = v^* \cdot S_0 + \kappa \sum_{n=1}^{N} \sigma_n \frac{(x_n - x_{n+1})^2}{V_n} + \lambda \sum_{n=1}^{N} x_n^2 \sigma_n^2.$$

The terminal conditions on x are the same as for the variance case:

$$x_0 = v^*, \; x_N = 0. \qquad \text{(A.27)}$$

To minimize C it is enough to cancel its derivatives with respect to any x_n:

$$\frac{\partial C}{\partial x_n} = 2\kappa \left(\frac{x_n - x_{n+1}}{V_n} \sigma_n - \frac{x_{n-1} - x_n}{V_{n-1}} \sigma_{n-1} \right) + 2\lambda x_n \sigma_n^2 = 0,$$

which gives rise to a recurrence formula in x:

Proposition 4 (Optimal trading rate for variance minimization) *The only possible trade scheduling for a mean-variance criterion is the solution of the recurrence equation*

$$x_{n+1} = \left(1 + \frac{\sigma_{n-1}}{\sigma_n} \cdot \frac{V_n}{V_{n-1}} + \frac{\lambda}{\kappa} \cdot \frac{V_n}{\sigma_n}\right) x_n - \frac{\sigma_{n-1}}{\sigma_n} \cdot \frac{V_n}{V_{n-1}} x_{n-1} \quad \text{(A.28)}$$

with the terminal conditions (A.27).

Various numerical methods can be used to solve the system (A.28) under (A.27), like:

- Minimizing x_N^2 as a function of x_1 (using for instance a gradient descent method [Amari, 1998]);
- A shooting method to solve (A.28), which we view as a discretization of a partial differential equation (again using x_1 as a parameter), iteratively (see [Labadie and Lehalle, 2012]).

All this stems from the fact that once x_1 is chosen (i.e. once the quantity to trade during the first slice is fixed), the recurrence (A.28) automatically leads to a unique value for x_N. On the one hand, if it is greater than zero, it means that the choice of x_1 was too large (i.e. the trading was too slow to be finished during the Nth slice); and on the other if it is lower than zero, it means the x_1 was too small (i.e. the trading went too fast according to our mean-variance criterion).

This optimality principle allows us to find the *"optimal trading schedule"* associated to any risk aversion parameter λ.

Figure A.11 gives some examples of trading curves associated to different values of λ. One can see that the larger λ (i.e. the more the trader fears market risk), the faster the execution. On the other hand, the smaller λ (i.e. the more the trader focuses on market impact), the more linear the execution profile. This is compatible with Propositions 1 and 3, that can now be seen as special cases of the generic Proposition 4.

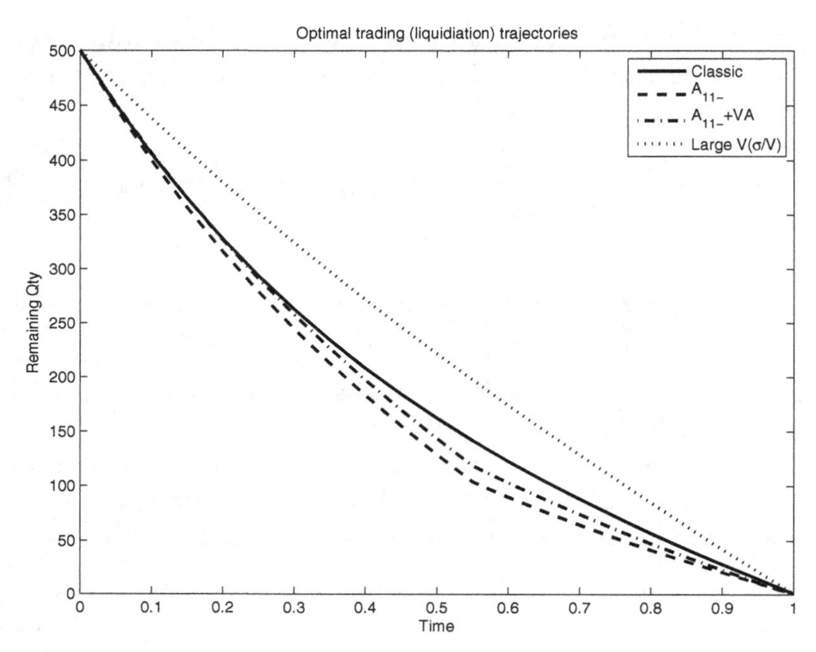

Figure A.11. Some optimal trading schedules associated with different risk aversion parameters.

More sophisticated theoretical frameworks have been proposed by academics: some inspired by stochastic control (like [Bouchard *et al.*, 2011]), others by stochastic algorithms (i.e. statistical learning, see [Laruelle *et al.*, 2013]). Market making has been formalized too (see [Guéant *et al.*, 2012a]).

A.7. Estimation of Proportion and its Confidence Intervals

In microstructure, we have to estimate proportions and probabilities on plenty of occasions: For example to estimate market shares, proportions of HFT in the market, probability to have a transaction at the bid or ask side, etc.

In statistics, the estimation of a proportion is generally done using a binomial distribution, namely an experiment which has two possible outcomes (labeled arbitrarily success (or 1) and failure (or 0)) is repeated a fixed number of times and the trials are assumed statistically independent, and the aim is to estimate the probability of success which is the same for each trial. Thus a good way to approximate this proportion is to consider the empirical mean of the trials. Formally, if we consider a sequence of n independent $\{0, 1\}$-valued random variables $X_1, \ldots, X_n$ (named Bernoulli trials), the estimation of the probability of success, denoted by p, will be $\hat{p} = \frac{1}{n}\sum_{k=1}^{n} X_k$ (see e.g., [Agresti and Caffo, 2000]). This estimator is unbiased, i.e., $\mathbb{E}[\hat{p}] = p$, and its variance is $\mathrm{Var}(\hat{p}) = \frac{p(1-p)}{n}$. Moreover, this estimator is consistent since by the strong law of large numbers (SLLN)

$$\hat{p} \xrightarrow[n\to\infty]{a.s.} p,$$

and we have also by the Central Limit Theorem (CLT) that

$$\sqrt{n}\frac{\hat{p} - p}{\sqrt{\frac{p(1-p)}{n}}} \xrightarrow[n\to\infty]{\mathcal{L}} \mathcal{N}(0, 1). \tag{A.29}$$

This last result justifies the normal approximation to the binomial distribution and allows us to build a confidence interval for this binomial proportion. However this approximation does not always work well, especially for situations with a small sample size and a proportion very close to zero or one, so several other formulas that perform better for these cases were proposed, but we do not mention them here because we are not faced with this situation (see for example [Agresti and Caffo, 2000] for small sample size).

From (A.29), we will derive a confidence interval for the true value of the probability of success p. As p is unknown, we have to approximate the variance of $\hat{p}$ by $\frac{\hat{p}(1-\hat{p})}{n}$ and we deduce that the appoximate confidence interval of p at level $1-\alpha$ (where α denotes the error) is

$$\hat{p} \pm z_{1-\alpha/2}\sqrt{\frac{\hat{p}(1-\hat{p})}{n}}$$

where $z_{1-\alpha/2}$ is the $1-\alpha/2$ percentile of a standard normal distribution. For example, for a 95% confidence level the error (α) is 5%, so $1-\alpha/2 = 0.975$ and $z_{1-\alpha/2} = 1.96$.

Remark. The central limit theorem applies well to a binomial distribution, even with a sample size less than 30, as long as the proportion is not too close to 0 or 1. For very extreme probabilities, though, a sample size of 30 or more may still be inadequate. The normal approximation fails totally when the sample proportion is exactly zero or exactly one. A frequently cited rule of thumb is that the normal approximation works well as long as $np > 5$ and $n(1-p) > 5$.

A.7.1. *Application to the estimation of the market share of venues on an asset*

If we want to estimate the market share of a venue on an asset, we may use the same idea as before by considering as estimator the ratio between the turnover of the asset on this venue and the global turnover of the asset (namely the sum of all the turnovers on the different venues). Formally, for an asset k, $k \in \{1,\ldots,K\}$, and a venue i, $i \in \{1,\ldots,I\}$, the estimated proportion is $\hat{p}_k^i = \frac{\text{turnover of } k \text{ on } i}{\sum_{i\in I} \text{turnover of } k \text{ on } i}$ (see Tables A.1 and A.2 for application to FSTE 100 and SBF 120).

A.7.2. *Aggregation or application to the market share on an index*

Consider an index made of K assets where for every $k \in \{1,\ldots,K\}$, the weight of the asset k in the index is w_k. Then the estimated market share of the index for a venue i, denoted by $\hat{p}^i$, $i \in \{1,\ldots,I\}$, is the aggregation of the different estimated market shares of the assets that composed the index $\hat{p}_k^i$, $k \in \{1,\ldots,K\}$, weighted by their own contribution in the index w_k, namely $\hat{p}^i = \sum_{k\in K} w_k \hat{p}_k^i$.

Table A.1. FSTE 100.

Venues	SETS	CHIXLO	TRQXLT	BATE	NAE
Market Shares	50.01%	34.01%	8.46%	7.42%	0.10%

Table A.2. SBF 120.

Venues	ENPA	CHIXPA	TRQXLT	BATE	EQTA
Market Shares	58.71%	27.06%	7.44%	4.90%	1.89%

Examples. To illustrate the estimation of the market shares of indexes, we have computed them for the FSTE100 and the SBF120 on five venues and the results are shown in Tables A.1 and A.2.

A.7.3. *Comparison of the estimators*

To compare the estimators $\hat{p}^i_k$ and $\hat{p}^i$ on a venue i, we will compute the expectation and the variance of the difference. First $\mathbb{E}\,[\hat{p}^i_k - \hat{p}^i] = p^i_k - p^i$ and by assuming that the sequence $(\hat{p}^i_k)_{k\in K}$ is independent, we have

$$
\begin{aligned}
\mathbb{E}\left[\left(\hat{p}^i_k - \hat{p}^i\right)^2\right] &= \mathbb{E}\left[\left(\hat{p}^i_k\right)^2\right] + \mathbb{E}\left[\left(\hat{p}^i\right)^2\right] - 2\mathbb{E}[\hat{p}^i_k \hat{p}^i] \\
&= \frac{p^i_k(1-p^i_k)}{n^i_k} + (p^i_k)^2 + \frac{p^i(1-p^i)}{n^i} + (p^i)^2 \\
&\quad -2\left(\sum_{j\neq k} w_j \mathbb{E}\left[\hat{p}^i_j\right]\mathbb{E}\left[\hat{p}^i_k\right] + w_k \mathbb{E}\left[\left(\hat{p}^i_k\right)^2\right]\right) \\
&= \frac{p^i_k(1-p^i_k)}{n^i_k} + (p^i_k)^2 + \frac{p^i(1-p^i)}{n^i} + (p^i)^2 \\
&\quad -2\left(\sum_{j\neq k} w_j p^i_j p^i_k + w_k \frac{p^i_k(1-p^i_k)}{n^i_k} + w_k (p^i_k)^2\right)
\end{aligned}
$$

$$= \frac{p_k^i(1-p_k^i)}{n_k^i} + (p_k^i)^2 + \frac{p^i(1-p^i)}{n^i} + (p^i)^2$$
$$-2\left(p^i p_k^i + w_k \frac{p_k^i(1-p_k^i)}{n_k^i}\right).$$

So we obtain for the variance the following result

$$\mathrm{Var}(\hat{p}_k^i - \hat{p}^i) = (1-2w_k)\frac{p_k^i(1-p_k^i)}{n_k^i} + \frac{p^i(1-p^i)}{n^i}.$$

Thus if $w_k < 0.5$, the variance between the two estimators is greater than the one of the estimation of the index market share, and when $w_k > 0.5$ the variance is smaller.

A.8. Gini Coefficient and Kolmogorov-Smirnov Test

These two tools allow us to examine the repartition of the different types of operators or actors on the market (HFT, investors...) or operators.

A.8.1. *Gini coefficient*

The Gini coefficient is a measure of the degree of inequality of income distribution in a given society, developed by the Italian statistician C. Gini in [Gini, 1912]. It is a number ranging from 0 to 1, where 0 means perfect equality (everyone has an exactly equal income) and 1 expresses total inequality (one person has all income, others have nothing, extreme case of master and slaves).

The Gini coefficient is calculated from the function (whose graph is the Lorenz curve) that maps each share of the population ordered by increasing income, the proportion that its revenues. It considers

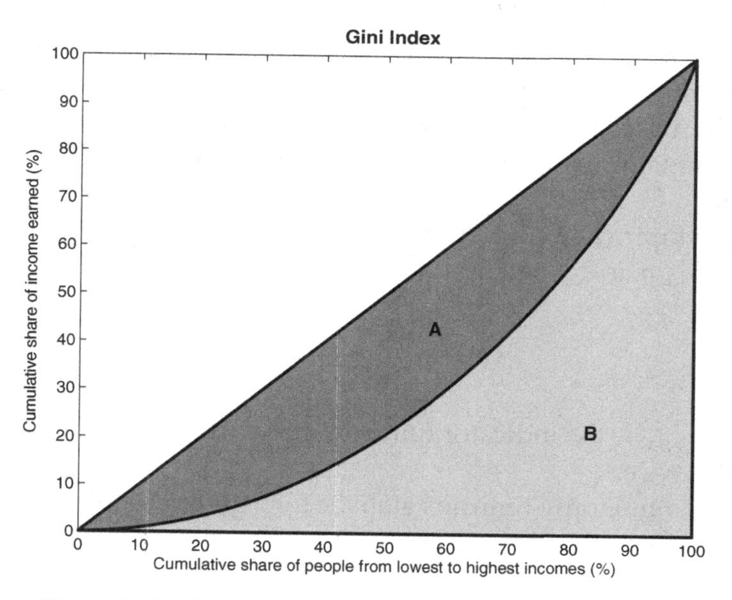

Figure A.12. Graphical representation of the Gini coefficient.

Note: The graph shows that the Gini coefficient is equal to the area marked A divided by the sum of the areas marked A and B. that is, $G = A/(A + B)$. It is also equal to $2 * A$, as $A + B = 0.5$ (since the axes scale from 0 to 1).

the inequality by the deviation from the Lorenz curve of equal distribution (dotted): The ratio of the surface A between the Lorenz curve of the situation under study (in bold) and triangle surface $A+B$:

$$G = A/(A+B) = A/(1/2) = 2A = 2(A+B) - 2B = 1 - 2B$$

where $A+B$ is the half of the square triangle 1x1.

The Gini coefficient is equal to the difference between one and twice the integral of the function represented by the Lorenz curve.

An alternative approach would be to consider the Gini coefficient as half of the relative mean difference, which is mathematically equivalent. The mean difference is the average absolute difference between two items selected randomly from a population, and the relative mean difference is the mean difference divided by the average, to normalize for scale.

A.8.2. *Kolmogorov-Smirnov test*

In statistics, the Kolmogorov-Smirnov test is a hypothesis test used to determine if a sample follows a known probability distribution given by its continuous distribution function, or if two samples follow the same distribution (see [Kolmogorov, 1933] for the original paper).

The empirical distribution function F_n for n i.i.d. observations $X_k, 1 \leq k \leq n$, is defined as

$$F_n(x) = \frac{1}{n} \sum_{k=1}^{n} \mathbf{1}_{\{X_k \leq x\}},$$

where $\mathbf{1}_{\{X_k \leq x\}}$ is the indicator function, equal to 1 if $X_k \leq x$ and equal to 0 otherwise.

The Kolmogorov-Smirnov statistic for a given cumulative distribution function $F(x)$ is

$$D_n = \sup_x |F_n(x) - F(x)| .$$

By the Glivenko-Cantelli theorem, if the sample comes from distribution $F(x)$, then D_n converges to 0 almost surely.

The null hypothesis H_0 is that the sample comes from the supposed continuous distribution $F(x)$,

$$\sqrt{n}D_n \xrightarrow[n\to\infty]{\mathcal{L}} K,$$

where K is a random variable with Kolmogorov distribution whose cumulative distribution function is given by

$$F_K(t) = \mathbb{P}(K \leq t) = 1 - 2\sum_{k\geq 1}(-1)^{k-1}e^{-2k^2x^2}$$

$$= \frac{\sqrt{2\pi}}{x}\sum_{k\geq 1}e^{-(2k-1)^2\pi^2/(8x^2)},$$

which does not depend on F.

The goodness-of-fit test or the Kolmogorov-Smirnov test is constructed by using the critical values of the Kolmogorov distribution. The null hypothesis is rejected at level α if

$$\sqrt{n}D_n > k_{1-\alpha},$$

where $k_{1-\alpha}$ is the $(1-\alpha)$-quantile of the Kolmogorov distribution, namely $\mathbb{P}(K \leq k_{1-\alpha}) = 1-\alpha$.

Two-sample Kolmogorov-Smirnov test. The Kolmogorov-Smirnov test may also be used to test whether two data samples $(X_1, \ldots, X_n)$ and $(Y_1, \ldots, Y_m)$ come from the same distribution (without specifying what that common distribution is). In this case, the Kolmogorov-Smirnov statistic is

$$D_{n,m} = \sup_x |F_n^X(x) - F_m^Y(x)|,$$

where F_n^X and F_m^Y are the empirical distribution functions of $(X_1, \ldots, X_n)$ and $(Y_1, \ldots, Y_m)$ sample respectively. The null hypothesis is rejected at level α if $\sqrt{\frac{nm}{n+m}}D_{n,m} > k_{1-\alpha}$.

A.8.3. *Practical implementation*

We will compare the market share for the SBF120 on Euronext Paris (ENPA) and Chi-X. We plot the evolution of their distribution

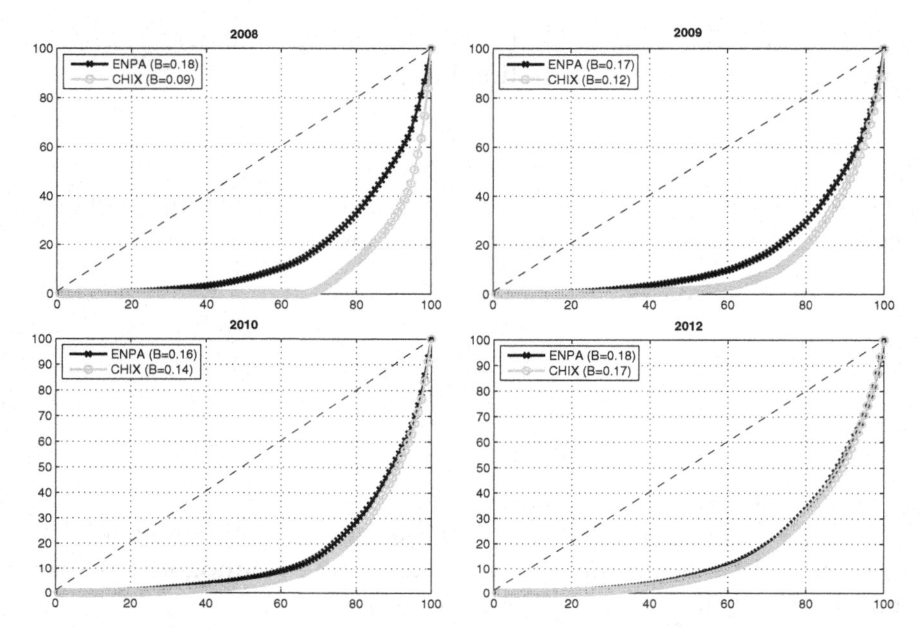

Figure A.13. Evolution of the Gini index of ENPA and CHIX for the SBF120 between 2008 and 2012.

Table A.3. Computation of the Gini index for ENPA and CHIX on SBF120 between 2008 and 2012.

Gini index	2008	2009	2010	2012
ENPA	0.64	0.66	0.68	0.64
CHIX	0.82	0.76	0.72	0.66

between 2008 and 2012 (see Figure A.13) and compute their associated Gini index (the value of area B is indicated in brackets in the legend) (see Table A.3).

We note that the market share of Chi-X has increased between 2008 and 2012 to be close to the one of Euronext Paris. To compare these two distributions, we will conduct a Kolmogorov-Smirnov test to check if the market shares of the two venues have the same distribution (see Table A.4). The null hypothesis H_0 is rejected for

Table A.4. Computation of the Kolmogorov-Smirnov statistic for ENPA and CHIX on SBF120 between 2008 and 2012. Test results for the threshold $\alpha = 5\%$.

Year	2008	2009	2010	2012
KS Stat.	0.6637	0.2348	0.1207	0.0833
H_0 $\alpha = 5\%$	Rejected	Rejected	Accepted	Accepted
p-value	$7.96.10^{-23}$	0.0028	0.3458	0.7816

2008 and 2009, thus we cannot conclude that they have the same distribution. But in 2010 and 2012, H_0 is accepted, so the market share for the SBF120 on ENPA and CHI-X have the same distribution.

A.9. Simple Linear Regression Model

In microstructure, a linear regression model allows us to exhibit linear dependence between two financial indicators: For example between the spread and the volatility, the market share and the spread, the daily turnover and the spread or electronic expansion and trade size.

More generally in statistics and econometrics, a linear regression model is a regression model of a dependent variable on one or more explanatory variables in which it is assumed that the function linking predictors to the dependent variable is linear in its parameters (see e.g. [Tassi, 2004, Bourbonnais, 2011]).

Formally, we model the relationship between a random variable y and a random variable x. In general, the linear model can be written as follows

$$y = a_0 + a_1 x + \epsilon,$$

where y is the dependent variable, the vector x denotes the explanatory variable, ϵ denotes the error term (sometimes called disturbance). Assume we have data on the variables y and x, so we want to estimate the parameters a_0 and a_1.

In general, the linear regression model means a model in which the conditional expectation of y given x is an affine transformation of x. However, we can also consider models in which it is the conditional median of y given x or any quantile of the distribution of y given x is an affine transformation of x.

The linear regression model is often estimated by the least squares method but there are also many other methods to estimate this model. One can for example estimate the model by maximum likelihood or by Bayesian inference. Although they are often presented together the linear model and least squares method does not represent the same thing. The linear model refers to a class of models which can be estimated by many methods and least squares method is a method of estimation. It can be used to estimate different types of models.

A.9.1. *Model presentation*

Consider the following simple linear model

$$y_i = a_0 + a_1 x_i + \epsilon_i, \quad 1 \le i \le n,$$

where $y, x \in \mathbb{R}^n$ are observed, $\epsilon \in \mathbb{R}^n$ is a random vector denoting the modeling error and a_0, a_1 are the model parameters.

We make the following assumptions:

- The variable x is observed without error,
- the model is well-specified in mean: $\mathbb{E}[\epsilon_i] = 0, 1 \le i \le n$,
- the model is homoscedastic: $\mathbb{E}[\epsilon_i^2] = \sigma_\epsilon^2, 1 \le i \le n$,
- the errors are not correlated: $\mathbb{E}[\epsilon_i \epsilon_j] = 0, i \ne j, 1 \le i, j \le n$,
- x and ϵ are not correlated: $\mathbb{E}[x_i \epsilon_i] = 0, 1 \le i, j \le n$.

Denote by $\hat{a}_0$ and $\hat{a}_1$ the estimators of the model parameters a_0 and a_1 respectively. By the ordinary least squares estimation method, we determine $\hat{a}_0$ and $\hat{a}_1$ by minimizing the global quadratic error $S = \sum_{i=1}^n \epsilon_i^2 = \sum_{i=1}^n (y_i - a_0 - a_1 x_i)^2$ with $\frac{\partial S}{\partial a_0} = 0$ and $\frac{\partial S}{\partial a_1} = 0$. Thus we obtain, by setting $\bar{x} = \frac{1}{n} \sum_{i=1}^n x_i$ and $\bar{y} = \frac{1}{n} \sum_{i=1}^n y_i$ (the empirical means of x and y respectively),

$$\hat{a}_1 = \frac{\sum_{i=1}^n (x_i - \bar{x})(y_i - \bar{y})}{\sum_{i=1}^n (x_i - \bar{x})^2}$$

$$= \frac{\sum_{i=1}^n x_i y_i - n\bar{x}\bar{y}}{\sum_{i=1}^n x_i^2 - n\bar{x}^2} \quad \text{and} \quad \hat{a}_0 = \bar{y} - \hat{a}_1 \bar{x}.$$

We then defined the estimated model by $\hat{y}_i = \hat{a}_0 + \hat{a}_1 x_i, 1 \le i \le n$ and the residual term $e_i = y_i - \hat{y}_i, 1 \le i \le n$.

Estimator properties. The estimators of the model parameters are unbiased, i.e. $\mathbb{E}[\hat{a}_0] = a_0$ and $\mathbb{E}[\hat{a}_1] = a_1$, and we can compute their variances and their covariance

$$\sigma_{\hat{a}_0}^2 = \text{Var}(\hat{a}_0) = \frac{\sigma_\epsilon^2}{n} \frac{\sum_{i=1}^n x_i^2}{\sum_{i=1}^n (x_i - \bar{x})^2}, \quad \sigma_{\hat{a}_1}^2 = \text{Var}(\hat{a}_1) = \frac{\sigma_\epsilon^2}{\sum_{i=1}^n (x_i - \bar{x})^2}$$

and

$$\text{Cov}(\hat{a}_0, \hat{a}_1) = -\sigma_\epsilon^2 \frac{\bar{x}}{\sum_{i=1}^n (x_i - \bar{x})^2}.$$

As σ_ϵ^2 is unknown, we have to estimate it to approximate the variances of the estimations of the model parameters. By using the unbiased empirical variance $\hat{\sigma}_\epsilon^2 = \frac{1}{n-2}\sum_{i=1}^n \epsilon_i^2$ and by replacing σ_ϵ^2 by the estimation $\hat{\sigma}_\epsilon^2$ in the above expressions for the variances of $\hat{a}_0$ and $\hat{a}_1$, we obtain the estimators $\hat{\sigma}_{\hat{a}_0}^2$ and $\hat{\sigma}_{\hat{a}_1}^2$ respectively.

Distribution of $\hat{a}_0$ and $\hat{a}_1$. Assume that $\epsilon_i \overset{\mathcal{L}}{\sim} \mathcal{N}(0,\sigma_\epsilon^2)$, $1 \le i \le n$ (this assumption let's us check that the estimators obtained by the least square method are equal to those of maximum likehood). Then, for $k = 0, 1$,

- $\frac{\hat{a}_k - a_k}{\sigma_{\hat{a}_k}} \overset{\mathcal{L}}{\sim} \mathcal{N}(0,1)$,
- $\frac{\hat{a}_k - a_k}{\hat{\sigma}_{\hat{a}_k}} \overset{\mathcal{L}}{\sim} \mathcal{T}_{(n-2)}$,

where $\mathcal{T}_{(n-2)}$ denotes the Student-t distribution with $n-2$ degrees of freedom.

Fitting quality and variance analysis. The equation of variance analysis reads

$$\underbrace{\sum_{i=1}^n (y_i - \bar{y})^2}_{TV} = \underbrace{\sum_{i=1}^n (\hat{y}_i - \bar{\hat{y}})^2}_{EV} + \underbrace{\sum_{i=1}^n \epsilon_i^2}_{RV},$$

i.e. the global sum of squares (or total variability (TV)) is equal to the sum of the regression squares (or explained variability (EV)) plus the sum of the residual squares (or residual variability (RV)).

The determination coefficient R^2 is defined by $R^2 = \frac{EV}{TV} = 1 - \frac{RV}{TV} \le 1$. For a simple linear model, we check that $R^2 = r^2$, where r^2 is the coefficient of linear correlation

$$r = \frac{\sum_{i=1}^n (x_i - \bar{x})(y_i - \bar{y})}{\sqrt{\sum_{i=1}^n (x_i - \bar{x})^2}\sqrt{\sum_{i=1}^n (y_i - \bar{y})^2}}.$$

A.9.2. *Application to relation between spread and volatility*

Consider the volatility σ and the spread ψ of an asset. Our aim is to check if the relation between them is linear, *i.e.* if we have $\psi = a_0 + a_1\sigma + \epsilon$. To this end, we illustrate this idea on RIO TINTO by

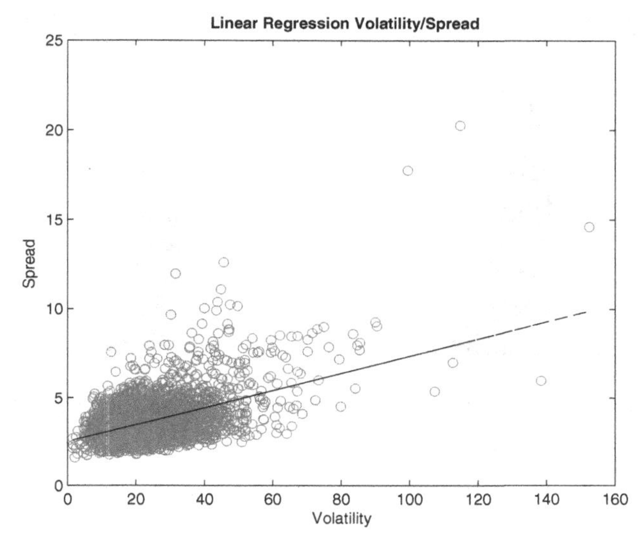

Figure A.14. Linear regression $\psi = a_0 + a_1\sigma + \epsilon$. $\hat{a}_0 = 2.4894$, $\hat{a}_1 = 0.0485$, $R^2 = 0.2404$.

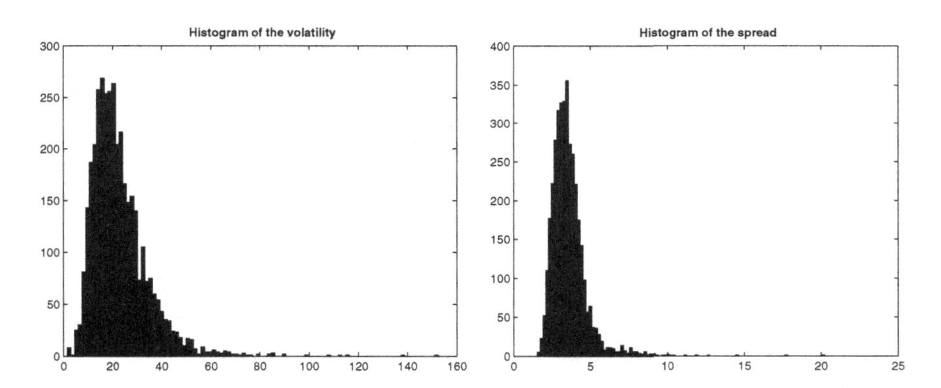

Figure A.15. Histograms of the volatility and the spread for the RIO TINTO.

using volatilities and spreads computed for 15-minute intervals since January 2012.

Let us check the distribution of the observed variables σ and ψ.

We see that the distributions of the volatility and the spread are not Gaussian, but look log-normal. To confirm this hypothesis, let us plot the histogram of the logarithm of these two quantities.

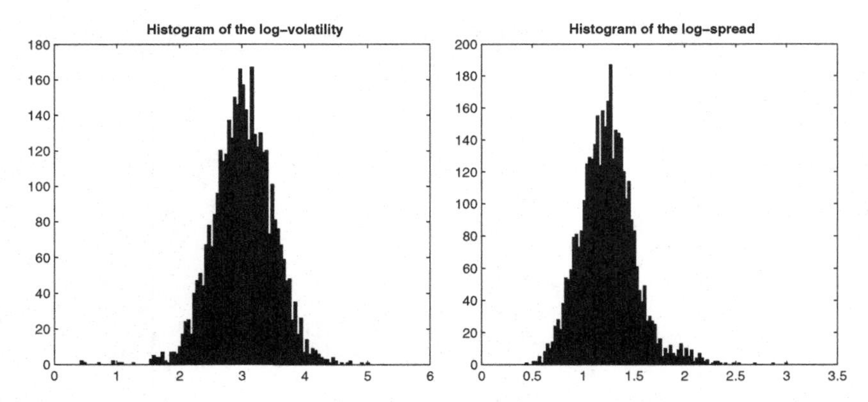

Figure A.16. Histograms of the log-volatility and the log-spread for the RIO TINTO.

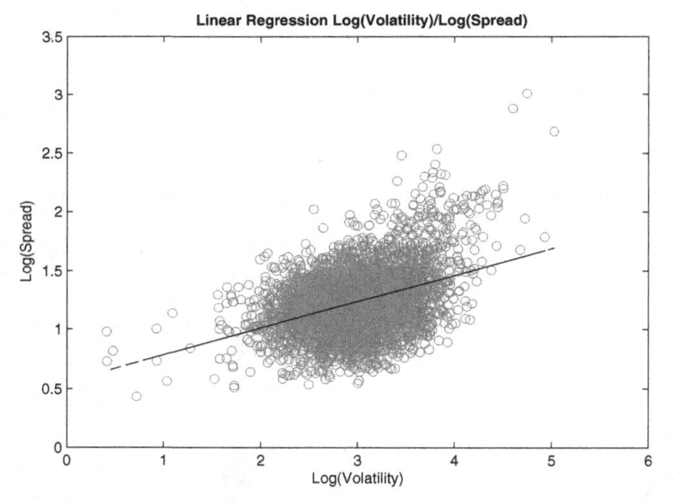

Figure A.17. Linear regression $\log \psi = a_0 + a_1 \log \sigma + \epsilon$. $\hat{a}_0 = 0.5609$, $\hat{a}_1 = 0.2252$, $R^2 = 0.1553$.

These distributions better fit with Gaussian distribution than in the previous case. Thus if we do the linear regression between the log-volatility and the log-spread, we obtain the following result If we go back to the initial variables ψ and σ, we then obtain the following expression

$$\psi = A_0 \sigma^{a_1} e^{\epsilon}, \quad \text{where } A_0 = e^{a_0},$$

which is no longer linear, but a multiplicative model where the error term is also multiplicative. To build $\hat{\psi}$ as a predictor of ψ so that $\mathbb{E}[\hat{\psi}] = \mathbb{E}[\psi]$, one needs to remark that if $\epsilon \overset{\mathcal{L}}{\sim} \mathcal{N}(0, \sigma_\epsilon^2)$, then

$$\mathbb{E}[\psi] = \mathbb{E}\left[A_0 \sigma^{a_1} e^{\epsilon}\right] = A_0 \sigma^{a_1} \mathbb{E}[e^{\epsilon}] = A_0 \sigma^{a_1} e^{\frac{\sigma_\epsilon^2}{2}}.$$

Thus the unbiased predictor of ψ reads

$$\hat{\psi} = \hat{A}_0 \sigma^{\hat{a}_1} e^{\frac{\hat{\sigma}_\epsilon^2}{2}}.$$

We can compute the determination coefficient associated with this multiplicative model, namely

$$R'^2 = \frac{\sum_{i=1}^{n} (\hat{\psi}_i - \bar{\hat{\psi}})^2}{\sum_{i=1}^{n} (\psi_i - \bar{\psi})^2} = \frac{\sum_{i=1}^{n} (e^{\hat{a}_0} \sigma_i^{\hat{a}_1} e^{\frac{\hat{\sigma}_\epsilon^2}{2}} - \bar{\hat{\psi}})^2}{\sum_{i=1}^{n} (\psi_i - \bar{\psi})^2} = 0.1097.$$

A.10. Time Series and Seasonalities

In microstructure, we can use time series techniques to model many indicators like the volatility, the spread, the price, the volume, etc. Very often, we may observe and model seasonalities in time series (daily, weekly, monthly, yearly), like for the traded volume (as illustrated below).

A.10.1. *Introduction to time series*

In statistics, signal processing, econometrics and mathematical finance, a time series is a sequence of data points, measured typically at successive time instants spaced at uniform time intervals (see e.g. [Brockwell and Davis, 1991, Hamilton, 1993]). We denote it by $(X_t)_{t\geq 1}$. We distinguish in general three constitutive effects of a series:

- A long-term trend C_t;
- A seasonal effect S_t that appears at regular intervals, and this effect results in a component of the series called seasonal component;
- An unexplained effect ε_t: this effect, which we assume is generally induced by chance, occurs by accidental variations.

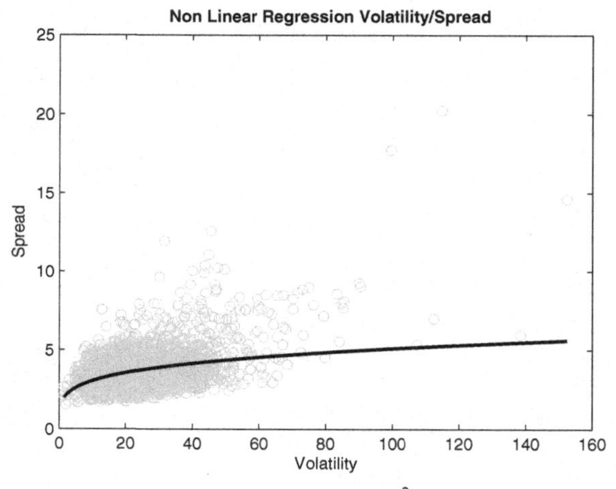

Figure A.18. Non Linear regression $\hat{\psi} = \hat{A}_0 \sigma^{\hat{a}_1} e^{\frac{\hat{\sigma}_\epsilon^2}{2}}$. $\hat{a}_0 = 0.5609$, $\hat{a}_1 = 0.2252$, $\hat{\sigma}_\epsilon = 0.2509$, $R'^2 = 0.1097$.

A time series model is an equation indicating how the components are articulated relative to each other to form the series. There are many models, among them two simple classical models:

- The additive model: $X_t = C_t + S_t + \varepsilon_t$;
- The multiplicative model: $X_t = C_t S_t + \varepsilon_t$.

Definition 2 (Moving Average)

1. *A* centered moving average *of odd length* $2k+1$ *at time* t *is the average value* MA_t *of observations* $X_{t-k}, \ldots, X_t, \ldots, X_{t+k}$

$$MA_t = \frac{X_{t-k} + \cdots + X_t + \cdots + X_{t+k}}{2k+1}.$$

2. *A* centered moving average *of even length* $2k$ *at time* t *is the average value* MA_t *of observations* $X_{t-k}, \ldots, X_t, \ldots, X_{t+k}$, *with the first and last observations weighted by* 0.5

$$MA_t = \frac{0.5X_{t-k} + X_{t-k+1} + \cdots + X_t + \cdots + X_{t+k-1} + 0.5X_{t+k}}{2k}.$$

In the first formula, the number of summands is equal to $2k+1$ — this is a real average. In the second, the sum of the coefficients is equal to $2k$, since the first and last are equal to 0.5 — this is a weighted average. In both cases, the number of observations taken into account before time t is equal to the number of observations taken into account after time t — this is why the averages are called centered.

Generally one can not calculate moving average at $t = 1$, $t = 2, \ldots, t = k$ since the formulas can be applied only if one knows X_{t-k}. Similarly, if T is the total number of observations, one can calculate $MA_T, \ldots, MA_{T-k+1}$ since we must know X_{t+k}. The advantage of moving averages is to smooth the irregular while preserving linear trends. Indeed if the trend of a time series X_t is linear and has the equation $C_t = bt + a$, the moving averages tend to have the same behavior and are even closer if the moving average is long.

Application to deseasonality

In both models presented (additive and multiplicative), the length of the moving averages should be absolutely equal to the period of seasonal variations. Indeed moving averages of a series subject to seasonal variations of period p are not subject to seasonal variations if their length is equal to the period p (and more generally if their length is a multiple of the period).

For a period p, we set $t = (i-1)p + j$ and denote by X_{ij} the observation $X_t = X_{(i-1)p+j}$.

Additive model. Generally, an additive model reads

$$\forall 1 \le i \le n, \quad \forall 1 \le j \le p, \quad X_{ij} = C_{ij} + S_j + \varepsilon_{ij}.$$

The term S_j characterizes the seasonal variation at time j of each period i. We can compute the difference between observation and the trend

$$\forall 1 \le i \le n, \quad \forall 1 \le j \le p, \quad X_{ij} - C_{ij} = S_j + \varepsilon_{ij}.$$

For the same seasonality, the difference between observation and the trend is just nearly constant and equal to S_j (assuming that the irregular component is relatively small). Earlier we saw that the moving averages of length l equal to the period of seasonal variations are approximations of the trend. We can therefore consider that the difference between an observation X_{ij} and the corresponding moving average MA_{ij} is roughly constant for fixed j

$$\forall 1 \le i \le n, \quad \forall 1 \le j \le p, \quad X_{ij} - MA_{ij} \approx S_j.$$

Differences $X_{ij} - MA_{ij}$ are approximations of the coefficients S_j. Their average (or median), for each j, gives a first estimate $\hat{S}_j$

$$\forall 1 \le j \le p, \quad \hat{S}_j = \frac{1}{n} \sum_{i=1}^{n} (X_{ij} - MA_{ij}).$$

We will finally obtain the final estimates S_j by centering these terms $\hat{S}_j$, namely

$$\forall 1 \le j \le p, \quad S_j = \hat{S}_j - \frac{1}{p}\sum_{k=1}^{p} \hat{S}_k.$$

Multiplicative model. A multiplicative model reads

$$\forall 1 \le i \le n, \quad \forall 1 \le j \le p, \quad X_{ij} = C_{ij}S_j + \varepsilon_{ij}.$$

To quantify the seasonal variations, we consider the following ratios

$$\forall 1 \le i \le n, \quad \forall 1 \le j \le p, \quad \frac{X_{ij}}{C_{ij}} = S_j + \frac{\varepsilon_{ij}}{C_{ij}}.$$

Considering that accidental variations ε_{ij} are small compared to the trend C_{ij} and using the approximation of the trend by moving averages, this leads to the following approximation

$$\forall 1 \le i \le n, \quad \forall 1 \le j \le p, \quad \frac{X_{ij}}{MA_{ij}} \approx S_j.$$

We obtain initial estimates $\hat{S}_j$ of seasonal coefficients by calculating the mean (or median) of ratios, namely

$$\forall 1 \le j \le p, \quad \hat{S}_j = \frac{1}{n}\sum_{i=1}^{n} \frac{X_{ij}}{MA_{ij}}.$$

By analogy with the seasonal coefficients in the additive model, with mean equal to 0, we look for final estimates of S_j with average equal to 1

$$\forall 1 \le j \le p, \quad S_j = \frac{\hat{S}_j}{\frac{1}{p}\sum_{k=1}^{p} \hat{S}_k}.$$

Thus $\sum_{j=1}^{p} S_j = \frac{\sum_{j=1}^{p} \hat{S}_j}{\frac{1}{p}\sum_{k=1}^{p} \hat{S}_k} = p$.

A.10.2. *Example of volume model*

Let $n \in \{1,\ldots,N\}$ denote the time slot, $d \in \{1,\ldots,D\}$ the day, $m \in \{1,\ldots,12\}$ the month and $y \in \{1,\ldots,Y\}$ the year. We model the traded volume of year y, month m, day d, hour n by the following random variable

$$V(y,m,d,n,\omega) = (f(n) + g(d,n))F(m)G(y)v(n,\omega),$$

where $f(n)$ is the mean effect of the time slot, $g(d,n)$ is the mean effect for day d at time n (to model some effect arriving at particular days), $F(m)$ is the mean monthly effect, $G(y)$ the mean yearly effect and $v(n,\omega)$ is the random variable modeling the volume level of day n.

$$\begin{aligned}
V^D(y,m,d,\omega) &= \sum_{n=1}^{N} V(y,m,d,n,\omega) \\
&= F(m)G(y)\left(\underbrace{\sum_{n=1}^{N} f(n)v(n,\omega)}_{\tilde{f}(\omega)} + \underbrace{\sum_{n=1}^{N} g(d,n)v(n,\omega)}_{\tilde{g}(d,\omega)}\right) \\
&= F(m)G(y)\left(\tilde{f}(\omega) + \tilde{g}(d,\omega)\right).
\end{aligned}$$

$$\begin{aligned}
V^M(y,m,\omega) &= \sum_{d=1}^{D} V^D(y,m,d,\omega) \\
&= F(m)G(y)\underbrace{\sum_{d=1}^{D}\left(\tilde{f}(\omega) + \tilde{g}(d,\omega)\right)}_{H(\omega)} \\
&= G(y)F(m)H(\omega).
\end{aligned}$$

By assuming that $\mathbb{E}[H] = 1$, we obtain that $\mathbb{E}[V^M(y, m, \cdot)] = G(y)F(m)$. Furthermore assume that $\sum_{m=1}^{M} F(m) = 1$, thus

$$V^Y(y, \omega) = \sum_{m=1}^{M} V^M(y, m, \omega) = G(y)H(\omega) \sum_{m=1}^{M} F(m) = G(y)H(\omega)$$

and $\mathbb{E}[V^Y(y, \cdot)] = G(y)$.

Illustration of daily and yearly seasonality on real data. We use here the traded volume of TOTAL over the period from 02/01/2007 to 01/06/2012. The first figure illustrates the daily seasonality and the second one the yearly seasonality.

We observe that the five days of the week look similar, but there is a slight bump at noon on Friday: this is due to some financial events that happen on some Fridays, namely derivative expiry. Thus the average profile of the day may be modified by these kinds of financial events, that's why we put on the above model the additional effect $g(d, n)$ to take into account these modifications.

This figure illustrates the yearly seasonality in the traded volume of Total from 2007 to 2011.

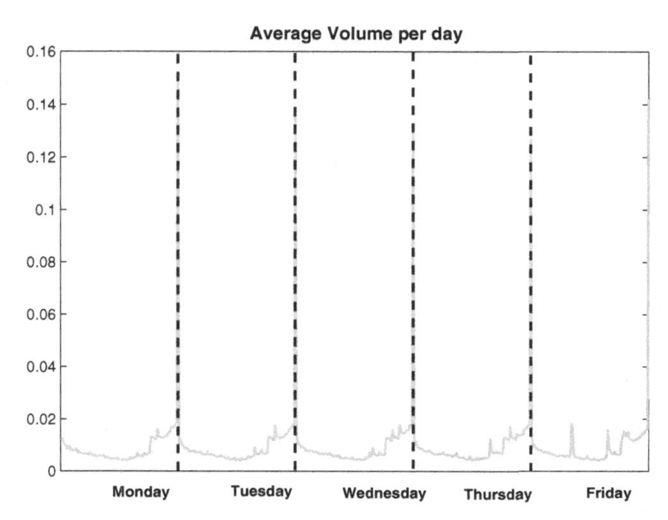

Figure A.19. Intraday seasonality for each day of a week of volume for TOTAL from 02/01/2007 to 01/06/2012.

A.11. Clusters of Liquidity

The aim of this section is to give an example of modeling for the number of transactions by observing some properties like clusters. To illustrate this phenomena, we plot the number of transactions for Total on a Dark Pool Chi-Delta.

We now introduce point processes, then Hawkes processes used in the recent microstructure literature to model the price dynamics (see e.g. [Bacry *et al.*, 2012]). This is a new stochastic model for the variations of asset prices at the tick-by-tick level. Its construction is based on marked point processes and relies on linear self and mutually exciting stochastic intensities as introduced by Hawkes. The advantage of this model is that it can reproduce microstructure noise and the Epps effect while preserving a standard Brownian diffusion behavior on large scales.

A.11.1. *Introduction to point processes*

For a review on point processes, we refer the reader to [Daley and Vere-Jones, 2003a, Daley and Vere-Jones, 2003b].

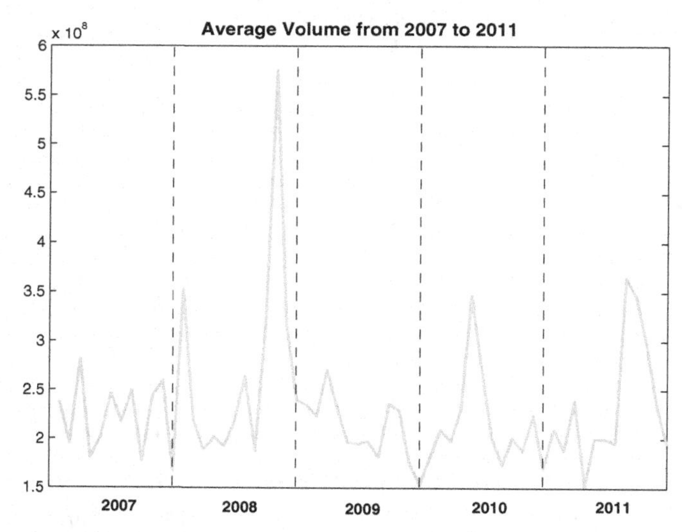

Figure A.20. Seasonality per year of volume for TOTAL from 02/01/2007 to 31/12/2011.

Definition 3 (Simple point processes). *Let $(\Omega, \mathcal{A}, \mathbb{P})$ be some probability space. Let $(\tau_i)_{i \geq 1}$ be a sequence of non-negative random variables such that $\forall i \geq 1$, $\tau_i < \tau_{i+1}$. We call $(\tau_i)_{i \geq 1}$ a (simple)* point process *on $\mathbb{R}_+$. In particular, the variables τ_i can represent the times of occurrence of transactions, or arrival of limit orders in an orderbook, etc. We start counting events with index 1. If needed, we will assume that $\tau_0 = 0$.*

Definition 4 (Counting process). *Let $(\tau_i)_{i \geq 1}$ be a point process. The right-continuous process*

$$N_t = \sum_{i \geq 1} \mathbf{1}_{\tau_i \leq t}$$

is called the counting process *associated with $(\tau_i)_{i \geq 1}$.*

Definition 5 (Duration). *The process $(\Delta \tau_i)_{i \geq 1}$ defined by*

$$\forall i \geq 1, \quad \Delta \tau_i = \tau_i - \tau_{i-1}$$

is called the duration process *associated with $(\tau_i)_{i \geq 1}$.*

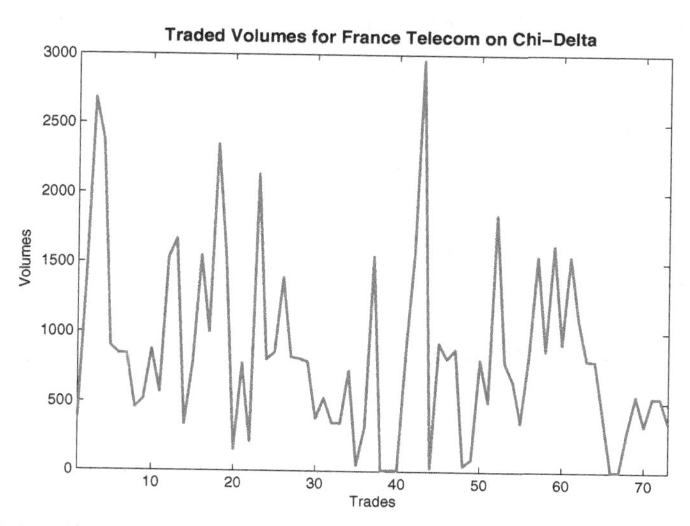

Figure A.21. Illustration of traded volume for France Telecom on Chi-Delta, 23/07/2012.

Definition 6 (Intensity process). *Let N be a point process adapted to a filtration $\mathcal{F}_t$. The left-continuous* intensity process *is defined as*

$$\lambda(t|\mathcal{F}_t) = \lim_{h \downarrow 0} \mathbb{E}\left[\frac{N_{t+h} - N_t}{h} \mid \mathcal{F}_t\right],$$

or equivalently

$$\lambda(t|\mathcal{F}_t) = \lim_{h \downarrow 0} \frac{1}{h}\mathbb{P}\left(N_{t+h} - N_t > 0|\mathcal{F}_t\right).$$

Intensity depends on the choice of filtration, but we will always assume that the filtration used is the natural one for the process N, denoted $\mathcal{F}_t^N$. We will therefore write $\lambda(t)$ instead of $\lambda(t|\mathcal{F}_t^N)$.

Example: Homogeneous Poisson Process. Let $\lambda \in \mathbb{R}_+^*$. A Poisson process with constant rate λ is a point process defined by

$$\mathbb{P}(N_{t+h} - N_t = 1|\mathcal{F}_t) = \lambda h + o(h),$$
$$\mathbb{P}(N_{t+h} - N_t > 1|\mathcal{F}_t) = o(h).$$

- The intensity does not depend on the history of the process N, and the probability of occurrence of an event in $(t, t+h]$ is independent of $\mathcal{F}_t$.
- Durations $(\Delta\tau_i)_{i\geq 1}$ of a homogeneous Poisson process are independent and identically distributed (i.i.d.) according to an exponential distribution with parameter λ.
- This process is Markovian and very often used in queueing theory (when the consumption and the service are assumed to be independent).

Stochastic Time Change. The *integrated intensity* function Λ is defined as

$$\forall i \geq 1, \quad \Lambda(\tau_{i-1}, \tau_i) = \int_{\tau_{i-1}}^{\tau_i} \lambda(s)ds.$$

The following theorem, called time change theorem, illustrates the fact that any point process comes down to a Poisson process up to a time change. This result is the equivalent of the Dubins-Schwarz

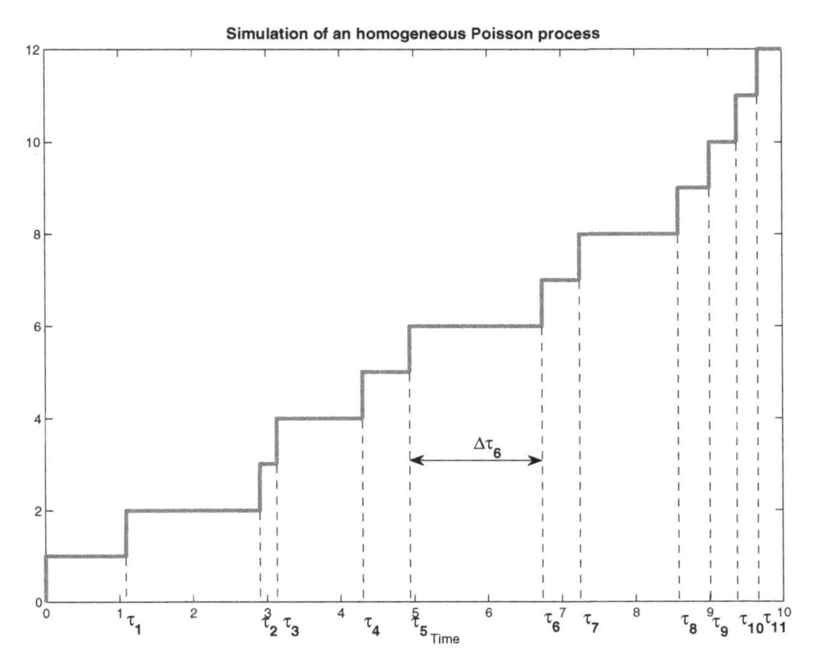

Figure A.22. Illustration of a homogeneous Poisson process with parameter $\lambda = 1$: events $(\tau_i)_{i\geq 1}$, counting process N_t and duration process $(\Delta\tau_i)_{i\geq 1}$.

theorem for martingales, namely every continuous local $(\mathcal{F}_t)$-martingale M is of the form $M_t = B_{\langle M\rangle_t}$, $t \geq 0$, where $(B_s)_{s\geq 0}$ is a $\mathcal{F}_{\tau_s}$-Brownian motion (with $\tau_s = \inf\{t : \langle M\rangle_t > s\}$).

Theorem 1 (Time change theorem). *Let N be a point process on $\mathbb{R}_+$ such that $\int_0^\infty \lambda(s)ds = 1$. Let t_τ be the stopping time defined by*

$$\int_0^{t_\tau} \lambda(s)ds = \tau.$$

Then the process $\tilde{N}_\tau = N_{t_\tau}$ is a homogeneous Poisson process with constant intensity $\lambda = 1$.

A.11.2. *One-dimensional Hawkes processes*

When the data that we want to model are not Markovian, namely they have some clusters, we do not use Poisson processes to model

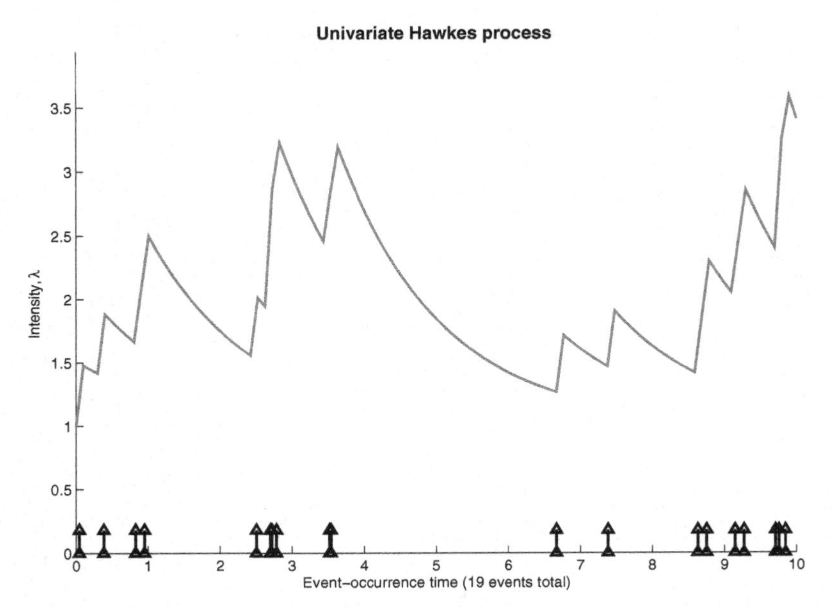

Figure A.23. Simulation of a one-dimensional Hawkes process with parameters $P = 1$, $\lambda_0 = 1$, $\alpha = 0.5$, $\beta = 0.7$ (see e.g. [Møller and Rasmussen, 2005] for simulation).

them. Thus we introduce a new type of processes recently used in microstructure and called Hawkes processes.

Definition 7 (Linear self-exciting process). *A general definition for a linear self-exciting process N reads*

$$\lambda(t) = \lambda_0(t) + \int_{-\infty}^{t} \nu(t-s)dN_s = \lambda_0(t) + \sum_{t_i<t} \nu(t-\tau_i),$$

where $\lambda_0 : \mathbb{R} \to \mathbb{R}_+$ is a deterministic base intensity and $\nu : \mathbb{R}_+ \to \mathbb{R}_+$ expresses the positive influence of the past events τ_i on the current value of the intensity process.

Hawkes (1971) proposes an exponential kernel $\nu(t) = \sum_{j=1}^{P} \alpha_j e^{-\beta_j t}\mathbf{1}_{\mathbb{R}_+}(t)$, so that the intensity of the model becomes

$$\lambda(t) = \lambda_0(t) + \int_0^t \sum_{j=1}^{P} \alpha_j e^{-\beta_j(t-s)} dN_s = \lambda_0(t) + \sum_{t_i<t}\sum_{j=1}^{P} \alpha_j e^{-\beta_j(t-\tau_i)}.$$

The simplest version with $P = 1$ and $\lambda_0(t)$ constant is defined as

$$\lambda(t) = \lambda_0(t) + \int_0^t \alpha e^{-\beta(t-s)} dN_s = \lambda_0(t) + \sum_{\tau_i < t} \alpha e^{-\beta(t-\tau_i)}.$$

Stationarity. Assuming stationarity gives $\mathbb{E}[\lambda(t)] = \mu$ constant. Thus,

$$\begin{aligned}\mu = \mathbb{E}[\lambda(t)] &= \mathbb{E}\left[\lambda_0 + \int_{-\infty}^t \nu(t-s) dN_s\right] \\ &= \lambda_0 + \mathbb{E}\left[\int_{-\infty}^t \nu(t-s)\lambda(s) ds\right] \\ &= \lambda_0 + \int_{-\infty}^t \nu(t-s)\mu ds = \lambda_0 + \mu \int_0^\infty \nu(u) du,\end{aligned}$$

which gives

$$\mu = \frac{\lambda_0}{1 - \int_0^\infty \nu(u) du}. \tag{A.30}$$

The stationarity condition for a 1D-Hawkes process reads $\sum_{j=1}^P \frac{\alpha_j}{\beta_j} < 1$. Equation (A.30) immediately gives for the one-dimensional Hawkes process with $P = 1$ the unconditional expected value of the intensity process

$$\mathbb{E}[\lambda(t)] = \frac{\lambda_0}{1 - \alpha/\beta}.$$

Example of calibration of Hawkes process on real data. We calibrate a 1D-Hawkes process on traded volumes of Figure A.11 and we present a path of the calibrated process.

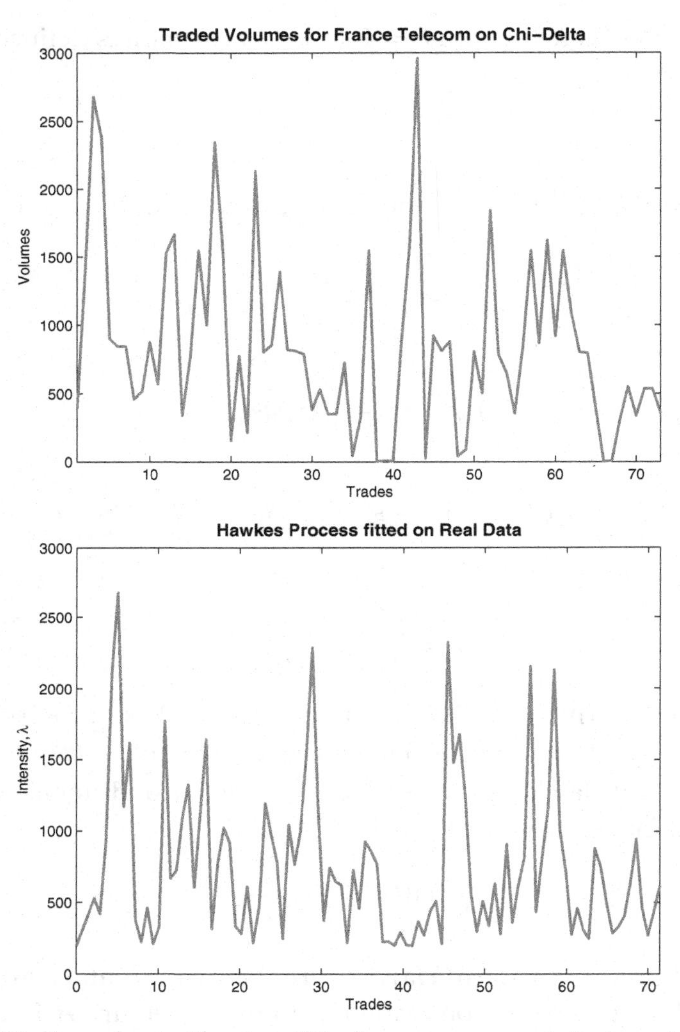

Figure A.24. Example of calibration of Hawkes process on traded volume for France Telecom on Chi-Delta for 23/07/2012, $\lambda_0 = 140$, $\alpha = 250$, $\beta = 300$.

A.12. Signature Plot and Epps Effect

A.12.1. *Volatility and signature plot*

Let S be the price process, $X = \log S$ be the log-price process and Δ the discretization step over a time period $[0, T]$. Set for every $j \in 1, \dots, T/\Delta$, $r_\Delta(j) = X_{\Delta j} - X_{\Delta(j-1)}$ the log-price increments. Thus, in the Itô semi-martingale framework, the integrated variance reads

$$\int_0^T \sigma_s^2 ds = \lim_{\Delta \to 0} \sum_{j=1}^{T/\Delta} r_\Delta(j)^2.$$

Consequently, a "natural" estimator for the integrated variance is $\hat{V}_R(\Delta) = \sum_{j=1}^{T/\Delta} r_\Delta(j)^2$. This estimator is consistent since $\hat{V}_R(\Delta) \xrightarrow[\Delta \to 0]{\mathbb{P}} \int_0^T \sigma_s^2 ds$.

They are many other ways to estimate the volatility: for example by using the minimum and the maximum of the price (see [Garman and Klass, 1980]), by considering multi-scale (see [Zhang *et al.*, 2005, Aït-Sahalia and Jacod, 2007]) or by bid-ask modeling (see [Robert and Rosenbaum, 2012]).

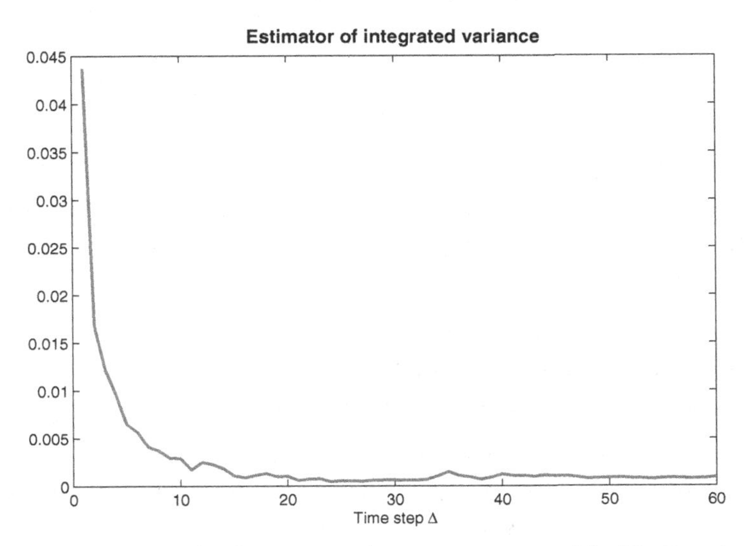

Figure A.25. Estimator for the integrated variance computed for Rio Tinto between 03/01/2012 and 19/06/2012 according to the time discretization step.

Observations and microstructure. A model for log-price observation X may be $X = M + \varepsilon$, where M is a semi-martingale and ε is the noise. Consequently

$$r_\Delta(j) = M_{\Delta j} - M_{\Delta(j-1)} + \varepsilon_{\Delta j} - \varepsilon_{\Delta(j-1)} = r_\Delta^M(j) + \eta_\Delta(j).$$

Thus the realized varince reads

$$\hat{V}_R(\Delta) = \sum_{j=1}^{T/\Delta} r_\Delta(j)^2 = \sum_{j=1}^{T/\Delta} r_\Delta^M(j)^2 + \sum_{j=1}^{T/\Delta} \eta_\Delta(j)^2 + \sum_{j=1}^{T/\Delta} r_\Delta^M(j)\eta_\Delta(j).$$

This estimator diverges when $\Delta \to 0$.

A.12.2. *Correlation and Epps effect*

Let X^1 and X^2 be two log-price processes. Then the covariance between the two assets reads

$$\int_0^T \rho_s \sigma_s^1 \sigma_s^2 ds = \lim_{\Delta \to 0} \sum_{j=1}^{T/\Delta} r_\Delta^1(j) r_\Delta^2(j).$$

Thus, an estimator for the realized covariance may be written as $\hat{C}_R(\Delta) = \sum_{j=1}^{T/\Delta} r_\Delta^1(j) r_\Delta^2(j)$. This estimator is consistent since $\hat{C}_R(\Delta) \xrightarrow[\Delta \to 0]{\mathbb{P}} \int_0^T \rho_s \sigma_s^1 \sigma_s^2 ds$.

The problem is that we must have synchronous data, but the quotations and transactions are asynchronous.

Epps effect. Epps (1979) (see [Epps, 1979]): "Correlations among price changes [...] are found to decrease with the length of the interval for which the price changes are measured." Many explanations were proposed:

- "Lead-lag" effect for the assets in the same sector,
- asynchronicity of transactions,
- "tick" effect and other microstructure effects.

The correlation estimator for high-frequency data is studied in many publications, for example [Barndorff-Nielsen and Shephard, 2004, Hayashi and Yoshida, 2005, Zhang, 2010].

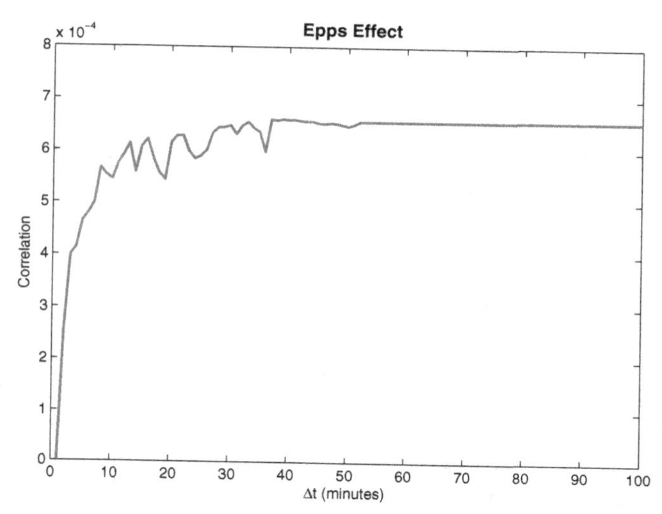

Figure A.26. Estimator for the correlation between Total and France Telecom on Euronext Paris on the period from 23/07/2012 to 27/07/2012 as a function of time discretization step.

A.13. Averaging Effect

The aim of this section is to show the effect of averaging and to warn of its use by illustrating it with the linear regression (see Section A.9). In microstructure the mean is often used to show the average profile of different quantities: for example, the average intraday volatility, the average intraday traded volume, etc.

A.13.1. *Mean versus path*

To show that the average profile of a quantity does not mean that this profile exists in the real world, we plot above the average intraday volatility of an asset on 3 months and a path of this intraday volatility on a day of this period Figure A.27 shows the effect of averaging and the difference between the two profiles: the volatility on 25/05/2012 does not have the same behavior as the mean on the period.

A.13.2. *Regression of average quantities versus mean of the regressions*

Consider an index I made up of N stocks where the weight of stock k is denoted by w_k and its price process by $S^k = (S_t^k)_{t\geq 0}$, $1 \leq k \leq N$.

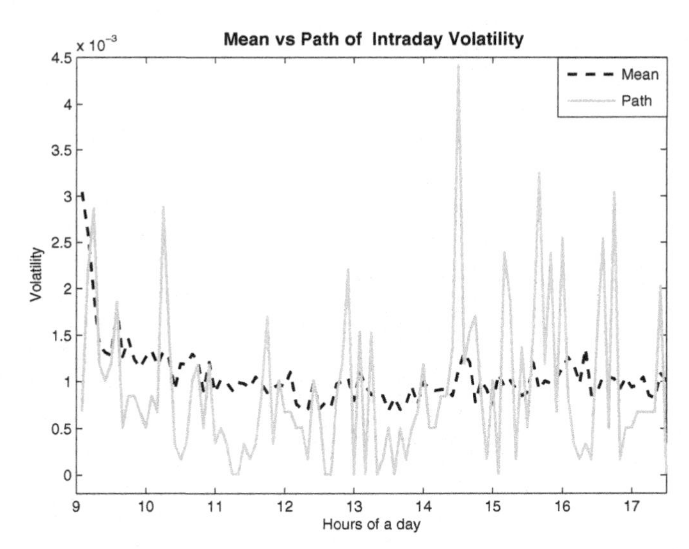

Figure A.27. Mean of intraday volatility of Adidas between 27/04/2012 and 27/07/2012 and realization of the intraday volatility on 25/05/2012.

Then the index process is a weighted average of the N price processes and reads

$$I = (I_t)_{t \geq 0} \quad \text{where } \forall t \geq 0, \quad I_t = \sum_{k=1}^{N} w_k S_t^k.$$

Denote by σ^I the volatility of the index and by ψ^I its spread (respectively σ^k and ψ^k the volatility and the spread of the stock k, $1 \leq k \leq N$). Note that we have

$$\psi^I = \sum_{k=1}^{N} w_k \psi^k$$

but this relation is not true for the volatility.

Now, as in Section A.9, we make the linear regression between the volatility and the spread for the index and for each stock, namely

$$\psi^I = a_0^I + a^I \sigma^I + \epsilon^I$$

and for every $k \in \{1, \ldots, N\}$,

$$\psi^k = a_0^k + a^k \sigma^k + \epsilon^k$$

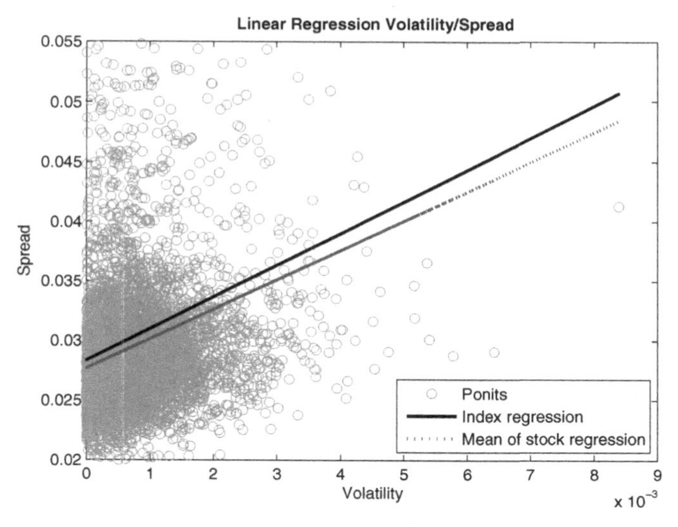

Figure A.28. Linear regression volatility/spread for the DAX and the average regression for the stocks on data from 27/04/2012 to 27/07/2012: $\hat{a}_0^I = 0.0283$, $\hat{a}_1^I = 2.6641$, $\bar{a}_0 = 0.0277$, $\bar{a}_1 = 2.4734$.

and we compare the coefficients of the regression on the index quantities ($\hat{a}_0^I$ and $\hat{a}_1^I$) with the weighted average of the coefficients of the regressions on the stocks quantities ($\bar{a}_0 = \sum_{k=1}^N w_k \hat{a}_0^k$ and $\bar{a}_1 = \sum_{k=1}^N w_k \hat{a}_0^k$).

Numerical example with the DAX. The results we obtained on the DAX and on its components are shown in the figure below. We see that the regression coefficients for the index are higher than the weighted average of those of the stocks — this is due to the index volatility which is not the weighted average of the stock volatilities.

Appendix B

Glossary

This glossary is sorted by themes, and its entries are reported in the index such that the reader can go through it to have a general view on main terms used in the book. Alternatively, the reader can refer to the index and jump directly to the term.

Price Formation Process. The price formation process covers all events occurring during trading that result in a constantly evolving market price. Such events are, for instance: Insertion of new orders or cancellation of orders, or matching of opposite orders.

Walrasian Equilibrium — An equilibrium between consumers and producers to set a perfect match between supply and demand.

Fair Price — The *fair price*, or *latent price* is a theoretical price figuring where the price could be if all the offer and demand could be instantaneously confronted, with no friction.

Fixing and Continuous Auctions — Electronic markets implement mainly two kind of auctions:

- Fixing auctions having two phases: A pre-fixing one, during which market participants can send and modify orders with no interaction; and the fixing itself, computing a market clearing price targeting a Walrasian equilibrium.
- Continuous auctions during which any order interacts with others as soon as it hits the matching engine of the trading facility.

Market Transparency — An electronic market provides pre-trade transparency when it discloses to market participants the state of its orderbook. It can be just the best bid and ask prices, or the full quotes (best bid and ask prices and sizes), or even more than the one price limit and associated sizes. It can provide post-trade transparency disseminating the price and size of transactions occurring in its matching engine.

Market and Limit Orders — When a market participant send an order to the matching engine of a trading facility, it can label it with some properties giving complementary instructions. A market order will consume liquidity at any price, hence it will definitely consume liquidity. A limit order has a limit price that cannot be exceeded. Usually market participants send limit orders when then plan to act as liquidity providers. Nevertheless to limit the price impact of an order, it is possible to use a limit order with a *marketable price*.

Another possible important property of an order is its disclosed quantity: Any order with a disclosed quantity lower than its size is an iceberg order. Only a fraction of the parent order will be visible in the pre-trade transparency information. As soon as its visible part is consumed, another fraction of the order will be disclosed, until it will be fully filled.

Regulation. Regulation organizes the market design, to ensure the efficiency of the price formation process.

Reg NMS — Regulation National Market System is a regulation promulgated by the SEC in 2005 that seeks to encourage competition among individual markets and among individual orders. It contains the trade-through rule, the access rule (addressing access to market data), the sub-penny rule (establishing minimum pricing increments) and market data rules.

Consolidated Tape — This is the electronic service that provides last sale and trade data for issues admitted on US exchanges, consolidating all markets and driving the trade-through rule.

Trade-Through Rule — The trade through rule mandates that when a stock is traded in more than one market, transactions may not occur in one market if a better price is offered on another market. There is a mandatory re-routing of the order to other markets.

MiFID — The Markets in Financial Instruments Directive, applied since November 2007, is part of the European Commission's drive to improve competition among European financial markets. This Directive was revised during 2011 and led to a draft of "MiFID 2", which will come up for a vote in 2013.

LIS (Large in Scale) — An order is considered to be large in scale compared with the normal market size if it is equal to or larger than the minimum order size specified in Table 2 in Annex II of the MiFID Implementing Regulation.

ESMA (The European Securities and Markets Authority) — It has been touted by the European Commission as a replacement for the CESR, with additional responsibilities. The ESMA will be responsible for safeguarding the integrity and stability of the financial system, the transparency of markets and financial products, and the protection of investors, as well as preventing regulatory arbitrage and guaranteeing a level playing field.

CESR (The Committee of European Securities Regulators) — Its role is to improve coordination among securities regulators, act as an advisory group to assist the European Commission, and work to ensure more consistent and timely day-to-day implementation of community legislation in the Member States.

SEC (Securities and Exchange Commission) — The US Securities and Exchange Commission's mission is to protect investors, maintain fair, orderly and efficient markets, and facilitate capital formation.

Trading Venues. MiFID removes domestic exchange concentration rules and recognizes three types of trading destinations: Regulated

Markets (RMs), Multilateral Trading Facilities (MTFs) and Systematic Internalisers (SIs). Everything else is over-the-counter (OTC).

Primary Market — Also called new issue market. Securities are issued for the first time in these markets. In this study, Euronext Paris, the London Stock Exchange, and Xetra are examples of primary markets.

MTF (Multilateral Trading Facility) — A multilateral system operated by an investment firm or a market operator which brings together multiple third-party buying and selling interests in financial instruments in a way that results in a contract. Chi-X, Turquoise and BATS are the MTFs studied here.

ECN (Electronic Communication Network) — This is a type of computer system that facilitates trading of financial products outside of stock exchanges. ECNs are the equivalent of MTFs in the US.

ATS (Alternative Trading Venue) — The ATS acronym is often use in the US to qualify trading facilities that are not exchanges. Not to be mistake with Average Trade Size.

Lit pool — A trading destination with a visible order book.

Dark pool — A trading destination that does not disclose its order book.

SOR (Smart Order Router) — A device routing an order across a given set of trading destinations according to a disclosed execution policy. It can split an order into smaller ones to spray all available destinations if needed.

BCN (Broker crossing network) — This is an alternative trading system that matches buy and sell orders electronically for execution without first routing the order to an exchange or other displayed market. The order is either anonymously placed in a black box or flagged to other participants of the crossing network. Its advantage is to enable large block order execution without impacting the public quote.

Matching Engine — This is the software device holding all pending trades for every listed stock on the trading destination and matching orders to compute possible transactions. Once the match is made, information about the completed transaction flows out of the matching engine.

Co-hosting, Co-location — Market operator services enabling market participants to have their computers or trading software in the same location than the matching engine of a trading facility.

Latency — The latency to a trading facility is the time taken for a message to travel from a market participant to the matching engine of the facility. Trading venues often measure the latency for a participant being as close as possible to their matching engine (typically a co-located participant). It is thus needed for a participant to add to this figure the network latency and the internal latency of a trading system to obtain the full latency he is submitted to.

Execution Costs and Market Depth Measurements. Execution costs are a mixture of fees, bid-ask spread, price impact, market impact, opportunity risk and market risk.

Market Risk — Measurement of the uncertainty in the price moves.

Price Impact — Impact of the volume of an order on the market price.

Market Impact — Impact of the volume of a large order (possibly split in smaller liquidity consuming or providing child orders). The market impact has two components: first a temporary impact, followed by a decay. The reminding price move being the permanent component of the impact.

Tick Size — The minimal difference allowed between two different prices. It is defined by the trading rules of each trading destination.

Decimalization — The decimalization of the tick sizes happend in 2001 on the US Equity market when the tick size has been set at one penny, instead of largest values it had before. The decrease of the tick size in other regions is often named a *"decimalization phase"* even if not setting the tick at one penny.

LOB (Limit Order Book) — This is a record of unexecuted limit orders maintained by trading destinations.

BBO (Best Bid and Offer) — The highest bid or lowest offer price available in a market at a specific time. The *Touch* is the best bid for a buy order and the best ask for a sell order. The *Best Opposite* is the best ask for a buy order and the best bid for a sell order.

Bid-Ask Spread — The bid-ask spread is the distance between the best bid and the best ask; it can be expressed in a currency or in basis points. The *Mid Price* is the middle of the bid-ask spread.

VWAS (Volume-Weighted Average Spread) — The middle of the bid-ask spread at each trade, weighted by the volume of the trade.

Market Depth — This is the size of an order needed to move the market by a given increment. If the market is deep, a large order is needed to change the price. Market Depth closely relates to the notion of liquidity.

Average daily number of trades — The higher it is, the more active the trading on a stock. It contributes positively to the liquidity of a stock.

ATS (Average trade size) — Mean trading size in euros. This can be considered the "natural size" of orders on the venue. Not to be mistaken for an Alternative Trading System.

% Time at E/N-BBO — This is the proportion of the day during which the venue offers a spread equal to the European or National Best Bid and Offer (EBBO for Europe and NBBO for the US).

Adverse Selection — In general, adverse selection is used to describe an insurance phenomenon in which people that want to have health insurance are more likely to have health problems, and so are typically the kind of people you do not want to insure because of the risk. In this context, this term refers to a market process in which buyers and sellers have asymmetric information. Adverse selection can occur in Dark Pools, for example. If your order is completely filled, this implies that the counterparty had more liquidity than you. It can be assumed that the other side, being even larger, will be likely to cause market impact and thus push the price against you. The fact that your order was filled is an indicator that you actually did not want it to be filled (it would have been better to wait until the price had been pushed and then to cross).

Opportunity Costs — The opportunity costs are the counterpart of the adverse selection costs: A trader will suffer from adverse selection cost if, given that he obtained a transaction, the price is more favorable few minutes later. He will suffer from opportunity costs if given that he decided to not trade, the price is worst few minutes later.

bp (Basis Point) — One hundredth of one percent: 1/100/100.

Bibliography

Admati, A. R. and Pfleiderer, P. (1988). A theory of intraday patterns: Volume and price variability. *The Review of Financial Studies*, 1(1): 3–40.

Agresti, A. and Caffo, B. (2000). Simple and effective confidence intervals for proportions and dierences of proportions result from adding two successes and two failures. *The American Statistician*, 54(4): 280–288.

Ahn, H.-J., Cao, C. Q., and Choe, H. (1996). Tick size, spread, and volume. *Journal of Financial Intermediation*, 5(1): 2–22.

Aït-Sahalia, Y. and Jacod, J. (2007). Volatility estimators for discretely sampled Lévy processes. *The Annals of Statistics*, 35(1): 355–392.

Aitken, M. and Comerton-Forde, C. (2005). Do reductions in tick sizes influence liquidity? *Accounting and Finance*, 45(2): 171–184.

Akerlof, G. A. (1970). The market for "lemons": Quality uncertainty and the market mechanism. *The Quarterly Journal of Economics*, 84(3): 488–500.

Almgren, R. F. and Chriss, N. (2000). Optimal execution of portfolio transactions. *Journal of Risk*, 3(2): 5–39.

Amari, S.-i. (1998). Natural gradient works efficiently in learning. *Neural Computation*, 10(2): 251–276.

Angel, J. J. (1997). Tick size, share prices, and stock splits. *The Journal of Finance*, 52(2): 655–681.

Arnold, V. I. (2011). *Dynamics, Statistics and Projective Geometry of Galois Fields* (1st Edition). United Kingdom: Cambridge University Press.

Azencott, R., Beri, A., Gadhyan, Y., Joseph, N., Lehalle, C.-A., and Rowley, M. (2013). Realtime market microstructure analysis: Online transaction cost analysis. Technical report, arxiv.

Bacidore, J., Battalio, R. H., and Jennings, R. H. (2003). Order submission strategies, liquidity supply, and trading in pennies on the New York stock exchange. *Journal of Financial Markets*, 6(3): 337–362.

Bacry, E., Delattre, S., Hoffmann, M., and Muzy, J. F. (2012). Modelling microstructure noise with mutually exciting point processes. *Quantitative Finance*, 13(1): 1–13.

Barndorff-Nielsen, O. E. and Shephard, N. (2004). Econometric analysis of realised covariation: High frequency based covariance, regression and correlation in financial economics. *Econometrica,* 72: 885–925.

Batali, J. (1983). Computational introspection. Technical report, MIT CSAIL.

Bats, Nasdaq, and Nyse (2010). Petition for sub-penny quotes. Technical report.

Bellman, R. (1956). Dynamic programming and lagrange multipliers. *Proceedings of the National Academy of Sciences of the United States of America,* 42(10): 767–769.

Benzécri, J.-P. (1973). *L'analyse des données.* France: Dunod.

Bertrand, P. (2010). Clustering systems with or without overlapping clusters and their dissimilarities. *Mathématiques et science humaines,* 190: 59–87.

Bertsimas, D. and Lo, A. W. (1998). Optimal control of execution costs. *Journal of Financial Markets,* 1(1): 1–50.

Biau, G., Devroye, L., and Lugosi, G. (2008). On the performance of clustering in hilbert spaces. *Information Theory, IEEE Transactions,* 54(2): 781–790.

Billingsley, P. (1978). *Ergodic theory and information.* R. E. Krieger Publishing Company.

Bollen, N. P. B. and Busse, J. A. (2006). Tick size and institutional trading costs: Evidence from mutual funds. *Journal of Financial and Quantitative Analysis,* 41(04): 915–937.

Bouchard, B., Dang, N.-M., and Lehalle, C.-A. (2011). Optimal control of trading algorithms: A general impulse control approach. *SIAM J. Financial Mathematics,* 2: 404–438.

Bouchaud, J. P., Mezard, M., and Potters, M. (2002). Statistical properties of stock order books: Empirical results and models. *Quantitative Finance,* 2(4).

Bourbonnais, R. (2011). *Économétrie.* France: Dunod.

Bourghelle, D. and Declerck, F. (2004). Why markets should not necessarily reduce the tick size. *Journal of Banking and Finance,* 28(2): 373–398.

Bremaud, P. (1981). *Point Processes and Queues: Martingale Dynamics.* Springer, 1st Edition.

Brockwell, P. J. and Davis, R. A. (1991). *Time series: Theory and methods.* Springer-Verlag.

Brogaard, J., Baron, M., and Kirilenko, A. (2012). The trading profits of high frequency traders. In Abergel, F., Bouchaud, J.-P., Foucault, T., Lehalle, C.-A. and Rosenbaum, M., editors, *Market Microstructure: Confronting Many Viewpoints* United Kingdom: Wiley.

Buti, S., Rindi, B., and Werner, I. M. (2010). Diving into dark pools. *Social Science Research Network Working Paper Series.*

Chakravarty, S., Panchapagesan, V., and Wood, R. A. (2005). Did decimalization hurt institutional investors? *Journal of Financial Markets,* 8(4): 400–420.

Cleveland, W. S. (1988). *The Collected Works of John W. Tukey: Graphics 1965-1985, Volume V (Statistics/probability Series).* United Kingdom: Chapman and Hall/CRC.

Cohen, Y. and Wolcough, A. (2012). New standards for market data. Technical report, etrading software.

Coughenour, J. F. and Harris, L. (2004). Specialist profits and the minimum price increment. *Social Science Research Network Working Paper Series.*

Daley, D. J. and Vere-Jones, D. (2003a). *An Introduction to the Theory of Point Processes, Volume I: Elementary Theory and Methods.* Springer, 2nd edition.

Daley, D. J. and Vere-Jones, D. (2003b). *An Introduction to the Theory of Point Processes, Volume II: General Theory and Structure (Probability and Its Applications)* (2nd Edition), Springer.

Dayri, K. and Rosenbaum, M. (2012). Large tick assets: Implicit spread and optimal tick size. Technical report.

Delassus, R. and Tyc, S. (2011). Sub-penny trading in us equity markets. In Abergel, F., Chakrabarti, B. K., Chakraborti, A. and Mitra, M., editors, *Econophysics of Order-driven Markets*, pp. 31–47. Milan: Springer.

Epps, T. W. (1979). Co-movements in stock prices in the very short run. *Journal of the American Statistical Association*, 74(366): 291–298.

Feynman, R. P., Leighton, R. B., and Sands, M. (1989). *The Feynman Lectures on Physics: Commemorative Issue, Volume 1*. United Kingdom: Addison Wesley.

Foucault, T., Kadan, O., and Kandel, E. (2009). Liquidity cycles and make/take fees in electronic markets. *Social Science Research Network Working Paper Series.*

Foucault, T. and Menkveld, A. J. (2008). Competition for order flow and smart order routing systems. *The Journal of Finance*, 63(1): 119–158.

Gabaix, X., Gopikrishnan, P., Plerou, V., and Stanley, H. E. (2006). Institutional investors and stock market volatility. *The Quarterly Journal of Economics*, 121(2): 461–504.

Garman, M. B. and Klass, M. J. (1980). On the estimation of security price volatilities from historical data. *Journal of Business*, 53(1): 67–78.

Garvey, R. and Wu, F. (2007). Market transparency and institutional trader behavior after a tick change. *The Journal of Trading*, 2(1): 35–48.

Gini, C. (1912). *Variabilità e mutabilità*. Rome: Libreria Eredi Virgilio Veschi.

Goldstein, M. A. and Kavajecz (2000). Eighths, sixteenths, and market depth: Changes in tick size and liquidity provision on the nyse. *Journal of Financial Economics*, 56(1): 125–149.

Grossman, S. J. and Stiglitz, J. E. (1980). On the impossibility of informationally efficient markets. *The American Economic Review*, 70(3): 393–408.

Guéant, O., Lehalle, C.-A., and Fernandez-Tapia, J. (2012a). Dealing with the inventory risk. A solution to the market making problem. *Mathematics and Financial Economics.*

Guéant, O., Lehalle, C.-A., and Fernandez-Tapia, J. (2012b). Optimal Execution with Limit Orders. *SIAM Journal on Financial Mathematics.*

Hamilton, J. D. (1993). *Time Series Analysis.* New Jersey: Princeton University, 1st edition.

Harris, L. (1996). *Does a large Minimum price variation encourage order exposure.* New York Stock Exchange.

Harris, L. (2002). *Trading and Exchanges: Market Microstructure for Practitioners.* New York: Oxford University Press.

Harris, L. E. (1994). Minimum price variations, discrete bid-ask spreads, and quotation sizes. *Review of Financial Studies*, 7(1): 149–178.

Hayashi, T. and Yoshida, N. (2005). On covariance estimation of non-synchronously observed diffusion processes. *Bernoulli*, 11(2): 359–379.

Jain, P. C. and Joh, G.-H. (1988). The dependence between hourly prices and trading volume. *The Journal of Financial and Quantitative Analysis*, 23(3): 269–283.

Jickling, M. (2005). The trade-through rule. Technical report, US Congress.

Johnson, B. (2010). *Algorithmic Trading and DMA: An Introduction to Direct Access Trading Strategies*. 4Myeloma Press.

Jones, C. M. and Lipson, M. L. (2001). Sixteenths: Direct evidence on institutional execution costs. *Journal of Financial Economics*, 59(2): 253–278.

Kandel, E., Rindi, B., and Bosetti, L. (2008). The effect of a closing call auction on market quality and trading strategies. *Social Science Research Network Working Paper Series*.

Karatzas, I. and Shreve, S. E. (1991). *Brownian Motion and Stochastic Calculus (Graduate Texts in Mathematics)*. Springer, 2nd edition.

Kirilenko, A. A., Kyle, A. P., Samadi, M., and Tuzun, T. (2010). The Flash Crash: The impact of high frequency trading on an electronic market. *Social Science Research Network Working Paper Series*.

Kolmogorov, A. N. (1933). Sulla determinazione empirica di una legge di distribuzione. *Giornale dell'Istituto Italiano degli Attuari*, 4: 83–91.

Labadie, M. and Lehalle, C.-A. (2012). Optimal starting times, stopping times and risk measures for algorithmic trading. Technical report, arvix.

Laruelle, S., Lehalle, C.-A., and Pagès, G. (2011). Optimal split of orders across liquidity pools: A stochatic algorithm approach. *SIAM Journal on Financial Mathematics*, 2(1): 1042–1076.

Laruelle, S., Lehalle, C.-A., and Pagès, G. (2013). Optimal posting price of limit orders: Learning by trading. *Mathematics and Financial Economics*, 7(3): 359–403.

Leber, C., Geib, B., and Litz, H. (2011). High frequency trading acceleration using fpgas. In *2011 21st International Conference on Field Programmable Logic and Applications*, pages 317–322. IEEE.

Lehalle, C.-A. (2008). Rigorous optimisation of intra day trading. *Wilmott Magazine*.

Lehalle, C.-A. (2009). Rigorous strategic trading: Balanced portfolio and mean-reversion. *The Journal of Trading*, 4(3): 40–46.

Lehalle, C.-A. (2012). *Market Microstructure Knowledge Needed to Control an Intra-day Trading Process*. In Foque, J.-P. and Langsam, J. A., editors, *Handbook on Systemic Risk*. United Kingdom: Cambridge University Press.

Lehalle, C.-A. and Burgot, R. (2008). New trading behaviours in a post-mifid liquidity landscape.

Lehalle, C.-A. and Burgot, R. (2009a). The established liquidity fragmentation affects all investors. Technical report, CA Cheuvreux.

Lehalle, C.-A. and Burgot, R. (2009b). Making sense of liquidity fragmentation. Technical report, CA Cheuvreux.

Lehalle, C.-A. and Burgot, R. (2010). Market microstructure: A paradigm shift. Technical report, CA Cheuvreux.

Lehalle, C.-A., Burgot, R., Lasnier, M., and Pelin, S. (2010a). Regulatory adjustments: A new hope. Technical report, CA Cheuvreux.

Lehalle, C.-A., Burgot, R., Lasnier, M., and Pelin, S. (2012). A global menu for optimal trading. Technical report, CA Cheuvreux.

Lehalle, C.-A., Guéant, O., and Razafinimanana, J. (2010b). High frequency simulations of an order book: A two-scales approach. In Abergel, F., Chakrabarti, B. K., Chakraborti, A., and Mitra, M., editors, *Econophysics of Order-Driven Markets*, Milan: Springer.

Madhavan, A. (2011). Exchange-traded funds, market structure and the Flash Crash. *Social Science Research Network Working Paper Series*.

Markowitz, H. (1952). Portfolio selection. *The Journal of Finance*, 7(1): 77–91.

Menkveld, A. J. (2010). High frequency trading and the new-market makers. *Social Science Research Network Working Paper Series*.

Menkveld, A. J. and Yueshen, B. (2012). Middlemen interaction and its effect on market quality. *Social Science Research Network Working Paper Series*.

Menkveld, A. J. and Yueshen, B. (2013). Anatomy of the Flash Crash. *Social Science Research Network Working Paper Series*.

Møller, J. and Rasmussen, J. G. (2005). Perfect simulation of hawkes processes. *Advances in Applied Probability*, 37(3): 629–646.

Moro, E., Vicente, J., Moyano, L. G., Gerig, A., Farmer, J. D., Vaglica, G., Lillo, F., and Mantegna, R. N. (2009). Market impact and trading profile of hidden orders in stock markets. *Physical Review E*, 80(6); DOI: 10.1103/PhysRevE.80.066102.

O'Hara, M. (1998). *Market Microstructure Theory*. United Kingdom: Wiley.

O'Hara, M. (2010). What is a quote? *The Journal of Trading*, 5(2): 10–16.

Robert, C. Y. and Rosenbaum, M. (2012). Volatility and covariation estimation when microstructure noise and trading times are endogenous. *Mathematical Finance*, 22(1): 133–164.

Rosenbaltt Securities Inc. (2012). Dark pools: 2011 in review. Technical report.

SEC (2012). Report to congress on decimalization. Technical report.

Shannon, C. E. (1948). A mathematical theory of communication. *Bell System Technical Journal*, 27: 379–423, 623–656.

Smith, E., Farmer, D. J., Gillemot, L., and Krishnamurthy, S. (2003). Statistical theory of the continuous double auction. *Quantitative Finance*, 3(6): 481–514.

Sussman, A., Tabb, L., and Iati, R. US equity high frequency trading: Strategies, sizing and market structure. Technical report, TABB Group.

Tassi, P. (2004). *Méthodes statistiques*. France: Economica.

Tufte, E. R. (2001). *The Visual Display of Quantitative Information*, Graphics Pr, 2nd edition.

U.S. Securities & Exchange Commission (2010a). Concept release on equity market structure. Technical report, U.S. Securities & Exchange Commission.

U.S. Securities & Exchange Commission (2010b). Findings regarding the market events of may 6, 2010. Technical report, U.S. Commodity Futures Trading Commission, U.S. Securities & Exchange Commission.

van Kervel, V. (2012). Liquidity: What you see is what you get? Tiburg University, Working Paper

Werner, I. M. (2003). Execution quality for institutional orders routed to NASDAQ dealers before and after decimals. *Social Science Research Network Working Paper Series*.

Wu, Y., Krehbiel, T., and Brorsen, B. W. (2011). Impacts of tick size reduction on transaction costs. *International Journal of Economics and Finance*, 3(6): 57–65.

Wyart, M., Bouchaud, J.-P., Kockelkoren, J., Potters, M., and Vettorazzo, M. (2008). Relation between bid-ask spread, impact and volatility in order-driven markets. *Quantitative Finance*, 8(1): 41–57.

Zhang, L. (2011). Estimating covariation: Epps effect and microstructure noise. *Journal of Econometrics* 160(1): 33–47.

Zhang, L., Mykland, P. A., and Aït-Sahalia, Y. (2005). A tale of two time scales: Determining integrated volatility with noisy high frequency data. *Journal of the American Statistical Association*, 100(472): 1394–1411.

Zhu, H. (2010). Do dark pools harm price discovery? *Social Science Research Network Working Paper Series*.

Index